Using MPI

Scientific and Engineering Computation
Janusz Kowalik, editor

Data-Parallel Programming on MIMD Computers, Philip J. Hatcher and Michael J. Quinn, 1991

Unstructured Scientific Computation on Scalable Multiprocessors, edited by Piyush Mehrotra, Joel Saltz, and Robert Voigt, 1992

Parallel Computational Fluid Dynamics: Implementation and Results, edited by Horst D. Simon, 1992

Enterprise Integration Modeling: Proceedings of the First International Conference, edited by Charles J. Petrie, Jr., 1992

The High Performance Fortran Handbook, Charles H. Koelbel, David B. Loveman, Robert S. Schreiber, Guy L. Steele Jr. and Mary E. Zosel, 1994

PVM: Parallel Virtual Machine–A Users' Guide and Tutorial for Network Parallel Computing, Al Geist, Adam Beguelin, Jack Dongarra, Weicheng Jiang, Bob Manchek, and Vaidy Sunderam, 1994

Practical Parallel Programming, Gregory V. Wilson, 1995

Enabling Technologies for Petaflops Computing, Thomas Sterling, Paul Messina, and Paul H. Smith, 1995

An Introduction to High-Performance Scientific Computing, Lloyd D. Fosdick, Elizabeth R. Jessup, Carolyn J. C. Schauble, and Gitta Domik, 1995

Parallel Programming Using C++, edited by Gregory V. Wilson and Paul Lu, 1996

Using PLAPACK: Parallel Linear Algebra Package, Robert A. van de Geijn, 1997

Fortran 95 Handbook, Jeanne C. Adams, Walter S. Brainerd, Jeanne T. Martin, Brian T. Smith, Jerrold L. Wagener, 1997

MPI—The Complete Reference: Volume 1, The MPI Core, Marc Snir, Steve Otto, Steven Huss-Lederman, David Walker, and Jack Dongarra, 1998

MPI—The Complete Reference: Volume 2, The MPI-2 Extensions, William Gropp, Steven Huss-Lederman, Andrew Lumsdaine, Ewing Lusk, Bill Nitzberg, William Saphir, and Marc Snir, 1998

A Programmer's Guide to ZPL, Lawrence Snyder, 1999

How to Build a Beowulf, Thomas L. Sterling, John Salmon, Donald J. Becker, and Daniel F. Savarese, 1999

Using MPI: Portable Parallel Programming with the Message-Passing Interface, second edition, William Gropp, Ewing Lusk, and Anthony Skjellum, 1999

Using MPI-2: Advanced Features of the Message-Passing Interface, William Gropp, Ewing Lusk, and Rajeev Thakur, 1999

Using MPI

Portable Parallel Programming with the Message-Passing Interface

Second Edition

William Gropp
Ewing Lusk
Anthony Skjellum

The MIT Press
Cambridge, Massachusetts
London, England

This book was set in LaTeX by the authors and was printed and bound in the United States of America.

Library of Congress Cataloging-in-Publication Data

Gropp, William.
Using MPI : portable parallel programming with the message-passing interface / William Gropp, Ewing Lusk, Anthony Skjellum.—2nd ed.
p. cm.—(Scientific and engineering computation)
Includes bibliographical references and index.
ISBN 0-262-57134-X (set : pbk. : alk. paper)—0-262-57132-3 (v. 1 : pbk. : alk. paper)
1. Parallel programming (Computer science). 2. Parallel computers—programming. 3. Computer interfaces. I. Lusk, Ewing. II. Skjellum, Anthony. III. Title. IV. Series.
QA76.642.G76 1999
005.2'75—dc21 99-16613
CIP

To Patty, Brigid, and Jennifer

Contents

Series Foreword

The world of modern computing potentially offers many helpful methods and tools to scientists and engineers, but the fast pace of change in computer hardware, software, and algorithms often makes practical use of the newest computing technology difficult. The Scientific and Engineering Computation series focuses on rapid advances in computing technologies and attempts to facilitate transferring these technologies to applications in science and engineering. It will include books on theories, methods, and original applications in such areas as parallelism, large-scale simulations, time-critical computing, computer-aided design and engineering, use of computers in manufacturing, visualization of scientific data, and human-machine interface technology.

The series will help scientists and engineers to understand the current world of advanced computation and to anticipate future developments that will impact their computing environments and open up new capabilities and modes of computation.

This book in the series describes how to use the Message-Passing Interface (MPI), a communication library for both parallel computers and workstation networks. MPI has been developed as a standard for message passing and related operations. Its adoption by both users and implementors is providing the parallel programming community with the portability and features needed to develop application programs and parallel libraries that tap the power of today's (and tomorrow's) high-performance computers.

Janusz S. Kowalik

Preface to the Second Edition

When *Using MPI* was first published in 1994, the future of MPI was unknown. The MPI Forum had just concluded its work on the Standard, and it was not yet clear whether vendors would provide optimized implementations or whether users would select MPI for writing new parallel programs or would port existing codes to MPI.

Now the suspense is over. MPI is available everywhere and widely used, in environments ranging from small workstation networks to the very largest computers in the world, with thousands of processors. Every parallel computer vendor offers an MPI implementation, and multiple implementations are freely available as well, running on a wide variety of architectures. Applications large and small have been ported to MPI or written as MPI programs from the beginning, and MPI is taught in parallel programming courses worldwide.

In 1995, the MPI Forum began meeting again. It revised in a compatible way and significantly extended the MPI specification, releasing version 1.2 (covering the topics included in the original, 1.0 specification) and version 2.0 (covering entirely new topics) in the summer of 1997. In this book, we update the original *Using MPI* to reflect these later decisions of the MPI Forum. Roughly speaking, this book covers the use of MPI 1.2, while *Using MPI 2* (published by MIT Press as a companion volume to this book) covers extensions in MPI 2.0. New topics in MPI-2 include parallel I/O, one-sided operations, and dynamic process management. However, many topics relevant to the original MPI functions were modified as well, and these are discussed here. Thus this book can be viewed as the up-to-date version of the topics covered in the original edition.

About the Second Edition

This second edition of *Using MPI: Portable Programming with the Message-Passing Interface* contains many changes from and additions to the first edition.

- We have added many new examples and have added additional explanations to the examples from the first edition.
- A section on common errors and misunderstandings has been added to several chapters.
- We have added new material on the performance impact of choices among alternative MPI usages.
- A chapter on implementation issues has been added to increase understanding

of how and why various MPI implementations may differ, particularly with regard to performance.

- Since "Fortran" now means Fortran 90 (or Fortran 95 [1]), all Fortran examples have been updated to Fortran 90 syntax. We do, however, explain the small modifications necessary to run the examples in Fortran 77.
- C++ bindings are given for all functions described in this book and some C++ examples are included in the text.
- We have added the new functions from the MPI 1.2 specification, and also those from MPI 2.0 whose exposition seems to belong with functions from MPI 1.2.
- We describe new tools in the MPE toolkit, reflecting their evolution since the publication of the first edition.
- The chapter on converting to MPI from earlier message-passing systems has been greatly revised, now that many of those systems have been completely supplanted by MPI. We include a comparison of MPI syntax and semantics with PVM, since conversion of programs from PVM to MPI is still going on. We also compare MPI with the use of Unix sockets.
- Some functions in MPI 1.0 are now deprecated, since better definitions have now been made. These are identified and their replacements described.
- Errors, particularly those in the example programs, have been corrected.

Our order of presentation again is guided by the level of complexity in the algorithms we study. This tutorial approach differs substantially from that given in more formal presentations of the MPI standard such as [118].

We begin in Chapter 1 with a brief overview of the current situation in parallel computing environments, the message-passing model, and the process that produced MPI. Chapter 2 introduces the basic concepts that arise from the message-passing model itself, and how MPI augments these basic concepts to create a full-featured, high-performance-capable interface.

In Chapter 3 we set the pattern for the remaining chapters. We present several examples and the small number of MPI functions that are required to express them. We describe how to execute the examples using the model MPI implementation and how to investigate the performance of these programs using a graphical performance-analysis tool. We conclude with an example of a large-scale application, a nuclear structure code from Argonne National Laboratory, written using only the MPI functions introduced in this chapter.

Chapter 4 rounds out the basic features of MPI by focusing on a particular application prototypical of a large family: solution of the Poisson problem. We introduce MPI's facilities for application-oriented process structures called virtual topologies. Using our performance analysis tools, we illustrate how to improve performance using slightly more advanced MPI message-passing functions. We conclude with a discussion of a production code currently being used to investigate the phenomenon of high-temperature superconductivity.

Some of the more advanced features for message passing provided by MPI are covered in Chapter 5. We use the N-body problem as a setting for much of the discussion. We complete our discussion of derived datatypes and demonstrate the use of the MPE graphics library with a version of Mandelbrot set computation.

We believe that the majority of programmers of parallel computers will, in the long run, access parallelism through libraries. Indeed, enabling the construction of robust libraries is one of the primary motives behind the MPI effort, and perhaps its single most distinguishing feature when compared with other parallel programming environments. In Chapter 6 we address this issue with a series of examples.

MPI contains a variety of advanced features that will only have been touched on or presented in their simplest form at this point in the book. Some of these features include elaborate collective data-distribution and data-collection schemes, error handling, and facilities for implementing client-server applications. In Chapter 7 we fill out the description of these features using further examples taken from applications. We also discuss in detail MPI's environmental-inquiry functions.

In Chapter 8 we discuss what one finds "under the hood" in implementations of MPI. Understanding the choices available to MPI implementors can provide insight into the behavior of MPI programs in various computing environments.

Chapter 9 presents a comparison of MPI with two other systems often used to implement a message-passing model of computation. PVM is a system that predated MPI and is still widely used. The "socket" interface on both Unix and Microsoft systems is the operating system's way of communicating among processes on different machines.

We recognize that message passing, as a computational paradigm, is not the last word in parallel computing. We briefly explore the topics of active messages, threads, distributed shared memory, and other items in Chapter 10. We also attempt to predict future development and extensions of MPI.

The appendixes for the most part contain information on the software used in running and studying the examples in this book. Appendix A provides the language bindings for the C, C++, and Fortran versions of all of the MPI routines. Appendix B describes briefly the architecture of MPICH, a freely available MPI implementation. It also describes how to obtain, build, and run MPICH Appendix C describes how to obtain and use the Multiprocessing Environment (MPE) library along with the `upshot` program visualization program that we use in this book. Appendix D describes how to obtain supplementary material for this book, including complete source code for the examples, and related MPI materials that are available via anonymous `ftp` and the World Wide Web. Appendix E discusses some issues of C and Fortran that are relevant to MPI and may be unfamiliar to some readers.

Acknowledgments for the Second Edition

We thank Peter Lyster of NASA's Goddard Space Flight Center for sharing his marked-up copy of the first edition of *Using MPI* with us. We thank Puri Bangalore, Nicholas Carriero, Robert van de Geijn, Peter Junglas, David Levine, Bryan Putnam, Bill Saphir, David J. Schneider, Barry Smith, and Stacey Smith for sending in errata for the first edition (and anyone that we've forgotten), and Anand Pillai for correcting some of the examples in Chapter 6. The reviewers of the prospectus for this book offered many helpful suggestions for topics. We thank Gail Peiper for her careful and knowledgeable editing.

Preface to the First Edition

About This Book

During 1993, a broadly based group of parallel computer vendors, software writers, and application scientists collaborated on the development of a standard portable message-passing library definition called MPI, for Message-Passing Interface. MPI is a specification for a library of routines to be called from C and Fortran programs. As of mid-1994, a number of implementations are in progress, and applications are already being ported.

Using MPI: Portable Parallel Programming with the Message-Passing Interface is designed to accelerate the development of parallel application programs and libraries by demonstrating how to use the new standard. It fills the gap among introductory texts on parallel computing, advanced texts on parallel algorithms for scientific computing, and user manuals of various parallel programming languages and systems. Each topic begins with simple examples and concludes with real applications running on today's most powerful parallel computers. We use both Fortran (Fortran 77) and C. We discuss timing and performance evaluation from the outset, using a library of useful tools developed specifically for this presentation. Thus this book is not only a tutorial on the use of MPI as a language for expressing parallel algorithms, but also a handbook for those seeking to understand and improve the performance of large-scale applications and libraries.

Without a standard such as MPI, getting specific about parallel programming has necessarily limited one's audience to users of some specific system that might not be available or appropriate for other users' computing environments. MPI provides the portability necessary for a concrete discussion of parallel programming to have wide applicability. At the same time, MPI is a powerful and complete specification, and using this power means that the expression of many parallel algorithms can now be done more easily and more naturally than ever before, without giving up efficiency.

Of course, parallel programming takes place in an environment that extends beyond MPI. We therefore introduce here a small suite of tools that computational scientists will find useful in measuring, understanding, and improving the performance of their parallel programs. These tools include timing routines, a library to produce an event log for post-mortem program visualization, and a simple real-time graphics library for run-time visualization. Also included are a number of utilities that enhance the usefulness of the MPI routines themselves. We call the union of these libraries MPE, for MultiProcessing Environment. All the example programs and tools are freely available, as is a model portable implementation of MPI itself developed by researchers at Argonne National Laboratory and Mississippi State University [63].

Our order of presentation is guided by the level of complexity in the parallel algorithms we study; thus it differs substantially from the order in more formal presentations of the standard.

[To preclude possible confusion on the part of the reader, the outline of the first edition that occurred here has been omitted.]

In addition to the normal subject index, there is an index for the definitions and usage examples for the MPI functions used in this book. A glossary of terms used in this book may be found before the appendices.

We try to be impartial in the use of Fortran and C for the book's examples; many examples are given in each language. The MPI standard has tried to keep the syntax of its calls similar in Fortran and C; for the most part they differ only in case (all capitals in Fortran, although most compilers will accept all lower case as well, while in C only the "MPI" and the next letter are capitalized), and in the handling of the return code (the last argument in Fortran and the returned value in C). When we need to refer to an MPI function name without specifying whether it is Fortran or C, we will use the C version, just because it is a little easier to read in running text.

This book is not a reference manual, in which MPI routines would be grouped according to functionality and completely defined. Instead we present MPI routines informally, in the context of example programs. Precise definitions are given in [98]. Nonetheless, to increase the usefulness of this book to someone working with MPI, we have provided for each MPI routine that we discuss a reminder of its calling sequence, in both Fortran and C. These listings can be found set off in boxes scattered throughout the book, located near the introduction of the routines they contain. In the boxes for C, we use ANSI C style declarations. Arguments that can be of several types (typically message buffers) are typed as `void*`. In the Fortran boxes the types of such arguments are marked as being of type `<type>`. This means that one of the appropriate Fortran data types should be used. To find the "binding box" for a given MPI routine, one should use the appropriate bold-face reference in the Function Index (**f77** for Fortran, **C** for C). Another place to find this information is in Appendix A, which lists all MPI functions in alphabetical order.

Acknowledgments

Our primary acknowledgment is to the Message Passing Interface Forum (MPIF), whose members devoted their best efforts over the course of a year and a half to producing MPI itself. The appearance of such a standard has enabled us to collect and coherently express our thoughts on how the process of developing application programs and libraries for parallel computing environments might be carried out. The aim of our book is to show how this process can now be undertaken with more ease, understanding, and probability of success than has been possible before the appearance of MPI.

The MPIF is producing both a final statement of the standard itself and an annotated reference manual to flesh out the standard with the discussion necessary for understanding the full flexibility and power of MPI. At the risk of duplicating acknowledgments to be found in those volumes, we thank here the following MPIF participants, with whom we collaborated on the MPI project. Special effort was exerted by those who served in various positions of responsibility: Lyndon Clarke, James Cownie, Jack Dongarra, Al Geist, Rolf Hempel, Steven Huss-Lederman, Bob Knighten, Richard Littlefield, Steve Otto, Mark Sears, Marc Snir, and David Walker. Other participants included Ed Anderson, Joe Baron, Eric Barszcz, Scott Berryman, Rob Bjornson, Anne Elster, Jim Feeney, Vince Fernando, Sam Fineberg, Jon Flower, Daniel Frye, Ian Glendinning, Adam Greenberg, Robert Harrison, Leslie Hart, Tom Haupt, Don Heller, Tom Henderson, Alex Ho, C.T. Howard Ho, John Kapenga, Bob Leary, Arthur Maccabe, Peter Madams, Alan Mainwaring, Oliver McBryan, Phil McKinley, Charles Mosher, Dan Nessett, Peter Pacheco, Howard Palmer, Paul Pierce, Sanjay Ranka, Peter Rigsbee, Arch Robison, Erich Schikuta, Ambuj Singh, Alan Sussman, Robert Tomlinson, Robert G. Voigt, Dennis Weeks, Stephen Wheat, and Steven Zenith.

While everyone listed here made positive contributions, and many made major contributions, MPI would be far less important if it had not had the benefit of the particular energy and articulate intelligence of James Cownie of Meiko, Paul Pierce of Intel, and Marc Snir of IBM.

Support for the MPI meetings came in part from ARPA and NSF under grant ASC-9310330, NSF Science and Technology Center Cooperative Agreement No. CCR-8809615, and the Commission of the European Community through Esprit Project P6643. The University of Tennessee kept MPIF running financially while the organizers searched for steady funding.

The authors specifically thank their employers, Argonne National Laboratory and Mississippi State University, for the time and resources to explore the field of parallel computing and participate in the MPI process. The first two authors were supported by the U.S. Department of Energy under contract W-31-109-Eng-38. The third author was supported in part by the NSF Engineering Research Center for Computational Field Simulation at Mississippi State University.

The MPI Language Specification is copyrighted by the University of Tennessee and will appear as a special issue of *International Journal of Supercomputer Applications*, published by MIT Press. Both organizations have dedicated the language definition to the public domain.

We also thank Nathan Doss of Mississippi State University and Hubertus Franke of the IBM Corporation, who participated in the early implementation project that has allowed us to run all of the examples in this book. We thank Ed Karrels, a student visitor at Argonne, who did most of the work on the MPE library and the profiling interface examples. He was also completely responsible for the new version of the `upshot` program for examining logfiles.

We thank James Cownie of Meiko and Brian Grant of the University of Washington for reading the manuscript and making many clarifying suggestions. Gail Pieper vastly improved the prose. We also thank those who have allowed us to use their research projects as examples: Robert Harrison, Dave Levine, and Steven Pieper.

Finally we thank several Mississippi State University graduate students whose joint research with us (and each other) have contributed to several large-scale examples in the book. The members of the *Parallel Scientific Computing* class in the Department of Computer Science at MSU, spring 1994, helped debug and improve the model implementation and provided several projects included as examples in this book. We specifically thank Purushotham V. Bangalore, Ramesh Pankajakshan, Kishore Viswanathan, and John E. West for the examples (from the class and research) that they have provided for us to use in the text.

Using MPI

1 Background

In this chapter we survey the setting in which the MPI Standard has evolved, from the current situation in parallel computing and the prevalence of the message-passing model for parallel computation to the actual process by which MPI was developed.

1.1 Why Parallel Computing?

Fast computers have stimulated the rapid growth of a new way of doing science. The two broad classical branches of theoretical science and experimental science have been joined by *computational* science. Computational scientists simulate on supercomputers phenomena too complex to be reliably predicted by theory and too dangerous or expensive to be reproduced in the laboratory. Successes in computational science have caused demand for supercomputing resources to rise sharply over the past ten years.

During this time parallel computers have evolved from experimental contraptions in laboratories to become the everyday tools of computational scientists who need the ultimate in computer resources in order to solve their problems.

Several factors have stimulated this evolution. It is not only that the speed of light and the effectiveness of heat dissipation impose physical limits on the speed of a single computer. (To pull a bigger wagon, it is easier to add more oxen than to grow a gigantic ox.) It is also that the cost of advanced single-processor computers increases more rapidly than their power. (Large oxen are expensive.) And price/performance ratios become really favorable if the required computational resources can be found instead of purchased. This factor has caused many sites to exploit existing workstation networks, originally purchased to do modest computational chores, as SCANs (SuperComputers At Night) by utilizing the workstation network as a parallel computer. And most recently, as personal computer (PC) performance has increased and prices have fallen steeply, both for the PCs themselves and the network hardware necessary to connect them, dedicated clusters of PC workstations have provided significant computing power on a budget. The largest of these clusters, assembled out of commercial, off-the-shelf (COTS) parts, are beginning to seriously compete with offerings from traditional supercomputer vendors. One particular flavor of this approach, involving open source system software and dedicated networks, has acquired the name "Beowulf" [120]. Finally, the growth in performance and capacity of wide-area networks (WANs) has made it possible to write applications that span the globe. Many researchers are exploring the concept of a "grid" [40] of computational resources and connections that is in some ways analogous to the electric power grid.

Thus, considerations of both peak performance and price/performance are pushing large-scale computing in the direction of parallelism. So why hasn't parallel computing taken over? Why isn't everyone writing parallel programs?

1.2 Obstacles to Progress

Barriers to the widespread use of parallelism are in all three of the usual large subdivisions of computing: hardware, algorithms, and software.

In the hardware arena, we are still trying to build intercommunication networks (often called switches) that keep up with speeds of advanced single processors. Although not needed for every application (many successful parallel programs use Ethernet for their communication environment and some even use electronic mail), in general, faster computers require faster switches to enable most applications to take advantage of them. Over the past five years much progress has been made in this area, and today's parallel supercomputers have a better balance between computation and communication than ever before. This balance is now being extended into the networked-workstation and PC cluster environment as well, through the growth of higher-speed local (and even wide-area) networks.

Algorithmic research has contributed as much to the speed of modern parallel programs as has hardware engineering research. Parallelism in algorithms can be thought of as arising in three ways: from the physics (independence of physical processes), from the mathematics (independence of sets of mathematical operations), and from the programmer's imagination (independence of computational tasks). A bottleneck occurs, however, when these various forms of parallelism in algorithms must be *expressed* in a real program to be run on a real parallel computer. At this point, the problem becomes one of software.

The biggest obstacle to the spread of parallel computing and its benefits in economy and power is the problem of inadequate software. The author of a parallel algorithm for an important computational science problem may find the current software environment obstructing rather than smoothing the path to use of the very capable, cost-effective hardware available.

Part of the obstruction consists of what is not there. Compilers that automatically parallelize sequential algorithms remain limited in their applicability. Although much research has been done, and parallelizing compilers work well on some programs, the best performance is still obtained when the programmer himself supplies the parallel algorithm. If parallelism cannot be provided automatically by compilers, what about libraries? Here there has been some progress, but the barriers to writing libraries that work in multiple environments are great. The requirements of libraries and how these requirements are addressed by MPI are the subject matter of Chapter 6.

Other parts of the obstruction consist of what *is* there. The ideal mechanism for communicating a parallel algorithm to a parallel computer should be expressive, efficient, and portable. Current mechanisms all represent compromises among these three goals. Some vendor libraries are efficient but not portable, and in most cases minimal with regard to expressiveness. High-level languages emphasize portability over efficiency. And programmers are never satisfied with the expressivity of their programming language. (Turing completeness is necessary, but not sufficient.)

MPI is a compromise too, of course, but its design has been guided by a vivid awareness of these goals in the context of the next generation of parallel systems. It is portable. It has been designed to impose no semantic restrictions on efficiency; that is, nothing in the design (as opposed to a particular implementation) forces a loss of efficiency. Moreover, the deep involvement of vendors in MPI's definition has ensured that vendor-supplied MPI implementations can be efficient. As for expressivity, MPI is designed to be a convenient, complete definition of the message-passing model, the justification for which we discuss in the next section.

1.3 Why Message Passing?

To put our discussion of message passing in perspective, we briefly review informally the principal parallel computational models. Then we will focus on the advantages of the message-passing model.

1.3.1 Parallel Computational Models

A *computational model* is a conceptual view of the types of operations available to the program. It does not include the specific syntax of a particular programming language or library, and it is (almost) independent of the underlying hardware that supports it. That is, any of the models we discuss can be implemented on any modern parallel computer, given a little help from the operating system. The effectiveness of such an implementation, however, depends on the gap between the model and the machine.

Parallel computational models form a complicated structure. They can be differentiated along multiple axes: whether memory is physically shared or distributed, how much communication is in hardware or software, exactly what the unit of execution is, and so forth. The picture is made confusing by the fact that software can provide an implementation of any computational model on any hardware. This section is thus not a taxonomy; rather, we wish to define our terms in order to delimit clearly our discussion of the message-passing model, which is the focus of MPI.

Data parallelism. Although parallelism occurs in many places and at many levels in a modern computer, one of the first places it was made available to the programmer was in vector processors. Indeed, the vector machine began the current age of supercomputing. The vector machine's notion of operating on an array of similar data items in parallel during a single operation was extended to include the operation of whole programs on collections of data structures, as in SIMD (single-instruction, multiple-data) machines like the ICL DAP and the Thinking Machines CM-2. The parallelism need not necessarily proceed instruction by instruction in lock step for it to be classified as data parallel. Data parallelism is now more a programming style than a computer architecture, and the CM-2 is extinct.

At whatever level, the model remains the same: the parallelism comes entirely from the data; the program itself looks very much like a sequential program. The partitioning of data that underlies this model may be done by a compiler; the High Performance Fortran (HPF) Standard [87] specifies a set of additions to Fortran that help a compiler with the data-partitioning process.

Compiler directives such as those defined by OpenMP [103, 104] allow the programmer a way to provide hints to the compiler on where to find data parallelism in sequentially coded loops.

Shared memory. Parallelism that is not determined implicitly by data independence but is explicitly specified by the programmer is *control* parallelism. One simple model of control parallelism is the shared-memory model, in which each processor has access to all of a single, shared address space at the usual level of load and store operations. A schematic diagram of this arrangement is shown in Figure 1.1. Access to locations manipulated by multiple processes is coordinated by some form of locking, although high-level languages may hide the explicit use of locks. Early examples of this model were the Denelcor HEP and Alliant family of shared-memory multiprocessors, as well as Sequent and Encore machines. The Cray parallel vector machines, as well as the SGI Power Challenge series, are also of this same model. Now there are many small-scale shared-memory machines, often called "symmetric multiprocessors" (SMP's).

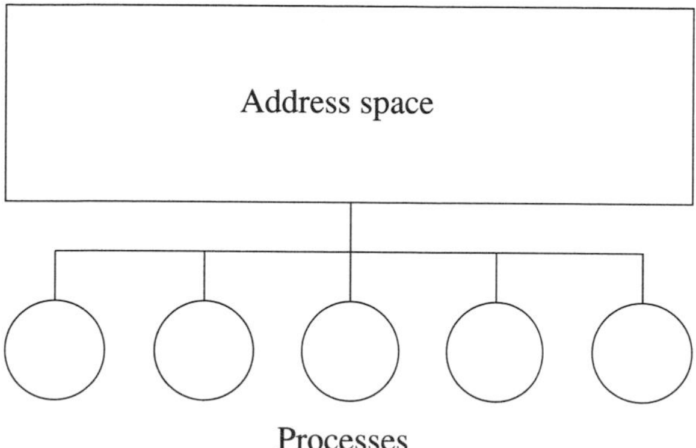

Figure 1.1
The shared-memory model

It is difficult (and expensive) to make "true" shared-memory machines with more than a few tens of processors. To achieve the shared-memory model with large numbers of processors, one must allow some memory references to take longer than others. The BBN family (GP-1000, TC-2000) maintained the shared-memory model on hardware architectures that provided nonuniform memory access (NUMA). These were followed by the Kendall Square family of machines. The current exponents of this approach are SGI, with its Origin series of computers, and the Hewlett-Packard Exemplar machines. For a discussion of a different version of this method of providing shared memory, see [73].

A variation on the shared-memory model occurs when processes have both a local memory (accessible by only one process) and also share a portion of memory (accessible by some or all of the other processes). The Linda programming model [21] is of this type.

Message passing. The message-passing model posits a set of processes that have only local memory but are able to communicate with other processes by sending and receiving messages. It is a defining feature of the message-passing model that data transfer from the local memory of one process to the local memory of another requires operations to be performed by both processes. Since MPI is a specific realization of the message-passing model, we discuss message passing in detail below.

In Figure 1.2 we don't show a specific communication network because it is not part of the computational *model*. The Intel IPSC/860 had a hypercube topology, the Intel Paragon (and its big brother, the ASCI TFLOPS machine) are mesh-connected, and machines such as the Meiko CS-2, Thinking Machines CM-5,

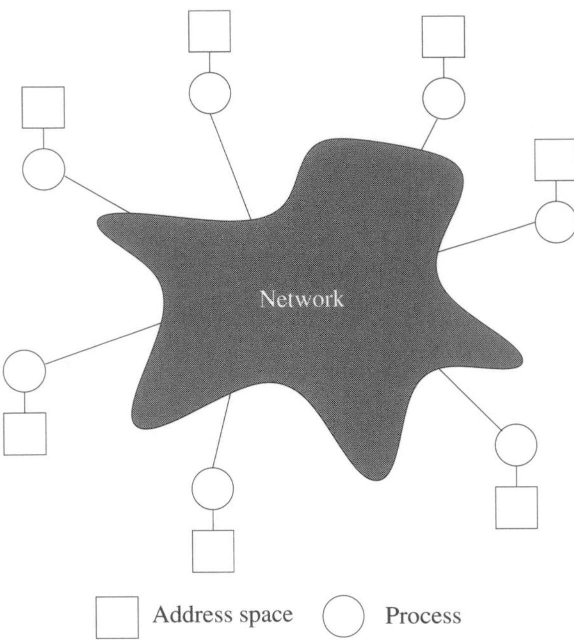

Figure 1.2
The message-passing model

and IBM SP-1 had various forms of multilevel switches that went a long way toward making the precise connection topology irrelevant to the programmer. Now message-passing models (represented by MPI) are implemented on a wide variety of hardware architectures.

Remote memory operations. Halfway between the shared-memory model, where processes access memory without knowing whether they are triggering remote communication at the hardware level, and the message-passing model, where both the local and remote processes must participate, is the remote memory operation model. This model is typified by *put* and *get* operations on such current machines as the Cray T3E. In this case one process can access the memory of another without that other's participation, but it does so explicitly, not the the same way it accesses its local memory. A related type of operation is the "active message" [126], which causes execution of a (typically short) subroutine in the address space of the other process. Active messages are often used to facilitate *remote memory copying*, which can be thought of as part of the active-message model. Such remote memory copy operations are exactly the "one-sided" sends and receives unavailable in the message-passing model. The first commercial machine to popularize this model was the TMC CM-5, which used active messages both directly and as an implementation layer for the TMC message-passing library.

MPI-style remote memory operations are part of the MPI-2 Standard and are described, along with the other parts of MPI-2, in [55] and [66]. Hardware support for one-sided operations, even on "commodity" networks, is now arriving. In addition to proprietary interfaces like IBM's LAPI [113], there are emerging industry standards such as the Virtual Interface Architecture (VIA) [125], that have the potential to bring good support for remote memory access operations even to inexpensive parallel computers.

Threads. Early forms of the shared-memory model provided processes with separate address spaces, which could obtain shared memory through explicit memory operations, such as special forms of the C `malloc` operation. The more common version of the shared-memory model now specifies that all memory be shared. This allows the model to be applied to multithreaded systems, in which a single process (address space) has associated with it several program counters and execution stacks. Since the model allows fast switching from one thread to another and requires no explicit memory operations, it can be used portably in Fortran programs. The difficulty imposed by the thread model is that any "state" of the program defined by the value of program variables is shared by all threads simultaneously, although in most thread systems it is possible to allocate thread-local memory. The most widely used thread model is specified by the POSIX Standard [84]. A higher-level approach is programming with threads is also offered by OpenMP [103, 104].

Combined models. Combinations of the above models are also possible, in which some clusters of processes share memory with one another but communicate with other clusters via message passing (Figure 1.3), or in which single processes may be multithreaded (separate threads share memory) yet not share memory with one another. Such a model is not yet widely available but is appearing rapidly from two different directions:

- As processors become cheaper, it becomes feasible to add them to the nodes of existing distributed-memory machines. This will affect even Beowulf-style systems as commodity PC's become small-scale symmetric multiprocessors.

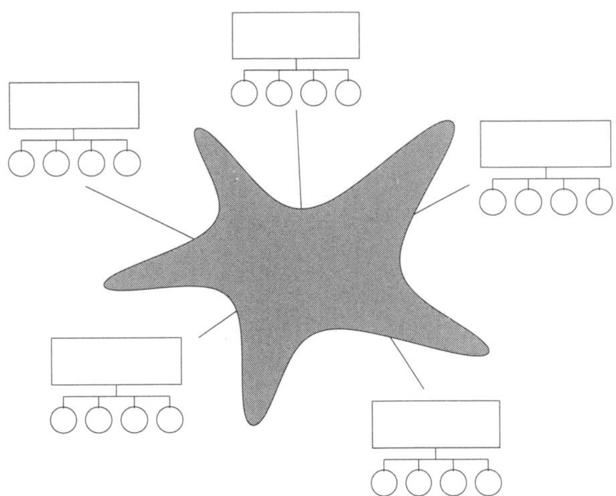

Figure 1.3
The cluster model

- Workstation vendors, such as Sun, DEC, and SGI, are now offering shared-memory multiprocessor versions of their standard products. These machines on a high-speed network represent early platforms for the combined model.

All three of the world's largest parallel machines provide a combined model at the hardware level, even though they are currently being programmed largely with MPI.

- The ASCI Red machine at Sandia has two processors per node (memory system). Although the second processor is there primarily to function as a communication processor, some applications have been coded so as to use it for computation.
- The ASCI Blue Mountain machine at Los Alamos consists (as of this writing) of many SGI Origin computers of 128 nodes each, connected by a HiPPI network. Each Origin is a NUMA shared-memory machine. SGI's future direction seems headed toward slightly smaller shared-memory machines, with more of them in the network.
- The ASCI Blue Pacific machine at Livermore is an IBM SP with nodes consisting of four-processor SMPs. The future direction for this machine seems to be to increase the number of processors on a node.

MPI implementations can take advantage of such hybrid hardware by utilizing the shared memory to accelerate message-passing operations between processes that share memory.

These combined models lead to software complexity, in which a shared-memory approach (like OpenMP) is combined with a message-passing approach (like MPI). Whether performance gains will outweigh the cost of the resulting complexity on large applications is still being explored.

The description of parallel computing models we have given here has focused on what they look like to the programmer. The underlying hardware for supporting these and future models continues to evolve. One direction being explored is multithreading at the hardware level, as exemplified by the Tera MTA product (architecturally descended from the Denelcor HEP) and the HTMT (Hybrid Technology Multithreaded) [83] architecture currently being explored as a research project.

1.3.2 Advantages of the Message-Passing Model

In this book we focus on the message-passing model of parallel computation, and in particular the MPI instantiation of that model. While we do not claim that the message-passing model is uniformly superior to the other models, we can say here why it has become widely used and why we can expect it to be around for a long time.

Universality. The message-passing model fits well on separate processors connected by a (fast or slow) communication network. Thus, it matches the hardware of most of today's parallel supercomputers, as well as the workstation networks and dedicated PC clusters that are beginning to compete with them. Where the machine supplies extra hardware to support a shared-memory model, the message-passing model can take advantage of this hardware to speed data transfer.

Expressivity. Message passing has been found to be a useful and complete model in which to express parallel algorithms. It provides the control missing from the data-parallel and compiler-based models in dealing with data locality. Some find its anthropomorphic flavor useful in formulating a parallel algorithm. It is well suited to adaptive, self-scheduling algorithms and to programs that can be made tolerant of the imbalance in process speeds found on shared networks.

Ease of debugging. Debugging of parallel programs remains a challenging research area. While debuggers for parallel programs are perhaps easier to write for the shared-memory model, it is arguable that the debugging process itself is easier in the message-passing paradigm. This is because one of the most common causes of error is unexpected overwriting of memory. The message-passing model, by controlling memory references more explicitly than any of the other models (only one process has direct access to any memory location), makes it easier to locate erroneous memory reads and writes. Some parallel debuggers even can display message queues, which are normally invisible to the programmer.

Performance. The most compelling reason that message passing will remain a permanent part of the parallel computing environment is performance. As modern CPUs have become faster, management of their caches and the memory hierarchy in general has become the key to getting the most out of these machines. Message passing provides a way for the programmer to explicitly associate specific data with processes and thus allow the compiler and cache-management hardware to function fully. Indeed, one advantage distributed-memory computers have over even the largest single-processor machines is that they typically provide more memory and more cache. Memory-bound applications can exhibit superlinear speedups when ported to such machines. And even on shared-memory computers, use of the message-passing model can improve performance by providing more programmer control of data locality in the memory hierarchy.

This analysis explains why message passing has emerged as one of the more widely used paradigms for expressing parallel algorithms. Although it has shortcomings, message passing comes closer than any other paradigm to being a standard approach for the implementation of parallel applications.

1.4 Evolution of Message-Passing Systems

Message passing has only recently, however, become a standard for *portability*, in both syntax and semantics. Before MPI, there were many competing variations on the message-passing theme, and programs could only be ported from one system to another with difficulty. Several factors contributed to the situation.

Vendors of parallel computing systems, while embracing standard sequential languages, offered different, proprietary message-passing libraries. There were two (good) reasons for this situation:

- No standard emerged, and—until MPI—no coherent effort was made to create one. This situation reflected the fact that parallel computing is a new science, and experimentation has been needed to identify the most useful concepts.

• Without a standard, vendors quite rightly treated the excellence of their proprietary libraries as a competitive advantage and focused on making their advantages unique (thus nonportable).

To deal with the portability problem, the research community contributed a number of libraries to the collection of alternatives. The better known of these are PICL [48], PVM [9], PARMACS [12], p4 [13, 19, 20], Chameleon [71], Zipcode [117], and TCGMSG [74]; these libraries were publicly available and some of them are still widely used. Many other experimental systems, of varying degrees of portability, have been developed at universities. In addition, commercial portable message-passing libraries were developed, such as Express [25], with considerable added functionality. These portability libraries, from the user's point of view, also competed with one another, and some users were driven to then write their own meta-portable libraries to hide the differences among them. Unfortunately, the more portable the code thus produced, the less functionality in the libraries the code could exploit, because it must be a least common denominator of the underlying systems. Thus, to achieve portable syntax, one must restrict oneself to deficient semantics, and many of the performance advantages of the nonportable systems are lost.

Sockets, both the Berkeley (Unix) variety and Winsock (Microsoft) variety, also offer a portable message-passing interface, although with minimal functionality. We analyze the difference between the socket interface and the MPI interface in Chapter 9.

1.5 The MPI Forum

The plethora of solutions being offered to the user by both commercial software makers and researchers eager to give away their advanced ideas for free necessitated unwelcome choices for the user among portability, performance, and features.

The user community, which quite definitely includes the software suppliers themselves, determined to address this problem. In April 1992, the Center for Research in Parallel Computation sponsored a one-day workshop on Standards for Message Passing in a Distributed-Memory Environment [127]. The result of that workshop, which featured presentations of many systems, was a realization both that a great diversity of good ideas existed among message-passing systems and that people were eager to cooperate on the definition of a standard.

At the Supercomputing '92 conference in November, a committee was formed to define a message-passing standard. At the time of creation, few knew what the outcome might look like, but the effort was begun with the following goals:

- to define a portable standard for message passing, which would not be an official, ANSI-like standard, but would attract both implementors and users;
- to operate in a completely open way, allowing anyone to join the discussions, either by attending meetings in person or by monitoring e-mail discussions; and
- to be finished in one year.

The MPI effort was a lively one, as a result of the tensions among these three goals. The MPI Forum decided to follow the format used by the High Performance Fortran Forum, which had been well received by its community. (It even decided to meet in the same hotel in Dallas.)

The MPI standardization effort has been successful in attracting a wide class of vendors and users because the MPI Forum itself was so broadly based. The parallel computer vendors were represented by Convex, Cray, IBM, Intel, Meiko, nCUBE, NEC, and Thinking Machines. Members of the groups associated with the portable software libraries were also present: PVM, p4, Zipcode, Chameleon, PARMACS, TCGMSG, and Express were all represented. Moreover, a number of parallel application specialists were on hand. In addition to meetings every six weeks for more than a year, there were continuous discussions via electronic mail, in which many persons from the worldwide parallel computing community participated. Equally important, an early commitment to producing a model implementation [69] helped demonstrate that an implementation of MPI was feasible.

The MPI Standard [98] was completed in May of 1994. This book is a companion to the Standard itself, showing how MPI is *used*, and how its advanced features are exploited, in a wide range of situations.

During the 1993–1995 meetings of the MPI Forum, several issues were postponed in order to reach early agreement on a core of message-passing functionality. The Forum reconvened during 1995–1997 to extend MPI to include remote memory operations, parallel I/O, dynamic process management, and a number of features designed to increase the convenience and robustness of MPI. Although some of the results of this effort are described in this book, most of them are covered formally in [55] and described in a more tutorial approach in [64].

2 Introduction to MPI

In this chapter we introduce the basic concepts of MPI, showing how they arise naturally out of the message-passing model.

2.1 Goal

The primary goal of the MPI specification is to demonstrate that users need not compromise among efficiency, portability, and functionality. Specifically, users can write portable programs that still take advantage of the specialized hardware and software offered by individual vendors. At the same time, advanced features, such as application-oriented process structures and dynamically managed process groups with an extensive set of collective operations, can be expected in every MPI implementation and can be used in every parallel application program where they might be useful. One of the most critical families of users is the parallel library writers, for whom efficient, portable, and highly functional code is extremely important. MPI is the first specification that allows these users to write truly portable libraries. The goal of MPI is ambitious, but because the collective effort of collaborative design and competitive implementation has been successful, it has removed the need for alternatives to MPI as means of specifying message-passing algorithms to be executed on any computer platform that implements the message-passing model.

This tripartite goal—portability, efficiency, functionality—has forced many of the design decisions that make up the MPI specification. We describe in the following sections just how these decisions have affected both the fundamental *send* and *receive* operations of the message-passing model and the set of advanced message-passing operations included in MPI.

2.2 What Is MPI?

MPI is not a revolutionary new way of programming parallel computers. Rather, it is an attempt to collect the best features of many message-passing systems that have been developed over the years, improve them where appropriate, and standardize them. Hence, we begin by summarizing the fundamentals of MPI.

- MPI is a library, not a language. It specifies the names, calling sequences, and results of subroutines to be called from Fortran programs, the functions to be called from C programs, and the classes and methods that make up the MPI C++ library. The programs that users write in Fortran, C, and C++ are compiled with ordinary compilers and linked with the MPI library.

• MPI is a specification, not a particular implementation. As of this writing, all parallel computer vendors offer an MPI implementation for their machines and free, publicly available implementations can be downloaded over the Internet. A correct MPI program should be able to run on all MPI implementations without change.
• MPI addresses the message-passing model. Although it is far more than a minimal system, its features do not extend beyond the fundamental computational model described in Chapter 1. A computation remains a collection of *processes* communicating with *messages*.

The structure of MPI makes it straightforward to port existing codes and to write new ones without learning a new set of fundamental concepts. Nevertheless, the attempts to remove the shortcomings of existing systems have made even the basic operations a little different. We explain these differences in the next section.

2.3 Basic MPI Concepts

Perhaps the best way to introduce the basic concepts in MPI is first to derive a minimal message-passing interface from the message-passing model itself and then to describe how MPI extends such a minimal interface to make it more useful to application programmers and library writers.

In the message-passing model of parallel computation, the processes executing in parallel have separate address spaces. Communication occurs when a portion of one process's address space is copied into another process's address space. This operation is cooperative and occurs only when the first process executes a *send* operations and the second process executes a *receive* operation. What are the minimal arguments for the send and receive functions?

For the sender, the obvious things that must be specified are the data to be communicated and the destination process to which the data is to be sent. The minimal way to describe data is to specify a starting address and a length (in bytes). Any sort of data item might be used to identify the destination; typically it has been an integer.

On the receiver's side, the minimum arguments are the address and length of an area in local memory where the received variable is to be placed, together with a variable to be filled in with the identity of the sender, so that the receiving process can know which process sent it the message.

Although an implementation of this minimum interface might be adequate for some applications, more features usually are needed. One key notion is that of *matching*: a process must be able to control which messages it receives, by screening them by means of another integer, called the *type* or *tag* of the message. Since we are soon going to use "type" for something else altogether, we will use the word "tag" for this argument to be used for matching. A message-passing system is expected to supply queuing capabilities so that a receive operation specifying a tag will complete successfully only when a message sent with a matching tag arrives. This consideration adds the tag as an argument for both sender and receiver. It is also convenient if the source can be specified on a receive operation as an additional screening parameter.

Finally, it is useful for the receive to specify a maximum message size (for messages with a given tag) but allow for shorter messages to arrive, in which case the actual length of the message received needs to be returned in some way.

Now our minimal message interface has become

```
send(address, length, destination, tag)
```

and

```
receive(address, length, source, tag, actlen)
```

where the `source` and `tag` in the receive can be either input arguments used to screen messages or special values used as "wild cards" to indicate that messages will be matched from any source or with any tag, in which case they will be filled in with the actual tag and destination of the message received. The argument `actlen` is the length of the message received. Typically it is considered an error if a matching message is received that is too long, but not if it is too short.

Many systems with variations on this type of interface were in use when the MPI effort began. Several of them were mentioned in the preceding chapter. Such message-passing systems proved extremely useful, but they imposed restrictions considered undesirable by a large user community. The MPI Forum sought to lift these restrictions by providing more flexible versions of each of these parameters, while retaining the familiar underlying meanings of the basic *send* and *receive* operations. Let us examine these parameters one by one, in each case discussing first the original restrictions and then the MPI version.

Describing message buffers. The `(address, length)` specification of the message to be sent was a good match for early hardware but is not really adequate for two different reasons:

- Often, the message to be sent is *not contiguous*. In the simplest case, it may be a row of a matrix that is stored columnwise. More generally, it may consist of an irregularly dispersed collection of structures of different sizes. In the past, programmers (or libraries) have provided code to pack this data into contiguous buffers before sending it and to unpack it at the receiving end. However, as communications processors began to appear that could deal directly with strided or even more generally distributed data, it became more critical for performance that the packing be done "on the fly" by the communication processor in order to avoid the extra data movement. This cannot be done unless the data is described in its original (distributed) form to the communication library.

• The past few years have seen a rise in the popularity of *heterogeneous computing* [18]. The popularity comes from two sources. The first is the distribution of various parts of a complex calculation among different semi-specialized computers (e.g., SIMD, vector, graphics). The second is the use of workstation networks as parallel computers. Workstation networks, consisting of machines acquired over time, are frequently made up of a variety of machine types. In both of these situations, messages must be exchanged between machines of different architectures, where `(address, length)` is no longer an adequate specification of the semantic content of the message. For example, with a vector of floating-point numbers, not only may the floating-point formats be different, but even the length may be different. This situation is true for integers as well. The communication library can do the necessary conversion *if* it is told precisely what is being transmitted.

The MPI solution, for both of these problems, is to specify messages at a higher level and in a more flexible way than `(address, length)` to reflect the fact that a message contains much more structure than just a string of bits. Instead, an MPI message buffer is defined by a triple `(address, count, datatype)`, describing `count` occurrences of the data type `datatype` starting at `address`. The power of this mechanism comes from the flexibility in the values of datatype.

To begin with, datatype can take on the values of elementary data types in the host language. Thus `(A, 300, MPI_REAL)` describes a vector `A` of 300 real numbers in Fortran, regardless of the length or format of a floating-point number. An MPI implementation for heterogeneous networks guarantees that the same 300 reals will be received, even if the receiving machine has a very different floating-point format.

The full power of data types, however, comes from the fact that users can construct their own data types using MPI routines and that these data types can describe noncontiguous data. Details of how to construct these "derived" data types are given in Chapter 5.

Separating Families of Messages. Nearly all message-passing systems have provided a `tag` argument for the *send* and *receive* operations. This argument allows the programmer to deal with the arrival of messages in an orderly way, even if the arrival of messages is not in the order desired. The message-passing system queues messages that arrive "of the wrong tag" until the program(mer) is ready for them. Usually a facility exists for specifying wild-card tags that match any tag.

This mechanism has proven necessary but insufficient, because the arbitrariness of the tag choices means that the entire program must use tags in a predefined, coherent way. Particular difficulties arise in the case of libraries, written far from the application programmer in time and space, whose messages must not be accidentally received by the application program.

MPI's solution is to extend the notion of tag with a new concept: the *context*. Contexts are allocated at run time by the system in response to user (and library) requests and are used for matching messages. They differ from tags in that they are allocated by the system instead of the user and no wild-card matching is permitted.

The usual notion of message tag, with wild-card matching, is retained in MPI.

Naming Processes. Processes belong to *groups*. If a group contains n processes, then its processes are identified within the group by *ranks*, which are integers from 0 to $n-1$. There is an initial group to which all processes in an MPI implementation belong. Within this group, then, processes are numbered similarly to the way in which they are numbered in many previous message-passing systems, from 0 up to 1 less than the total number of processes.

Communicators. The notions of context and group are combined in a single object called a *communicator*, which becomes an argument to most point-to-point and collective operations. Thus the `destination` or `source` specified in a send or receive operation always refers to the rank of the process in the group identified with the given communicator.

That is, in MPI the basic (blocking) *send* operation has become

```
MPI_Send(address, count, datatype, destination, tag, comm)
```

where

- `(address, count, datatype)` describes `count` occurrences of items of the form `datatype` starting at `address`,
- `destination` is the rank of the destination in the group associated with the communicator `comm`,

- `tag` is an integer used for message matching, and
- `comm` identifies a group of processes and a communication context.

The *receive* has become

```
MPI_Recv(address, maxcount, datatype, source, tag, comm, status)
```

where

- `(address, maxcount, datatype)` describe the receive buffer as they do in the case of `MPI_Send`. It is allowable for less than `maxcount` occurrences of `datatype` to be received. The arguments `tag` and `comm` are as in `MPI_Send`, with the addition that a wildcard, matching any tag, is allowed.
- `source` is the rank of the source of the message in the group associated with the communicator `comm`, or a wildcard matching any source,
- `status` holds information about the actual message size, source, and tag.

The source, tag, and count of the message actually received can be retrieved from `status`.

Several early message-passing systems returned the "status" parameters by separate calls that implicitly referenced the most recent message received. MPI's method is one aspect of its effort to be reliable in the situation where multiple threads are receiving messages on behalf of a process.

2.4 Other Interesting Features of MPI

Our focus so far has been on the basic *send* and *receive* operations, since one may well regard as the most fundamental new feature in MPI the small but important way in which each of the arguments of the "traditional" send/receive was modified from the minimal message-passing interface we described at the beginning of this section. Nevertheless, MPI is a large specification and offers many other advanced features, including the following:

Collective communications. Another proven concept from early message-passing libraries is the notion of *collective operation*, performed by all the processes in a computation. Collective operations are of two kinds:

- *Data movement* operations are used to rearrange data among the processes. The simplest of these is a broadcast, but many elaborate scattering and gathering operations can be defined (and are supported in MPI).

• *Collective computation* operations (minimum, maximum, sum, logical OR, etc., as well as user-defined operations).

In both cases, a message-passing library can take advantage of its knowledge of the structure of the machine to optimize and increase the parallelism in these operations.

MPI has an extremely flexible mechanism for describing data movement routines. These are particularly powerful when used in conjunction with the derived datatypes.

MPI also has a large set of collective computation operations, and a mechanism by which users can provide their own. In addition, MPI provides operations for creating and managing groups in a scalable way. Such groups can be used to control the scope of collective operations.

Virtual topologies. One can conceptualize processes in an application-oriented topology, for convenience in programming. Both general graphs and grids of processes are supported in MPI. Topologies provide a high-level method for managing process groups without dealing with them directly. Since topologies are a standard part of MPI, we do not treat them as an exotic, advanced feature. We use them early in the book (Chapter 4) and freely from then on.

Debugging and profiling. Rather than specifying any particular interface, MPI requires the availability of "hooks" that allow users to intercept MPI calls and thus define their own debugging and profiling mechanisms. In Chapter 7 we give an example of how to write such hooks for visualizing program behavior.

Communication modes. MPI has both the blocking send and receive operations described above and nonblocking versions whose completion can be tested for and waited for explicitly. It is possible to test and wait on multiple operations simultaneously. MPI also has multiple communication *modes.* The *standard* mode corresponds to current common practice in message-passing systems. The *synchronous* mode requires sends to block until the corresponding receive has occurred (as opposed to the standard mode blocking send, which blocks only until the buffer can be reused). The *ready* mode (for sends) is a way for the programmer to notify the system that the receive has been posted, so that the underlying system can use a faster protocol if it is available. The *buffered* mode provides user-controllable buffering for send operations.

Support for libraries. The structuring of all communication through communicators provides to library writers for the first time the capabilities they need to write parallel libraries that are completely independent of user code and inter-operable with other libraries. Libraries can maintain arbitrary data, called *attributes*, associated with the communicators they allocate, and can specify their own error handlers. The tools for creating MPI parallel libraries that take advantage of these features are described in Chapters 6 and 7.

Support for heterogeneous networks. MPI programs can run on networks of machines that have different lengths and formats for various fundamental datatypes, since each communication operation specifies a (possibly very simple) structure and all the component datatypes, so that the implementation always has enough information to do data format conversions if they are necessary. MPI does not specify how these conversions are done, however, thus allowing a variety of optimizations. We discuss heterogeneity specifically in Chapter 7.

Processes and processors. The MPI standard talks about *processes*. A process is a software concept, and represents an address space and one or more threads (each thread has a program counter). In contrast, a *processor* is a piece of hardware containing a central processing unit capable of executing a program. Some MPI implementations will limit an MPI program to one MPI process per processor; others will allow multiple MPI processes on each processor. In fact, some implementations limit an MPI program to one MPI process per node, where a node is a single symmetric multiprocessor (SMP) containing multiple processors.

An MPI process is usually the same as a process in the operating system, but that isn't required by the MPI standard. See [29] for an example where one Unix process contains multiple MPI processes.

2.5 Is MPI Large or Small?

Perhaps the most fundamental decision for the MPI Forum was whether MPI would be "small and exclusive," incorporating the minimal *intersection* of existing libraries, or "large and inclusive," incorporating the *union* of the functionality of existing systems.

In the end, although some ideas were left out, an attempt was made to include a relatively large number of features that had proven useful in various libraries and

MPI_Init	Initialize MPI
MPI_Comm_size	Find out how many processes there are
MPI_Comm_rank	Find out which process I am
MPI_Send	Send a message
MPI_Recv	Receive a message
MPI_Finalize	Terminate MPI

Table 2.1
The six-function version of MPI

applications. At the same time the number of *ideas* in MPI is small; the number of functions in MPI comes from combining a small set of orthogonal concepts.

To demonstrate just how little one needs to learn to write MPI programs, we present here a list of the indispensable functions, the ones that the programmer really cannot do without. There are six. With only these functions a vast number of useful and efficient programs can be written. The other functions add flexibility (datatypes), robustness (nonblocking send/receive), efficiency ("ready" mode), modularity (groups, communicators), or convenience (collective operations, topologies). Nonetheless, one can forego all of these concepts and use only the six routines from MPI shown in Table 2.1 to write complete message passing programs with just these six functions.

The designers of MPI attempted to make the features of MPI consistent and orthogonal. Hence users can incrementally add sets of functions to their repertoire as needed, without learning everything at once. For example, for collective communication, one can accomplish a lot with just `MPI_Bcast` and `MPI_Reduce`, as we show in Chapter 3. The next addition to one's repertoire is likely to be the nonblocking operations, which we discuss in Chapter 4, followed by derived datatypes, introduced in Chapter 4 and explored in more depth in Chapter 5. The unfolding of topics in this book will be driven by examples that motivate the introduction of MPI routines a little at a time.

2.6 Decisions Left to the Implementor

The MPI Standard does not specify *every* aspect of a parallel program. Some aspects of parallel programming that are left to the specific implementation are as follows:

- Process startup is left to the implementation. This strategy allows considerable flexibility in how an MPI program is executed, at some cost in portability of the parallel programming environment.[1]

- Although MPI specifies a number of error codes, the implementation is allowed to return a richer set of error codes than is specified in the Standard.
- The amount of system buffering provided for messages is implementation dependent, although users can exert some control if they choose. We describe what we mean by buffering and techniques for dealing with the buffering problem in Chapter 4. Chapter 8 contains a look at buffering issues from the implementor's point of view.
- Further issues, including some impacting performance, that come up when one looks more deeply into implementation issues are covered in Chapter 8.

The implementation used in the preparation of examples used in this book is MPICH [63], a freely available, portable implementation of MPI. Instructions for obtaining MPICH and the source code for the examples used here are given in Appendix D. Information on other implementations of MPI can be found on the Web at `http://www.mcs.anl.gov/mpi`.

[1]The capability of MPI programs to start new processes dynamically during the computation is added to MPI in the MPI-2 part of the Standard. This capability is covered in the companion volume to this book [66].

3 Using MPI in Simple Programs

In this chapter we introduce the most basic MPI calls and use them to write some simple parallel programs. Simplicity of a parallel algorithm does not limit its usefulness, however: even a small number of basic routines are enough to implement a major application. We also demonstrate in this chapter a few of the tools that we use throughout this book to study the behavior of parallel programs.

3.1 A First MPI Program

For our first parallel program, we choose a "perfect" parallel program: it can be expressed with a minimum of communication, load balancing is automatic, and we can verify the answer. Specifically, we compute the value of π by numerical integration. Since

$$\int_0^1 \frac{1}{1+x^2}dx = \arctan(x)|_0^1 = \arctan(1) - \arctan(0) = \arctan(1) = \frac{\pi}{4},$$

we will integrate the function $f(x) = 4/(1+x^2)$. To do this integration numerically, we divide the interval from 0 to 1 into some number n of subintervals and add up the areas of the rectangles as shown in Figure 3.1 for $n = 5$. Larger values of the parameter n will give us more accurate approximations of π. This is not, in fact, a very good way to compute π, but it makes a good example.

To see the relationship between n and the error in the approximation, we write an interactive program in which the user supplies n and the program first computes an approximation (the parallel part of the program) and then compares it with a known, highly accurate approximation to π.

The parallel part of the algorithm occurs as each process computes and adds up the areas for a different subset of the rectangles. At the end of the computation, all of the local sums are combined into a global sum representing the value of π. Communication requirements are consequently simple. One of the processes (we'll call it the master) is responsible for communication with the user. It obtains a value for n from the user and broadcasts it to all of the other processes. Each process is able to compute which rectangles it is responsible for from n, the total number of processes, and its own rank. After reporting a value for π and the error in the approximation, the master asks the user for a new value for n.

The complete program is shown in Figure 3.2. In most of this book we will show only the "interesting" parts of programs and refer the reader to other sources for the complete, runnable version of the code. For our first few programs, however,

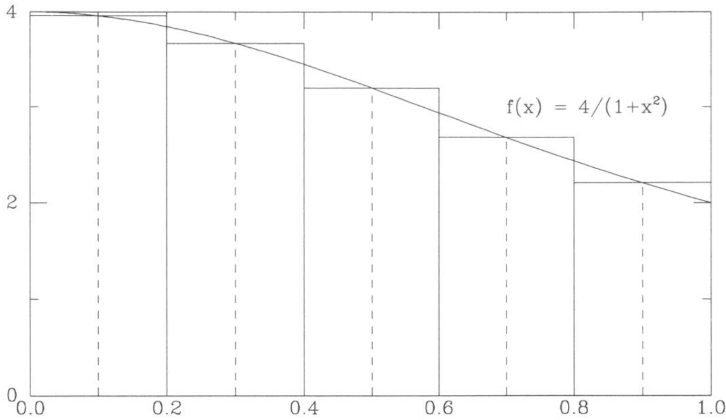

Figure 3.1
Integrating to find the value of π

we include the entire code and describe it more or less line by line. In the directory of programs that accompanies this book, the `pi` program is available as '`simplempi/pi.f`'. See Appendix D for details of how to obtain this code, other examples, and an implementation of MPI. Instructions for running this implementation of MPI are given in Appendix B.

Our program starts like any other, with the `program main` statement. Fortran 77 programs require the include file

```
include "mpif.h"
```

and Fortran 90 programs may use either `include "mpif.h"` or, if the MPI implementation supports it, the MPI module

```
use mpi
```

The include file or module is necessary in every MPI Fortran program and subprogram to define various constants and variables. For Fortran 77 compilers that do not support the `include` directive, the contents of this file must be inserted by hand into each function and subroutine that uses MPI calls. In this book, all of the examples use `use mpi` because the MPI module provides valuable checking for correct argument types and counts. However, if your MPI implementation does not provide an MPI module, you can use the `mpif.h` include file.

```
      program main
      use mpi
!     Use the following include if the mpi module is not available
!     include "mpif.h"
      double precision  PI25DT
      parameter        (PI25DT = 3.141592653589793238462643d0)
      double precision  mypi, pi, h, sum, x, f, a
      integer n, myid, numprocs, i, ierr
!                                 function to integrate
      f(a) = 4.d0 / (1.d0 + a*a)

      call MPI_INIT(ierr)
      call MPI_COMM_RANK(MPI_COMM_WORLD, myid, ierr)
      call MPI_COMM_SIZE(MPI_COMM_WORLD, numprocs, ierr)

 10   if ( myid .eq. 0 ) then
         print *, 'Enter the number of intervals: (0 quits) '
         read(*,*) n
      endif
!                                 broadcast n
      call MPI_BCAST(n,1,MPI_INTEGER,0,MPI_COMM_WORLD,ierr)
!                                 check for quit signal
      if ( n .le. 0 ) goto 30
!                                 calculate the interval size
      h = 1.0d0/n
      sum  = 0.0d0
      do 20 i = myid+1, n, numprocs
         x = h * (dble(i) - 0.5d0)
         sum = sum + f(x)
 20   continue
      mypi = h * sum
!                                 collect all the partial sums
      call MPI_REDUCE(mypi,pi,1,MPI_DOUBLE_PRECISION,MPI_SUM,0, &
                      MPI_COMM_WORLD,ierr)
!                                 node 0 prints the answer.
      if (myid .eq. 0) then
         print *, 'pi is ', pi, ' Error is', abs(pi - PI25DT)
      endif
      goto 10
 30   call MPI_FINALIZE(ierr)
      stop
      end
```

Figure 3.2
Fortran program for calculating π

After a few lines of variable definitions, we get to three lines that will probably be found near the beginning of every Fortran MPI program:

```
call MPI_INIT( ierr )
call MPI_COMM_RANK( MPI_COMM_WORLD, myid, ierr )
call MPI_COMM_SIZE( MPI_COMM_WORLD, numprocs, ierr )
```

The call to MPI_INIT is required in every MPI program and must be the first MPI call.[1] It establishes the MPI "environment." Only one invocation of MPI_INIT can occur in each program execution. Its only argument is an error code. Every Fortran MPI subroutine returns an error code in its last argument, which is either MPI_SUCCESS or an implementation-defined error code. In this example (and in many of our examples) we will be sloppy and not test the return codes from our MPI routines, assuming that they will always be MPI_SUCCESS. This approach will improve readability of the code at the expense of possible debugging time. We will discuss later (in Section 7.7) how to check, handle, and report errors.

As described in Chapter 2, all MPI communication is associated with a *communicator* that describes the communication context and an associated group of processes. In this program we will be using only the default communicator, predefined and named MPI_COMM_WORLD, that defines one context and the set of all processes. MPI_COMM_WORLD is one of the items defined in 'mpif.h'.

The call MPI_COMM_SIZE returns (in numprocs) the number of processes that the user has started for this program. Precisely how the user caused these processes to be started depends on the implementation, but any program can find out the number with this call. The value numprocs is actually the size of the group associated with the default communicator MPI_COMM_WORLD. We think of the processes in any group as being numbered with consecutive integers beginning with 0, called *ranks*. By calling MPI_COMM_RANK, each process finds out its rank in the group associated with a communicator. Thus, although each process in this program will get the same number in numprocs, each will have a different number for myid.

Next, the master process (which can identify itself by using myid) gets a value for n, the number of rectangles, from the user. The line

```
call MPI_BCAST(n,1,MPI_INTEGER,0,MPI_COMM_WORLD,ierr)
```

sends the value of n to all other processes. Note that *all* processes call MPI_BCAST, both the process sending the data (with rank zero) and all of the other processes in

[1] An exception is the MPI_Initialized routine, which a library can call to determine whether MPI_Init has been called. See Section 7.8.2.

MPI_COMM_WORLD.[2] The MPI_BCAST results in every process (in the group associated with the communicator given in the fifth argument) ending up with a copy of n. The data to be communicated is described by the address (n), the datatype (MPI_INTEGER), and the number of items (1). The process with the original copy is specified by the fourth argument (0 in this case, the master process, which just reads it from the user). (MPI assigns a type to every data item. MPI datatypes are described in full in Section 5.1.)

Thus, after the call to MPI_BCAST, all processes have n and their own identifiers, which is enough information for each one to compute its contribution, mypi. Each process computes the area of every numprocs'th rectangle, starting with myid+1. Next, all of the values of mypi held by the individual processes need to be added up. MPI provides a rich set of such operations, using the MPI_REDUCE routine, with an argument specifying which arithmetic or logical operation is being requested. In our case the call is

```
call MPI_REDUCE(mypi,pi,1,MPI_DOUBLE_PRECISION,MPI_SUM,0, &
                MPI_COMM_WORLD,ierr)
```

The first two arguments identify the source and result addresses, respectively. The data being collected consists of 1 (third argument) item of type MPI_DOUBLE_PRECISION (fourth argument). The operation is addition (MPI_SUM, the next argument), and the result of the operation is to be placed in pi on the process with rank 0 (fifth argument). The last two arguments are the communicator and error return code, as usual. The first two arguments of MPI_REDUCE must not overlap (i.e., must be different variables or sections of an array). A full list of the operations is presented in Section 7.3.2; user-defined operations are discussed in Section 7.3.2.

All processes then return to the top of the loop (the master prints the answer first). The MPI_BCAST causes all the processes except the master to wait for the next value of n.

When the user types a zero in response to the request for a number of rectangles, the loop terminates and all processes execute

```
call MPI_FINALIZE(ierr)
```

This call must be made by every process in an MPI computation. It terminates the

[2]In some other message-passing systems, messages sent with a broadcast can be received with a receive, just like a message sent with a send. In MPI, communication involving more than two processes is *collective*, and all participating processes call the same routine. MPI_BCAST is an example of a collective communication routine.

MPI_INIT(ierror)
    integer ierror

MPI_COMM_SIZE(comm, size, ierror)
    integer comm, size, ierror

MPI_COMM_RANK(comm, rank, ierror)
    integer comm, rank, ierror

MPI_BCAST(buffer, count, datatype, root, comm, ierror)
    <type> buffer(*)
    integer count, datatype, root, comm, ierror

MPI_REDUCE(sendbuf, recvbuf, count, datatype, op, root, comm, ierror)
    <type> sendbuf(*), recvbuf(*)
    integer count, datatype, op, root, comm, ierror

MPI_FINALIZE(ierror)
    integer ierror

Table 3.1
Fortran bindings for routines used in the `pi` program

MPI "environment"; with few exceptions, no MPI calls may be made by a process after its call to `MPI_FINALIZE`. In particular, `MPI_INIT` cannot be called again.

The Fortran bindings for the MPI routines used in this section are summarized in Table 3.1. In the tables of Fortran bindings, the expression `<type>` stands for any Fortran datatype, such as `INTEGER` or `DOUBLE PRECISION`.

3.2 Running Your First MPI Program

The way in which MPI programs are "launched" on a particular machine or network is not itself part of the MPI standard. Therefore it may vary from one machine to another. Several existing MPI implementations have used a syntax like

```
mpirun -np 4 pi
```

Recently the MPI Forum settled on a standard that recommended, but did not require, the syntax

```
mpiexec -n 4 pi
```

instead. See [64] for a complete discussion of the options for `mpiexec`. You can use `mpiexec` with MPICH.

Other MPI implementations may require different commands to start MPI programs; often `man mpi` will give tell you how to run programs. The MPI-2 standard strongly encourages implementors to provide an `mpiexec` command that provices a uniform interface to starting MPI programs.

3.3 A First MPI Program in C

In this section we repeat the program for computing the value of π, but this time in C rather than Fortran. In general, every effort was made in MPI to keep the Fortran and C bindings similar. The primary difference is that error codes are returned as the value of C functions instead of in a separate argument. In addition, the arguments to most functions are more strongly typed than they are in Fortran, having specific C types such as `MPI_Comm` and `MPI_Datatype` where Fortran has integers. The included file is, of course, different: '`mpi.h`' instead of the `mpi` module (or '`mpif.h`' in Fortran 77). Finally, the arguments to `MPI_Init` are different, so that a C program can take advantage of command-line arguments. An MPI implementation is expected to remove from the `argv` array any command-line arguments that should be processed by the implementation before returning control to the user program and to decrement `argc` accordingly. Note that the arguments to `MPI_Init` in C are the *addresses* of the usual `main` arguments `argc` and `argv`. New for MPI-1.2 implementations, one is allowed to pass `NULL` for both of these addresses. The C++ equivalent is to have two bindings for `MPI_Init`, one with `argc` and `argv` and one without. You may find, however that your implementation of MPI does not (yet) support this option.

The program is shown in Figure 3.3, and definitions of the C versions of the MPI routines used in this program are given in Table 3.2.

3.4 A First MPI Program in C++

Here we repeat the π-calculating program, this time in C++, to illustrate the new C++ bindings that were added to the MPI Standard as part of the MPI-2 effort.

The MPI Forum had three basic alternatives to choose from in deciding how users would use MPI in C++ programs.

- The easiest (from the Forum's point of view) would be to just use the C bindings as they stood. Functions written C can be called from C++ by defining them as

```
#include "mpi.h"
#include <math.h>
int main( int argc, char *argv[] )
{
    int n, myid, numprocs, i;
    double PI25DT = 3.141592653589793238462643;
    double mypi, pi, h, sum, x;
    MPI_Init(&argc,&argv);
    MPI_Comm_size(MPI_COMM_WORLD,&numprocs);
    MPI_Comm_rank(MPI_COMM_WORLD,&myid);
    while (1) {
        if (myid == 0) {
            printf("Enter the number of intervals: (0 quits) ");
            scanf("%d",&n);
        }
        MPI_Bcast(&n, 1, MPI_INT, 0, MPI_COMM_WORLD);
        if (n == 0)
            break;
        else {
            h   = 1.0 / (double) n;
            sum = 0.0;
            for (i = myid + 1; i <= n; i += numprocs) {
                x = h * ((double)i - 0.5);
                sum += (4.0 / (1.0 + x*x));
            }
            mypi = h * sum;
            MPI_Reduce(&mypi, &pi, 1, MPI_DOUBLE, MPI_SUM, 0,
                       MPI_COMM_WORLD);
            if (myid == 0)
                printf("pi is approximately %.16f, Error is %.16f\n",
                       pi, fabs(pi - PI25DT));
        }
    }
    MPI_Finalize();
    return 0;
}
```

Figure 3.3
C program for calculating π

```
int MPI_Init(int *argc, char ***argv)

int MPI_Comm_size(MPI_Comm comm, int *size)

int MPI_Comm_rank(MPI_Comm comm, int *rank)

int MPI_Bcast(void *buf, int count, MPI_Datatype datatype, int root,
              MPI_Comm comm)

int MPI_Reduce(void *sendbuf, void *recvbuf, int count, MPI_Datatype datatype,
               MPI_Op op, int root, MPI_Comm comm)

int MPI_Finalize()
```

Table 3.2
C bindings for routines used in the `pi` program

"external C" functions. It was decided that this approach would be a disappointment to C++ programmers, who are used to the convenience of C++. Besides, MPI has an object-oriented design, and it would be a shame not to express this design explicitly in an object-oriented language like C++.

- An alternate approach would be to define a complete class library in which all of the power of C++ would be used to free the C++ bindings from the structure of the C and Fortran bindings. The Forum decided that further research was needed before standardization of such a library. An example of such a library is OOMPI [119].
- An intermediate approach would be to exploit MPI's object-oriented structure to define classes and methods that closely followed the structure of the C and Fortran bindings.

The C++ bindings for MPI take the third approach. Most C functions become members of C++ classes that one can identify informally in the C bindings as objects. For example, `MPI::COMM_WORLD` is an instance of the communicator class, and both `Get_rank` and `Get_size` are methods on it. All classes, together with methods without an obvious class to attach them to, belong to the `MPI` name space.

The C++ version of our program for calculating π is shown in Figure 3.4. It is much the same as the C version shown in Figure 3.3. The differences are as follows.

The call to `MPI_Init` has become `MPI::Init`, with nearly the same arguments (because the C++ binding uses reference parameters, it isn't necessary or correct to pass the address of the arguments). Instead of passing the address of a variable to be

```
#include <math.h>
#include "mpi.h"

int main(int argc, char *argv[])
{
    int n, rank, size, i;
    double PI25DT = 3.141592653589793238462643;
    double mypi, pi, h, sum, x;

    MPI::Init(argc, argv);
    size = MPI::COMM_WORLD.Get_size();
    rank = MPI::COMM_WORLD.Get_rank();

    while (1) {
        if (rank == 0) {
            cout << "Enter the number of intervals: (0 quits)"
                 << endl;
            cin >> n;
        }

        MPI::COMM_WORLD.Bcast(&n, 1, MPI::INT, 0);
        if (n==0)
            break;
        else {
            h = 1.0 / (double) n;
            sum = 0.0;
            for (i = rank + 1; i <= n; i += size) {
                x = h * ((double)i - 0.5);
                sum += (4.0 / (1.0 + x*x));
            }
            mypi = h * sum;

            MPI::COMM_WORLD.Reduce(&mypi, &pi, 1, MPI::DOUBLE,
                                   MPI::SUM, 0);
            if (rank == 0)
                cout << "pi is approximately " << pi
                     << ", Error is " << fabs(pi - PI25DT)
                     << endl;
        }
    }
    MPI::Finalize();
    return 0;
}
```

Figure 3.4
C++ program for calculating π

```
void MPI::Init(int& argc, char**& argv)

void MPI::Init()

int MPI::Comm::Get_rank() const

int MPI::Comm::Get_size() const

void MPI::Intracomm::Bcast(void* buffer, int count,
                const Datatype& datatype, int root) const

void MPI::Intracomm::Reduce(const void* sendbuf, void* recvbuf, int count,
                const Datatype& datatype, const Op& op, int root) const

void MPI::Finalize()
```

Table 3.3
C++ bindings for routines used in the `pi` program

filled in with the value of the size of `MPI_COMM_WORLD`, we invoke the method `Get_size` on the object `MPI::COMM_WORLD`, and it returns the size of the `MPI::COMM_WORLD` communicator as its value. Here we see one of the big differences between C and C++. In C, the return value of each function is reserved for the error code, and the default error behavior (when the error code is not `MPI_SUCCESS`) is for all processes to abort. An alternative is to return error codes. How to control error behavior is described in Chapter 7. In C++, the default error handling is the same (all processes abort) but the alternative is not to return an error code but rather to throw an exception. This is in keeping with C++-style error handling.

The call to `Get_rank` is similar to the call to `Get_size`; it returns the rank as the value of the function. The other calls are to `Bcast` and `Reduce`, invoked as methods on `MPI::COMM_WORLD`. These are the obvious C++ analogues of their C counterparts. `MPI::Finalize` finishes up. The C++ bindings for the functions used in the π program are shown in Table 3.4. Note that there are two alternatives for `MPI::Init`: one has the usual command line arguments; the other has none. This is the C++ way of saying that the command-line arguments are optional; in C it is allowed to pass `NULL` for both `&argc` and `&argv`. The reasons why `MPI_Bcast` and `MPI_Reduce` are presented here as methods on an `Intercomm` class instead of on a `Comm` class are discussed in Chapter 6.

double precision **MPI_WTIME**()
double precision **MPI_WTICK**()

Table 3.4
Fortran binding for MPI timing routines

double **MPI_Wtime**()
double **MPI_Wtick**()

Table 3.5
C binding for MPI timing routines

3.5 Timing MPI Programs

Sequential algorithms are tested for correctness by seeing whether they give the right answer. For parallel programs, the right answer is not enough: one wishes to decrease the execution time. Therefore, measuring speed of execution is part of testing the program to see whether it performs as intended.

Many operating systems and libraries provide timing mechanisms, but so far all of those that both are portable and provide access to high resolution clocks are cumbersome to use. Therefore MPI provides a simple routine that can be used to time programs or sections of programs.

`MPI_Wtime()` returns a double-precision floating-point number that is the time in seconds since some arbitrary point of time in the past. The point is guaranteed not to change during the lifetime of a process. Thus, a time interval can be measured by calling this routine at the beginning and end of a program segment and subtracting the values returned. Making this a floating-point value allows the use of high-resolution timers if they are supported by the underlying hardware, although no particular resolution is specified. MPI provides a function to find out what the resolution is. This function, called `MPI_Wtick`, has no arguments. It returns a floating-point number that is the time in seconds between successive ticks of the clock. The bindings are shown in Tables 3.4, 3.5, and 3.6. The values returned by `MPI_Wtime` are not synchronized with other processes. That is, you cannot compare a value from `MPI_Wtime` from process 8 with a value from process 2. Only the difference in values of `MPI_Wtime`, taken on the same process, has any meaning.[3]

[3]If in fact the values of `MPI_Wtime` are synchronized among the processes, the MPI implementation sets an *attribute* to indicate this. This will be discussed in Section 7.8.

```
double MPI::Wtime()

double MPI::Wtick()
```

Table 3.6
C++ bindings for MPI timing routines

Suppose we wished to measure the *speedup* obtained by our program for computing π. Since this program is written as an interactive program, we wish to time only the section that does internal communications and computation. We don't want to include time spent waiting for user input. Figure 3.5 shows how the central part of our π program is modified to provide timings. Then, by running it with varying numbers of processes, we can measure speedup. Speedup for p processors is normally defined as

$$\frac{\text{time for 1 process}}{\text{time for } p \text{ processes}}$$

Thus, a nearly perfect speedup would be a phrase like "speedup of 97.8 with 100 processors."

3.6 A Self-Scheduling Example: Matrix-Vector Multiplication

So far, we have been able to write a "message-passing" program without explicitly sending and receiving messages. The next example will illustrate such explicit point-to-point communication and, at the same time illustrate one of the most common of parallel algorithm prototypes: the *self-scheduling*, or *master-slave*, algorithm. We will demonstrate the self-scheduling prototype first in the context of matrix-vector multiplication, for simplicity, but the same abstract algorithm has been used in many other contexts. In fact, it is the type of algorithm used in this chapter's major application, described in Section 3.12.

This example was chosen not because it illustrates the best way to parallelize this particular numerical computation (it doesn't), but because it illustrates the basic MPI *send* and *receive* operations in the context of a fundamental type of parallel algorithm, applicable in many situations.

The idea is that one process, which we call the master process, is responsible for coordinating the work of the others. This mechanism is particularly appropriate when the other processes (the *slave* processes) do not have to communicate with one another and when the amount of work that each slave must perform is difficult to predict. In the case of matrix-vector multiplication, the first criterion holds but

```
      double precision starttime, endtime
      ...
      starttime = MPI_WTIME()
!                                    broadcast n
      call MPI_BCAST(n,1,MPI_INTEGER,0,MPI_COMM_WORLD,ierr)
!                                    check for quit signal
      if ( n .le. 0 ) goto 30
!                                    calculate the interval size
      h   = 1.0d0/n
      sum = 0.0d0
      do 20 i = myid+1, n, numprocs
         x   = h * (dble(i) - 0.5d0)
         sum = sum + f(x)
 20   continue
      mypi = h * sum
!                                    collect all the partial sums
      call MPI_REDUCE(mypi,pi,1,MPI_DOUBLE_PRECISION,MPI_SUM,0, &
                      MPI_COMM_WORLD,ierr)
!                                    node 0 prints the answer.
      endtime = MPI_WTIME()
      if (myid .eq. 0) then
         print *, 'pi is ', pi, 'Error is ', abs(pi - PI25DT)
         print *, 'time is ', endtime-starttime, ' seconds'
      endif
      go to 10
```

Figure 3.5
Timing the program for calculating π

not the second. We can, of course, take the view that we might be computing on a network of workstations with varying loads, and so even if equal amounts of work were assigned, the time it takes for each slave to complete its task might vary widely. In any event, the point of this example is the use of the MPI *send* and *receive* routines to express the master-slave parallel algorithm, rather than the matrix-vector multiplication itself.

In our example of multiplying a matrix by a vector, a unit of work to be given out will consist of the dot product of one row of the matrix **A** with the (column) vector **b**. The master begins by broadcasting **b** to each slave. It then sends one row of the matrix **A** to each slave. At this point the master begins a loop, terminated when it has received all of the entries in the product. The body of the loop consists of receiving one entry in the product vector from whichever slave sends one, then sending the next task to that slave. In other words, completion of one task by a slave is considered to be a request for the next task. Once all tasks have been handed out, termination messages are sent instead.

Each slave, after receiving the broadcast value of **b**, also enters a loop, terminated by the receipt of the termination message from the master. The body of the loop consists of receiving a row of **A**, forming the dot product with **b**, and sending the answer back to the master.

Although the master and slaves execute distinct algorithms, and in some environments it is possible to have them compiled into separate executable files, the more portable and convenient alternative is to combine them into a single program, with a test near the beginning to separate the master code from the slave code.

We present the code here in three chunks: the code executed by all processes, the code executed only by the master, and the code executed only by the slaves. The code that is executed by all processes is shown in Figure 3.6. It does not contain any MPI calls that we have not already seen.

Now we fill in the sections carried out by the master and slaves. The way in which the master obtains the matrix **A** and the vector **b** is irrelevant, so we don't show their initialization here. We have arbitrarily made **A** of size 100×100, just to be specific. The code for the master is shown in Figure 3.7 on page 40. The new MPI call is the *send* operation, which the master uses to send a row of **A** to a slave. In this first version we pack the data into a contiguous buffer before sending it. (Later, in Section 5.2, we will show how MPI can do this for us.) Then the message is sent with

```
tag  = i
dest = i
call MPI_SEND(buffer, cols, MPI_DOUBLE_PRECISION, dest, &
              tag, MPI_COMM_WORLD, ierr)
```

The first three arguments, `buffer`, `cols`, and `MPI_DOUBLE_PRECISION`, describe the message in the usual MPI way: address, count, and datatype. The next argument, `i`, is the destination, an integer specifying the rank of the destination process in the group associated with the communicator given by the argument `MPI_COMM_WORLD`. Next comes an integer message type, or *tag*, in MPI terminology. We use the tag in this case to send a little extra information along with the row, namely, the row number. The slave will send this number back with the dot product it computes, so the master will know where to store the answer in the vector **c**. Of course, we are assuming that there are enough tag values to keep track of the rows

```
      program main
      use mpi
      integer MAX_ROWS, MAX_COLS, rows, cols
      parameter (MAX_ROWS = 1000, MAX_COLS = 1000)
      double precision a(MAX_ROWS,MAX_COLS), b(MAX_COLS), c(MAX_ROWS)
      double precision buffer(MAX_COLS), ans

      integer myid, master, numprocs, ierr, status(MPI_STATUS_SIZE)
      integer i, j, numsent, sender
      integer anstype, row

      call MPI_INIT( ierr )
      call MPI_COMM_RANK( MPI_COMM_WORLD, myid, ierr )
      call MPI_COMM_SIZE( MPI_COMM_WORLD, numprocs, ierr )
      master = 0
      rows   = 100
      cols   = 100

      if ( myid .eq. master ) then
!        master initializes and then dispatches
         ...
      else
!        slaves receive b, then compute dot products until done message
         ...
      endif

      call MPI_FINALIZE(ierr)
      stop
      end
```

Figure 3.6
Fortran program for matrix-vector multiplication: common part

of **A**. MPI guarantees that at least the values from 0 to 32767 are valid, which will suffice for small tests of this program. (More tag values might be available; see Section 7.8 for how to find out.) We reserve tag value 0 for the termination message. Finally, a communicator is specified (in this case the "default" communicator `MPI_COMM_WORLD`, whose group includes all processes), and a place (`ierr`) in which to return an error code. (We will consider error codes in more detail in Section 7.7.)

The responses from the slaves are received by the line

```
call MPI_RECV(ans, 1, MPI_DOUBLE_PRECISION, MPI_ANY_SOURCE, &
              MPI_ANY_TAG, MPI_COMM_WORLD, status, ierr)
```

This is a *blocking* receive; that is, control is not returned to the user program until the message has been received. The first three arguments specify a place to put the message. Here it is a single double-precision number, the dot product of one row of **A** with **b**. The master process can also specify that it wishes to wait for a message from a specific process. Here it does not wish to be so selective, so it uses the predefined value `MPI_ANY_SOURCE` to indicate that it will accept messages from any process associated with the `MPI_COMM_WORLD` communicator. The use of `MPI_ANY_TAG` indicates that any row is acceptable.

The argument `status` is an output argument that provides information about the message that is received (including the source, tag, and length). In Fortran, it is an array of integers of size `MPI_STATUS_SIZE`. It is declared in the user's program. Here we have called it `status`. The entry `status(MPI_SOURCE)` is filled in with the rank of the process that sent the message. It is important here because we will send the next unit of work (the next row) to that slave. We also need to know the value of `status(MPI_TAG)` in order to know where to store the answer in the vector **c**. In C, `status` is a structure of type `MPI_Status`; the element `status.MPI_SOURCE` is the source, and the element `status.MPI_TAG` is the tag value. In C programs, the status is usually passed by reference (that is, `&status`). In Fortran and C, other entries in `status` are used to determine the number of items that were actually received with the routine `MPI_Get_count`, which we will discuss in Section 7.1.3. In C++, `status` is an object of type `MPI::Status`. Instead of referencing elements of a status structure, in C++ you use member functions to set and get the values. These are shown in Table 3.7.

After all rows have been sent, the master sends a message with tag `0` to the slaves to tell them they are finished. The content of this message is irrelevant; all the information is carried by the tag. In fact, since the content of the message is irrelevant, we send a message of zero length by setting the count field to `0`.

```
!     master initializes and then dispatches
!     initialize a and b  (arbitrary)
      do 20 j = 1,cols
         b(j) = 1
         do 10 i = 1,rows
            a(i,j) = i
 10      continue
 20   continue
      numsent = 0
!     send b to each slave process
      call MPI_BCAST(b, cols, MPI_DOUBLE_PRECISION, master, &
                     MPI_COMM_WORLD, ierr)
!     send a row to each slave process; tag with row number
      do 40 i = 1,min(numprocs-1,rows)
         do 30 j = 1,cols
            buffer(j) = a(i,j)
 30      continue
         call MPI_SEND(buffer, cols, MPI_DOUBLE_PRECISION, i, &
                       i, MPI_COMM_WORLD, ierr)
         numsent = numsent+1
 40   continue
      do 70 i = 1,rows
         call MPI_RECV(ans, 1, MPI_DOUBLE_PRECISION, &
                       MPI_ANY_SOURCE, MPI_ANY_TAG, &
                       MPI_COMM_WORLD, status, ierr)
         sender     = status(MPI_SOURCE)
         anstype    = status(MPI_TAG)       ! row is tag value
         c(anstype) = ans
         if (numsent .lt. rows) then        ! send another row
            do 50 j = 1,cols
               buffer(j) = a(numsent+1,j)
 50         continue
            call MPI_SEND(buffer, cols, MPI_DOUBLE_PRECISION, &
                          sender, numsent+1, MPI_COMM_WORLD, ierr)
            numsent = numsent+1
         else      ! Tell sender that there is no more work
            call MPI_SEND(MPI_BOTTOM, 0, MPI_DOUBLE_PRECISION, &
                          sender, 0, MPI_COMM_WORLD, ierr)
         endif
 70   continue
```

Figure 3.7
Fortran program for matrix-vector multiplication: master part

int MPI::Status::Get_source() const

void MPI::Status::Set_source(int source)

int MPI::Status::Get_tag() const

void MPI::Status::Set_tag(int tag)

Table 3.7
C++ bindings for accessing the source and tag fields of a `status` object

MPI_SEND(buf, count, datatype, dest, tag, comm, ierror)
<type> buf(*)
integer count, datatype, dest, tag, comm, ierror

MPI_RECV(buf, count, datatype, source, tag, comm, status, ierror)
<type> buf(*)
integer count, datatype, source, tag, comm,
status(MPI_STATUS_SIZE), ierror

Table 3.8
Fortran bindings for send and receive routines

The slave code is given in Figure 3.8. It is a simple loop in which a message is received from the master and then is acted upon. Whether the message is a row to work on or a termination message is determined by its tag, which is available in `status(MPI_TAG)`.

If the message is a row (the tag is nonzero), then the dot product with **b** is computed and sent back to the master, and the slave waits for another task with `MPI_RECV`. Otherwise the slave branches to the `MPI_FINALIZE` in the code shared by master and slave.

The new routines used in in this example are the basic *send* and *receive* routines. Their Fortran, C, and C++ bindings are given in Tables 3.8, 3.9, and 3.10, respectively.

Now that we have discussed `MPI_Send` and `MPI_Recv`, we have covered all of the six functions listed in Chapter 2 as the minimal subset of MPI.

```
!         slaves receive b, then compute dot products until
!         done message received
          call MPI_BCAST(b, cols, MPI_DOUBLE_PRECISION, master, &
                         MPI_COMM_WORLD, ierr)
          if (rank .gt. rows)
             goto 200               ! skip if more processes than work
 90       call MPI_RECV(buffer, cols, MPI_DOUBLE_PRECISION, master, &
                       MPI_ANY_TAG, MPI_COMM_WORLD, status, ierr)
          if (status(MPI_TAG) .eq. 0) then
             go to 200
          else
             row = status(MPI_TAG)
             ans = 0.0
             do 100 i = 1,cols
                ans = ans+buffer(i)*b(i)
 100         continue
             call MPI_SEND(ans, 1, MPI_DOUBLE_PRECISION, master, &
                           row, MPI_COMM_WORLD, ierr)
             go to 90
          endif
 200      continue
```

Figure 3.8
Fortran program for matrix-vector multiplication: slave part

int **MPI_Send**(void *buf, int count, MPI_Datatype datatype, int dest, int tag, MPI_Comm comm)

int **MPI_Recv**(void *buf, int count, MPI_Datatype datatype, int source, int tag, MPI_Comm comm, MPI_Status *status)

Table 3.9
C bindings for send and receive routines

void MPI::Comm::Recv(void* buf, int count, const Datatype& datatype, int source, int tag, Status& status) const

void MPI::Comm::Send(const void* buf, int count, const Datatype& datatype, int dest, int tag) const

Table 3.10
C++ bindings for send and receive routines

3.7 Studying Parallel Performance

In this section we study the behavior of parallel programs in more depth than just by timing them as we did in Section 3.5. We will begin with a very simple example of *scalability analysis*, applied to matrix-vector and matrix-matrix multiplication. This is an interesting and deep topic in its own right (see, for example, [38] or [88]). We can convey the flavor of an analysis by looking at the program we have just written. We will then switch from an analytical approach to an experimental one, and show how to instrument a program so that it produces a log that we can study with graphical tools. The tools we describe here are in the MPE library.

3.7.1 Elementary Scalability Calculations

Scalability analysis is the estimation of the computation and communication requirements of a particular problem and the mathematical study of how these requirements change as the problem size and/or the number of processes changes. As an elementary example, let us look at the matrix-vector multiplication algorithm that we have just presented. The amount of computation is easy to estimate. Let us suppose, for simplicity, that the matrix $\mathbf{A}$ is square, of size $n \times n$. Then for each element of the product $\mathbf{c}$ of $\mathbf{A}$ and $\mathbf{b}$, we have to perform n multiplications, and $n-1$ additions. There are n elements of $\mathbf{c}$, so the total number of floating-point operations is

$$n \times (n + (n-1)) = 2n^2 - n.$$

For simplicity, we assume that additions and multiplications take the same amount of time, which we call T_{calc}. We assume further that the total computation time is dominated by the floating-point operations. Thus our rough estimate for computation time is $(2n^2 - n) \times T_{calc}$.

Now let us estimate the communication costs. Let us not count the cost of sending $\mathbf{b}$ to each slave process, assuming that it arrived there some other way (perhaps it is computed there). Then the number of floating-point numbers that have to be communicated is n (to send a row of $\mathbf{A}$), + 1 (to send the answer back) for each element of $\mathbf{c}$, for a grand total of

$$n \times (n+1) = n^2 + n.$$

If we assume that the time it takes to communicate a floating-point number is T_{comm}, the total communication time is roughly $(n^2 + n) \times T_{comm}$.

Therefore the ratio of communication to computation is

$$\left(\frac{n^2+n}{2n^2-n}\right)\times\left(\frac{T_{comm}}{T_{calc}}\right).$$

Since the cost of a single floating-point operation is usually much less than the cost of communicating one floating-point number, we hope to make this ratio as small as possible. Often by making a problem larger, one can reduce to insignificance the communication overhead. Here the bad news is that it doesn't happen in this case. The ratio T_{comm}/T_{calc} is roughly independent of n. (For the purposes of this analysis, we will ignore the effects of message sizes on communication costs; more detail is presented in Section 4.6.) As n gets larger, the ratio $\frac{n^2+n}{2n^2-n}$ just gets closer to $\frac{1}{2}$. This means that communications overhead will always be a problem in this simplistic algorithm for matrix-vector multiply. (In Chapter 4, we will discuss the effect of message size on the communication cost.)

Better news is provided by a similar analysis of matrix-*matrix* multiplication. We can easily modify our matrix-vector algorithm to multiply two matrices instead. The vector **b** becomes a matrix **B**, we still distribute a copy of **B** to all the slave processes, and we collect back a whole row of the product matrix **C** from each process. The slave code is shown in Figure 3.9, and the master code is modified accordingly. (We save listing of the whole program until later, when we show the instrumented version.)

Now let us do the scalability analysis for this (still not so very good) algorithm for matrix multiplication. For simplicity, let us again suppose that **A** is square and that **B** is square as well. Then the number of operations for each element of **C** is (as before) n multiplications and $n-1$ adds, but now there are n^2 elements of **C** to be computed, as opposed to n. Therefore, the number of floating-point operations is

$$n^2\times(2n-1)=2n^3-n^2.$$

The number of floating-point numbers communicated for each row is n (to send the row of **A**, plus n to send the row of **C** back), and there are n rows, so

$$n\times 2n$$

is the answer. Now the ratio of communication to computation is

$$\left(\frac{2n^2}{2n^3-n^2}\right)\times\left(\frac{T_{comm}}{T_{calc}}\right),$$

which approaches $1/n$ as n becomes large. Therefore for this problem we should expect communication overhead to play a smaller role than in large problems.

```
!     slaves receive B, then compute rows of C until done message
      do 85 i = 1,bcols
         call MPI_BCAST(b(1,i), brows, MPI_DOUBLE_PRECISION, &
                        master, MPI_COMM_WORLD, ierr)
 85   continue
 90   call MPI_RECV(buffer, acols, MPI_DOUBLE_PRECISION, master, &
                    MPI_ANY_TAG, MPI_COMM_WORLD, status, ierr)
      if (status(MPI_TAG) .eq. 0) then
         go to 200
      else
         row = status(MPI_TAG)
         do 100 i = 1,bcols
            ans(i) = 0.0
            do 95 j = 1,acols
               ans(i) = ans(i) + buffer(j)*b(j,i)
 95         continue
 100     continue
         call MPI_SEND(ans, bcols, MPI_DOUBLE_PRECISION, master, &
                       row, MPI_COMM_WORLD, ierr)
         go to 90
      endif
 200  continue
```

Figure 3.9
Matrix-matrix multiplication: slave part

3.7.2 Gathering Data on Program Execution

Timing results provide some insight into the performance of our program, and our programs so far have not been difficult to understand. But suppose that we need to see in detail just what the sequence of events was, just what amounts of time were spent on each phase of the computation, and just how long each individual communication operation took. The easiest way to understand this data at a glance would be through a graphical tool of some kind.

Several projects have been developed to create files of events with associated time stamps and then examine them in post-mortem fashion by interpreting them graphically on a workstation. Such files are called *logfiles*. The ability to generate logfiles automatically was an important component of one of the early portable programming libraries, PICL (for Portable *Instrumented* Communication Library) [48, 49]. Its latest logfile format has been proposed as a standard [130], and its logfile presentation program ParaGraph [76, 77] is widely used. An MPI version, MPICL, was recently released [131].

In this book we will use some simple tools for creating logfiles and viewing them. We treat the library for creation of logfiles as separate from the message-passing library. Viewing the logfile is independent of its creation, and multiple tools can be used. In the next few sections we describe routines in the MPE library for explicit logging of programmer-chosen events under program control, and we use the matrix-matrix multiplication program as an example. These routines will be used in Chapter 7 to build a completely automatic logging mechanism based on the standard MPI profiling interface.

The logfile viewing program we use is called `upshot`; it is a simple graphical display of parallel time lines and state durations, based on an earlier program of the same name [80]. `Upshot` is distributed with the model implementation of MPI and is a Tcl/Tk script [106], so it is easy to customize and extend. Further description of `upshot` is given in Appendix C.[4]

A recent addition to our toolkit is a program similar to `upshot`, written in Java and therefore called `Jumpshot` [132].

3.7.3 Instrumenting a Parallel Program with MPE Logging

Although there are advantages to having logfile creation and logfile examination be parts of a single integrated system, we separate them so that they can undergo separate development. We present in this section the MPE library for logfile creation. It is designed to coexist with any MPI implementation and is being distributed along with the model version of MPI. It is also used in the automatic instrumentation techniques for MPI programs discussed in Chapter 7. Reference bindings for MPE are given in Appendix C. Here we describe the routines needed to instrument a program with explicit, programmer-controlled events. In Chapter 7 we show how automatic logging can be done, with a decrease in programmer involvement but a corresponding decrease in flexibility.

Generally speaking, we need to call the `MPE_Log_event` routine only when we wish to record a log. The time-stamp and process identifier are collected automatically; the user specifies an event type and optionally can also supply one integer data item and one (short) character string. In addition, each process must call `MPE_Init_log` to prepare for logging, and `MPE_Finish_log` to merge the files being stored locally at each process into a single logfile, which is written out. `MPE_-`

[4]The strange name "Upshot" has arisen historically. Once there was a program called "Gist" that was written at BBN for the Butterfly software environment. It inspired a program written at Argonne, and the thesaurus suggested "Upshot" as related to "Gist."

Stop_log can be used to suspend logging, although the timer continues to run. MPE_Start_log causes logging to resume.

3.7.4 Events and States

The programmer chooses whatever non-negative integers are desired for event types; the system attaches no particular meaning to event types. Events are considered to have no duration. To measure duration of program states, pairs of events are specified as the beginnings and endings of *states*. A state is defined by the MPE_-Describe_state routine, which specifies the starting and ending event types. For the benefit of a logfile display program, whatever it might be, MPE_Describe_state also adds a state name and a color (and a bitmap pattern for use by monochrome displays) for the state. The corresponding MPE_Describe_event provides an event description for an event type. Note that this differs from the approach taken in [130], for example, where every "event" has duration. We treat events as atomic, and we define states, whether long or short, in terms of events.

3.7.5 Instrumenting the Matrix-Matrix Multiply Program

Now let us instrument the matrix-matrix multiply program using these routines. The first decision to make is which events to log. In this example it is easier first to decide on the states to be visualized and then to provide starting and ending events for each state. We could get a reasonably complete picture of the matrix-matrix multiply by measuring in the master program

- broadcast of **B**,
- sending each row of **A**,
- receiving each row of **C**,

and in the slave program

- receipt of **B** (by broadcast),
- receipt of each row of **A**,
- computation of the row of **C**,
- sending each row of **C** back to the master.

The overall framework of the instrumented version of our matrix-matrix multiplication program is shown in Figure 3.10. This is much the same as Figure 3.6, except for some changes to the program variables to reflect the fact that this is matrix-matrix instead of matrix-vector multiplication. The logging setup section just before the main if that separates master and slave does the MPE_INIT_LOG

```
!     matmat.f - matrix - matrix multiply,
!     simple self-scheduling version
      program main
      use mpi
      integer MAX_AROWS, MAX_ACOLS, MAX_BCOLS
      parameter (MAX_AROWS = 20, MAX_ACOLS = 1000, MAX_BCOLS = 20)
      double precision a(MAX_AROWS,MAX_ACOLS), b(MAX_ACOLS,MAX_BCOLS)
      double precision c(MAX_AROWS,MAX_BCOLS)
      double precision buffer(MAX_ACOLS), ans(MAX_ACOLS)
      double precision starttime, stoptime
      integer myid, master, numprocs, ierr, status(MPI_STATUS_SIZE)
      integer i, j, numsent, sender
      integer anstype, row, arows, acols, brows, bcols, crows, ccols
      call MPI_INIT( ierr )
      call MPI_COMM_RANK( MPI_COMM_WORLD, myid, ierr )
      call MPI_COMM_SIZE( MPI_COMM_WORLD, numprocs, ierr )
      arows  = 10
      acols  = 20
      brows  = 20
      bcols  = 10
      crows  = arows
      ccols  = bcols
      call MPE_INIT_LOG()
      if ( myid .eq. 0 ) then
         call MPE_DESCRIBE_STATE(1, 2, "Bcast",   "red:vlines3")
         call MPE_DESCRIBE_STATE(3, 4, "Compute","blue:gray3")
         call MPE_DESCRIBE_STATE(5, 6, "Send",    "green:light_gray")
         call MPE_DESCRIBE_STATE(7, 8, "Recv",    "yellow:gray")
      endif
      if ( myid .eq. 0 ) then
!        master initializes and then dispatches ...
      else
!        slaves receive b, then compute rows of c ...
      endif
      call MPE_FINISH_LOG("pmatmat.log")
      call MPI_FINALIZE(ierr)
      stop
      end
```

Figure 3.10
Matrix-matrix multiplication with logging: common part

and then defines four states, for broadcasting, computing, sending and receiving. For example, the line

```
call MPE_DESCRIBE_STATE(1, 2, "Bcast", "red:vlines3", ierror)
```

defines the "Bcast" state as the time between events of type 1 and events of type 2. We will use those event types to bracket the MPI_BCAST call in the program. The name of the state will be used in the logfile display program (whatever it may be) to label data associated with this state. The last argument is a hint to the display program about how we wish this state displayed. Here we are requesting "red" on a color display and the bitmap pattern "vlines3" on a black-white-display. The black-and-white (bitmap) versions are the ones used in this book. Calling the MPE_DESCRIBE_STATE routine just inserts a record into the logfile that the display program can use if it wishes to do so.

At the end of the computation, the call to MPE_FINISH_LOG gathers the log buffers from all the processes, merges them based on the time-stamps, and process 0 writes the logfile to the file named as the argument of MPE_FINISH_LOG.

Code specific to the master process is shown in Figure 3.11. We have just inserted calls to MPE_LOG_EVENT before and after each of the sections of code that we wish to be represented as a state, using the event types that we chose above. In addition, we have in some cases added data in the integer data field (the loop index in this case).

We log in the "receive" event the loop index we have reached, and in the "received" event the number of the row that was received. We have not really used the character data field here, since we have not varied it according to the individual event being logged; here it is merely echoing the event type.

Code specific to the slave process is shown in Figure 3.12. Again, the placement of calls to MPE_LOG_EVENT is routine.

3.7.6 Notes on Implementation of Logging

It is important for accuracy that logging of an event be a low-overhead operation. MPE_Log_event stores a small amount of information in memory, which is quite fast. During MPE_Finish_log, these buffers are merged in parallel, and the final buffer, sorted by time-stamp, is written out by process 0.

One subtle aspect of collecting logs with time-stamps is the necessity of relying on local clocks. On some parallel computers there are synchronized clocks, but on others the clocks are only approximately synchronized. On workstation networks, the situation is much worse, and clocks even drift with respect to each other as well.

```
!       master initializes and then dispatches
        .... initialization of a and b, broadcast of b
        numsent = 0
!       send a row of a to each other process; tag with row number
!       For simplicity, assume arows .ge. numprocs - 1
        do 40 i = 1,numprocs-1
           do 30 j = 1,acols
 30           buffer(j) = a(i,j)
           call MPE_LOG_EVENT(5, i, "send", ierr)
           call MPI_SEND(buffer, acols, MPI_DOUBLE_PRECISION, i, &
                         i, MPI_COMM_WORLD, ierr)
           call MPE_LOG_EVENT(6, i, "sent", ierr)
 40        numsent = numsent+1
        do 70 i = 1,crows
           call MPE_LOG_EVENT(7, i, "recv", ierr)
           call MPI_RECV(ans, ccols, MPI_DOUBLE_PRECISION, &
                MPI_ANY_SOURCE, MPI_ANY_TAG, MPI_COMM_WORLD, status, &
                ierr)
           sender     = status(MPI_SOURCE)
           anstype    = status(MPI_TAG)
           call MPE_LOG_EVENT(8, anstype, "recvd", ierr)
           do 45 j = 1,ccols
 45           c(anstype,j) = ans(j)
           if (numsent .lt. arows) then
              do 50 j = 1,acols
 50              buffer(j) = a(numsent+1,j)
              call MPE_LOG_EVENT(5, i, "send", ierr)
              call MPI_SEND(buffer, acols, MPI_DOUBLE_PRECISION, &
                            sender, numsent+1, MPI_COMM_WORLD, ierr)
              call MPE_LOG_EVENT(6, i, "sent", ierr)
              numsent = numsent+1
           else
              call MPE_LOG_EVENT(5, 0, "send", ierr)
              call MPI_SEND(1.0, 1, MPI_DOUBLE_PRECISION, sender, &
                            0, MPI_COMM_WORLD, ierr)
              call MPE_LOG_EVENT(6, 0, "sent", ierr)
           endif
 70     continue
```

Figure 3.11
Matrix-matrix multiplication with logging: master part

```
!       slaves receive b, then compute rows of c until done message
        call MPE_LOG_EVENT(1, 0, "bstart")
        do 85 i = 1,bcols
        call MPI_BCAST(b(1,i), brows, MPI_DOUBLE_PRECISION, master, &
                       MPI_COMM_WORLD, ierr)
 85     continue
        call MPE_LOG_EVENT(2, 0, "bend")
        call MPE_LOG_EVENT(7, i, "recv")
 90     call MPI_RECV(buffer, acols, MPI_DOUBLE_PRECISION, master, &
                      MPI_ANY_TAG, MPI_COMM_WORLD, status, ierr)
        if (status(MPI_TAG) .eq. 0) then
           go to 200
        else
           row = status(MPI_TAG)
           call MPE_LOG_EVENT(8, row, "recvd")
           call MPE_LOG_EVENT(3, row, "compute")
           do 100 i = 1,bcols
              ans(i) = 0.0
              do 95 j = 1,acols
                 ans(i) = ans(i) + buffer(j)*b(j,i)
 95           continue
 100       continue
           call MPE_LOG_EVENT(4, row, "computed")
           call MPE_LOG_EVENT(5, row, "send")
           call MPI_SEND(ans, bcols, MPI_DOUBLE_PRECISION, master, &
                         row, MPI_COMM_WORLD, ierr)
           call MPE_LOG_EVENT(6, row, "sent")
           go to 90
        endif
 200    continue
```

Figure 3.12
Matrix-matrix multiplication: slave part

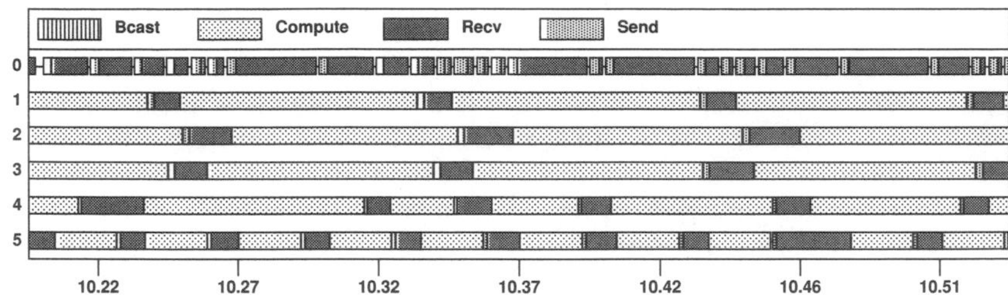

Figure 3.13
Upshot output

To compensate for this situation, the time-stamps are postprocessed with respect to synchronizations at `MPE_Init_log` and `MPE_Finish_log`. Postprocessing, which includes aligning and stretching the time axes of each process so that the `MPE_-Init_log` and `MPE_Finish_log` take place at the same time, is done as part of `MPE_Finish_log`. MPI itself is used to combine the logs, and the combining process is done in parallel, with the logfile itself written out by the process with rank 0 in `MPI_COMM_WORLD`.

3.7.7 Examining Logfiles with Upshot

After an MPI program instrumented with the MPE logging routines has completed, the directory where it executed contains a file of events sorted by time, with time adjusted to correct for offset and drift. We can write many programs to extract useful data from this file. One that we describe here and use from time to time in the rest of this book is the graphical display program `upshot`. A sample of `upshot` output is shown in Figure 3.13, which displays a portion of the logfile collected while running the matrix-matrix multiplication program on six Suns on an Ethernet. One can tell which one was the Sparc-10; the others were Sparc-2's.

Upshot displays parallel time lines, with states indicated by colored bars on color displays and patterns of dots or lines on monochrome displays (like the page of this book). Time-stamp values, adjusted to start at 0, are shown along the bottom of the frame. A particular view is shown in Figure 3.13, but what is missing there is the `upshot` control window for horizontal and vertical zooming in and out and scrolling forward and backward in time. Such adjustment of the view is necessary in order to glean both fine detail and summary impressions from the same logfile. Details of `upshot`'s control window, together with other features such as a state histogram display, can be found in Appendix C.4.

Of course, the information in logfiles can be displayed in simple summary form as well, without graphics. The model implementation contains, in addition to `upshot`, a short program called `states`. If we run `states` on the logfile that produced Figure 3.13, we get

```
State:   Time:
Bcast    0.146799
Compute  0.044800
Send     0.030711
Recv     0.098852
------------------
Total:   0.321162
```

Such summary information is a crude form of profiling; it tells us where the program is spending its time. Note that since the events and states may be described by the programmer and are not tied to the message-passing library, the MPE library can be useful in studying aspects of an algorithm that have nothing to do with interprocess communication.

3.8 Using Communicators

Up to this point, all of our examples have used `MPI_COMM_WORLD` as an argument to nearly every MPI call. What is it for, if it is always the same? In this section we describe *communicators*, which are perhaps the most pervasive and distinguishing feature of the MPI library specification. While a more comprehensive discussion of the purpose and use of communicators occurs in Chapter 6, we give here an extremely simple example that illustrates some of the MPI functions dealing with groups and communicators.

The example will illustrate the Monte Carlo method of integration. We will use it to find (again) the value of π. This will not be a particularly good way to find the value of π, but it will provide us with a simple example. To make it more interesting, we will introduce here some of the MPE real-time graphics operations, so that we can watch our program in action.

In Figure 3.14, if the radius of the circle is 1, then the area is π and the area of the square around it is 4. Therefore the ratio r of the area of the circle to that of the square is $\pi/4$. We will compute the ratio r by generating random points (x, y) in the square and counting how many of them turn out to be in the circle (by determining for each one whether $x^2 + y^2 < 1$. Then $\pi = 4r$. The testing of these

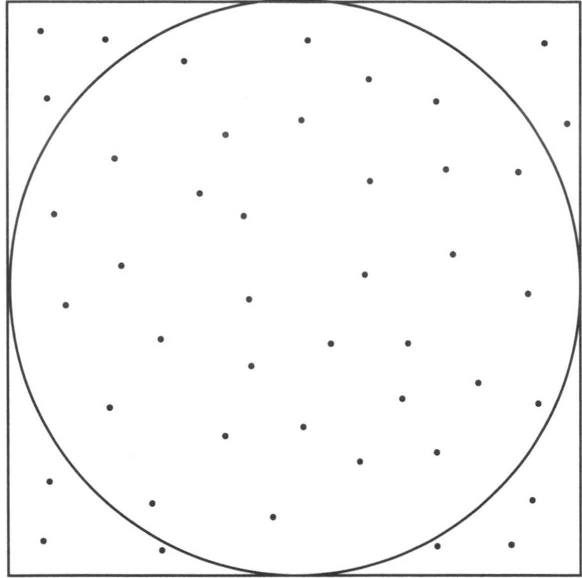

Figure 3.14
Monte Carlo computation of π

points is highly parallelizable.

The issue of parallel random number generators is too deep for us here (see [2] or [15] for discussions of the topic). To avoid the issue, we will use only one random number generator and devote a separate process to it. This process will generate the random numbers and will hand them out to the other processes for evaluation and display. Since the other processes will need to perform collective operations that do not involve this random number "server," we need to define a communicator whose group (see Chapter 2 for a brief discussion of groups) does not include it. The program itself is shown in Figures 3.15 through 3.18. This example is in C and has two purposes: to illustrate the use of a nondefault communicator, and to demonstrate the use of the MPE graphics library. We delay discussion of the graphics routines until the next section. The code that illustrates communicator manipulation is as follows:

```
MPI_Comm world, workers;
MPI_Group world_group, worker_group;
int ranks[1];
```

```
MPI_Init(&argc,&argv);
world  = MPI_COMM_WORLD;
MPI_Comm_size(world,&numprocs);
MPI_Comm_rank(world,&myid);
server = numprocs-1;              /* last process is server */

MPI_Comm_group( world, &world_group );
ranks[0] = server;
MPI_Group_excl( world_group, 1, ranks, &worker_group );
MPI_Comm_create( world, worker_group, &workers );
MPI_Group_free(&worker_group);
MPI_Group_free(&world_group);
```

The new feature here is that we have *two* communicators, `world` and `workers`. The communicator `workers` will contain all the processes except the random number server. This code illustrates how to build a communicator that has all the processes except the server process in it. To do this, we deal explicitly with the *group* of processes associated with the default communicator `MPI_COMM_WORLD`. Let us go through this code line by line.

Two communicators, `world` and `workers`, are declared, along with two groups of processes, `world_group` and `worker_group`. In C, an MPI group is described by a `MPI_Group` type. After the required call to `MPI_Init`, we assign `MPI_COMM_WORLD` to `world`. We find out how many processes there are with the call to `MPI_Comm_size`, and we assign to `server` the rank of the last process in the original group. The next few lines of code build the communicator that has as its group all of the processes except the random number server. First we extract from the `MPI_COMM_WORLD` communicator its group, which contains all processes. This is done with a call to `MPI_Comm_Group`. It returns in `world_group` the group of all processes. Next we build a new group. Groups can be manipulated in many ways (see Chapter 7), but here the simplest approach is to use `MPI_Group_excl`, which takes a given group and forms a new group by excluding certain of the original group's members. The members to be excluded are specified with an array of ranks; here we exclude a single process. Then the call to `MPI_Group_excl` returns in `worker_group` the new group, containing all the processes except the random number server. We create the new communicator from `MPI_COMM_WORLD` by calling `MPI_Comm_create` with the old communicator and the new group, getting back the new communicator in `workers`. This is the communicator we will use for collective operations that do not involve the random number server. At the end of the program, we release this

```
/* compute pi using Monte Carlo method */
#include <math.h>
#include "mpi.h"
#include "mpe.h"
#define CHUNKSIZE      1000
/* message tags */
#define REQUEST  1
#define REPLY    2
int main( int argc, char *argv[] )
{
    int iter;
    int in, out, i, iters, max, ix, iy, ranks[1], done, temp;
    double x, y, Pi, error, epsilon;
    int numprocs, myid, server, totalin, totalout, workerid;
    int rands[CHUNKSIZE], request;
    MPI_Comm world, workers;
    MPI_Group world_group, worker_group;
    MPI_Status status;

    MPI_Init(&argc,&argv);
    world  = MPI_COMM_WORLD;
    MPI_Comm_size(world,&numprocs);
    MPI_Comm_rank(world,&myid);
    server = numprocs-1;        /* last proc is server */
    if (myid == 0)
        sscanf( argv[1], "%lf", &epsilon );
    MPI_Bcast( &epsilon, 1, MPI_DOUBLE, 0, MPI_COMM_WORLD );
    MPI_Comm_group( world, &world_group );
    ranks[0] = server;
    MPI_Group_excl( world_group, 1, ranks, &worker_group );
    MPI_Comm_create( world, worker_group, &workers );
    MPI_Group_free(&worker_group);
```

Figure 3.15
Monte Carlo computation of π: beginning

```
if (myid == server) {          /* I am the rand server */
    do {
        MPI_Recv(&request, 1, MPI_INT, MPI_ANY_SOURCE, REQUEST,
                 world, &status);
        if (request) {
            for (i = 0; i < CHUNKSIZE; i++)
                    rands[i] = random();
            MPI_Send(rands, CHUNKSIZE, MPI_INT,
                     status.MPI_SOURCE, REPLY, world);
        }
    }
    while( request>0 );
}
```

Figure 3.16
Monte Carlo computation of π: server

communicator with a call to MPI_Comm_free. Finally, since we needed only the group worker_group in order to create the workers communicator, we may now release it by calling MPI_Group_free.

The code that "tidies up" by freeing the group and communicator that we created during the run merits further discussion, because it illustrates an important point: communicators contain internal references to groups. When we extract the group explicitly, by a call to MPI_Comm_group, we create another *reference* to the group. Later on, when we call MPI_Group_free with this reference, we are freeing the *reference*, which becomes invalid, but we are not destroying the group itself, since there is another reference inside the communicator. For this reason, we may actually call

```
MPI_Group_free(&worker_group);
```

and

```
MPI_Comm_free(&workers);
```

in either order; the group does not cease to exist until both references to the group have been freed. As an aid to safe programming, MPI sets the arguments to a free call to a special null object; this makes it easier to detect the inadvertent use of an (now) invalid object. These null objects have names (so that one can test for them); they are MPI_GROUP_NULL and MPI_COMM_NULL. Others will be introduced as they are needed.

```
    else {                            /* I am a worker process */
        request = 1;
        done = in = out = 0;
        max  = INT_MAX;          /* max int, for normalization */
        MPI_Send( &request, 1, MPI_INT, server, REQUEST, world );
        MPI_Comm_rank( workers, &workerid );
        iter = 0;
        while (!done) {
            iter++;
            request = 1;
            MPI_Recv( rands, CHUNKSIZE, MPI_INT, server, REPLY,
                     world, &status );
            for (i=0; i<CHUNKSIZE; ) {
                x = (((double) rands[i++])/max) * 2 - 1;
                y = (((double) rands[i++])/max) * 2 - 1;
                if (x*x + y*y < 1.0)
                    in++;
                else
                    out++;
            }
            MPI_Allreduce(&in, &totalin, 1, MPI_INT, MPI_SUM,
                          workers);
            MPI_Allreduce(&out, &totalout, 1, MPI_INT, MPI_SUM,
                          workers);
            Pi = (4.0*totalin)/(totalin + totalout);
            error = fabs( Pi-3.141592653589793238462643);
            done = (error < epsilon || (totalin+totalout) > 1000000);
            request = (done) ? 0 : 1;
            if (myid == 0) {
                printf( "\rpi = %23.20f", Pi );
                MPI_Send( &request, 1, MPI_INT, server, REQUEST,
                         world );
            }
            else {
                if (request)
                    MPI_Send(&request, 1, MPI_INT, server, REQUEST,
                             world);
            }
        }
    }
```

Figure 3.17
Monte Carlo computation of π: workers

```
    if (myid == server) {          /* I am the rand server */
      ...
    } else {                          /* I am a worker process */
      ...
    }
    if (myid == 0) {
        printf( "\npoints: %d\nin: %d, out: %d, <ret> to exit\n",
                totalin+totalout, totalin, totalout );
        getchar();
    }
    MPI_Comm_free(&workers);
    MPI_Finalize();
}
```

Figure 3.18
Monte Carlo computation of π: ending

The other new MPI library call introduced in this example is `MPI_Allreduce`. This differs from the `MPI_Reduce` that we have seen before in that the result of the reduction operation is available in all processes, not just in the one specified as root. Depending on implementation, `MPI_Allreduce` may be more efficient than the equivalent `MPI_Reduce` followed by an `MPI_Bcast`. Here we use it to test whether it is time to stop. We have provided an error value on the command line, and each process compares the current value of π with the precalculated value we have put into the program.

The specific bindings for the functions used in the Monte Carlo example are shown in Tables 3.11, 3.12, and 3.13. The C++ binding for `MPI_Allreduce` may appear strange at first. It is shown as a method belonging to the class `MPI::Intracomm` instead of the class `MPI::Comm`. The explanation is that there are two subclasses of the communicator class, *intracommunicators* and *intercommunicators*. The communicators we have been dealing with so far are intracommunicators; intercommunicators will be discussed in Chapter 7. The behavior of `Allreduce` depends on which kind of communicator it is called with. The C++ classes involved here are discussed in more detail in Section 6.2.2.

3.9 Another Way of Forming New Communicators

The preceding example was useful in introducing the notions of MPI groups and communicators. However, there is a slightly easier way of creating new communi-

```
int MPI_Allreduce(void *sendbuf, void *recvbuf, int count,
              MPI_Datatype datatype, MPI_Op op, MPI_Comm comm)

int MPI_Comm_group(MPI_Comm comm, MPI_Group *group)

int MPI_Group_excl(MPI_Group group, int n, int *ranks, MPI_Group *newgroup)

int MPI_Group_free(MPI_Group *group)

int MPI_Comm_create(MPI_Comm comm, MPI_Group group,
              MPI_Comm *newcomm)

int MPI_Comm_free(MPI_Comm *comm)
```

Table 3.11
C bindings for new routines needed by Monte Carlo

```
MPI_ALLREDUCE(sendbuf, recvbuf, count, datatype, op, comm, ierror)
              <type> sendbuf(*), recvbuf(*)
              integer count, datatype, op, comm, ierror

MPI_COMM_GROUP(comm, group, ierror)
              integer comm, group, ierror

MPI_GROUP_EXCL(group, n, ranks, newgroup, ierror)
              integer group, n, ranks(*), newgroup, ierror

MPI_GROUP_FREE(group, ierror)
              integer group, ierror

MPI_COMM_CREATE(comm, group, newcomm, ierror)
              integer comm, group, newcomm, ierror

MPI_COMM_FREE(comm, ierror)
              integer comm, ierror
```

Table 3.12
Fortran bindings for new routines needed by Monte Carlo

```
void MPI::Intracomm::Allreduce(const void* sendbuf, void* recvbuf, int count,
                const Datatype& datatype, const Op& op) const

Group MPI::Comm::Get_group() const

Group MPI::Group::Excl(int n, const int ranks[]) const

void MPI::Group::Free()

Intracomm MPI::Intracomm::Create(const Group& group) const

void MPI::Comm::Free()
```

Table 3.13
C++ bindings for new routines needed by Monte Carlo

```
int MPI_Comm_split(MPI_Comm oldcomm, int color, int key,
                MPI_Comm *newcomm)
```

Table 3.14
C binding for splitting communicators

cators containing a subset of the processes in an existing communicator.

`MPI_Comm_split` is a collective operation taking as input a communicator and two integers, called the `color` and the `key`, returning a new communicator. All the processes that pass in the same value of color will be placed in the same communicator, and that communicator will be the one returned to them. The C binding for `MPI_Comm_split` is shown in Table 3.14.

The key argument is used to assign ranks to the processes in the new communicator. If all processes passing the same value of color also pass the same value of key, then they are given ranks in the new communicator that are in the same order as their ranks in the old communicator. If they pass in different values for key, then these values are used to determine their order in the new communicator.

Note that `MPI_Comm_split` creates several new communicators (one for each color value) but each process is given access only to one of the new communicators, the one whose group the process belongs to.

The Fortran and C++ bindings for `MPI_Comm_split` are shown in Tables 3.15 and 3.16. Note the economy of the C++ binding for `Split` compared to the Fortran and C bindings. Since it need not return an error code it is free to return the new communicator. Furthermore, it will be invoked as a method on the old communicator. Therefore instead of four or five arguments it has only two.

MPI_COMM_SPLIT(oldcomm, color, key, newcomm, ierror)
integer oldcomm, color, key, newcomm, ierror

Table 3.15
Fortran binding for splitting communicators

Intracomm MPI::Intracomm::Split(int color, int key) const

Table 3.16
C++ binding for splitting communicators

The alternative way of creating new communicators out of MPI_COMM_WORLD simplifies our program substantially. Instead of manipulating the groups of the communicators directly, we create the communicator for the workers by having all of them pass to MPI_Comm_split the same color value, but one that is different from that passed in by the server. All the code involving group extraction and the call to MPI_Comm_create is replaced by

```
color = (myid == server);
MPI_Comm_split(world, color, 0, &workers);
```

3.10 A Handy Graphics Library for Parallel Programs

A second reason for including this Monte Carlo example is that it allows us to introduce in its simplest possible form the MPE graphics library. In many programs, parallel or not, it would be convenient to provide some simple graphics output. The X Window System (X11) provides this capability, but it has a steep learning curve. We decided that in order to better represent some of the computations in the examples in this book, it would be useful to add to the model implementation a simple graphics interface. One unusual aspect of this library is that it allows shared access by parallel processes to a single X display. It is not the case that graphics output is explicitly sent via MPI to a single process that does the X graphics; rather, the processes may do parallel updates to a shared X display, which need not be associated with any of the processes in the MPI program. On the other hand, when they need to communicate, they use an MPI communicator for this purpose.

We can animate the Monte Carlo program with only four calls: to initialize shared access to an X display, to free it, to draw points, and to update the display with the points that have been drawn. All processes declare

```
MPE_XGraph graph;
```

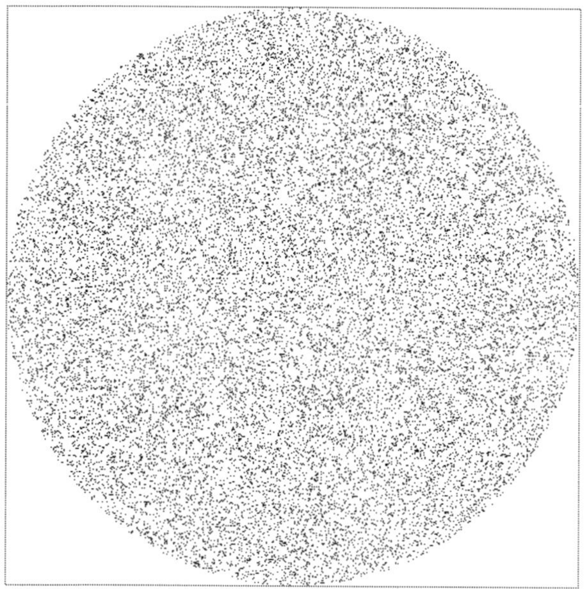

Figure 3.19
Monte Carlo computation of π: output

which defines a "handle" to a graphics object that will be manipulated by the MPE graphics routines. The type `MPE_XGraph` is defined in the file 'mpe.h', which must be included. At the beginning of the program, all processes might do

```
MPE_Open_graphics(&graph, MPI_COMM_WORLD, (char *)0, -1, -1,
                  WINDOW_SIZE, WINDOW_SIZE, MPE_GRAPH_INDEPENDENT);
```

which initializes this handle. The arguments in this case specify that the communicator `MPI_COMM_WORLD` will be used for communication for this graphics object, that the default display from the user's environment should be used as the X display (`(char *)0` as third argument instead of a display name), and that the user will be asked to place the window that is created. One could specify a location (x,y) by using nonnegative integers instead of (-1, -1). The rest of the arguments specify that the window will be square with side `WINDOW_SIZE` and that graphics operations will not be collective. For details, see Appendix C.

At the end of the program, each process does

```
MPE_Close_graphics(&graph);
```

to terminate access to the display. The only drawing command in this program is used to draw single points on the display. We will draw the points that lie within the circle of radius 1. Therefore, as more points are generated, we expect to see a rounder and rounder circle emerge. We can see this happening in Figure 3.19. The subroutine call that draws a point is

```
MPE_Draw_point(graph,
               (int)(WINDOW_SIZE/2 + x*WINDOW_SIZE/2),
               (int)(WINDOW_SIZE/2 - y*WINDOW_SIZE/2),
               MPE_BLACK);
```

which draws a point at the two coordinates given by its second and third arguments, in the color given by its last argument (of type `MPE_Color`). Finally, the line

```
MPE_Update( graph );
```

causes all of the drawing actions that may have been buffered up to this point to be flushed to the display. We can cut down on traffic to the X server by calling this only after a large number of calls to `MPE_Draw_point`. In our program, `MPE_Update` is called after each process has finished with one batch of points.

3.11 Common Errors and Misunderstandings

Experience with helping people learn MPI has helped us identify a set of mistakes that users often make. In this section we call your attention to some of them in the hope that we can help you avoid them right from the beginning.

Forgetting `ierr` in Fortran. Perhaps the most common error made in MPI programs written in Fortran is to forget the last argument, where the error code is returned. some compilers, particularly for Fortran 90, will catch this for you at compile time, but others will not, leading to hard-to-find errors.

Misdeclaring `status` in Fortran. When an `MPI_Recv` returns, certain information has been stored in the `status` argument. `Status` is an *array* of integers (of size `MPI_STATUS_SIZE`), *not* a single integer. Many compilers will not complain about this, but running the program will definitely lead to an unexpected memory overwrite and mysterious behavior.

Misdeclaring string variables in Fortran. In Fortran, strings are not the same as arrays of characters. Although this is not really an MPI issue, MPI does use string variables, and so this error sometimes happens when someone uses MPI for the first time. A ten-character string `a` in Fortran should be declared as something like

```
character*10 a
```

and definitely *not*

```
character a(10)
```

The latter is an array of characters, not a single character string variable.

Expecting `argc` and `argv` to be passed to all processes. The arguments to `MPI_Init` in C are `&argc` and `&argv`. this *allows* the MPI implementation to fill these in on all processes, but the MPI Standard does not *require* it. Some implementations propagate `argc` and `argv` to all processes; some don't. The same is true for the environment (variables whose values are accessible by `getenv`); some implementations may start all processes with the environment in existence when `mpirun` or `mpiexec` is run, but others may not. A portable program will not rely on this feature. Remember that MPI does not assume it is running under Unix, and some MPI implementations run on Windows NT or Macintosh systems or in specialized (e.g., real-time) environments.

Doing things before `MPI_Init` or after `MPI_Finalize`. The MPI Standard says nothing about the situation before `MPI_Init` or after `MPI_Finalize`, not even how many processes are running. Doing anything whatsoever in your program during either of these periods may yield unexpected and implementation-dependent results. For example, `argc` and `argv` may not make any sense until after `MPI_Init` has processed them, and so an MPI application should not access them until then.

Matching `MPI_Bcast` with `MPI_Recv`. It is easy to think that `MPI_Bcast` is a "multiple send" operation, and that the recipients of the broadcast message should receive it with `MPI_Recv`. On the contrary, `MPI_Bcast` is a collective operation which must be called on all processes in the group of the specified communicator. It functions as a multi-send on the specified root process and as a receive on the others. The reason for this is that it allows for optimal performance. An `MPI_Recv` does not have to check whether the message it has just received is part of a broadcast than hence may have to be forwarded to other processes.

Assuming your MPI implementation is thread-safe. We discussed multithreading in Chapter 1. MPI was designed so that it could be implemented in a thread-safe manner (multiple threads could call MPI routines at the same time) but the Standard does not require it of implementations. If you use multithreading in your program (or even if your compiler generates multithreaded code for you) and your MPI implementation is not thread-safe, you may get unpredictable results. See *Using MPI-2* [66] for a discussion of the MPI-2 features that make MPI's interaction with threads more explicit.

3.12 Application: Quantum Monte Carlo Calculations in Nuclear Physics

Although we have presented only a few MPI routines in this chapter, they are enough to express quantum Monte Carlo applications in theoretical physics. Researchers in Argonne's Physics Division, in collaboration with colleagues at the University of Illinois at Urbana-Champaign and Los Alamos, are computing the properties of light (up to 40 neutrons and protons) nuclei using realistic two- and three-nucleon interactions. This research involves developing many-body methods for reliably computing the properties of a nucleus with complicated forces that are strongly dependent on the spins and charge states of the nucleons.

The methods used are described in [111], [129], and [112]. The newest calculations use the Green's function Monte Carlo (GFMC) method. They are the first calculations of nuclei with more than 3 nucleons, using realistic potentials, that give binding energies accurate to 1%. The calculations are done mainly on the IBM SP and SGI Onyx parallel computers at Argonne and can efficiently use as many nodes as are available (runs with 128 nodes have been made with speedups of 122).

The programs were originally developed for Cray computers and had been designed to use long vectors; significant modifications (required by the cache size and other considerations) were made to speed up the programs on the workstation architectures of modern parallel computers. The effort involved in adapting the programs to parallel processors was much less than this single-processor tuning.

For the older programs, the algorithm is a master-slave algorithm, just like our matrix-vector multiplication example in Section 3.6. The master generates positions or samples on a random walk and sends them to the slaves for the time-consuming (up to minutes per sample) task of evaluating the local energy. A reasonable run takes 5,000 to 10,000 Monte Carlo samples while searching for the best variational parameters; final runs can take about 50,000 samples. There is no requirement that the master receive the results in the order it sends positions to the slaves. Slaves that are busy with other work will automatically be used for fewer positions. There is no significant I/O; all of the I/O is done by the master node.

In the more recent GFMC program, the master initially sends a different list of starting configurations to each slave. The slaves then independently propagate their configurations and periodically return local energies to the master. However, during the propagation, configurations can be removed (because they have wandered into regions of low importance) or replicated (because they have discovered regions of high importance). Thus the load on each slave can change and from time to time the master instructs overloaded slaves to directly send some of their configurations to underloaded slaves. Hence both master-slave and slave-slave communication occurs.

The programs are of nontrivial size (typically 20,000 lines of Fortran), but as message-passing programs they are quite straightforward. The first program developed uses the same basic self-scheduling structure as the matrix-vector multiplication program shown in Figures 3.6, 3.7, and 3.8. It was originally written for the IBM SP1 using p4 and was ported to MPI in one afternoon. The explicitly MPI content of the GFMC program is also quite small.

3.13 Summary of a Simple Subset of MPI

In this chapter we have introduced basic MPI routines through very simple example programs. In particular, we have defined the six functions that make up the minimal MPI subset that we discussed in Chapter 2. We have added to those the two most common collective operations and the basic timing routine, and we have shown how to work with groups and communicators. We have also introduced a few useful tools: MPE logging, MPE graphics, and `upshot`. We will continue to use these tools as we look at more example programs in the chapters to come. Finally, we have summarized a few of the common problems that MPI beginners sometimes make.

In some ways we have already provided enough of the MPI library to write serious applications (such as the nuclear structure example of the preceding section). In other ways we have barely scratched the surface; MPI offers much more, as we will see in the upcoming chapters.

4 Intermediate MPI

In the preceding chapter we considered a number of straightforward parallel algorithms. We wrote parallel programs for these algorithms using straightforward MPI subroutine calls, and we verified with timing and program visualization tools that our programs behaved as we expected.

In this chapter we introduce several important issues that require more subtlety in our analysis and more precision in our tools. The mathematical problem we address here (the Poisson problem) is only a little more complicated than the problems of the preceding chapter, but the parallel algorithm, particularly the communication pattern, admits more options.

We introduce several new MPI routines. For example, since our mathematical problem takes place on a finite-difference computational grid, we introduce the MPI notion of *virtual topology*, which makes the allocation of processes to particular parts of a grid convenient to manage. We also describe many of the variations on the basic *send* and *receive* operations supported by MPI; indeed, the communication patterns needed here by our parallel algorithm motivated some of the more esoteric MPI features.

Our first goal in this chapter is thus to show how MPI enables efficient programs to be written concisely. A secondary goal is to explain some of the issues that arise in analyzing of communication patterns in grid-based problems.

We approach both of these goals by examining a number of programs for the 2-D and 3-D Poisson problem, a model partial differential equation. Because Fortran provides a much more convenient syntax for manipulating multidimensional arrays than does C, the bulk of the examples in this chapter are written in Fortran.

We also use the Poisson problem as a means to introduce the different mechanisms by which an MPI program can send data from one process to another, particularly with respect to both how data is buffered in the message passing system and how nonblocking communications can be used. By examining the different approaches in the context of a single application, we clarify the distinctions between these approaches. We begin by presenting the mathematical problem and an approach to solving it computationally. Then we describe MPI's virtual topology feature, which allows us to manage a grid of processes. As we progress, we introduce several new MPI functions while considering various ways of organizing the communications. Finally, to help in understanding the reasons for the different implementation choices, we make another brief foray into scalability analysis.

This chapter may also be viewed as a discussion of the sparse matrix-vector product, because that is really the fundamental operation at work in these algorithms. While we will not discuss it in this book, the message-passing operations discussed in this chapter are the same as are used in implementing a parallel sparse matrix-vector product. The Jacobi method was chosen for its simplicity in the computational part of the program, allowing us to present a complete application.

4.1 The Poisson Problem

The Poisson problem is a simple partial differential equation (PDE) that is at the core of many applications. More elaborate problems and algorithms often have the same communication structure that we will use here to solve this problem. Thus, by studying how MPI can be used here, we are providing fundamentals on how communication patterns appear in more complex PDE problems. At the same time, we can demonstrate a wide variety of message-passing techniques and how MPI may be used to express them.

We emphasize that while the Poisson problem is a useful example for describing the features of MPI that can be used in solving partial differential equations and other problems that involve decomposition across many processes, the numerical techniques in this section are not the last word in solving PDEs and give poor performance relative to more recent and sophisticated methods. For information on more sophisticated, freely available parallel solvers for PDE's that use MPI, see [72]. For more details about the mathematical terminology used in this chapter, consult [89], among other sources.

The Poisson problem is expressed by the equations

$$\nabla^2 u = f(x,y) \text{ in the interior} \tag{4.1.1}$$

$$u(x,y) = g(x,y) \text{ on the boundary} \tag{4.1.2}$$

To simplify the discussion, we use the unit square as the domain.

To find an approximate solution to this problem, we define a square *mesh* (also called a *grid*) consisting of the points (x_i, y_j), given by

$$\begin{aligned} x_i &= \frac{i}{n+1}, i = 0, \ldots, n+1, \\ y_j &= \frac{j}{n+1}, j = 0, \ldots, n+1, \end{aligned}$$

where there are $n+2$ points along each edge of the mesh (see Figure 4.1). We will find an approximation to $u(x,y)$ only at the points (x_i, y_j). We use the shorthand $u_{i,j}$ to refer to the approximation to u at (x_i, y_j). The value $1/(n+1)$ is used frequently; we will denote it by h (following common practice). We can approximate (4.1.1) at each of these points with the formula [89]

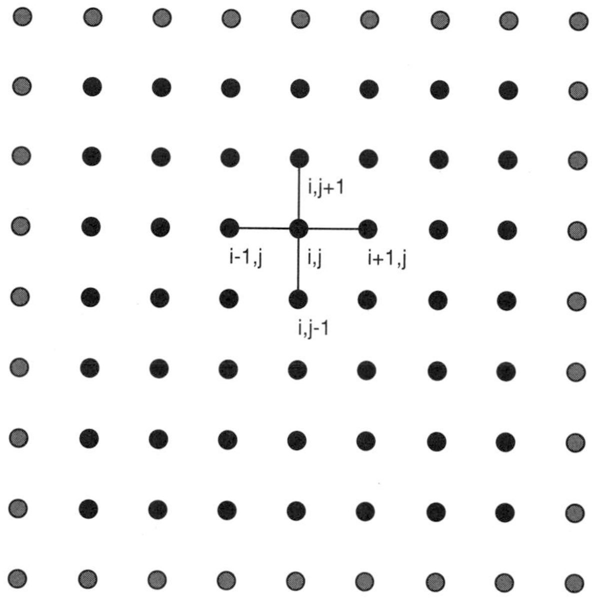

Figure 4.1
Five-point stencil approximation for 2-D Poisson problem, with $n = 7$. The boundaries of the domain are shown in gray.

$$\frac{u_{i-1,j} + u_{i,j+1} + u_{i,j-1} + u_{i+1,j} - 4u_{i,j}}{h^2} = f_{i,j}. \tag{4.1.3}$$

We wish to solve (4.1.3) for $u_{i,j}$ everywhere on the mesh. Since the formula involves u at five points, we must find some way to solve for u everywhere. One approach is to rewrite (4.1.3) as

$$u_{i,j} = \frac{1}{4}\left(u_{i-1,j} + u_{i,j+1} + u_{i,j-1} + u_{i+1,j} - h^2 f_{i,j}\right),$$

iterate by choosing values for all mesh points $u_{i,j}$, and then replace them by using[1]

$$u_{i,j}^{k+1} = \frac{1}{4}\left(u_{i-1,j}^k + u_{i,j+1}^k + u_{i,j-1}^k + u_{i+1,j}^k - h^2 f_{i,j}\right).$$

This process, known as *Jacobi iteration*, is repeated until the solution is reached. Fortran code for this is shown in Figure 4.2.

[1]The ways in which arrays and matrices correspond to one another and are laid out in memory by Fortran and C compilers are often a source of confusion. We discuss this topic in excruciating detail in Appendix E.

```
      integer i, j, n
      double precision u(0:n+1,0:n+1), unew(0:n+1,0:n+1)
      do 10 j=1, n
         do 10 i=1, n
            unew(i,j) = &
                0.25*(u(i-1,j)+u(i,j+1)+u(i,j-1)+u(i+1,j)) - &
                h * h * f(i,j)
 10   continue
```

Figure 4.2
Jacobi iteration

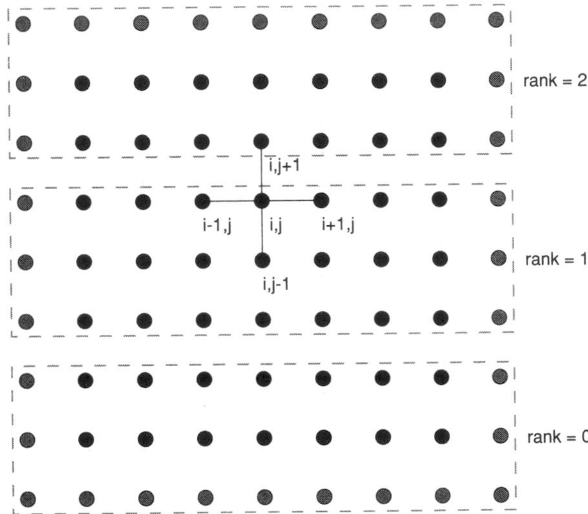

Figure 4.3
1-D decomposition of the domain

To parallelize this algorithm, we need to parallelize the loops in the code. To do this, we must distribute the data, in this case the arrays `u`, `unew`, and `f`, across the processes. Several approaches are possible.

One of the simplest decompositions is shown in Figure 4.3. In this decomposition, the physical domain is sliced into slabs, with the computations on each slab being handled by a different process.

It is easy to describe this decomposition in Fortran. On each process, the arrays are dimensioned as

```
double precision u(0:n+1,s:e)
```

```
      integer i, j, n
      double precision u(0:n+1,s:e), unew(0:n+1,s:e)
      do 10 j=s, e
         do 10 i=1, n
            unew(i,j) = &
                    0.25*(u(i-1,j)+u(i,j+1)+u(i,j-1)+u(i+1,j)) - &
                       h * h * f(i,j)
 10   continue
```

Figure 4.4
Jacobi iteration for a slice of the domain

where `s:e` indicates the values of j that this process is responsible for. This way of declaring `u` changes the code for the algorithm to that shown in Figure 4.4.

Unfortunately, a problem arises. The loop will require elements such as `u(i,s-1)`, that is, data from a different process. The rest of this chapter will discuss how to identify which process the data is from and how to get that data.

But first, let us fix our routine. Since the data is needed, we must expand our arrays to hold the data. In this case, a dimension of

```
double precision u(0:n+1,s-1:e+1)
```

is sufficient (see Figure 4.5). The elements of the array that are used to hold data from other processes are called *ghost points*. We will show how to get the data for these ghost points in Section 4.3.

4.2 Topologies

Our next task is deciding how to assign processes to each part of the decomposed domain. An extensive literature on this subject (e.g., [50, 68, 96]) exists. Handling this assignment of processes to regions is one of the services that MPI provides to the programmer, exactly because the best (or even a good) choice of decomposition depends on the details of the underlying hardware.

The description of how the processes in a parallel computer are connected to one another is often called the *topology* of the computer (or more precisely, of the interconnection network). In most parallel programs, each process communicates with only a few other processes; the pattern of communication is called an *application topology* or *virtual topology*. The relationships between the topology of the parallel computer's hardware and the application can be made in many ways; some are better than others.

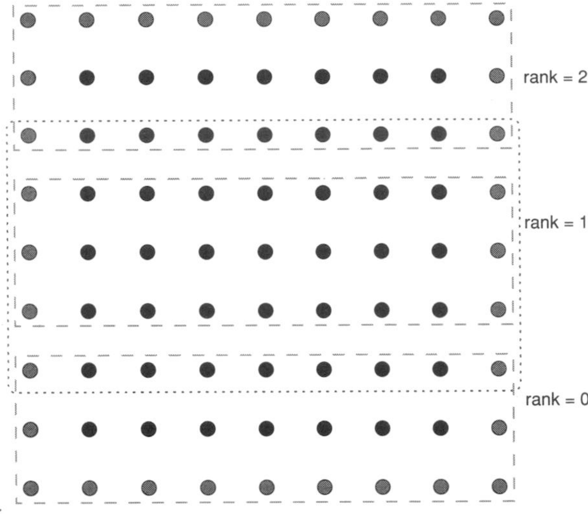

Figure 4.5
The computational domain, with ghost points, for one of the processes

For example, it may seem that simply assigning processes in increasing rank from the bottom is the best approach. On some parallel computers, however, this ordering can lead to performance degradation (see [81, 85] for more details). It is hard for anyone but the vendor to know the best way for application topologies to be fitted onto the physical topology of the parallel machine. MPI allows the vendor to help optimize this aspect of the program through implementation of the MPI topology functions.

The topology functions are sometimes treated as an "exotic" feature of MPI, but we introduce them here, early in the book, because they make many types of MPI programs easier to write.

MPI allows the user to define a particular application, or virtual, topology. An important virtual topology is the *Cartesian* topology. This is simply a decomposition in the natural coordinate (e.g., x, y) directions. A two-dimensional Cartesian decomposition is shown in Figure 4.6. Each element of the decomposition (rectangles in the figure) is labeled by a coordinate tuple indicating the position of the element in each of the coordinate directions. For example, the second process from the left and the third from the bottom is labeled `(1,2)`. (The indices start from zero, following the practice of C, rather than starting at one, which may be more natural for Fortran users.) MPI provides a collection of routines for defining, examining, and manipulating Cartesian topologies.

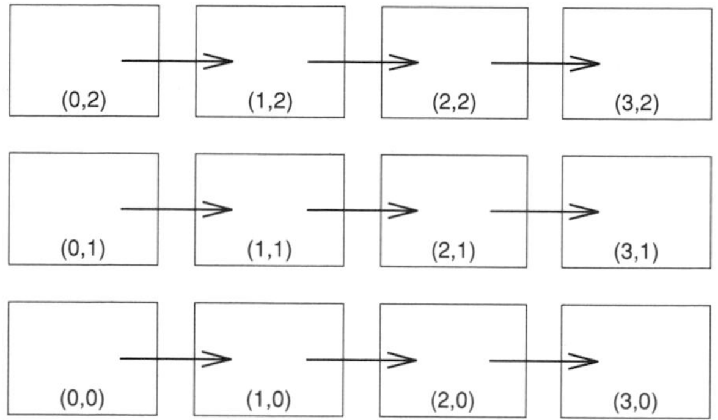

Figure 4.6
A two-dimensional Cartesian decomposition of a domain, also showing a shift by one in the first dimension. Tuples give the coordinates as would be returned by `MPI_Get_coords`.

The routine `MPI_Cart_create` creates a Cartesian decomposition of the processes, with the number of dimensions given by the `ndim` argument. The user can specify the number of processes in any direction by giving a positive value to the corresponding element of `dims`. For example, to form the decomposition shown in Figure 4.6, one can use the following code:

```
integer dims(2)
logical isperiodic(2), reorder

dims(1)       = 4
dims(2)       = 3
isperiodic(1) = .false.
isperiodic(2) = .false.
reorder       = .true.
ndim          = 2
call MPI_CART_CREATE( MPI_COMM_WORLD, ndim, dims, isperiodic, &
                      reorder, comm2d, ierr )
```

This creates a new communicator in the sixth argument from the communicator in the first argument. The new communicator has the Cartesian topology defined by the second through fifth arguments. The `isperiodic` argument indicates whether the processes at the "ends" are connected (for example, is the right neighbor of the process at the right end the *leftmost* process in that row?). This is useful for "periodic" domains. For example, in simulating the weather on the Earth within the temperate latitudes using a three-dimensional grid with the dimensions referring to east-west, north-south, and up-down, the first of these is periodic and the other two are not.

Note that we have not specified which process is assigned to each of the elements of the decomposition. By setting the argument `reorder` to `.true.`, we have allowed MPI to find a good way to assign the process to the elements of the decomposition.

In one dimension, we can simply use the rank in the new communicator, plus or minus one, to find our neighbors (and not use `MPI_Cart_create`). Even here, this may not be the best choice, because neighbors defined in this way may not be neighbors in the actual hardware. In more than one dimension, however, it is more difficult to determine the neighboring processes. The `reorder` argument, when true, lets MPI know that it may reorder the processes for better performance.

Fortunately, MPI provides a simple way to find the neighbors of a Cartesian mesh. The most direct way is to use the routine `MPI_Cart_get`. This routine returns values of the `dims` and `isperiodic` argument used in `MPI_Cart_create` as well as an array `coords` that contains the Cartesian coordinates of the calling process. For example, the code

```
call MPI_CART_GET( comm2d, 2, dims, isperiodic, coords, ierr )
print *, '(', coords(1), ',', coords(2), ')'
```

will print the coordinates of the calling process in the communicator `comm2d`. Another way is to use `MPI_Cart_coords`; this routine, given a rank in a communicator, returns the coordinates of the process with that rank. For example, to get the coordinates of the calling process, one can use

```
call MPI_COMM_RANK( comm2d, myrank, ierr )
call MPI_CART_COORDS( comm2d, myrank, 2, coords, ierr )
```

However, there is another way that is more closely related to what we are trying to accomplish. Each process needs to send and receive data from its neighbors. In the 1-D decomposition, these are the neighbors above and below. There are many ways to do this, but a simple one is illustrated in Figure 4.7. This represents a copy of the top row from one process to the bottom ghost-point row of the process above it, followed by a copy of the bottom row to the top ghost-point row of the process below. If we look at the first of these operations, we see that each process is both sending and receiving data. In fact, one way to look at this is that data is being shifted up from one process to another. This is a common operation, and MPI provides the routine `MPI_Cart_shift` that may be used to find the neighbors.

Figure 4.6 shows a (nonperiodic) shift by one in the first dimension in a two-dimensional Cartesian grid. `MPI_Cart_shift` may be used to find the destination

MPI_CART_CREATE(commold, ndims, dims, isperiodic, reorder, newcomm,ierror) integer commold, ndims, dims(*), newcomm, ierror logical isperiodic(*),reorder
MPI_CART_SHIFT(comm, direction, shift, src, dest, ierror) integer comm, direction, shift, src, dest, ierror
MPI_CART_GET(comm, maxdims, dims, isperiodic, coords, ierror) integer comm, maxdims, dims(*), coords(*), ierror logical isperiodic(*)
MPI_CART_COORDS(comm, rank, maxdims, coords, ierror) integer comm, rank, maxdims, coords(*), ierror

Table 4.1
Fortran bindings for topology routines

and source of a shift for each process. For example, the process at Cartesian coordinates $(1, 1)$ has destination at $(2, 1)$ and source at $(0, 1)$. This gives the neighbors to the left (the rank of the process at coordinates $(0, 1)$) and to the right (the rank of the process at coordinates $(2, 1)$).

What happens for a right shift at the right edge? For example, what is the right neighbor of $(3, 0)$ in Figure 4.6? If the grid were periodic, the right neighbor would be $(0, 0)$. In our application, however, the grid is not periodic, and thus there is no neighbor. This is indicated by the value MPI_PROC_NULL. This value is a valid source for all the MPI receive routines and a valid destination for all the MPI send routines. The behavior of an MPI_Send or MPI_Recv with MPI_PROC_NULL as a source or destination is identical to code of this form:

```
if (source .ne. MPI_PROC_NULL) then
    call MPI_SEND( ..., source, ... )
endif
```

We will exploit MPI_PROC_NULL when we write the code to move data between the processes.

The last routine that we need in defining the decomposition helps us determine the array limits (s and e in the sample code), given the Cartesian coordinate of the process and the size of the array (n in our sample). Because it is a common need, we have provided MPE_Decomp1d. To determine the values of s and e, we use

```
call MPE_DECOMP1D( n, nprocs, myrank, s, e )
```

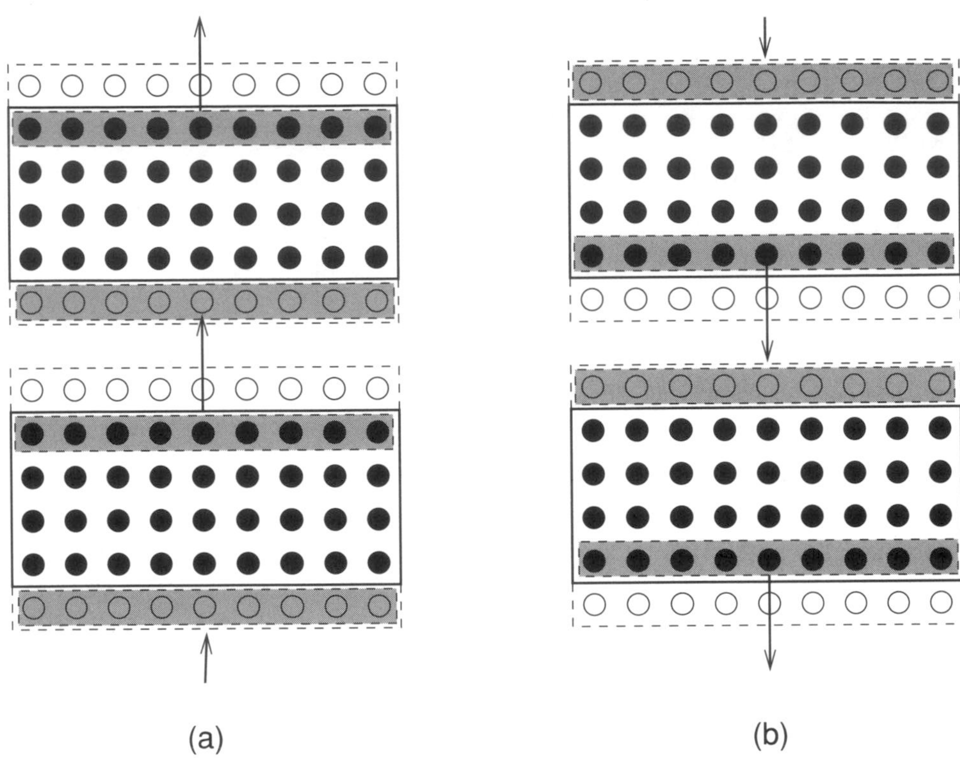

Figure 4.7
Two-step process to transfer data. Ghost point areas are shown in dashed boxes; data to be moved is shaded. The mesh points are shown as block circles; the ghost points in the mesh are shown as unfilled circles.

```
int MPI_Cart_create(MPI_Comm comm_old, int ndims, int *dims,int *isperiodic,
                    int reorder, MPI_Comm *new_comm)

int MPI_Cart_shift(MPI_Comm comm, int direction, int displ,int *src, int *dest)

int MPI_Cart_get(MPI_Comm comm, int maxdims, int *dims, int *isperiodic,
                 int *coords)

int MPI_Cart_coords(MPI_Comm comm, int rank, int maxdims, int *coords)
```

Table 4.2
C bindings for topology routines

Cartcomm MPI::Intracomm::Create_cart(int ndims, const int dims[], const bool isperiodic[], bool reorder) const
void MPI::Cartcomm::Shift(int direction, int disp, int& rank_source, int& rank_dest) const
void MPI::Cartcomm::Get_topo(int maxdims, int dims[], bool isperiodic[], int coords[]) const
void MPI::Cartcomm::Get_coords(int rank, int maxdims, int coords[]) const

Table 4.3
C++ bindings for topology routines

where `nprocs` is the number of processes in the Cartesian coordinate, `myrank` is the Cartesian coordinate of the calling process, and `n` is the size of the array (assumed to run from `1` to `n`). `MPE_Decomp1d` computes values for `s` and `e`. If `n` is evenly divisible by `nprocs`, this routine isn't really needed; in that case we can use have

```
s = 1 + myrank * (n / nprocs)
e = s + (n / nprocs) - 1
```

In the case where `nprocs` does not evenly divide `n`, the most obvious choice is

```
s = 1 + myrank * floor(n / nprocs)
if (myrank .eq. nprocs - 1) then
     e = n
else
     e = s + floor (n / nprocs) - 1
endif
```

where `floor(x)` returns the largest integer value that is no greater than `x`. The special case for the last process is needed to ensure that all points between 1 and n are assigned to some process. However, this simple formula does not provide an even decomposition of points among the processes. To see why, consider using these formulas with `size=64` and `n=127`. Every process gets $\text{floor}(n/size) = 1$ elements except for the last, which gets $e - s + 1 = n - 63 * \text{floor}(n/size) = 64$ elements. `MPE_Decomp1d` in this case gives processes 0 through 62 two elements and gives the last process a single element. By using `MPE_Decomp1d`, we are ensured that if

MPI_SENDRECV(sendbuf, sendcount, sendtype, dest, sendtag, recvbuf,
recvcount, recvtype, source, recvtag, comm, status, ierror)
<type> sendbuf(*), recvbuf(*)
integer sendcount, sendtype, dest, sendtag, recvcount, recvtype,
source, recvtag, comm, status(MPI_STATUS_SIZE), ierror

MPI_ISEND(buf, count, datatype, dest, tag, comm, request, ierror)
<type> buf(*)
integer count, datatype, dest, tag, comm, request, ierror

MPI_IRECV(buf, count, datatype, source, tag, comm, request,ierror)
<type> buf(*)
integer count, datatype, source, tag, comm, request, ierror

MPI_WAIT(request, status, ierror)
integer request,status(MPI_STATUS_SIZE), ierror

MPI_TEST(request, flag, status, ierror)
logical flag
integer request, status(MPI_STATUS_SIZE), ierror

MPI_WAITALL(count, array_of_requests, array_of_statuses,ierror)
integer count, array_of_requests(*),
array_of_statuses(MPI_STATUS_SIZE,*), ierror

MPI_WAITANY(count, array_of_requests, index, status, ierror)
integer count, array_of_requests(*), index,
status(MPI_STATUS_SIZE), ierror

Table 4.4
Fortran bindings for various data exchange routines

```
int MPI_Sendrecv(void *sendbuf, int sendcount,MPI_Datatype sendtype, int dest,
                 int sendtag, void *recvbuf, int recvcount, MPI_Datatype recvtype,
                 int source, MPI_Datatype recvtag, MPI_Comm comm,
                 MPI_Status *status)

int MPI_Isend(void* buf, int count, MPI_Datatype datatype, int dest, int tag,
              MPI_Comm comm, MPI_Request *request)

int MPI_Irecv(void* buf, int count, MPI_Datatype datatype, int source, int tag,
              MPI_Comm comm, MPI_Request *request)

int MPI_Wait(MPI_Request *request, MPI_Status *status)

int MPI_Test(MPI_Request *request, int *flag, MPI_Status *status)

int MPI_Waitall(int count, MPI_Request *array_of_requests,
                MPI_Status *array_of_statuses)

int MPI_Waitany(int count, MPI_Request *array_of_requests, int *index,
                MPI_Status *status)
```

Table 4.5
C bindings for various data exchange routines

`nprocs` does not evenly divide `n`, we will still get correct decomposition of the data, with good load balancing.[2]

Now that we know how the data is decomposed among the processes, and how the processes are ranked in the decomposition, we can write the routine to get the data that we need. For each process, we must get the ghost-point data for the `s-1` row from the process below and the data for the `e+1` row from the process above. Many methods exist to do even this simple operation, and we will investigate several of them through the course of this chapter.

4.3 A Code for the Poisson Problem

In this section we will assemble the pieces of the code that we have defined, as well as the first version of the MPI routines needed to exchange the ghost points between the processes.

[2] `MPE_Decomp1d` is not very complex, but it uses `mod(n,nprocs)` and some tests to get a good decomposition and is just clever enough to be hidden in a separate routine.

void MPI::Comm::Sendrecv(const void *sendbuf, int sendcount,
const Datatype& sendtype, int dest, int sendtag, void *recvbuf,
int recvcount, const Datatype& recvtype, int source, int recvtag,
Status& status) const

Request MPI::Comm::Isend(const void* buf, int count,
const Datatype& datatype, int dest, int tag) const

Request MPI::Comm::Irecv(void* buf, int count, const Datatype& datatype,
int source, int tag) const

void MPI::Request::Wait(Status& status)

void MPI::Request::Wait()

bool MPI::Request::Test(Status& status)

bool MPI::Request::Test()

void MPI::Request::Waitall(int count, Request array_of_requests[],
Status array_of_statuses[])

void MPI::Request::Waitall(int count, Request array_of_requests[])

int MPI::Request::Waitany(int count, Request array_of_requests[],
Status& status)

int MPI::Request::Waitany(int count, Request array_of_requests[])

Table 4.6
C++ bindings for various data exchange routines

The only piece of this code that we have not yet described is the routine to exchange data between the processes. The rest of this chapter will be concerned with different ways to perform this communication operation, and it will pay particular attention to some subtle issues that are often ignored in discussions of message passing. With the warning that we are about to embark on a long journey, we start with perhaps the simplest approach, shown in Figure 4.8.

In this routine, each process sends data to the process on top and then receives data from the process below it. The order is then reversed, and data is sent to the process below and received from the process above. We will see below that, while this strategy is simple, it is not necessarily the best way to implement the exchange of ghost points.

```
      subroutine exchng1( a, nx, s, e, comm1d, nbrbottom, nbrtop )
      use mpi
      integer nx, s, e
      double precision a(0:nx+1,s-1:e+1)
      integer comm1d, nbrbottom, nbrtop
      integer status(MPI_STATUS_SIZE), ierr
!
      call MPI_SEND( a(1,e), nx, MPI_DOUBLE_PRECISION, &
                     nbrtop, 0, comm1d, ierr )
      call MPI_RECV( a(1,s-1), nx, MPI_DOUBLE_PRECISION, &
                     nbrbottom, 0, comm1d, status, ierr )
      call MPI_SEND( a(1,s), nx, MPI_DOUBLE_PRECISION, &
                    nbrbottom, 1, comm1d, ierr )
      call MPI_RECV( a(1,e+1), nx, MPI_DOUBLE_PRECISION, &
                    nbrtop, 1, comm1d, status, ierr )
      return
      end
```

Figure 4.8
Code to exchange data for ghost points using blocking sends and receives

We now have all of the pieces needed to put together our first version of the Poisson solver program. This program uses `MPI_Cart_create` to create the decomposition of processes and the routine `MPE_Decomp1d` to determine the decomposition of the arrays. The routine `onedinit` simply initializes the elements of the arrays `a`, `b`, and `f`. The solution is computed alternately in the array `a` and then `b`; this is why there are two calls to `exchng1` and `sweep1d` in the loop. The iteration is terminated when the difference between two successive approximations to the solution is less than 1×10^{-5}. The difference between the local parts of `a` and `b` is computed with the routine `diff`; the routine `MPI_Allreduce` is used to ensure that all processes compute the same value for the difference in all of the elements. The program prints both the progress of the iterations and the final iteration count. A do-loop with a maximum iteration count ensures that the program terminates even if the iteration is not converging. The computational part of the program is shown in Figure 4.9.

Let's run this program, using the MPI profiling interface and the graphical tools to understand the behavior. Using the "automatic" profiling method described in Chapter 7, we use the MPE profiling files `mpe_proff.o` and `mpe_prof.o` to generate a logfile of the communication. The '`Makefile`' in '`intermediate`' contains a target for '`oned`'; this is the first version of our Poisson solver. To run it, we give the

```
! Get a new communicator for a decomposition of the domain
! and my position in it
      call MPI_CART_CREATE( MPI_COMM_WORLD, 1, numprocs, .false., &
                            .true., comm1d, ierr )
      call MPI_COMM_RANK( comm1d, myid, ierr )
      call MPI_CART_SHIFT( comm1d, 0,  1, nbrbottom, nbrtop, ierr )
! Compute the actual decomposition
      call MPE_DECOMP1D( ny, numprocs, myid, s, e )
! Initialize the right-hand-side (f) and the initial solution guess (a)
      call ONEDINIT( a, b, f, nx, s, e )
!
! Actually do the computation.  Note the use of a collective operation to
! check for convergence, and a do-loop to bound the number of iterations.
!
      do 10 it=1, maxit
!                    get ghost points
        call EXCHNG1( a, nx, s, e, comm1d, nbrbottom, nbrtop )
!                    perform one Jacobi "sweep"
        call SWEEP1D( a, f, nx, s, e, b )
!                    repeat to get a solution back into array a
        call EXCHNG1( b, nx, s, e, comm1d, nbrbottom, nbrtop )
        call SWEEP1D( b, f, nx, s, e, a )
!                    check for convergence
        diffw = DIFF( a, b, nx, s, e )
        call MPI_ALLREDUCE( diffw, diffnorm, 1, MPI_DOUBLE_PRECISION, &
                            MPI_SUM, comm1d, ierr )
        if (diffnorm .lt. 1.0e-5) goto 20
        if (myid .eq. 0) print *, 2*it, ' Difference is ', diffnorm
10     continue
      if (myid .eq. 0) print *, 'Failed to converge'
20    continue
      if (myid .eq. 0) then
         print *, 'Converged after ', 2*it, ' Iterations'
      endif
```

Figure 4.9
Implementation of the Jacobi iteration

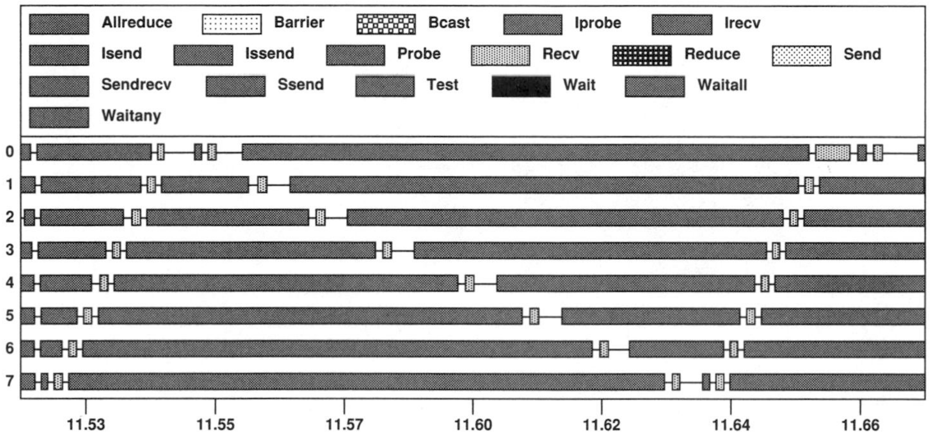

Figure 4.10
Communication in a single iteration for send followed by receive

command

```
mpiexec -n 8 oned
```

Using the MPE logging tools described in Section 3.7.3, we can get a graphical display of the communication. One output from `upshot` is shown in Figure 4.10. Note that the communication is entirely sequential! What went wrong?

Although this is a frequently used communication pattern, it is not a safe one, particularly for large values of `nx` (long messages). The reason is that the amount of parallelism depends in a subtle way on the amount of buffering provided by the message passing system, which is not explicitly specified by MPI and may be difficult to determine. Let us suppose that we run this on a system with a small amount of system buffer space or with a large message size. Then we will get the behavior displayed in Figure 4.10.

Looking at the `upshot` output gives us a clue to what has happened. The sends do not complete until the matching receives are take place on the destination process. Since one process (the "top" process) does not send to anyone in the first step, it can receive from the process below it, thus allowing that process to receive from below it, etc. This produces a staircase pattern of sends and receives. We illustrate this in Figure 4.11.

Before we go any further, we need to understand in more detail what happens when we ask MPI (or any message-passing system) to send a message.

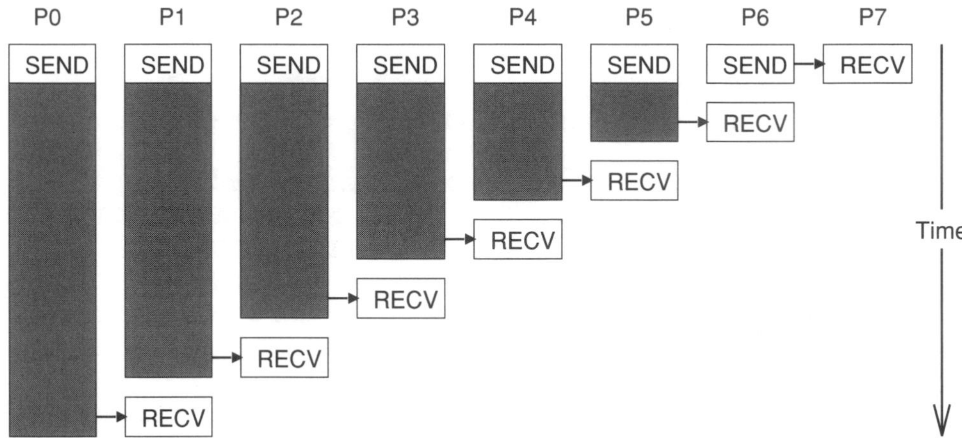

Figure 4.11
Sequentialization caused by sends blocking until the matching receive is posted. The shaded area indicates the time a process is idle, waiting for the send to be allowed to transfer data to the neighboring process

Consider the following code:

```
if (rank .eq. 0) then
    call MPI_Send( sbuffer, ..., 1, ... )
else
    call MPI_Recv( rbuffer, ..., 0, ... )
endif
```

What happens on the process with rank zero?

The easy answer is that the message in `sbuffer` is sent to process one. But what if process one is not ready to receive it? Perhaps process one is still computing a previous result. What can process zero do? There are three possibilities: process zero can stop and wait until process one is ready to receive the message, it can copy the message out of `sbuffer` into some internal buffer (which may be located on process zero, process one, or somewhere else) and return from the `MPI_Send` call, or it can fail.

There are good arguments for the first two of these. The argument for the second case is the easiest: as long as there is space available to hold a copy of the message, the message-passing system should provide this service to the programmer rather than forcing the process to stop dead in its tracks until the matching receive is called.

The argument for the first case is, in part, a rebuttal to this. What if there isn't enough space available? We don't want the computation to fail just because the matching receive has not yet been made; perhaps that `MPI_Recv` is about to be called. Since we cannot guarantee that there will be enough space to store a copy of an arbitrary message, why not simply say that we will never copy the message into internal storage?

The MPI Forum had long and impassioned discussions about these choices; in the end, both interpretations were allowed. That is, an MPI implementation is permitted to copy the message to be sent into internal storage in order to permit the `MPI_Send` to return, but it is not required to do so. If the MPI implementation does copy the send buffer into internal storage, we say that it *buffers* the data. Different buffering strategies provide differing levels of convenience and performance. However, it is incorrect for an MPI program to require buffering in `MPI_Send`.

The third case is also interesting because it allows for certain performance improvements. The use of this kind of send operation is described in Section 7.1.5.

For large applications that are already using a large amount of memory, even requiring the message-passing system to use all "available" memory may not provide enough memory to make this code work. For example, consider a value of `nx` in the above example that represents more memory space than is free on the process. There is no place to store this message on the sending process, and, until the receiver begins the matching receive, there is no place to store the message on the receiving process. For large applications that are already using large amounts of memory, the value of `nx` that triggers this situation may be quite small. Once the receive is issued, however, we know that there is enough space to receive, since the receiver supplies the buffer in the call to the receive.

The performance problem shown here is even more dangerous. As we saw, the code runs (it does not deadlock) but it does not execute in parallel.

All of these issues suggest that programmers should be aware of the pitfalls in assuming that the system will provide adequate buffering. In the next few sections, we will describe ways in which the MPI programmer can ensure that the correct parallel execution of a program does not depend on the amount of buffering, if any, provided by the message-passing system.

Ordered send and receive. One of the easiest ways to correct for a dependence on buffering is to order the sends and receives so that they are paired. That is, the sends and receives are ordered so that if one process is sending to another, the destination will do a receive that matches that send before doing a send of its own. The code for this approach is shown in Figure 4.12. In this code, the even processes

MPI_BSEND(buf, count, datatype, dest, tag, comm, ierror) <type> buf(*) integer count, datatype, dest, tag, comm, ierror
MPI_BUFFER_ATTACH(buffer, size, ierror) <type> buffer(*) integer size, ierror
MPI_BUFFER_DETACH(buffer, size, ierror) <type> buffer(*) integer size, ierror

Table 4.7
Fortran bindings for buffer operations

(in Cartesian coordinates) send first, and the odd processes receive first.

Figure 4.13 shows the communication pattern in a single iteration of the Jacobi code when using this approach.

Combined send and receive. Pairing the sends and receives is effective but can be difficult to implement when the arrangement of processes is complex (for example, with an irregular grid). An alternative is to use the MPI routine `MPI_Sendrecv`. This routine allows you to send and receive data without worrying about deadlock from a lack of buffering. Each process then sends to the process below it and receives from the process above it. The code fragment for this sequence of operations is shown in Figure 4.14.

Buffered sends. Instead of requiring the programmer to determine a safe ordering of the send and receive operations, MPI allows the programmer to provide a buffer into which data can be placed until it is delivered (or at least left the buffer). The change to the exchange routine is simple; one just replaces the `MPI_Send` calls with `MPI_Bsend`. The resulting routine is shown in Figure 4.15.

In addition to the change to the exchange routine, MPI requires that the programmer provide the storage into which the message may be placed with the routine `MPI_Buffer_attach`. This buffer should be large enough to hold all of the messages that must be sent before the matching receives are called. In our case, we need a buffer of `2*nx` double precision values. We can provide this with code like the following:

```
      subroutine exchng1( a, nx, s, e, comm1d, nbrbottom, nbrtop )
      use mpi
      integer nx, s, e
      double precision a(0:nx+1,s-1:e+1)
      integer comm1d, nbrbottom, nbrtop, rank, coord
      integer status(MPI_STATUS_SIZE), ierr
!
      call MPI_COMM_RANK( comm1d, rank, ierr )
      call MPI_CART_COORDS( comm1d, rank, 1, coord, ierr )
      if (mod( coord, 2 ) .eq. 0) then
        call MPI_SEND( a(1,e), nx, MPI_DOUBLE_PRECISION, &
                       nbrtop, 0, comm1d, ierr )
        call MPI_RECV( a(1,s-1), nx, MPI_DOUBLE_PRECISION, &
                       nbrbottom, 0, comm1d, status, ierr )
        call MPI_SEND( a(1,s), nx, MPI_DOUBLE_PRECISION, &
                       nbrbottom, 1, comm1d, ierr )
        call MPI_RECV( a(1,e+1), nx, MPI_DOUBLE_PRECISION, &
                       nbrtop, 1, comm1d, status, ierr )
      else
        call MPI_RECV( a(1,s-1), nx, MPI_DOUBLE_PRECISION, &
                       nbrbottom, 0, comm1d, status, ierr )
        call MPI_SEND( a(1,e), nx, MPI_DOUBLE_PRECISION, &
                       nbrtop, 0, comm1d, ierr )
        call MPI_RECV( a(1,e+1), nx, MPI_DOUBLE_PRECISION, &
                       nbrtop, 1, comm1d, status, ierr )
        call MPI_SEND( a(1,s), nx, MPI_DOUBLE_PRECISION, &
                       nbrbottom, 1, comm1d, ierr )
      endif
      return
      end
```

Figure 4.12
Exchange routine with paired sends and receives

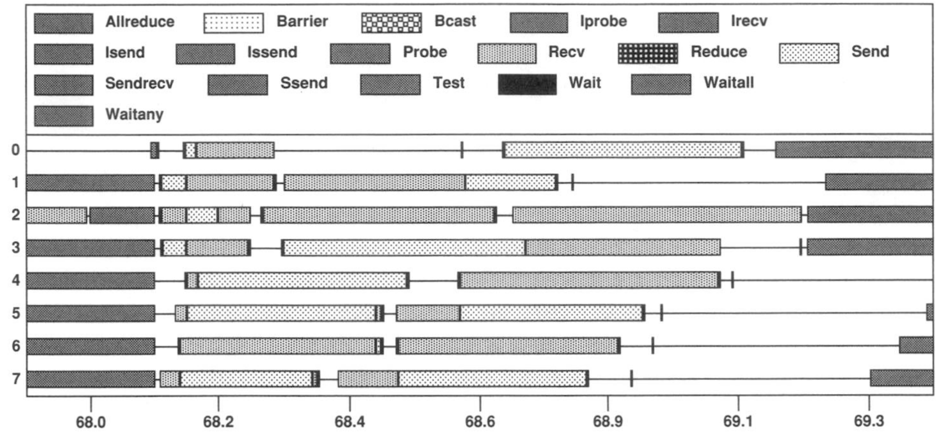

Figure 4.13
Communication in a single iteration with paired sends and receives

```
      subroutine exchng1( a, nx, s, e, comm1d, nbrbottom, nbrtop )
      use mpi
      integer nx, s, e
      double precision a(0:nx+1,s-1:e+1)
      integer comm1d, nbrbottom, nbrtop
      integer status(MPI_STATUS_SIZE), ierr
!
      call MPI_SENDRECV( &
                a(1,e), nx, MPI_DOUBLE_PRECISION, nbrtop, 0, &
                a(1,s-1), nx, MPI_DOUBLE_PRECISION, nbrbottom, 0, &
                comm1d, status, ierr )
      call MPI_SENDRECV( &
                a(1,s), nx, MPI_DOUBLE_PRECISION, nbrbottom, 1, &
                a(1,e+1), nx, MPI_DOUBLE_PRECISION, nbrtop, 1, &
                comm1d, status, ierr )
      return
      end
```

Figure 4.14
Exchange routine with send-receive

int **MPI_Bsend**(void* buf, int count, MPI_Datatype datatype, int dest, int tag, MPI_Comm comm)
int **MPI_Buffer_attach**(void* buffer, int size)
int **MPI_Buffer_detach**(void* buffer, int* size)

Table 4.8
C bindings for buffering routines. Note that even though the buffer argument in `MPI_Buffer_detach` is typed as `void *`, it is really a pointer to a pointer and is typed as `void *` to simplify its use.

void MPI::Comm::Bsend(const void* buf, int count, const Datatype& datatype, int dest, int tag) const
void MPI::Attach_buffer(void* buffer, int size)
int MPI::Detach_buffer(void*& buffer)

Table 4.9
C++ bindings for buffering routines

```
subroutine exchng1( a, nx, s, e, comm1d, nbrbottom, nbrtop )
use mpi
integer nx, s, e
double precision a(0:nx+1,s-1:e+1)
integer comm1d, nbrbottom, nbrtop
integer status(MPI_STATUS_SIZE), ierr

call MPI_BSEND( a(1,e), nx, MPI_DOUBLE_PRECISION, nbrtop, &
                0, comm1d, ierr )
call MPI_RECV( a(1,s-1), nx, MPI_DOUBLE_PRECISION, nbrbottom, &
               0, comm1d, status, ierr )
call MPI_BSEND( a(1,s), nx, MPI_DOUBLE_PRECISION, nbrbottom, &
                1, comm1d, ierr )
call MPI_RECV( a(1,e+1), nx, MPI_DOUBLE_PRECISION, nbrtop, &
               1, comm1d, status, ierr )
return
end
```

Figure 4.15
Exchange routine with buffered sends

```
double precision buffer(2*MAXNX+2*MPI_BSEND_OVERHEAD)
...
call MPI_BUFFER_ATTACH( buffer, &
                        2*MAXNX*8+2*MPI_BSEND_OVERHEAD*8, ierr )
```

The "8" here is the number of bytes in a double-precision value; this value could also be computed with `MPI_Type_extent`, as described in Chapter 5, or with the MPI-2 function `MPI_SIZEOF` (for Fortran only).

Note that extra space is allocated in the buffer. For each message that is sent with `MPI_Bsend`, an extra amount of space, of `MPI_BSEND_OVERHEAD` bytes, must be allocated. An MPI implementation uses this within the `MPI_Bsend` routine to manage the buffer space and the communication (e.g., it may allocate an `MPI_Request` within the buffer area). The code here actually allocates eight times as much space for this overhead than is needed; this is done to simplify the declaration, which would otherwise have to be something like

```
double precision buffer(2*MAXNX+2*((MPI_BSEND_OVERHEAD+7)/8))
```

Once a program no longer needs to use a buffer (or wishes to reclaim it for other use), the routine `MPI_Buffer_detach` should be called. The bindings for these routines are shown in Tables 4.8, 4.7, and 4.9. (The reason for the `buffer` and `size` arguments in `MPI_Buffer_detach` is that C programmers can use these to find out the location and size of an existing buffer.) It is important to remember that buffering may incur a performance penalty (extra effort copying data to and from the buffer), and may expose the program to failure if the amount of needed buffering is not calculated correctly.

One final caution when using `MPI_Bsend` is needed. One might think that a loop like the following could be used to send 100 bytes at each iteration of the loop:

```
   size = 100 + MPI_BSEND_OVERHEAD
   call MPI_BUFFER_ATTACH( buf, size, ierr )
   do 10 i=1, n
       call MPI_BSEND( sbuf, 100, MPI_BYTE, 0, dest, &
                       MPI_COMM_WORLD, ierr )
       ... other work
10 continue
   call MPI_BUFFER_DETACH( buf, size, ierr )
```

The problem with this code is the message sent in the ith step of the loop may not have been delivered when the next call to `MPI_Bsend` occurs in the $i+1^{st}$ step. To use MPI_Bsend correctly in this case, either the buffer given specified with MPI_-Buffer_attach must be large enough to hold *all* of the data sent (in this case, $n * 100+$MPI_BSEND_OVERHEAD), or the buffer attach and detach must be moved inside of the loop.

An alternative to using the buffered send involves using communications operations that do not block but permit the program to continue to execute instead of waiting for communications to complete. This approach also allows the program to compute while waiting for the communications to complete. However, the ability to overlap computation with communication is just one reason to consider the nonblocking operations in MPI; the ability to prevent one communication operation from preventing others from finishing is just as important.

4.4 Using Nonblocking Communications

On most parallel computers, moving data from one process to another takes more time than moving or manipulating data within a single process. For example, on one modern parallel computer, each process can compute up to 500 million floating-point results per second, but can only move roughly ten million words per second between processes.[3] To keep a program from being slowed down (also described as "starved for data"), many parallel computers allow users to start sending (and receiving) several messages and to proceed with other operations. Programmers who have used "asynchronous I/O" will recognize this approach as a way of compensating for the relatively slow speed of access to external information (disks in the case of I/O, another process in the case of message passing). MPI supports this approach by providing *nonblocking* sends and receives.

Nonblocking routines also solve the problem of buffering, by providing a way to defer completion of communication until the user, through an MPI receive operation, provides a place for a message to be received into. Many MPI concepts have this property of solving two problems.

The routine MPI_Isend begins the nonblocking send operation. The arguments are the same as for MPI_Send with the addition of a *handle* as the next to last argument (the last argument in C). The two routines also behave similarly except that, for MPI_Isend, the buffer containing the message to be sent must not be modified until the message has been delivered (more precisely, until the operation

[3]This apparent mismatch of capabilities reflects underlying engineering and physical realities and is a major reason that the message-passing approach, which keeps the programmer reminded of the cost of accessing remote data, has been a successful way to program parallel computers.

is complete, as indicated by one of the MPI_Wait or MPI_Test routines). In C, the type of this handle is MPI_Request.

The *handle* argument is used to determine whether an operation has completed. The easiest way to test is with MPI_Test:

```
      call MPI_ISEND( buffer, count, datatype, dest, tag, &
                      comm, request, ierr )
       < do other work >
10    call MPI_TEST( request, flag, status, ierr )
      if (.not. flag) goto 10
```

Often, one wishes to wait until the send completes. Rather than writing the loop in the previous example, one can use MPI_Wait instead:

```
call MPI_WAIT( request, status, ierr )
```

Once a nonblocking operation is complete (e.g., MPI_Wait returns or MPI_Test returns with flag = .true.), the request is set to MPI_REQUEST_NULL.

The routine MPI_Irecv begins the nonblocking receive operation. It has one additional argument, the handle, just as MPI_Isend does. It also has one *less* argument: the status argument, which is used to return information on the completed receive, is deleted from the argument list. Just as for MPI_Isend, MPI_Test may be used to test for the completion of a receive started with MPI_Irecv, and MPI_Wait may be used to wait for the completion of such a receive. The status arguments of these two routines return the information on the completed receive in the same form as MPI_Recv does for a blocking receive.

In many cases, one wishes to test or wait for many nonblocking operations. Although one can simply loop through the operations, this approach is inefficient, since this forces the user's program to be constantly executing rather than waiting (possibly without consuming CPU time) for the "next" message. MPI provides a way to wait for all or any of a collection of nonblocking operations (with MPI_Waitall and MPI_Waitany) and to test all or any of a collection of nonblocking operations (with MPI_Testall and MPI_Testany). For example, to start two nonblocking receives and then wait on them, one can use

```
call MPI_IRECV( ..., requests(1), ierr )
call MPI_IRECV( ..., requests(2), ierr )
...
call MPI_WAITALL( 2, requests, status, ierr )
```

Here, status must be an array of two MPI_status objects; it can be declared with

```
      subroutine exchng1( a, nx, s, e, comm1d, &
                          nbrbottom, nbrtop )
      use mpi
      integer nx, s, e
      double precision a(0:nx+1,s-1:e+1)
      integer comm1d, nbrbottom, nbrtop
      integer status_array(MPI_STATUS_SIZE,4), ierr, req(4)
!
      call MPI_IRECV ( &
           a(1,s-1), nx, MPI_DOUBLE_PRECISION, nbrbottom, 0, &
           comm1d, req(1), ierr )
      call MPI_IRECV ( &
           a(1,e+1), nx, MPI_DOUBLE_PRECISION, nbrtop, 1, &
           comm1d, req(2), ierr )
      call MPI_ISEND ( &
           a(1,e), nx, MPI_DOUBLE_PRECISION, nbrtop, 0, &
           comm1d, req(3), ierr )
      call MPI_ISEND ( &
           a(1,s), nx, MPI_DOUBLE_PRECISION, nbrbottom, 1, &
           comm1d, req(4), ierr )
!
      call MPI_WAITALL ( 4, req, status_array, ierr )
      return
      end
```

Figure 4.16
Row-exchange routine using nonblocking operations

```
integer status(MPI_STATUS_SIZE,2)
```

With these routines, we can rewrite the exchange routine `exchng1` using nonblocking operations, as shown in Figure 4.16. This approach allows for both sends and receives to take place at the same time. In principle, this approach can be almost twice as fast as the version in Figure 4.12, though few existing systems support this (don't forget that MPI was designed to support current and future message-passing systems). In the next section, we try them out and see what happens.

Note that in order to overlap communication and computation, we must make further changes to our program. In particular, we need to change the `sweep` program to allow us to do some of the work while we wait for data to arrive. We will come back to nonblocking operations in Section 4.9, where we discuss overlapping

P	Blocking Send	Ordered Send	Sendrecv	Buffered Bsend	Noblock Isend
1	5.38	5.54	5.54	5.38	5.40
2	2.77	2.88	2.91	2.75	2.77
4	1.58	1.56	1.57	1.50	1.51
8	1.15	0.947	0.931	0.854	0.849
16	1.18	0.574	0.534	0.521	0.545
32	1.94	0.443	0.451	0.452	0.397
64	3.73	0.447	0.391	0.362	0.391

Table 4.10
Timings for variants of the 1-D decomposition of the Poisson problem

communication with computation.

4.5 Synchronous Sends and "Safe" Programs

What can we do to ensure that a program does not depend on buffering? In general, this is equivalent to the Turing halting-problem and is hence unanswerable, but in many special cases it is possible to show that if the program runs successfully with no buffering, it will run with any amount of buffering. MPI provides a way to send a message so that the send does not return until the destination begins to receive the message (in addition, just like `MPI_Send`, it doesn't return until the send buffer is available for reuse by the programmer). The routine is `MPI_Ssend`. The arguments to this send are identical to `MPI_Send`. Note that it is permissible for an MPI operation to implement `MPI_Send` with `MPI_Ssend`; thus, for maximum portability, one should ensure that any use of `MPI_Send` can be replaced with `MPI_Ssend`. Programs that do not require buffering (or, with `MPI_Bsend`, only the amount of buffering made available) for their correct operation are sometimes called *safe*.

4.6 More on Scalability

Because we have encapsulated the routines to exchange data between the processes, it is a simple matter to link the program with different methods and to compare them. Table 4.10 shows the results for one particular parallel computer and MPI implementation.

Before going on, we note that each iteration of the loop calls `MPI_Allreduce`. This routine can take a significant amount of time; on networks of workstations,

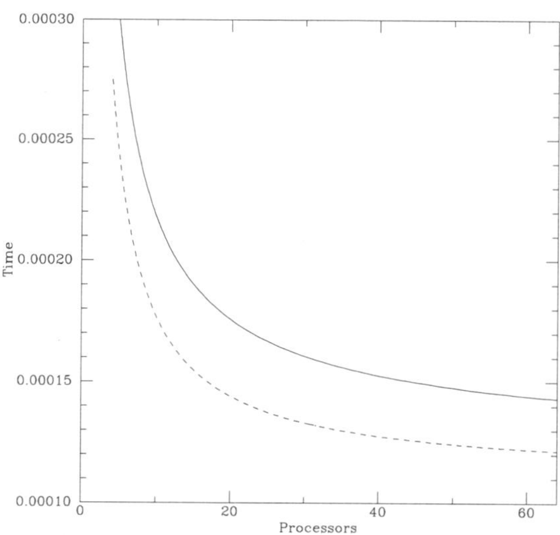

Figure 4.17
Predicted time for a 1-D (dashed) and 2-D (solid) decomposition of the 2-D Poisson problem

it can take many milliseconds. In many applications, the effective cost of the `MPI_Allreduce` is reduced by taking a number of iterations without computing the difference between successive iterates; this approach works because the Jacobi method converges very slowly.

A quick examination of Table 4.10 reveals a number of interesting features. First, with the exception of the blocking sends, the performance of the other methods is roughly the same. The blocking sends case shows the lack of parallelism in the communication; with 32 processes, the computation actually takes longer than with 4 processes. More serious is the poor performance of the other methods. At 64 processes, the program is running only about fourteen times as fast as for a single process, for an efficiency of about 20%.

To understand the performance of these methods, we perform a simple scalability analysis similar to the one in Chapter 3. We will need a slightly more sophisticated model of communication cost than that used in Chapter 3. There, we used T_{comm} as the time to send a word. We will replace T_{comm} with $s + rn$ as the time to send n bytes; for n large, we have $T_{comm} \approx r * n$. The term s is the latency or startup time; it can be thought of as the time to send a message containing no data beyond the message tag and source. The term r is the inverse rate; it is the time to send a single byte and is given by one over the bandwidth. For example, if the bandwidth of a connection is 100 MB/sec, $r = 1/(100\text{MB/sec}) = 10^{-8}$ sec/byte. Using this formula, we can easily see that the `exchng1d` routine in Figure 4.12 takes roughly $2(s + rn)$ time, where $n = 8$ `nx` (assuming 8-byte double-precision data).

In a two-dimensional decomposition, let there be p_x processes in the x direction and p_y processes in the y direction, with each process having the same number of mesh points. Then, with the exception of the processes on any edge of the domain, the amount of communication T_c is

$$T_c = 2\left(s + r\frac{n}{p_x}\right) + 2\left(s + r\frac{n}{p_y}\right).$$

If $p_x = p_y = \sqrt{p}$, this takes a particularly simple form:

$$T_c = 4\left(s + r\frac{n}{\sqrt{p}}\right).$$

Figure 4.17 shows the expected performance for both 1-D and 2-D decompositions of the domain, based on these estimates. The situation is even more extreme in 3-D, as shown in Figure 4.18. Note that, for small numbers of processes, this model suggests that a 1-D decomposition is actually better than a 2-D decomposition. Care must be exercised here, as our analysis is good in the 2-D case only for $p \geq 9$ since for $p < 9$ no process has four neighbors. More details on analyzing the communication in parallel codes for PDEs may be found in [54, 67]; an example of using these techniques to analyze a large application can be found in [38].

4.7 Jacobi with a 2-D Decomposition

Figures 4.17 and 4.18 and this scalability analysis suggest that we need to rewrite our program to use these higher-dimensional decompositions. Fortunately, MPI makes this task relatively easy. We will show how a few modifications to the program in Figure 4.9 change it from a one-dimensional to two-dimensional decomposition.

First, we let MPI compute the decomposition of the domain for us with `MPI_Cart_create`:

```
isperiodic(1) = .false.
isperiodic(2) = .false.
reorder       = .true.
call MPI_CART_CREATE( MPI_COMM_WORLD, 2, dims, isperiodic, &
                      reorder, comm2d, ierr )
```

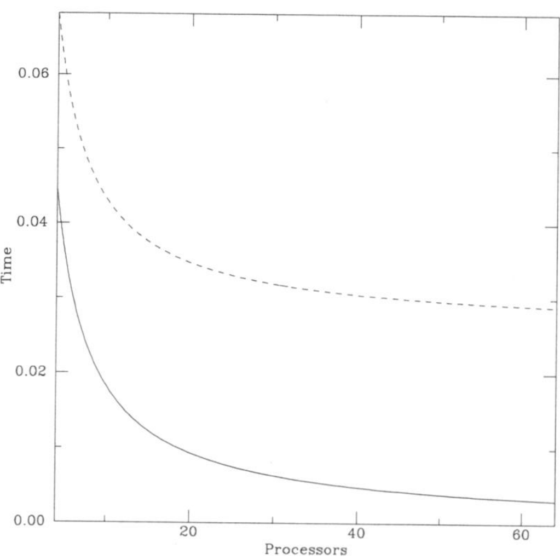

Figure 4.18
Predicted time for a 1-D (dashed) and 3-D (solid) decomposition of the 3-D Poisson problem

Compare this with the 1-D code in Section 4.2.

Next, we get left and right neighbors as well as the top and bottom neighbors:

```
call MPI_CART_SHIFT( comm2d, 0,  1, nbrleft, nbrright, ierr )
call MPI_CART_SHIFT( comm2d, 1,  1, nbrbottom, nbrtop, ierr )
```

We change the body of the sweep routine to

```
      integer i, j, n
      double precision u(sx-1:ex+1,sy-1:ey+1), &
                       unew(sx-1:ex+1,sy-1:ey+1)
      do 10 j=sy, ey
         do 10 i=sx, ex
            unew(i,j) = &
                0.25*(u(i-1,j)+u(i,j+1)+u(i,j-1)+u(i+1,j)) - &
                   h * h * f(i,j)
   10 continue
```

The last routine that we need to change is the data exchange routine (exchng1d in the 1-D examples). This is a little more difficult because, while the data sent to the top and bottom processes is stored contiguously in memory, the data sent to the left and right processes is not.

4.8 An MPI Derived Datatype

One of MPI's novel features is its use of a datatype associated with every message. Specifying the length of a message as a given count of occurrences of a given datatype is more portable than using length in bytes, since lengths of given types may vary from one machine to another. It also allows MPI to provide translations between machine formats.

So far all of our messages have consisted of contiguous areas in memory, so the basic datatypes such as `MPI_INTEGER` and `MPI_DOUBLE_PRECISION`, accompanied by a count, have been sufficient to describe our messages. In this section we introduce MPI's *derived datatypes*, which allow us to specify *noncontiguous* areas in memory, such as a row of an array stored columnwise (or, in our case, a column of an array stored rowwise).

This is a common situation, and MPI provides a mechanism for describing this kind of data layout. We begin by defining a new datatype that describes a group of elements that are separated by a constant amount in memory (a constant *stride*). We do this with the `MPI_Type_vector`:

```
call MPI_TYPE_VECTOR( ey - sy + 3, 1, ex - sx + 3, &
                      MPI_DOUBLE_PRECISION, stridetype, ierr )
call MPI_TYPE_COMMIT( stridetype, ierr )
```

The arguments to `MPI_Type_vector` describe a *block*, which consists of a number of (contiguous) copies of the input datatype given by the second argument. The first argument is the number of blocks; the second is the number of elements of the old datatype in each block (this is often one). The third argument is the *stride*; this is the distance in terms of the extent of the input datatype between successive elements. The old datatype is the fourth argument. The fifth argument is the created derived datatype. In this example, there is one double-precision item per block; the double-precision values are `ex + 1 - (sx - 1) + 1 = ex - sx + 3` apart, and there are `ey + 1 - (sy - 1) + 1 = ey - sy + 3` of them. Figure 4.19 illustrates an MPI vector datatype.

Note that after the new datatype is created with the `MPI_Type_vector` command, we *commit* it to the system with `MPI_Type_commit`. This routine takes the newly constructed datatype and gives the system the opportunity to perform any

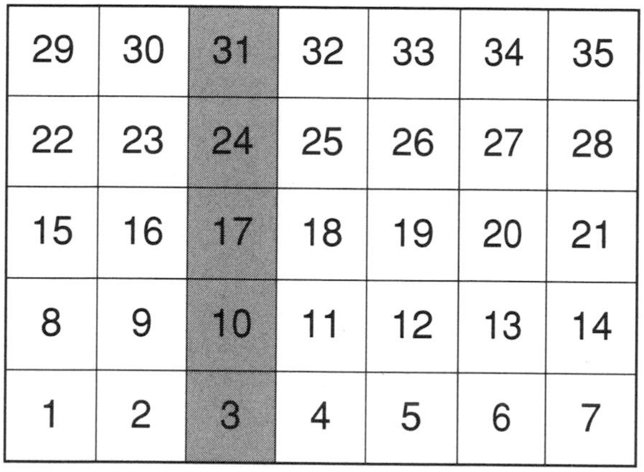

29	30	31	32	33	34	35
22	23	24	25	26	27	28
15	16	17	18	19	20	21
8	9	10	11	12	13	14
1	2	3	4	5	6	7

```
MPI_TYPE_VECTOR( 5, 1, 7, MPI_DOUBLE_PRECISION, newtype, ierr )
```

Figure 4.19
A strided data item (shaded) and its MPI definition. Numbers indicate consecutive memory locations.

performance optimizations that it may wish. All user-constructed data types must be committed before they can be used.

With this new datatype definition, the MPI code for sending a row differs from the code for sending a column only in the datatype argument. The final version of `exchng2d` is shown in Figure 4.20.

When a datatype is no longer needed, it should be freed with `MPI_Type_free`. The datatype variable (the first argument) is set to `MPI_TYPE_NULL` by `MPI_Type_free`. Bindings for these routines are shown in Tables 4.11, 4.12, and 4.13.

An alternative definition of the strided type, described in Section 5.4, allows the programmer to send any number of elements with the same datatype.

4.9 Overlapping Communication and Computation

Because of the time it can take to move data from one process to another, it is often advantageous to arrange the program so that some work can be done while the messages are "in transit." So far, we have used nonblocking operations to avoid deadlock in the communications. Here we describe some of the details in arranging a program so that computation and communication can take place simultaneously.

In the Jacobi method, the values of `unew` at points of the mesh that are interior to the domain on each process may be computed without needing any data from

```
      subroutine exchng2( a, sx, ex, sy, ey, &
                          comm2d, stridetype, &
                          nbrleft, nbrright, nbrtop, nbrbottom  )
      use mpi
      integer sx, ex, sy, ey, stridetype
      double precision a(sx-1:ex+1, sy-1:ey+1)
      integer nbrleft, nbrright, nbrtop, nbrbottom, comm2d
      integer status(MPI_STATUS_SIZE), ierr, nx
!
      nx = ex - sx + 1
!  These are just like the 1-d versions, except for less data
       call MPI_SENDRECV( a(sx,ey),  nx, MPI_DOUBLE_PRECISION, &
                         nbrtop, 0, &
                         a(sx,sy-1), nx, MPI_DOUBLE_PRECISION, &
                         nbrbottom, 0, comm2d, status, ierr )
       call MPI_SENDRECV( a(sx,sy),  nx, MPI_DOUBLE_PRECISION, &
                         nbrbottom, 1, &
                         a(sx,ey+1), nx, MPI_DOUBLE_PRECISION, &
                         nbrtop, 1, comm2d, status, ierr )
!
! This uses the vector datatype stridetype
       call MPI_SENDRECV( a(ex,sy),  1, stridetype, nbrright, 0, &
                          a(sx-1,sy), 1, stridetype, nbrleft, 0, &
                          comm2d, status, ierr )
       call MPI_SENDRECV( a(sx,sy),  1, stridetype, nbrleft,   1, &
                          a(ex+1,sy), 1, stridetype, nbrright, 1, &
                          comm2d, status, ierr )
       return
       end
```

Figure 4.20
Two-dimensional exchange with sendrecv

MPI_TYPE_VECTOR(count, blocklength, stride, oldtype, newtype, ierror) integer count, blocklength, stride, oldtype, newtype, ierror
MPI_TYPE_COMMIT(datatype, ierror) integer datatype, ierror
MPI_TYPE_FREE(datatype, ierror) integer datatype, ierror

Table 4.11
Fortran bindings for elementary MPI datatype routines

int **MPI_Type_vector**(int count, int blocklength, int stride, MPI_Datatype oldtype, MPI_Datatype *newtype)
int **MPI_Type_commit**(MPI_Datatype *datatype)
int **MPI_Type_free**(MPI_Datatype *datatype)

Table 4.12
C bindings for MPI elementary datatype routines

Datatype MPI::Datatype::Create_vector(int count, int blocklength, int stride) const
void MPI::Datatype::Commit()
void MPI::Datatype::Free()

Table 4.13
C++ bindings for MPI elementary datatype routines

any other process; this is shown in Figure 4.21.

We can arrange our computational task as follows: (1) indicate where to receive data from other processes; (2) begin sending data to the other processes; (3) compute with the local data; and (4) receive data from the other processes and finish computing with it. Separating the code into these four steps does increase the amount of code, but all of it is easily derived from our existing code. For example, Step 3 is given by the code in Figure 4.22.

All that we have done here is to select the part of the domain that is one away from the edges of the local domain, ensuring that all of the data is available.

The communication routines change in similar ways; in addition, the calls are

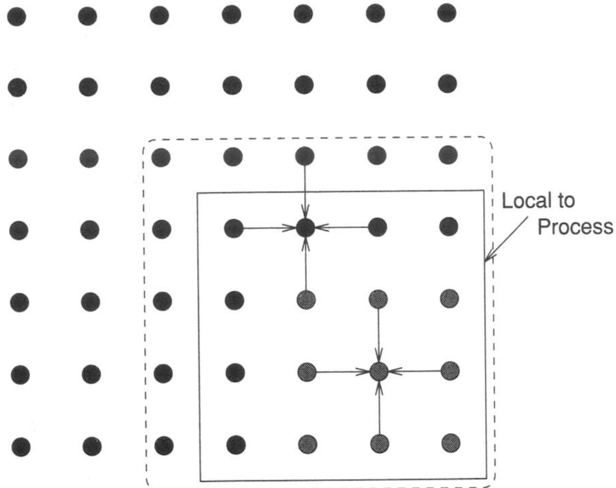

Figure 4.21
The shaded points show those mesh points whose computation does not depend on any data from other processes. The local domain is given by the solid outline; the domain with ghost points is given by the dashed box.

```
   integer i, j, n
   double precision u(sx-1:ex+1,sy-1:ey+1), &
                    unew(sx-1:ex+1,sy-1:ey+1)
   do 10 j=sy+1, ey-1
      do 10 i=sx+1, ex-1
         unew(i,j) = &
               0.25*(u(i-1,j)+u(i,j+1)+u(i,j-1)+u(i+1,j)) - &
                  h * h * f(i,j)
10 continue
```

Figure 4.22
Code to compute a Jacobi iteration with only local data

split into two sections of code, separated by the main computational section. The first part begins both the nonblocking sends and nonblocking receives:

```
call MPI_IRECV( ..., requests(1), ierr )
...
call MPI_ISEND( ..., requests(5), ierr )
```

These are followed by[4]

```
    do 100 k=1,8
        call MPI_WAITANY( 8, requests, idx, status, ierr )
!       Use tag to determine which edge
        goto (1,2,3,4,100,100,100,100), status(MPI_TAG,idx)
1       do 11 j=sy,ey
11          unew(si,j) = ...
        goto 100
2       do 21 j=sy,ey
21          unew(ei,j) = ...
        goto 100
3       do 31, i=sx,ex
31          unew(i,ej) = ...
        goto 100
4       do 41 i=sx,ex
41          unew(i,sj) = ...
        goto 100
100  continue
```

Here, `requests(1)` through `requests(4)` are receive handles, and `requests(5)` through `requests(8)` are send handles.

4.10 More on Timing Programs

Our simple code can also be used to solve time-dependent PDEs. Many discretizations for time-dependent PDEs require only the data that our Jacobi iteration needs. The only difference is that the `sweep` routines change and there is no longer any need for the `MPI_Allreduce` to check for convergence. However, this does raise

[4]For C programmers: the construction `goto (...), variable` is similar to the C `switch (variable)` except that the values are labels and the variable is in the range 1 to the number of labels.

an issue when timing this program: how do we know that everyone is done when we call MPI_Wtime? We can use the MPI routine MPI_Barrier to ensure that everyone has completed the computation. A barrier is a special collective operation that does not let the process continue until all processes in the communicator have called MPI_Barrier.

```
call MPI_Barrier( MPI_COMM_WORLD, ierr )
t1 = MPI_Wtime()
<do work>
call MPI_Barrier( MPI_COMM_WORLD, ierr )
total_time = MPI_Wtime() - t1
```

The barriers ensure that all processes have reached the same point in the code and are ready to proceed. Many of the collective operations (e.g., MPI_Allreduce) have the same property; that is, no process can exit the operation until all processes have entered. Note that this is not true for operations like MPI_Reduce, where only the root process must wait for all other processes to enter the MPI_Reduce call. The bindings for MPI_Barrier are shown in Tables 4.14, 4.15, and 4.16.

This simple timing code is in fact often too simple. There are a number of effects that can cause this code to produce misleading results. One well-known problem is that of cache: if the data needed for the work step will fit into cache, the first time this data is accessed, the time will often be dominated not by the work itself but by the time to load the data into cache. One less well-known but related problem is the demand-loading of code: in many systems, the machine instructions are not loaded from disk into memory until they are first referenced. Because this requires accessing a disk (or at least a remote file server), this can take a significant amount of time. Thus, it is better to use a loop such as the following:

```
   do 10 i=1,2
      call MPI_Barrier( MPI_COMM_WORLD, ierr )
      t1 = MPI_Wtime()
      <do work>
      call MPI_Barrier( MPI_COMM_WORLD, ierr )
      total_time = MPI_Wtime() - t1
10 continue
```

This simple code runs the test twice, discarding the result from the first test. More sophisticated testing methods are discussed in [61]. The chapter on measuring performance in [5] also contains valuable suggestions for acurately timing tests.

MPI_BARRIER(comm, ierr)
integer comm, ierr

Table 4.14
Fortran bindings for barrier routine

int **MPI_Barrier**(MPI_Comm comm)

Table 4.15
C binding for barrier routine

void **MPI::Intracomm::Barrier**() const

Table 4.16
C++ binding for barrier routine

4.11 Three Dimensions

So far, we have restricted ourselves to the 2-D problem. Now, we want to introduce the 3-D case and also show the problem in a C implementation. Even a relatively small 3-D problem having 100 grid points on a side involves 10^6 grid points; it is common to encounter one or two orders of magnitude more grid points than this in 3-D simulations. These problems are consequently ideal candidates for parallel computing. The flexibility of MPI makes generalizing our previous 2-D problem solutions to 3-D straightforward.

One complication in developing a 3-D code is the decomposition of the domain among the processes. As we would expect from the scalability analysis in this chapter, we should use a 3-D virtual topology. MPI provides the routine `MPI_Dims_create` to aid in generating a Cartesian virtual topology with any number of dimensions. This routine takes as input the total number of processes and the number of dimensions, and returns an array containing the Cartesian dimensions. These values may be used as the `dims` argument to `MPI_Cart_create`. The bindings are shown in Tables 4.17, 4.18, and 4.19.

4.12 Common Errors and Misunderstandings

As in the preceding chapter, we list a few common pitfalls associated with this chapter.

MPI_DIMS_CREATE(nnodes, ndims, dims, ierr)
integer nnodes, ndims, dims(*), ierr

Table 4.17
Fortran binding for MPI_DIMS_CREATE

int **MPI_Dims_create**(int nnodes, int ndims, int *dims)

Table 4.18
C binding for MPI_DIMS_CREATE

void **MPI::Compute_dims**(int nnodes, int ndims, int dims[])

Table 4.19
C++ binding for MPI_DIMS_CREATE

Not making programs safe. In Section 4.5 we identified the concept of "safe" programs; those that would still work if all blocking sends were replaced by synchronous sends. A program of the form

Process 0	Process 1
MPI_Send to process 1	MPI_Send to process 0
MPI_Recv from process 1	MPI_Recv from process 0

is inherently *unsafe*: it is certain to fail for some value of the length of the message, since there will not be enough system buffering for both messages to be copied out of the send buffers before being copied into the receive buffers. Many implementations have generous buffering, which can lull the programmer into a false sense of security. As messages get bigger, eventually the buffer limit will be reached and the program will fail. When exchanging messages between processes, it is better to write a safe program using one of the techniques described in this chapter.

- Interleave sends and receives so that one process is sending while the other is receiving.
- Use MPI_Sendrecv.
- Allocate one's own buffers with MPI_Buffer_attach.
- Use the nonblocking operations MPI_Isend and MPI_Irecv.

The most common and general approach is the last one.

Counting on the overlapping of communication and computation. The nonblocking operations are more important for allowing safe programs than for improving performance by overlapping communication and computation. Although we described in Section 4.9 how to structure our program to allow for such overlapping, many implementations cannot overlap without extra hardware in the form of a communication coprocessor. Use of the nonblocking operations *allows* an implementation to obtain extra performance by simultaneously communicating and computing, but it is not *required* to, and whether such overlapping is possible may depend on the hardware environment. If switching to non-blocking operations doesn't improve performance, it may not be your fault.

4.13 Application: Simulating Vortex Evolution in Superconducting Materials

As an example of an application that uses the techniques described in this chapter, we briefly discuss a model of superconductivity.

The time-dependent Ginzburg-Landau (TDGL) equation can be used for the numerical simulation of vortex dynamics and phase transitions in type-II superconductors. The TDGL equation provides a phenomenological description of the macroscopic properties of high-temperature superconductors and has been remarkably successful in explaining experimental results on phase transitions. The TDGL equation is a partial differential equation for the complex-valued order parameter with stochastic coefficients. This model uses a field description of vortices as described by the time-dependent Ginzburg-Landau equation in three dimensions.

A group at Argonne National Laboratory [45] has parallelized a three-dimensional TDGL program by partitioning the superconductor data structure among the processes. Each process's memory contains a "cubelet" of the original global data structure. Each process is then responsible for the time integration over its part of the superconductor. The time integration is done by using the forward Euler technique. Finite differences are used to approximate the derivatives using a box (27-point) stencil.

With this program, researchers have answered several questions about the behavior of high-temperature superconductors. The computations require very high resolution.

The update step for each cell requires values from neighboring cells. Because of the array decomposition, neighbors of some of the cells that a process has require values from cells stored in other processes' memories. To communicate these values, routines similar to the exchange routines described for the Poisson problem are used.

5 Advanced Message Passing in MPI

This chapter discusses some of the more advanced features from the MPI Standard that have not arisen in the discussion so far. The chapter also provides a more complete discussion of some features already introduced briefly. We use the opportunity to introduce several interesting example programs.

5.1 MPI Datatypes

One of MPI's unusual features is the introduction of a datatype argument for all messages sent and received. In the early chapters of this book, we relied primarily on elementary datatypes that correspond to the base datatypes in the host programming language—integers, floating-point numbers, and so forth, and arrays of these. In this section we discuss the complete set of datatypes and take the opportunity to describe the full power of MPI's derived datatype features. The examples we describe, the N-body problem and Mandelbrot computations, also allow us to exercise some more of the graphics part of the MPE library.

5.1.1 Basic Datatypes and Concepts

MPI provides a rich set of predefined datatypes. These include all of the basic datatypes in C (Table 5.1) and Fortran (Table 5.2). Included in both lists are two datatypes specific to MPI: `MPI_BYTE` and `MPI_PACKED`. `MPI_BYTE` refers to a *byte* that is defined as eight binary digits. Many C and Fortran programmers may wonder why this is needed when they have `MPI_CHAR` and `MPI_CHARACTER`, respectively. There are two reasons. First, while many implementations represent `char` and `character` as bytes, this representation is not required. A version of C for Japanese could choose 16-bit `char`s, for example. The second reason is that in a heterogeneous environment, machines may have different character sets. For example, a system that uses ASCII uses different bits to represent the character `A` than does a system that uses EBCDIC. `MPI_PACKED` is described in Section 5.2.3.

Tables 5.1 and 5.2 do not include the MPI datatypes that correspond to language datatypes that are not part of the language standard but are common extensions. Vendor-specific implementations of Fortran, in particular, often have additional datatypes. The most common is `DOUBLE COMPLEX`, the double precision counterpart to `COMPLEX`, which is not, in fact, part of Fortran 77. The MPI standard could hardly mandate datatypes not part of the language standards, and so such datatypes are not a *required* part of an MPI implementation. However, many Fortran implementations do support `DOUBLE COMPLEX`, along with types such as `REAL*8`

MPI Datatype	C Datatype
MPI_BYTE	
MPI_CHAR	signed char
MPI_DOUBLE	double
MPI_FLOAT	float
MPI_INT	int
MPI_LONG	long
MPI_LONG_LONG_INT	long long
MPI_LONG_DOUBLE	long double
MPI_PACKED	
MPI_SHORT	short
MPI_UNSIGNED_CHAR	unsigned char
MPI_UNSIGNED	unsigned int
MPI_UNSIGNED_LONG	unsigned long
MPI_UNSIGNED_SHORT	unsigned short

Table 5.1
Basic (predefined) MPI datatypes for C

(8-byte reals) and INTEGER*2 (2-byte integers). MPI defines the corresponding datatypes MPI_DOUBLE_COMPLEX, MPI_REAL8, and MPI_INTEGER2 (among others) as *optional* datatypes—an MPI implementation does not need to define them, but should use these names if it does.

In addition, MPI-2 introduced a few new basic predefined datatypes. These are shown in Table 5.3. In MPI-2, the types MPI_SIGNED_CHAR and MPI_UNSIGNED_-CHAR may be used in reduction operations (e.g., MPI_Allreduce) where it is treated as a (signed or unsigned) integer value.

As we have already seen in Section 4.8, it is often useful to define additional datatypes. MPI provides for arbitrary datatypes; the rest of this section concerns how MPI describes a general datatype.

In MPI, a datatype is an object consisting of a sequence of the basic datatypes (Tables 5.1 and 5.2) and displacements, in bytes, of each of these datatypes. These displacements are taken to be relative to the buffer that the datatype is describing (see Section 3.6). We will represent a datatype as a sequence of pairs of basic types and displacements as shown in (5.1.1); MPI calls this sequence the *typemap*.

$$\text{Typemap} = \{(type_0, disp_0), \ldots, (type_{n-1}, disp_{n-1})\} \tag{5.1.1}$$

For example, the type MPI_INT can be represented as the typemap (int,0).

The *type signature* of a datatype is just a list of the basic datatypes in a datatype:

MPI Datatype	Fortran Datatype
MPI_BYTE	
MPI_CHARACTER	CHARACTER
MPI_COMPLEX	COMPLEX
MPI_DOUBLE_PRECISION	DOUBLE PRECISION
MPI_INTEGER	INTEGER
MPI_LOGICAL	LOGICAL
MPI_PACKED	
MPI_REAL	REAL

Table 5.2
Basic (predefined) MPI datatypes for Fortran

MPI Datatype	C Datatype
MPI_WCHAR	wchar_t
MPI_SIGNED_CHAR	signed char
MPI_UNSIGNED_LONG_LONG	unsigned long long

Table 5.3
New C datatypes

Type signature $= \{type_0, \ldots, type_{n-1}\}$

The type signature controls how data items are interpreted when data is sent or received. In other words, it tells MPI how to interpret the bits in a data buffer. The displacements tell MPI where to find the bits (when sending) or where to put them (when receiving).

To illustrate how MPI assembles user-defined datatypes, we need to introduce a few terms. Let an MPI datatype have typemap given by (5.1.1). We define

$$lb(\text{Typemap}) = \min_j(disp_j) \tag{5.1.2}$$

$$ub(\text{Typemap}) = \max_j(disp_j + \texttt{sizeof}(type_j)) + pad \tag{5.1.3}$$

$$extent(\text{Typemap}) = ub(\text{Typemap}) - lb(\text{Typemap}) \tag{5.1.4}$$

lb is the *lower bound* of the displacements of the components of the datatype; it can be considered the location of the first byte described by the datatype. *ub* is the *upper bound* of the datatype; it can be considered the location of the last byte described by the datatype. The *extent* is the difference between these two, possibly increased to meet an alignment requirement. The `sizeof` operator in (5.1.3) is the size of the *basic* datatype in bytes.

To descuss the role of the "pad," we first need to discuss data *alignment*. Both C and Fortran require that the basic datatypes be properly aligned, that is, that the locations of, for example, an integer or a double-precision value occur only where allowed. Each implementation of these languages defines what is allowed (there are, of course, some restrictions). One of the most common requirements made by an implementation of these languages is that the address of an item in bytes be a multiple of the length of that item in bytes. For example, if an `int` takes four bytes, then the address of an `int` must be evenly divisible by four. This requirement is reflected in the definition of the extent of an MPI datatype. Consider the typemap

$$\{(int, 0), (char, 4)\} \tag{5.1.5}$$

on a computer that requires that `int`'s be aligned on 4-byte boundaries. This typemap has $lb = \min(0, 4) = 0$ and $ub = \max(0 + 4, 4 + 1) = 5$. But the next `int` can be placed with displacement eight from the `int` in the typemap. This makes the extent of this typemap *on the computer we are discussing* eight.

To find the extent of a datatype, MPI provides the routine `MPI_Type_extent`. The first argument is the MPI datatype; the extent is returned in the second argument. In C, the type of the second argument is `MPI_Aint`; this is an integer type that can hold an arbitrary address (on many but not all systems, this will be an `int`). The extents of the basic datatypes (those in Tables 5.1 and 5.2) are the same as the number of bytes in them.

The size of a datatype is the number of bytes that the data takes up. This is given by `MPI_Type_size`; the first argument is the datatype, and the size is returned in the second argument. The difference between the extent and size of a datatype is illustrated by the typemap in (5.1.5): the size is five bytes, but the extent (on a computer that requires `ints` be aligned on four-byte boundaries) is eight bytes. Rounding out the routines to get the properties of an MPI datatype are `MPI_Type_ub`, to get the upper bound, and `MPI_Type_lb`, to get the lower bound. Bindings for the datatype routines described here are given in Tables 5.4, 5.6, and 5.5.

One routine, `MPI_Type_count`, was defined by MPI-1 but was removed from MPI-1.1 because its definition was unclear. This function gave some information about the contents of a derived datatype; MPI-2 provides more powerful and useful routines for discovering the contents and structure of a datatype.

5.1.2 Derived Datatypes

The typemap is a completely general way of describing an arbitrary datatype. However, it may not be convenient, particularly if the resulting typemap contains

```
int MPI_Type_contiguous(int count, MPI_Datatype oldtype,
              MPI_Datatype *newtype)

int MPI_Type_extent(MPI_Datatype datatype, MPI_Aint *extent)

int MPI_Type_size(MPI_Datatype datatype, MPI_Aint *size)

int MPI_Type_lb(MPI_Datatype datatype, MPI_Aint *displacement)

int MPI_Type_ub(MPI_Datatype datatype, MPI_Aint *displacement)
```

Table 5.4
C bindings for MPI datatype routines

```
Datatype MPI::Datatype::Create_contiguous(int count) const

Aint MPI::Datatype::Get_extent() const

int MPI::Datatype::Get_size() const

Aint MPI::Datatype::Get_lb() const

Aint MPI::Datatype::Get_ub() const
```

Table 5.5
C++ bindings for MPI datatype routines

```
MPI_TYPE_CONTIGUOUS(count, oldtype, newtype, ierror)
              integer  count, oldtype, newtype, ierror

MPI_TYPE_EXTENT(datatype, extent, ierror)
              integer datatype, extent, ierror

MPI_TYPE_SIZE(datatype, size, ierror)
              integer datatype, size, ierror

MPI_TYPE_LB( datatype, displacement, ierror)
              integer datatype, displacement, ierror

MPI_TYPE_UB( datatype, displacement, ierror)
              integer datatype, displacement, ierror
```

Table 5.6
Fortran bindings for MPI datatype routines

large numbers of entries. MPI provides a number of ways to create datatypes without explicitly constructing the typemap.

Contiguous: This is the simplest constructor. It produces a new datatype by making `count` copies of an existing one, with the displacements incremented by the extent of the `oldtype`.

Vector: This is a slight generalization of the contiguous type that allows for regular gaps in the displacements. Elements are separated by multiples of the extent of the input datatype. See Section 4.8.

Hvector: This is like vector, but elements are separated by a specified number of bytes.

Indexed: In this datatype, an array of displacements of the input datatype is provided; the displacements are measured in terms of the extent of the input datatype. See Section 5.2.3.

Hindexed: This is like indexed, but the displacements are measured in bytes. See Section 5.2.4.

Struct: This provides a fully general description. In fact, if the input arguments consist of the basic MPI datatypes, the input is just the typemap. See Section 5.3.

We will describe the MPI functions that create these datatypes as we encounter them. We will discuss the contiguous type here, because that datatype explains how the `count` argument in MPI routines applies to these derived datatypes.

The routine `MPI_Type_contiguous` produces a new datatype by making `count` copies of an existing one, with the displacements incremented by the extent of the `oldtype`. For example, if the original datatype (`oldtype`) has typemap

$\{(int, 0), (double, 8)\}$,

then

```
MPI_Type_contiguous( 2, oldtype, &newtype );
```

produces a datatype `newtype` with typemap

$\{(int, 0), (double, 8), (int, 16), (double, 24)\}$.

When a `count` argument is used in an MPI operation, it is the same as if a contiguous type of the that size had been constructed. That is,

```
MPI_Send( buffer, count, datatype, dest, tag, comm );
```

is exactly the same as

```
MPI_Type_contiguous( count, datatype, &newtype );
MPI_Type_commit( &newtype );
MPI_Send( buffer, 1, newtype, dest, tag, comm );
MPI_Type_free( &newtype );
```

5.1.3 Understanding Extents

The extent of a datatype is probably the most misunderstood concept in MPI. The extent of a datatype is used by MPI communication routines to indicate where to find the "next" data item to send or put the "next" item received. For example

```
char *buffer;
MPI_Send( buffer, n, datatype, ... );
```

sends the same data (but in a single message, rather than `n` messages) as

```
char *buffer;
MPI_Type_extent( datatype, &extent );
for (i=0; i<n; i++) {
    MPI_Send( buffer + (i * extent), 1, datatype, ... );
}
```

To simplify this example, we have declared `buffer` as type `char` and assumed that `sizeof(char)` is one byte.

We can see from this that the extent of a datatype is *not* its size; it is closest to being the *stride* of a datatype: the distance (in bytes) to skip (stride) from the start of one instance of the datatype to the start of another instance of a datatype. We will come back to this topic in Section 5.4 where will see how to use the extent to send data separated by regular gaps.

5.2 The N-Body Problem

Many simulations involve computing the interaction of a large number of particles or objects. If the force between the particles is completely described by adding the forces between all pairs of particles, and the force between each pair acts along the line between them, this is called an N-body central force problem (often just an N-body problem). Such a problem is a good choice for parallelization, since it can be described with N items (the particles) but requires $\mathcal{O}(N^2)$ computation (all the pairs of particles). This means that we can expect good speedups for large problems because the communication between processes will be small relative to the computation.

In this section, we will use the N-body problem to describe a number of MPI features, including new collective operations, persistent communication requests, and new derived datatypes.

In implementing an N-body code, we need first to decide how the particles are distributed among the processes. One simple way is to divide the particles evenly among the processes. For example, if there are 1000 particles and 10 processes, we put the first 100 particles on process 0, the second 100 particles on process 1, and so forth. To compute the forces on the particles, each process must access all the particles on the other processes. (An important optimization involves exploiting the fact that the forces are equal and opposite; this can reduce the computation by a factor of two. For simplicity, we do not make use of this property.)

To begin with, we define a particle datatype. Let us assume that a particle is defined by the structure

```
typedef struct {
    double x, y, z;
    double mass;
} Particle;
```

and that the particles are stored in an array:

```
Particle particles[MAX_PARTICLES];
```

To send this data, we could just send four doubles for each particle, but it makes more sense in MPI to create a datatype for a particle consisting of four doubles:

```
MPI_Type_contiguous( 4, MPI_DOUBLE, &particletype );
MPI_Type_commit( &particletype );
```

(We should really use `MPI_Type_struct` to build this structure, but `MPI_Type_-contiguous` will work on almost any system for this particular case. We will cover the use of `MPI_Type_struct` in Section 5.3.)

5.2.1 Gather

The simplest approach is for all processes to exchange all the particles and then compute with them. In this approach, all processes will have copies of all of the particles, computing only the forces on the particles held locally.[1] For example, each process could do

```
Particle *(particleloc[]);
...
MPI_Comm_size( MPI_COMM_WORLD, &size );
for (i=0; i<size; i++) {
    MPI_Send( particles, count, particletype, i, 0,
              MPI_COMM_WORLD );
}
for (i=0; i<size; i++) {
    MPI_Recv( particleloc[i], MAX_PARTICLES, particletype, i, 0,
              MPI_COMM_WORLD, &status );
}
```

(For reasons that will soon be clear, we have deliberately left the sends and receives from a process to itself in this code.) This code has many problems: it does not scale (it takes time proportional to the number of processes), it may deadlock (because the code requires that `MPI_Send` provide buffering), and it needs the locations `particleloc[i]` computed before the code can be used. We could use the techniques in Chapter 4 to get around the deadlock (buffering) problem, but the other problems require more care. Fortunately, MPI provides routines to handle this common case. We will show how the routines `MPI_Allgather` and `MPI_Allgatherv` can be used to provide efficient ways to communicate data between processes.

First, let us handle the problem of determining how many particles each process has. Let each process have `count` contain the number of particles that it holds. We wish to fill an array `counts` such that `counts[i]` contains the number of particles on the $\mathtt{i}^{\text{th}}$ process. One way to do this is to gather all the data to a single process and then use `MPI_Bcast` to send the data to all the processes. The routine that accomplishes this is `MPI_Gather`.

```
int count, counts[];
...
root = 0;
MPI_Gather( &count, 1, MPI_INT, counts, 1, MPI_INT, root,
            MPI_COMM_WORLD );
MPI_Comm_size( MPI_COMM_WORLD, &size );
```

[1] This approach is suitable only for relatively small number of particles; it may be used if the forces are particularly complicated or if long spans of time need to be computed.

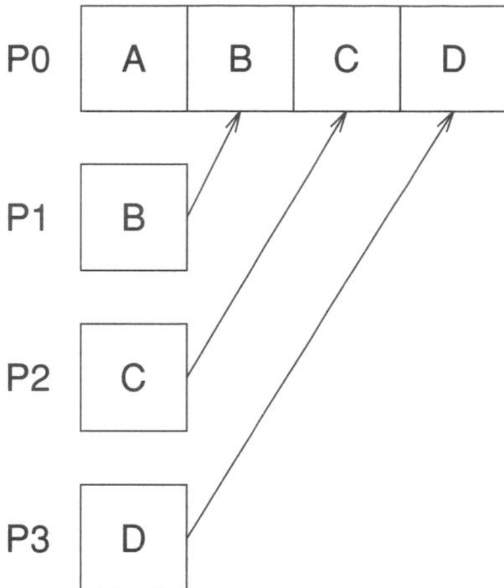

Figure 5.1
Data motion for a gather operation with p0 as root

```
MPI_Bcast( counts, size, MPI_INT, root, MPI_COMM_WORLD );
```

The gather operation takes the data being sent by the $\mathtt{i}^{\mathrm{th}}$ process and places it in the $\mathtt{i}^{\mathrm{th}}$ location in the receive buffer on the root process. Only the process designated as the root receives the data.

Tables 5.7, 5.8, and 5.9 show the bindings for the gather operations. The first three arguments describe the data to be sent; the fourth through sixth arguments describe the data to be received. For `MPI_Gather`, the seventh argument indicates which process will receive the data. `MPI_Gather` requires that all processes, including the root, send the same amount of data and that the type signature of the `sendtype` match that of the `recvtype`. The value of `recvcount` is the number of data items sent by any *one* process; usually, `sendtype = recvtype` and `sendcount = recvcount`. Once all the data has been gathered to a single process, the data can be distributed to all processes with the broadcast routine `MPI_Bcast`. Note also that the `recvbuf` is longer than the `sendbuf` except for the trivial case where the `sendcount` is zero.

Just as with `MPI_Reduce` and `MPI_Allreduce`, it can be more convenient and efficient to combine the gather and broadcast operations into a single operation. `MPI_Allgather` does this; the code for collecting the counts onto all processes is shown here:

```
int counts[MAX_PROCESSES];
```

```
int MPI_Gather(void *sendbuf, int sendcount,MPI_Datatype sendtype,
               void *recvbuf, int recvcount,MPI_Datatype recvtype, int root,
               MPI_Comm comm)

int MPI_Allgather(void *sendbuf, int sendcount,MPI_Datatype sendtype,
               void *recvbuf, int recvcount,MPI_Datatype recvtype,
               MPI_Comm comm)

int MPI_Allgatherv(void *sendbuf, int sendcount,MPI_Datatype sendtype,
               void *recvbuf, int *recvcounts, int *displs,MPI_Datatype recvtype,
               MPI_Comm comm)
```

Table 5.7
C bindings for N-body code

```
MPI_Allgather( &count, 1, MPI_INT, counts, 1, MPI_INT,
               MPI_COMM_WORLD );
```

Note that the `recvcount` argument is a scalar; it indicates the number of items received from *each* process, not the sum of the number of items received from all processes.

If all processes had the same number of particles, then we could use `MPI_Allgather` to get the particles:

```
MPI_Allgather( myparticles, count, particletype,
           allparticles, counts, particletype, MPI_COMM_WORLD );
```

In most cases, however, there will be different numbers of particles on each process. In this case, we can use a variant of `MPI_Allgather` that permits differing sizes of data to be sent from each process. The routine `MPI_Allgatherv` takes the lengths of each item to be received and the displacement relative to the receive buffer (in units of the extent of the receive datatype) where the item will be stored. That is, on the $\mathtt{i}^{th}$ process, `recvcount[i]` items are received into the receive buffer starting at location `recvbuf + displs[i]` (the value of `displs[i]` is relative to the datatype of the receive buffer). In our case, we wish to receive the particles into a single array `allparticles`. The displacement for the $\mathtt{i}^{th}$ process is simply the sum of counts for processes 0 through $i-1$. The code to gather all of the particles is

MPI_GATHER(sendbuf, sendcount, sendtype, recvbuf,recvcount, recvtype, root, comm, ierror)
<type> sendbuf(*), recvbuf(*)
integer sendcount, sendtype, recvcount, recvtype, root, comm, ierror

MPI_ALLGATHER(sendbuf, sendcount, sendtype, recvbuf,recvcount, recvtype, comm, ierror)
<type> sendbuf(*), recvbuf(*)
integer sendcount, sendtype, recvcount, recvtype, comm, ierror

MPI_ALLGATHERV(sendbuf, sendcount, sendtype,recvbuf, recvcounts, rdispls, recvtype, comm, ierror)
<type> sendbuf(*), recvbuf(*)
integer sendcount, sendtype,recvcounts(*), displs(*), recvtype, comm, ierror

Table 5.8
Fortran bindings for N-body code

void MPI::Intracomm::Gather(const void* sendbuf, int sendcount, const Datatype& sendtype, void* recvbuf, int recvcount, const Datatype& recvtype, int root) const

void MPI::Intracomm::Allgather(const void* sendbuf, int sendcount, const Datatype& sendtype, void* recvbuf, int recvcount, const Datatype& recvtype) const

void MPI::Intracomm::Allgatherv(const void* sendbuf, int sendcount, const Datatype& sendtype, void* recvbuf, const int recvcounts[], const int displs[], const Datatype& recvtype) const

Table 5.9
C++ findings for N-body code

```
displacements[0] = 0;
for (i=1; i<size; i++)
    displacements[i] = counts[i-1] + displacements[i-1];
MPI_Allgatherv( myparticles, count, particletype,
              allparticles, counts, displacements, particletype,
              MPI_COMM_WORLD );
```

5.2.2 Nonblocking Pipeline

In this section we present another approach to the communications in the N-body problem. When using MPI_Allgatherv, the computation and communication phases are distinct and nonoverlapping. A different approach is to use nonblocking communications, overlapping the communication with the computation. There are a number of ways to do this. One of the simplest is to create a *pipeline* where each process receives some data from the left and sends data to the right. While the data is arriving, computations on data previously received are carried out. This approach is shown below:

```
while (not done) {
    MPI_Irecv( buf1, ..., source=left, ..., &handles[0] );
    MPI_Isend( buf2, ..., dest=right, ..., &handles[1] );
    <compute with buf2>
    MPI_Waitall( 2, handles, statuses );
    <swap buf1 and buf2>
}
```

If enough data is being sent and the MPI implementation and computer hardware can effectively overlap computation and communication, this approach can be faster than using MPI_Allgatherv.

In many simulations, thousands to millions of these steps may be taken. As written above, each step requires the creation of a send and a receive request, with the same parameters being used in each cycle. In this situation, it is possible for a sophisticated MPI implementation to take advantage of the fact that the same operation is being performed many times. To express this, MPI provides routines to create "persistent" send and receive objects that can be used to perform the same operation multiple times. The form of the create call is very similar to a nonblocking send and receive; the only difference is that no communication takes place. Just as for the nonblocking operations MPI_Isend and MPI_Irecv, these routines return an MPI_Request. In order to begin communication with the request, the routine MPI_Start must first be called with the request. In order to complete the communication, one of the wait routines, such as MPI_Wait, must be called. Once a wait has succeeded with the request, MPI_Start may be called again. Multiple persistent communications may be initiated with MPI_Startall.

The code

```
MPI_Irecv( ..., &request );
```

is equivalent to

```
MPI_Recv_init( ..., &request );
MPI_Start( request );
```

An MPI_Wait on an MPI_Irecv request is equivalent to

```
MPI_Wait( &request, &status );
MPI_Request_free( &request );
```

In the N-body problem, the code is complicated by the fact that, if all processes do not have the same number of particles, then there must be a different MPI_-Request created for each number of particles (or, for simplicity, for each process). The code is shown in Figure 5.2.[2]

Note that we call the communication routines only size-1 times; we do not need to send the particles back to their original processes. A complete N-body code using this approach is available in 'advmsg/nbodypipe.c'. Bindings for the MPI routines used here are shown in Tables 5.10, 5.11, and 5.12.

5.2.3 Moving Particles between Processes

In many N-body problems, the force between the particles falls off rapidly with distance. At great enough distance, the influence of an individual particle becomes negligible. A number of algorithms have been devised to take advantage of this fact. They can reduce the order of the computation from $\mathcal{O}(N^2)$ to $\mathcal{O}(N \log N)$ [3, 8, 82] or even to $\mathcal{O}(N)$ [52]. All of these algorithms organize the particles into groups based on their location. For example, the domain may be divided into cells, and the cells assigned to processes as shown in Figure 5.3. One important step in the implementation of these algorithms is that of transferring particles from one process to another as they move. We will discuss several ways in which this can be accomplished in MPI.

[2]For Fortran programmers, the C expression a % b is roughly equivalent to the Fortran expression mod(a,b).

```
/* Setup */
for (i=0; i<size-1; i++) {
    MPI_Send_init( sendbuf, counts[(rank+i)%size],
                    particletype, right, i, MPI_COMM_WORLD,
                    &request[2*i] );
    MPI_Recv_init( recvbuf, counts[(rank+i-1+size)%size],
                   particletype, left, i, MPI_COMM_WORLD,
                   &request[2*i+1] );
    }
/* run pipeline */
while (!done) {
    <copy local particles into sendbuf>
    for (i=0; i<size; i++) {
        MPI_Status statuses[2];
        if (i != size-1)
            MPI_Startall( 2, &request[2*i] );
        <compute using sendbuf>
        if (i != size-1)
            MPI_Waitall( 2, &request[2*i], statuses );
        <copy recvbuf into sendbuf>
         }
    <compute new particle positions>
    }
/* Free requests */
for (i=0; i<2*(size-1); i++) {
    MPI_Request_free( &request[i] );
    }
```

Figure 5.2
Nonblocking pipeline implemented with MPI persistent communication objects

```
int MPI_Send_init(void* buf, int count, MPI_Datatype datatype, int dest, int tag,
              MPI_Comm comm, MPI_Request *request)

int MPI_Recv_init(void* buf, int count, MPI_Datatype datatype, int source,
              int tag, MPI_Comm comm, MPI_Request *request)

int MPI_Start(MPI_Request *request)

int MPI_Startall(int count, MPI_Request *array_of_requests)

int MPI_Request_free(MPI_Request *request)
```

Table 5.10
C bindings for nonblocking pipeline

```
MPI_SEND_INIT(buf, count, datatype, dest, tag, comm, request, ierror)
              <type> buf(*)
              integer request, count, datatype, dest, tag, comm, request, ierror

MPI_RECV_INIT(buf, count, datatype, source, tag, comm, request, ierror)
              <type> buf(*)
              integer count, datatype, source, tag, comm, request, ierror

MPI_START(request, ierror)
              integer request, ierror

MPI_STARTALL(count, array_of_requests, ierror)
              integer count, array_of_requests(*), ierror

MPI_REQUEST_FREE(request, ierror)
              integer request, ierror
```

Table 5.11
Fortran bindings for nonblocking pipeline

Prequest MPI::Comm::Send_init(const void* buf, int count,
const Datatype& datatype, int dest, int tag) const

Prequest MPI::Comm::Recv_init(void* buf, int count,
const Datatype& datatype, int source, int tag) const

void MPI::Prequest::Start()

void MPI::Prequest::Startall(int count, Prequest array_of_requests[])

void MPI::Request::Free()

Table 5.12
C++ bindings for nonblocking pipeline. Note that the C++ class for a persistent request is `Prequest`.

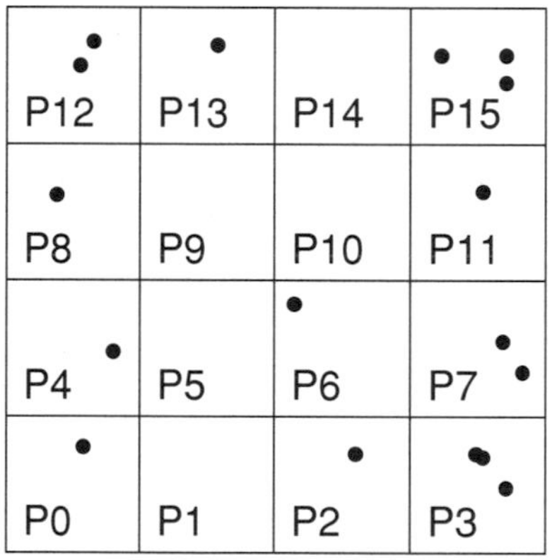

P12	P13	P14	P15
P8	P9	P10	P11
P4	P5	P6	P7
P0	P1	P2	P3

Figure 5.3
Sample of a decomposition of a domain into cells. The cells are labeled with process numbers and the dots are particles that belong to that process.

int **MPI_Type_indexed**(int count, int *array_of_blocklengths,
int *array_of_displacements, MPI_Datatype oldtype,
MPI_Datatype *newtype)

int **MPI_Get_count**(MPI_Status *status, MPI_Datatype datatype, int *count)

int **MPI_Probe**(int source, int tag, MPI_Comm comm, MPI_Status *status)

Table 5.13
C bindings used in moving particles

MPI_TYPE_INDEXED(count, array_of_blocklengths, array_of_displacements, oldtype, newtype, ierror)
integer count, array_of_blocklengths(*), array_of_displacements(*), oldtype, newtype, ierror

MPI_GET_COUNT(status, datatype, count, ierror)
integer status(*),datatype, count, ierror

MPI_PROBE(source, tag, comm, status, ierror)
integer source, tag, comm, status(MPI_STATUS_SIZE), ierror

Table 5.14
Fortran bindings used in moving particles

Datatype MPI::Datatype::Create_indexed(int count, const int array_of_blocklengths[], const int array_of_displacements[]) const

int MPI::Status::Get_count(const Datatype& datatype) const

void MPI::Comm::Probe(int source, int tag, Status& status) const

void MPI::Comm::Probe(int source, int tag) const

Table 5.15
C++ bindings used in moving particles

If the particles are all stored in a single array, say `Particles myparticles[]`, then the particles that need to be given to another process can be described by their indices into this array. MPI provides a way to describe the data to be moved directly in terms of these indices with `MPI_Type_indexed`. The input to this routine is the number of elements as the first argument, an array of block lengths (just as for `MPI_Type_vector`, these are often all ones) as the second argument, the array of index values as the third argument, and the type of the data to move as the fourth argument. The fifth argument is the new data type. Figure 5.4 shows how this routine can be used, and Figure 5.5 illustrates the relationship of the index values to the data that is to be moved. Note that this will work even if no particles leave the cell (`n_to_move=0`).

To receive, we can use

```
MPI_Recv( newparticles, MAX_PARTICLES, particletype,
          source, tag, comm, &status );
```

```
n_to_move = 0;
for (i=0; i<count; i++) {
    if (...particle exited cell...) {
        elmoffset[n_to_move] = i;
        elmsize[n_to_move]   = 1;
        n_to_move++;
    }
}
MPI_Type_indexed( n_to_move, elmsize, elmoffset,
                  particletype, &sendtype );
MPI_Type_commit( &sendtype );
MPI_Send( myparticles, 1, sendtype, dest, tag, comm );
MPI_Type_free( &sendtype );
```

Figure 5.4
Sketch of code to move particles from one process to another

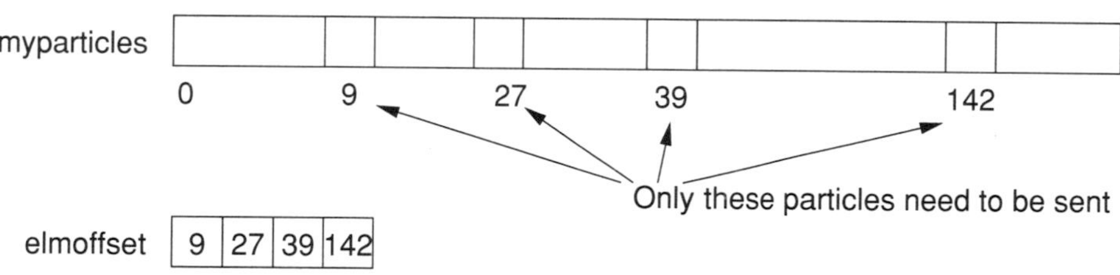

Figure 5.5
Illustration of the `array_of_displacements` argument in Figure 5.4

```
MPI_Get_count( &status, particletype, &number );
```

where `number` is the number of particles received. Here we use the routine `MPI_-Get_count` to determine how many particles were delivered. `MPI_Get_count` uses the information in the `status` returned from an MPI receive, probe, wait, or test together with a datatype (in the second argument) to determine what the output value is relative to. Note that the MPI datatype used in `MPI_Get_count` must be the same as the MPI datatype used in the MPI call that produced the `status` value; in this case, since `MPI_Recv` specified `particletype`, we must give `particletype` to `MPI_Get_count`. Bindings for these routines are given in Tables 5.13, 5.14, and 5.15.

This approach requires us to preallocate enough space to receive any number of particles. This is not always possible. What we need is some way to find out about a message before we receive it. The routine `MPI_Probe` allows us to do this. `MPI_-Probe` takes a source, tag, and communicator and returns an `MPI_Status`. In this

Thread 1	Thread 2
`MPI_Probe( s, t, comm, &st1 )`	`MPI_Probe( s, t, comm, &st2 )`
`MPI_Get_count( &st1, d, &n1 )`	`MPI_Get_count( &st2, d, &n2 )`
`MPI_Recv( a, n1, d, s, t, comm, &st )`	`MPI_Recv( b, n2, d, s, t, comm, &st )`

Figure 5.6
Two threads in the same MPI process receiving in the same communicator

MPI_Status, just as if the message had been received, are the message tag, source, and, using MPI_Get_count, length of the message. If the MPI_Probe is followed by a MPI_Recv using the same source, tag, and communicator, the MPI_Recv will receive the message that MPI_Probe told us about. Thus, we can use MPI_Get_count along with MPI_Probe to determine the amount of space that we need before we use MPI_Recv to receive the message. Since MPI_Probe and MPI_Iprobe return a status even when the message has not been received yet, they may be used to find out how large a pending message is and then allocate a buffer for it. This is one of the main situations where MPI_Probe is needed; MPI_Irecv will not do, because it requires preallocating the buffer into which the message is to be received. The code for this is

```
MPI_Probe( source, tag, comm, &status );
MPI_Get_count( &status, particletype, &number );
MPI_Type_extent( particletype, &extent );
newparticles = (Particle *)malloc( number * extent );
MPI_Recv( newparticles, number, particletype,
          source, tag, comm, &status );
```

A note on thread safety. This code shows one of the few places where the MPI design itself has a thread safety problem. Many MPI programs are run in an environment where there is one thread per process or where only one thread makes MPI calls, and in those situations, there is no problem with the above code.

However, if several threads are executing MPI calls, this code may not work. Consider the situation shown in Figure 5.6.

In this example, the two threads are trying to receive a message from the process at rank s in communicator comm with datatype d. Let us further assume that the process at rank s has sent two messages, one of length 1 and one of length 10. The possible outcomes are shown in Figure 5.7

Only cases one and four give what the programmer intended. In the other two

Case	Thread 1		Thread 2	
	Probe	Recv	Probe	Recv
1	1	1	10	10
2	1	10	1	1
3	1	1	1	10
4	10	10	1	1

Figure 5.7
Possible results for the code in Figure 5.6 showing the lengths of the message returned by the MPI_Probe and the MPI_Recv steps

Thread 1	Thread 2
`MPI_Probe( s, t, comm, &status1 )`	
`MPI_Get_count( &status1, d, &n1 )`	
	`MPI_Probe( s, t, comm, &status2 )`
Both `MPI_Probe` calls	see the same message
	`MPI_Get_count( &status2, d, &n2 )`
	`MPI_Recv( b, n2, d, s, t, comm, status )`
`MPI_Recv( a, n1, d, s, t, comm, status )`	

Figure 5.8
Possible execution sequence for the two threads in Figure 5.6

cases, the `MPI_Probe` and the `MPI_Recv` calls see separate messages. To see why, consider how case two might happen.

Figure 5.8 shows one possible execution sequence. Both threads call `MPI_Probe` before either call `MPI_Recv`; thus, both threads find out about the first message sent from the process at rank `s`, which has size one. Next, the second thread receives this message with `MPI_Recv`. Finally, the first thread attempts to receive a message with a count of `n1 = 1`. Unfortunately, since the first message has already been received, the first thread sees the second message, the one with length 10. This will generate an error of class `MPI_ERR_TRUNCATE`.

There are several ways to avoid this problem. The classic approach in multi-threaded programming is to use some mutual exclusion mechanism, such as locks, around the `MPI_Probe` to `MPI_Recv` to prevent any other thread from interfering. MPI offers another approach: since communication on different communicators is independent, as long as no communicator is used by more than one thread, no mutual exclusions are required. Thread safety issues are discussed in more detail in *Using MPI-2* [66].

```
int MPI_Type_create_indexed_block(int count, int blocklength,
        int *array_of_displacements, MPI_Datatype oldtype,
        MPI_Datatype *newtype)
```

Table 5.16
C binding for MPI-2 function for blocked, indexed datatypes

```
MPI_TYPE_CREATE_INDEXED_BLOCK(count, blocklength,
        array_of_displacements, oldtype, newtype, ierror)
        integer count, blocklength, array_of_displacement(*), oldtype,
            newtype, ierror
```

Table 5.17
Fortran binding for MPI-2 function for blocked, indexed datatypes

```
Datatype MPI::Datatype::Create_indexed_block( int count, int blocklength,
        const int array_of_displacements[]) const
```

Table 5.18
C++ binding for MPI-2 function for blocked, indexed datatypes

An MPI-2 alternative for `MPI_Type_indexed`. One cumbersome part of using `MPI_Type_indexed` is that for many applications, as in this example, the blocklengths are the same for all blocks. MPI-2 has a new routine that addresses this issue: `MPI_Type_create_indexed_block`. This routine is used in the same way as `MPI_Type_indexed`, except that the second argument in `MPI_Type_indexed`, `array_of_blocklengths`, is replaced by the scalar `blocklength`. The bindings for this routine are shown in Tables 5.16, 5.17, and 5.18.

Note that we have sent data, using a derived datatype, that was not stored contiguously in memory and received it into contiguous locations in memory. MPI requires only that the type signatures match, that is, the basic kinds of the data (e.g., integers match integers, reals match reals).

5.2.4 Sending Dynamically Allocated Data

In some implementations of N-body algorithms, the particles may be stored in dynamically allocated storage. In this case, there is no single buffer that we can use for the displacements to be relative to, as required by `MPI_Type_indexed`. We can use instead a special location, `MPI_BOTTOM`, and the absolute addresses (as given by `MPI_Address`) of the items. Since we will be computing the displacements as

```
MPI_Aint elmoffset[MAX_PARTICLES];
n_to_move  = 0;
while (particle) {
    if (particle exited cell) {
        MPI_Address( particle, &elmoffset[n_to_move] );
        elmsize[n_to_move] = 1;
        n_to_move++;
        <make sure to unlink particle and de-allocate>
    }
    else {
        particle = particle->next;
    }
}
MPI_Type_hindexed( n_to_move, elmsize, elmoffset,
                   particletype, &particlemsg );
MPI_Type_commit( &particlemsg );
MPI_Send( MPI_BOTTOM, 1, particlemsg, dest, tag, comm );
MPI_Type_free( &particlemsg );
```

Figure 5.9
Sketch of code to move dynamically allocated particles to other processes

addresses in bytes rather than as indexes into an array, we use `MPI_Type_hindexed`. This routine is identical to `MPI_Type_indexed` except that the third argument is measured in bytes rather than in elements. For example, if the particles are stored in a linked list whose elements are dynamically created, we can use the code in Figure 5.9.

The routine `MPI_Address` takes an item as the first argument and returns its address, with type (in C) of `MPI_Aint` as the second argument. Fortran programmers will appreciate this function, but C programmers may be a bit puzzled by its use, particularly in a C program. The reason is that in many C implementations, the value of a pointer (as an integer) is implemented as the address in memory of the item pointed at. However, this is not required in C, and there are important machines (for example, supercomputers with word, not byte, addressability and practically every personal computer on the planet) for which pointers are *not* addresses. Using `MPI_Address` in C programs helps maintain portability. Bindings for these routines are shown in Tables 5.19, 5.20, and 5.21.

```
int MPI_Address(void* location, MPI_Aint *address)

int MPI_Type_hindexed(int count, int *array_of_blocklengths,
                MPI_Aint *array_of_displacements, MPI_Datatype oldtype,
                MPI_Datatype *newtype)
```

Table 5.19
C bindings for sending dynamically allocated data

```
MPI_ADDRESS(location, address, ierror)
                <type> location
                integer address, ierror

MPI_TYPE_HINDEXED(count, array_of_blocklengths, array_of_displacements,
                oldtype, newtype, ierror)
                integer count, array_of_blocklengths(*), array_of_displacements(*),
                    oldtype, newtype, ierror
```

Table 5.20
Fortran bindings for sending dynamically allocated data

```
Aint MPI::Get_address(const void* location)

Datatype MPI::Datatype::Create_hindexed(int count,
                const int array_of_blocklengths[],
                const Aint array_of_displacements[]) const
```

Table 5.21
C++ bindings for sending dynamically allocated data

5.2.5 User-Controlled Data Packing

In some cases, it is easier to assemble a contiguous buffer to be sent rather than to create a special datatype. MPI provides routines to pack and unpack data consisting of any MPI datatype into and out of a user-provided buffer. The routine `MPI_Pack` allows the programmer to incrementally add data to a user-provided buffer. Data that has been packed may be sent and received with the datatype `MPI_PACKED`. The input to `MPI_Pack` is the data to pack, the number and datatype of the items, output buffer and the size of the output buffer in bytes, the current `position`, and the communicator. The `position` is also an output argument; it is one of the few arguments in MPI that is both input and output. The `position` value must be set to zero before the first call to `MPI_Pack` each time a buffer is to be filled up with data. `MPI_Pack` uses `position` to keep track of where in the output buffer it is. The value of `position` must be used as the `count` argument when sending a buffer that has been filled with `MPI_Pack`. The exact meaning of `position` is implementation dependent; for example, it need not be the number of bytes packed.

One question that must be answered is, How big a buffer do I need to hold the data? The routine `MPI_Pack_size` answers this question. This routine takes the number of elements, the MPI datatype of those elements, and the communicator in which they will be communicated, and returns the maximum number of bytes that will be required by `MPI_Pack` to hold the data.

The communicator is a required argument because in a heterogenous environment, that is, in an MPI program where `MPI_COMM_WORLD` contains processors with different data representations, the choice of representation for data to be sent in a communicator may depend on which processes are in a communicator. For example, consider the case where `MPI_COMM_WORLD` contains 64 processors of identical type and 1 processor that provides fast visualization but uses a different data representation. The program uses `MPI_Comm_split` to create a `compute` and a `graphics` communicator; the `compute` communicator contains the 64 identical processors. For the `compute` communicator, `MPI_Pack` can choose the native data representation for higher performance and efficiency. For `MPI_COMM_WORLD`, `MPI_Pack` may choose a different format.

A version of the code in Section 5.2.4 that uses `MPI_Pack` is shown in Figure 5.10. Receiving the particles is managed with `MPI_Unpack`, as shown in Figure 5.11. Note the use of `MPI_Get_count` to get the length of the packed buffer and the test of `position < length` to determine when all of the particles have been unpacked. Bindings for these routines are given in Tables 5.22, 5.23, and 5.24.

One can also receive a message assembled with `MPI_Pack` and sent with datatype `MPI_PACKED` with the appropriate datatype. In this case, we could use the `particletype` datatype:

```
Particle particles[MAX_PARTICLES];

position = 0;
particle = &particles[0];
MPI_Pack_size( MAX_SEND, particletype, comm, &bufsize );
buffer = malloc( (unsigned)bufsize );
while (particle) {
    if (particle exited cell) {
        MPI_Pack( particle, 1, particletype, buffer, bufsize,
              &position, comm );
        <make sure to unlink particle and de-allocate>
        }
    else {
        particle = particle->next;
        }
    }
MPI_Send( buffer, position, MPI_PACKED, dest, tag, comm );
```

Figure 5.10
Sketch of code to pack particles into an output buffer

```
MPI_Recv( buffer, maxcount, MPI_PACKED,
          source, tag, comm, &status );
MPI_Get_count( &status, MPI_PACKED, &length );
position = 0;
while (position < length) {
    MPI_Unpack( buffer, length, &position, &newparticle,
                1, particletype, comm );
    <add new particle to the list of particles>
    }
```

Figure 5.11
Sketch of code to unpack particles from a buffer

```
int MPI_Pack(void* inbuf, int incount, MPI_Datatype datatype, void *outbuf,
             int outsize, int *position, MPI_Comm comm)

int MPI_Unpack(void* inbuf, int insize, int *position, void *outbuf, int outcount,
             MPI_Datatype datatype, MPI_Comm comm)

int MPI_Pack_size(int incount, MPI_Datatype datatype, MPI_Comm comm,
             int *size)
```

Table 5.22
C bindings for buffer pack and unpack

```
MPI_PACK(inbuf, incount, datatype, outbuf, outcount, position, comm, ierror)
             <type> inbuf(*), outbuf(*)
             integer incount, datatype, outcount, position, comm, ierror

MPI_UNPACK(inbuf, insize, position, outbuf, outcount, datatype, comm, ierror)
             <type> inbuf(*), outbuf(*)
             integer insize, position, outcount, datatype, comm, ierror

MPI_PACK_SIZE(incount, datatype, comm, size, ierror)
             integer incount, datatype, comm, size, ierror
```

Table 5.23
Fortran bindings for buffer pack and unpack

```
void MPI::Datatype::Pack(const void* inbuf, int incount, void *outbuf,
             int outsize, int& position, const Comm &comm) const

void MPI::Datatype::Unpack(const void* inbuf, int insize, void *outbuf,
             int outcount, int& position, const Comm& comm) const

int MPI::Datatype::Pack_size(int incount, const Comm& comm) const
```

Table 5.24
C++ bindings for buffer pack and unpack

```
MPI_Recv( buffer, maxparticle, particletype,
          source, tag, comm, &status );
MPI_Get_count( &status, particletype, &newparticles );
```

Multiple buffers can be maintained, of course. For example, in traversing the data, we would probably keep data for each neighboring process in a separate buffer, each with a separate position variable.

5.3 Visualizing the Mandelbrot Set

No book on parallel programming would be complete without an example of Mandelbrot computation. In this section we use it to illustrate the use of MPI's derived datatypes along with the MPE real-time graphics library. For our example we use one of the many optimizations at the algorithm level that are possible for programs, parallel or not, that compute graphical representations of the Mandelbrot set.

The Mandelbrot set is a popular exercise for parallel computation because it is so obviously a parallel application, it introduces a load-balancing problem, and the results are fascinating to look at. To be at least a little original, we do it here with a slightly nonstandard algorithm. We would like to think we invented this trick, but we are not certain. Surely others have had the same idea.

Let z be a complex variable. That is, we think of z as a point (x, y) in the plane, with multiplication on points of the plane given by

$$(x_1, y_1) \cdot (x_2, y_2) = (x_1 x_2 - y_1 y_2, x_1 y_2 + x_2 y_1).$$

The *Mandelbrot set* $\mathcal{M}$ is defined in the following way. Given a complex number c, consider the function $f_c(z) = z^2 + c$. Then we can compute a series of points in the complex plane: $z_0 = 0$, $z_1 = f_c(0)$, $z_2 = f_c(z_1) = {f_c}^2(0)$, etc. This series either remains bounded, in which case c is in $\mathcal{M}$, or it gets farther and farther away from 0, in which case it is not. One can be prove that once a point in this sequence gets farther than a distance of 2 from the origin, the series becomes unbounded.

A "picture" of the Mandelbrot set can be made by plotting the points on the screen. Each pixel in the display corresponds to a point c in the complex plane and can be tested for membership in $\mathcal{M}$ by applying the function f_c repeatedly to 0. Either $|{f_c}^n(0)| > 2$ for some n, or some preset number of iterations has been reached, in which case we give up and declare that the point c is in $\mathcal{M}$ and color it, say, black. Details of the very complex boundary of $\mathcal{M}$ can be seen by "magnification," assigning the full area of the display to a small section of the complex plane. For more on the Mandelbrot set and related topics, see [93] or [110].

The region near the boundary of $\mathcal{M}$ is very interesting. Striking representations of this area can be made by assigning a color to the pixel representing point c according to the first value n for which $|{f_c}^n(0)| > 2$. As we explore the edge of $\mathcal{M}$ at greater and greater magnifications, we have a sense of exploring a huge universe of great variety. After a few random magnifications, we are likely to be looking at a part of the plane that no one has ever looked at before.

The calculation of each pixel's color value can be made independently of every other pixel's, so the program to compute such pictures is straightforwardly parallelizable, just by dividing up the screen into areas, one for each process. Unfortunately, this naive "prescheduled" approach works badly because of load imbalances. Some points escape the circle of radius 2 after only a few iterations, others take longer, and of course the points in $\mathcal{M}$ itself take the maximum number of iterations before we give up on them. As we magnify, we need more iterations to bring out detail, so some pixels may take thousands of times more iterations than others before we can assign them a color.

The most natural way to overcome this load-balancing problem is with self-scheduling. We divide up the screen into some moderately large number of squares and devote one process (the master) to sending them to the other processes (the slaves) for computation. Just as in the matrix-vector multiplication program in Chapter 3, completion of a task is a request for another assignment. Some tasks will take much longer than others (particularly the areas that are mostly black), but unless we have very bad luck, we will be able to keep all processes busy all the time.

We have included a parallel Mandelbrot program among the examples available with this book. It is too long to present here, but it has three interesting aspects that we will expand on below. Specifically, it illustrates

- the use of derived datatypes in MPI for sending scattered structures,
- an interesting technique for accelerating the computation, and
- a few more functions from the MPE graphics library.

During the initialization phase of the computation, the master process broadcasts a highly miscellaneous collection of data to the slaves. We can think of it as a C structure, although not all the data is stored as a single C structure. We could broadcast each of these parameters separately, which would be wasteful of messages (and be would expensive, because of the often high startup cost of sending a message), or we could rearrange them into arrays of `ints`, arrays of `doubles`, and

MPI_TYPE_HVECTOR(count, blocklength, stride, oldtype, newtype, ierror) integer count, blocklength, stride, oldtype, newtype, ierror **MPI_TYPE_STRUCT**(count, array_of_blocklengths, array_of_displacements, array_of_types, newtype, ierror) integer count, array_of_blocklengths(*), array_of_displacements(*), array_of_types(*), newtype, ierror

Table 5.25
Fortran bindings for MPI datatype routines

int **MPI_Type_hvector**(int count, int blocklength, MPI_Aint stride, MPI_Datatype oldtype, MPI_Datatype *newtype) int **MPI_Type_struct**(int count, int *array_of_blocklengths, MPI_Aint *array_of_displacements, MPI_Datatype *array_of_types, MPI_Datatype *newtype)

Table 5.26
C bindings for MPI datatype routines

so forth. The "MPI way" is to create a datatype that represents this structure and send it all at once.

The algorithm we use is illustrated in Figures 5.12, 5.13, and 5.14. The example code implements a method for accelerating the computation. The trick is based on the fact that except at the very lowest magnification, if the border of any square is made up of pixels all of which have the same color, then all the pixels in the interior of the square must have that color too. This can speed things up a great deal, especially for large areas of $\mathcal{M}$ itself. In order to dynamically adapt the sizes

Datatype MPI::Datatype::Create_hvector(int count, int blocklength, Aint stride) const **Datatype MPI::Datatype::Create_struct**(int count, const int array_of_blocklengths[], const Aint array_of_displacements[], const Datatype array_of_types[])

Table 5.27
C++ bindings for MPI datatype routines

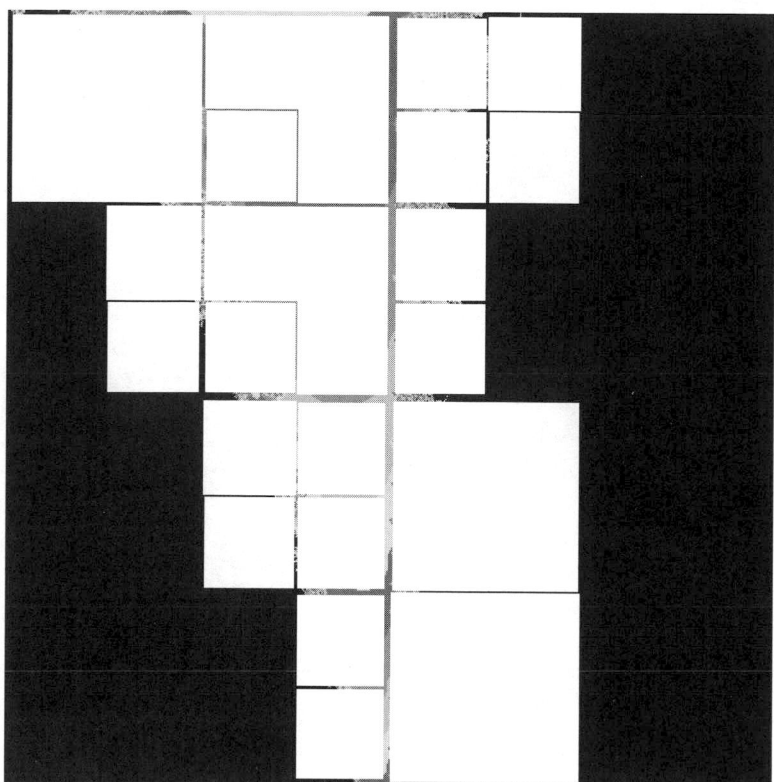

Figure 5.12
Box algorithm for Mandelbrot, starting

of the squares, we do the following.

The queue of tasks to be done is managed by the master and consists of squares whose colors are to be computed. Initially just one task is in the queue, the entire region selected for display. Given a square, we begin computing the colors of the pixels on its boundary. If we get all the way around the boundary without changing colors, then we color in the interior with the same color. If we come to a new color while computing the boundary, then we subdivide the square into four subsquares and send them back to the master as new tasks, while we carry on with the boundary. We carefully keep the squares nested tightly so that we never compute the color of any pixel more than once. There is a cutoff for subdivision so that when the squares get small enough, they are not subdivided further.

As the program runs, we watch the picture develop by using the MPE graphics

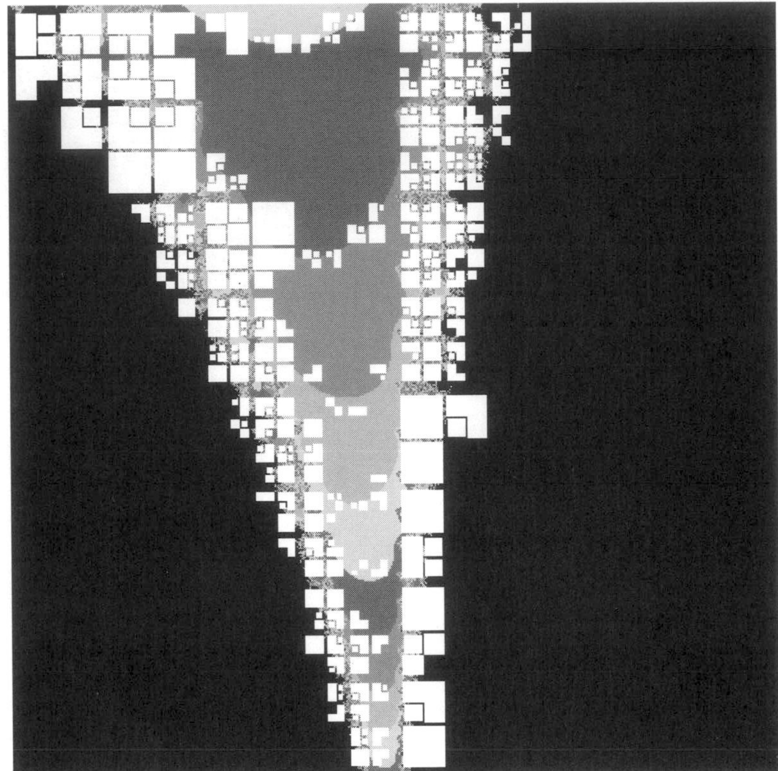

Figure 5.13
Box algorithm for Mandelbrot, a little later

library to see whether the program is proceeding as we expect. In addition to drawing individual points as we did in Chapter 3, we draw line segments as we are computing the boundaries of squares. Even when the boundary is not all of the same color, there are stretches of boundary that are, and they are displayed with

```
MPE_Draw_line( handle, x1, y1, x2, y2, color );
```

where `handle` is a pointer to an `MPE_XGraph` structure initialized with `MPE_Open_-graphics`; `x1,y1` and `x2,y2` are the endpoints of the line; and `color` is a color of type `MPE_Color`.

When we "win" and get to fill in a whole square, then we use

```
MPE_Fill_rectangle( handle, x, y, w, h, color );
```

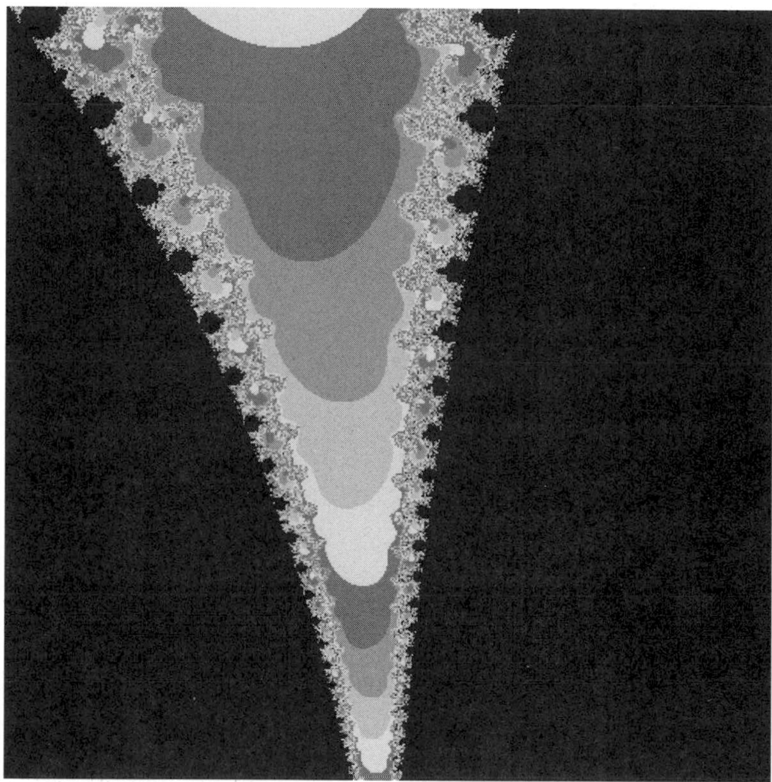

Figure 5.14
Mandelbrot, complete

where `x,y` is the position of the upper left corner of the rectangle, and `w` and `h` are the width and height of the rectangle, in pixels. When we draw only one point at a time, we use

```
MPE_Draw_point( handle, x, y, color );
```

where `x` and `y` are the coordinates of the point, in pixels.

Even these separate calls are "batched" in that we only call `MPE_Update` at the end of a task (an entire boundary, an entire square of the same color, or a small square of different colors). Figure 5.14 shows the completed picture.

We take this opportunity to introduce the most general of the MPI derived datatypes, which may be used for sending C structures or parts of them. The Mandelbrot program data structures contain a C structure that holds command line arguments, which specify a large number of options for the program. It is convenient to keep them in a structure so that they can easily be passed to various subroutines. MPI does not specify that all processes have access to the command line arguments through `MPI_Init`, so we broadcast them, assuming that at least the process with rank 0 in `MPI_COMM_WORLD` does get them when the program is started. After storing them in its copy of this structure, it broadcasts the structure to the other processes. The structure itself looks like the following:

```
struct {
    char      display[50];    /* Name of display */
    int       maxiter;        /* max # of iterations */
    double    xmin, ymin;     /* lower left corner of rectangle */
    double    xmax, ymax;     /* upper right corner */
    int       width;          /* of display in pixels */
    int       height;         /* of display in pixels */
} cmdline;
```

We would like to broadcast this structure with a single `MPI_Bcast`, taking advantage of MPI's facilities for dealing with alignment, mixed types, and heterogeneous communication. We show here two ways to do so.

`MPI_Type_struct` is very general. It allows us to describe as a single datatype as a collection of data items of various elementary and derived types. It considers the data to be composed of a set of "blocks" of data, each of which has a count and datatype associated with it and a location given as a displacement. The code to set up to broadcast the above structure would look like the following:

```
/* set up 4 blocks */
int          blockcounts[4] = {50,1,4,2};
MPI_Datatype types[4];
MPI_Aint     displs[4];
MPI_Datatype cmdtype;

/* initialize types and displs with addresses of items */
MPI_Address( &cmdline.display, &displs[0] );
MPI_Address( &cmdline.maxiter, &displs[1] );
MPI_Address( &cmdline.xmin,    &displs[2] );
MPI_Address( &cmdline.width,   &displs[3] );
types[0] = MPI_CHAR;
types[1] = MPI_INT;
```

```
types[2] = MPI_DOUBLE;
types[3] = MPI_INT;
```

The blockcounts array indicates how many elements there are for each corresponding type. In our example, we have char display[50], so the value of blockcounts[0] is 50. blockcounts[1] is one, matching the single int that is the next element (maxiter) in the structure. Following maxiter, there are four double values, starting with xmin, so blockcounts[2] is 4. Finally, there are two int values, so blockcounts[3] is 2.

Now we are ready to do the broadcast. First we adjust the displacement array so that the displacements are offsets from the beginning of the structure; that is, we make them relative to the beginning of the structure.

```
for (i = 3; i >= 0; i--)
    displs[i] -= displs[0];
```

Then we build the new type

```
MPI_Type_struct( 4, blockcounts, displs, types, &cmdtype );
MPI_Type_commit( &cmdtype );
```

and broadcast it from process zero to all others:

```
MPI_Bcast( &cmdline, 1, cmdtype, 0, MPI_COMM_WORLD );
```

There is an alternative to the way the displacements are presented. The displacements need not be relative to the beginning of a particular structure; they can be "absolute" addresses as well. In this case, we treat them as relative to the starting address in memory, given by MPI_BOTTOM. Using this technique, we can omit the loop that adjusts the displacements, leaving them as originally given by calls to MPI_Address, and change the MPI_Bcast to

```
MPI_Bcast( MPI_BOTTOM, 1, cmdtype, 0, MPI_COMM_WORLD );
```

5.3.1 Sending Arrays of Structures

When sending more than one struct, for example, when the count argument is greater than one, we may need an additional step when creating the datatype. Consider the datatype

```
struct {
    int a;
    char b;
} my_struct, struct_array[10];
```

```
int          blockcounts[2] = {1,1};
MPI_Datatype types[2];
MPI_Aint     displs[2];
MPI_Datatype structtype;

/* initialize types and displs with addresses of items */
MPI_Address( &my_struct.a, &displs[0] );
MPI_Address( &my_struct.b, &displs[1] );
types[0] = MPI_INT;
types[1] = MPI_CHAR;
/* Make displs relative */
displs[1] -= displs[0];
displs[0] = 0;
MPI_Type_struct( 2, blockcounts, displs, types, &structtype );
MPI_Type_commit( &structtype );
```

Figure 5.15
Code to construct a datatype for a structure. See also Section 5.6.

Given this structure, you might use the MPI code given in Figure 5.15 to create a datatype for it.

The code in this figure *might* work. To understand the problem, consider Figure 5.16. This figure shows one possible layout for the array `struct_array` in memory. As you can see, the end of the last element in `struct_array[i]` does not immediately precede the beginning of the first element in `struct_array[i+1]`.

Now, the MPI library may not know how the compiler has chosen to lay out structures in memory; some compilers have options by which one can choose among several different options (such as natural alignment, packed, packed on two-byte boundaries, etc.). Three possible alignments are shown in Figure 5.16. Thus, the MPI library may have to choose where the "natural" end of the structure is. The code that we used relies on MPI choosing correctly. For robust and portable code, one doesn't wish to rely on guessing correctly. How can we ensure that `structtype` is correct? We will see how to do this in the next section, but first we will look at another related case where gaps exist between the elements in a datatype.

5.4 Gaps in Datatypes

In Section 4.8 we introduced the `MPI_Type_vector` routine and used it to create a datatype for prespecified number of elements. What can you do if you want to

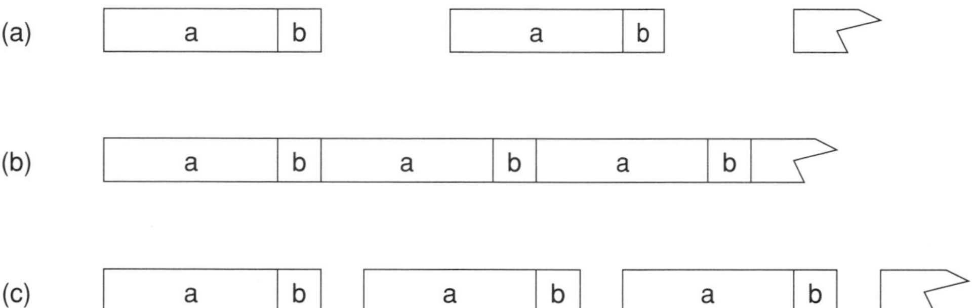

Figure 5.16
Three possible layouts of structure **struct_array** in memory: natural (a), packed (b), and packed on two-byte boundaries (c)

```
int          blens[2];
MPI_Aint     displs[2];
MPI_Datatype types[2], rowtype;
blens[0]  = 1;
blens[1]  = 1;
displs[0] = 0;
displs[1] = number_in_column * sizeof(double);
types[0]  = MPI_DOUBLE;
types[1]  = MPI_UB;
MPI_Type_struct( 2, blens, displs, types, &rowtype );
MPI_Type_commit( &rowtype );
```

Figure 5.17
Code to construct a general strided vector type

specify a variable number of elements?

We obviously wish to use the `count` argument of the send and receive routines, and so we need to describe a datatype that consists of the element followed by a "skip" to the next data element. We can define this by using `MPI_Type_struct` and a special MPI predefined datatype called `MPI_UB`. `MPI_UB` (for upper bound) is a datatype that has no size but serves as a way to change the extent of a datatype. By placing `MPI_UB` at a displacement that is the number of bytes between successive elements, we can skip over those bytes when using this datatype.

Figure 5.17 shows the code to create an MPI datatype for a double-precision array with `number_in_column` elements (assuming Fortran storage order for matrices).

This provides a good place to get a better understanding of the meaning of

```
MPI_Aint     displs;
MPI_Datatype rowtype;

displs = number_in_column * sizeof(double);
MPI_Type_create_resized( MPI_DOUBLE, (MPI_Aint)0, displs,
                         &rowtype );
MPI_Type_commit( &rowtype );
```

Figure 5.18
Code to construct a general strided vector using the MPI-2 approach. Compare with Figure 5.17.

extent and MPI contiguous datatypes. Consider this attempt to define a datatype to access the rows of a matrix stored columnwise:

```
MPI_Type_vector( 1, 1, number_in_column, MPI_DOUBLE, &rowtype2 );
MPI_Type_commit( &rowtype2 );
```

The intent is to use the `count` argument in a send to send the desired number of elements, just as with the datatype `rowtype` constructed above. However, the extent of `rowtype2` is the distance from the first to the last byte in the datatype; and since `rowtype2` contains only a single `double`, the extent is just the size of a `double`. Thus, a send or a receive using datatype `rowtype2` will use consecutive doubles, not doubles separated by `number_in_column` doubles.

The datatype `MPI_LB` is similar to `MPI_UB` except that it may be used to set the lower bound of a derived datatype. This also changes the extent of the datatypes.

5.4.1 MPI-2 Functions for Manipulating Extents

The use of `MPI_UB` and `MPI_LB` is deprecated in MPI-2. The reason is that these values are sticky: once a datatype contains an `MPI_UB` or `MPI_LB`, any datatype constructed from that datatype will also contain the `MPI_UB` and `MPI_LB` and will thus have the extent determined by the upper- or lower-bound markers, rather than by the displacements of the data items. Further, it is impossible to decrease the upper bound or increase the lower bound of a datatype that contains a `MPI_UB` or `MPI_LB`, respectively. Since the principal use of these special datatypes was to construct new datatypes with different extents, the MPI Forum added two new routines to change and discover the extent of a datatype.

The routine `MPI_Type_create_resized` takes an MPI datatype and creates a new datatype with different upper and lower bounds. Any previous upper and lower bounds are discarded. The MPI Forum strongly encourages the use of `MPI_-Type_create_resized` as a replacement for using `MPI_UB` and `MPI_LB` with `MPI_-`

```
int MPI_Type_create_resized(MPI_Datatype oldtype, MPI_Aint lb,
              MPI_Aint extent, MPI_Datatype *newtype)

int MPI_Type_get_true_extent(MPI_Datatype datatype, MPI_Aint *true_lb,
              MPI_Aint *true_extent)
```

Table 5.28
C bindings for MPI-2 datatype extent functions

```
MPI_TYPE_CREATE_RESIZED(oldtype, lb, extent, newtype, ierror)
              integer oldtype, newtype, ierror
              integer(kind=MPI_ADDRESS_KIND) lb, extent

MPI_TYPE_GET_TRUE_EXTENT(datatype, true_lb, true_extent, ierror)
              integer datatype, ierror
              integer(kind=MPI_ADDRESS_KIND) true_lb, true_extent
```

Table 5.29
Fortran bindings for MPI-2 datatype extent functions

```
Datatype MPI::Datatype::Resized(const MPI::Aint lb,
              const MPI::Aint extent) const

void MPI::Datatype::Get_true_extent(MPI::Aint& true_lb,
              MPI::Aint& true_extent) const
```

Table 5.30
C++ bindings for MPI-2 datatype extent functions

`Type_struct`. Of course, if your MPI implementation does not include this routine, you must continue to use the MPI-1 approach.

Figure 5.18 shows the MPI-2 approach for the code in Figure 5.17. The new type `rowtype` is not an exact replacement for the version in Figure 5.17 for the reasons mentioned above. However, for most uses, it accomplishes the same effect, and it may be implemented more efficiently.

Similarly, it is sometimes necessary to discover the true extent of a datatype, that is, the lower and upper bounds (or minimum and maximum displacements) used by a datatype. This is not possible in MPI-1: the routines `MPI_Type_ub` and `MPI_Type_lb` give the values only of the upper and lower bounds, which are the true values *only* if neither an `MPI_UB` or `MPI_LB` has been used in constructing the datatype. For this reason, the MPI Forum also deprecated these two routines, and added the routine MPI_Type_get_true_extent. This routine returns the lower bound and the extent of a datatype, ignoring any upper and lower bound markers (set either with explicit MPI_UB and MPI_LB or with MPI_Type_create_resized). Note that this value can be different from the value that MPI_Type_size returns: MPI_Type_size returns the number of bytes needed to represent the data values in the datatype *ignoring* the displacements; MPI_Type_get_true_extent effectively returns the number of bytes needed to hold a datatype including any gaps between data values caused by the displacements. For example, the vector type created with

```
call MPI_TYPE_VECTOR( 10, 1, 20, MPI_DOUBLE_PRECISION, &
                      vectype, ierr )
```

containing ten double precision values separated by a stride of 20 has a size (from MPI_Type_size) of 80 bytes (assuming 8 byte DOUBLE PRECISION) and a true extent of 1440 ($= (10-1) \times 20 \times 8 + 8$) bytes.

5.5 New MPI-2 Datatype Routines

In addition to the routines discussed in the preceding section, the MPI-2 Forum introduced replacements for several routines. The need for these new routines can be seen by looking at the use of MPI_Address in a Fortran program. Consider the following code fragment:

```
integer iadd, ierror
double precision a(10000)

call MPI_Address( a, iadd, ierror )
```

This seems quite simple. But there is a problem: let us assume that the machine that this is running on uses 64-bit pointers and that double precision is also implemented as 64-bit (e.g., using 64-bit IEEE floating-point arithmetic). This is becomming increasingly common as many computer systems move to 64-bit addresses.

However, the Fortran standard requires that integer and real data items have the same size and that double precision be twice the size of real. This forces[3] both integer and real to be 32 bits long in this case. The problem is that 64 bits is required to represent an address, but a Fortran integer on such systems is only

[3] Well, almost; in principle a compiler could work around this, but in reality all correct compilers use this rule.

MPI_GET_ADDRESS(location, address, ierror) <type> location(*) integer ierror integer(kind=MPI_ADDRESS_KIND) address
MPI_TYPE_CREATE_HVECTOR(count, blocklength, stide, oldtype, newtype, ierror) integer count, blocklength, oldtype, newtype, ierror integer(kind=MPI_ADDRESS_KIND) stride
MPI_TYPE_CREATE_HINDEXED(count, array_of_blocklengths, array_of_displacements, oldtype, newtype, ierror) integer count, array_of_blocklengths(*), oldtype, newtype, ierror integer(kind=MPI_ADDRESS_KIND) array_of_displacements(*)
MPI_TYPE_CREATE_STRUCT(count, array_of_blocklengths, array_of_displacements, array_of_types, newtype, ierror) integer count, array_of_blocklengths(*), array_of_types(*), newtype, ierror integer(kind=MPI_ADDRESS_KIND) array_of_displacements(*)

Table 5.31
Fortran bindings for MPI-2 replacements for some Datatype routines

32 bits long. As a result, `MPI_Address` cannot provide a usable value in the `iadd` argument. The MPI Forum fixed this problem by introducing new routines that use a different kind of integer in places where an address-valued integer is used (in the MPI C and C++ bindings, this is indicated by `MPI_Aint` rather than `int`). This integer type is indicated in Fortran with the type `INTEGER (KIND=MPI_ADDRESS_KIND)`. The replacement for `MPI_Address` is `MPI_Get_address`. Three other routines take address-sized arguments: `MPI_Type_hvector`, `MPI_Type_hindexed`, and `MPI_Type_struct`. These were replaced with `MPI_Type_create_hvector`, `MPI_Type_create_hindexed`, and `MPI_Type_create_struct`. The four new routines are shown in Table 5.31 for Fortran and in Table 5.32 for C. The C routines are exactly the same as the MPI-1 versions; the Fortran routines are the same except for the use of `MPI_ADDRESS_KIND` integer types for the address-valued arguments. Note that there are no C++ bindings for the MPI-1 versions of these routines.

The MPI Forum recommends that these routines be used in preference to the MPI-1 versions. You should do this when implementations of these routines (either as part of full or partial MPI-2 implementations) become widespread.

```
int MPI_Get_address(void *location, MPI_Aint *address)

int MPI_Type_create_hvector(int count, int blocklength, MPI_Aint stride,
              MPI_Datatype oldtype, MPI_Datatype *newtype)

int MPI_Type_create_hindexed(int count, int array_of_blocklengths[],
              MPI_Aint array_of_displacements[], MPI_Datatype oldtype,
              MPI_Datatype *newtype)

int MPI_Type_create_struct(int count, int array_of_blocklengths[],
              MPI_Aint array_of_displacements[], MPI_Datatype array_of_types[],
              MPI_Datatype *newtype)
```

Table 5.32
C bindings for MPI-2 replacements for some datatype routines

5.6 More on Datatypes for Structures

Now that we have seen how to specify a gap at the end of a datatype, we can see how to make the create a datatype for the `structtype` example in Figure 5.15. In MPI-1, we must use a third element in the struct definition that includes an `MPI_UB` as shown in Figure 5.19.

Of course, if `MPI_Type_create_resized` is available, it should be used instead of the `MPI_UB`. A possible refinement is to use the code in Figure 5.15, and compare the extent of this type with the size of the datatype. If the two are *not* equal, then it is necessary to resize the datatype. This is shown in Figure 5.20.

The MPI standard requires that MPI deliver exactly the data that is specified by a datatype. In other words, for structures that contain gaps or padding, MPI must not remove the "gaps." Hence, the MPI implementation needs to carefully skip over padding in a structure. The padding is of no importance to the application, but skipping over it might impose a significant performance penalty. There are two ways to improve the performance of an application that sends structures. The first and best is to rearrange the layout of the structure to eliminate any gaps. Often, this can be done by ordering the items in the structure so that the largest datatypes come first, followed by the next longest, and so on. For example, rearranging this structure

```
struct {
    int a;
    double b;
```

```
int          blockcounts[3] = {1,1,1};
MPI_Datatype types[3];
MPI_Aint     displs[3];
MPI_Datatype structtype;

/* initialize types and displs with addresses of items */
MPI_Address( &struct_array[0].a, &displs[0] );
MPI_Address( &struct_array[0].b, &displs[1] );
MPI_Address( &struct_array[1].a, &displs[2] );
types[0] = MPI_INT;
types[1] = MPI_CHAR;
types[2] = MPI_UB;
/* Make displs relative */
displs[1] -= displs[0];
displs[2] -= displs[0];
displs[0] = 0;
MPI_Type_struct( 3, blockcounts, displs, types, &structtype );
MPI_Type_commit( &structtype );
```

Figure 5.19
Code to construct a datatype for a structure that does not rely on MPI using the same rule for structure padding as the C compiler

```
    int c;
} struct_a;
```

to

```
struct {
    double b;
    int a;
    int c;
} struct_a;
```

will often yield a structure without gaps. To eliminate any padding at the end of the structure (see Section 5.3.1), adding a dummy declaration of a data item of the necessary size is a common approach.

A second approach is to forsake portability to heterogeneous systems of computers for performance by avoiding the use of `MPI_Type_struct` altogether, and send data of type `MPI_BYTE`, using the C `sizeof` operator to determine the size of the structure (again assuming that a `char` is one byte). While our preference is to

```
int          blockcounts[2] = {1,1};
MPI_Datatype types[2];
MPI_Aint     displs[2], s_extent;
MPI_Datatype structtype;

/* initialize types and displs with addresses of items */
MPI_Get_address( &struct_array[0].a, &displs[0] );
MPI_Get_address( &struct_array[0].b, &displs[1] );
types[0] = MPI_INT;
types[1] = MPI_CHAR;
/* Make displs relative */
displs[1] -= displs[0];
displs[0] = 0;
MPI_Type_create_struct( 2, blockcounts, displs, types,
                        &structtype );
/* Check that the datatype has the correct extent */
MPI_Type_extent( structtype, &s_extent );
if (s_extent != sizeof(struct_array[0])) {
    MPI_Datatype sold = structtype;
    MPI_Type_create_resized( sold, 0, sizeof(my_struct),
                             &structtype );
    MPI_Type_free( &sold );
    }
MPI_Type_commit( &structtype );
```

Figure 5.20
Code to construct a datatype for a structure that does not rely on MPI using the same rule for structure padding as the C compiler, using MPI-2 routines

write programs that are as portable as possible, using `MPI_BYTE` can be a reasonable choice when performance is an issue. Note that using `MPI_BYTE` does not offer a performance advantage over the predefined MPI datatypes such as `MPI_INT` or `MPI_DOUBLE_PRECISION`.

5.7 Deprecated Functions

Experience with MPI led to increased understanding of application needs and eventually an understanding of better ways to do things than the ways specified in the original (MPI-1) specification. At the same time, the MPI-2 Forum did not want to change the Standard in such a way that existing MPI programs would suddenly

Deprecated MPI-1	MPI-2 Replacement
MPI_ADDRESS	MPI_GET_ADDRESS
MPI_TYPE_HINDEXED	MPI_TYPE_CREATE_HINDEXED
MPI_TYPE_HVECTOR	MPI_TYPE_CREATE_HVECTOR
MPI_TYPE_STRUCT	MPI_TYPE_CREATE_STRUCT
MPI_TYPE_EXTENT	MPI_TYPE_GET_EXTENT
MPI_TYPE_UB	MPI_TYPE_GET_EXTENT
MPI_TYPE_LB	MPI_TYPE_GET_EXTENT
MPI_LB	MPI_TYPE_CREATE_RESIZED
MPI_UB	MPI_TYPE_CREATE_RESIZED
MPI_ERRHANDLER_CREATE	MPI_COMM_CREATE_ERRHANDLER
MPI_ERRHANDLER_GET	MPI_COMM_GET_ERRHANDLER
MPI_ERRHANDLER_SET	MPI_COMM_SET_ERRHANDLER
MPI_Handler_function	MPI_Comm_errhandler_fn
MPI_KEYVAL_CREATE	MPI_COMM_CREATE_KEYVAL
MPI_KEYVAL_FREE	MPI_COMM_FREE_KEYVAL
MPI_DUP_FN	MPI_COMM_DUP_FN
MPI_NULL_COPY_FN	MPI_COMM_NULL_COPY_FN
MPI_NULL_DELETE_FN	MPI_COMM_NULL_DELETE_FN
MPI_Copy_function	MPI_Comm_copy_attr_function
COPY_FUNCTION	COMM_COPY_ATTR_FN
MPI_Delete_function	MPI_Comm_delete_attr_function
DELETE_FUNCTION	COMM_DELETE_ATTR_FN
MPI_ATTR_DELETE	MPI_COMM_DELETE_ATTR
MPI_ATTR_GET	MPI_COMM_GET_ATTR
MPI_ATTR_PUT	MPI_COMM_SET_ATTR

Table 5.33
Deprecated functions, constants, and typedefs

lose their portability. Therefore it decided that certain functions would be "deprecated." This means that these functions are still part of the MPI Standard and implementations are required to support them, but that applications are encouraged to eventually abandon them in favor of new (MPI-2) ways of accomplishing the same things. The understanding is that in the long run these deprecated functions might disappear from the Standard. Here we take the opportunity to list (in Table 5.33 all the deprecated functions in MPI-1 and their MPI-2 replacements. For details on the MPI-2 functions, see [55].

5.8 Common Errors and Misunderstandings

This chapter has introduced at least one new topic that is the occasion for misunderstanding.

Confusing the specification of MPI datatypes with their implementation. MPI's datatypes *allow* optimized performance by telling the implementation exactly what the data layout is for a send or receive operation. With hardware support, using MPI datatypes can unleash extra performance. Even without hardware support, implementation of datatypes can be either sophisticated and fast or straightforward and slow. A poor implementation of datatypes can cause the user to prefer to create contiguous buffers and copy noncontiguous data into them "by hand." Our studies [65] show that there is much room for improvement in how MPI vendors implement datatypes, and we expect these improvements to eventually show up, as research on MPI implementations gradually permeates the entire MPI implementation community. Meanwhile, though it may be faster right now, on some MPI implementations, to pack buffers yourself, don't give up on MPI datatypes too soon!

6 Parallel Libraries

One of the primary motivations for MPI was to enable the development of parallel libraries. Libraries have been critical to the development of a software base for sequential computers. Lack of modularity in previous message-passing systems has hampered the comparable development of reliable parallel libraries, libraries that can be written independently of one another and of user code and still cooperate with one another in a single application.

We begin this chapter with a discussion of some of the issues that are raised by parallel libraries. We describe some of the shortcomings of previous message-passing systems when they are considered from the viewpoint of the library writer, and we point out features of the MPI definition that have been introduced to overcome these shortcomings. We then give an example of a simple library; it contains only two functions but illustrates a number of MPI's features that support libraries. We devote a section to the interplay between linear algebra and partial differential equations as an example of an area where parallel libraries are likely to be heavily used. We briefly describe some aspects of the use of MPI in the solution of a dense system of linear equations. We conclude the chapter with a discussion of general strategies for building parallel libraries.

6.1 Motivation

In this section we outline the motivation for libraries and describe the special design features that help in building parallel libraries.

6.1.1 The Need for Parallel Libraries

Software libraries offer several advantages:

- they ensure consistency in program correctness,
- they help guarantee a high-quality implementation,
- they hide distracting details and complexities associated with state-of-the-art implementations, and
- they minimize repetitive effort or haphazard results.

Even in sequential libraries, library writers incorporate numerous heuristics and domain-specific "tricks." With the addition of parallelism based on message passing, the "detail work" of typical numerical methods grows significantly, strongly motivating the development of parallel libraries that encapsulate and hide this complexity from the user. MPI is the underlying system library that will help make scientific as well as application-oriented parallel libraries both reliable and commonplace.

6.1.2 Common Deficiencies of Previous Message-Passing Systems

In the *sequential* Fortran and C environments, one can easily create libraries, because the stack-oriented procedural programming model has well-defined conditions about reasonable vs. erroneous programs. In the *distributed-memory, message-passing environment*, however, libraries are difficult to write with either vendor-supplied software or portability systems. The problem is one of modularity: a library needs a communication space isolated from the user's communication space precisely because it is a library. Its communication patterns are designed independently of the user code it is to be linked to.

The most obvious problem is that of having a message sent by the library accidentally received by user code, or vice versa. One might argue that tags could be used effectively to designate restrictions on message delivery. Such tags prove insufficient, however, for several reasons. First, more than one library (or invocation of the same library) could use the same tags. Second, wildcard receipt-selectivity on tags (e.g., `MPI_ANY_TAG`) destroys any promise of real protection that tags could otherwise afford. For this reason parallel libraries are often written in a style that strictly alternates execution of user code and library code, with care taken that no messages be in transit when control is passed from user to library and back (this state is often called *quiescence*). This type of design, inherited from the sequential case, introduces synchronization barriers that inhibit performance, and still leaves other problems unsolved.

This problem can be illustrated with a simple example. Let's assume that the program calls two routines, `SendRight` and `SendEnd`. These two routines are shown in Figure 6.1. Two possible execution sequences for these routines are shown in Figure 6.2. In part (b) of this figure, the messages are received by the wrong routine because the message from routine `SendEnd` on process zero arrives at process two before the message from `SendRight` on process one arrives at process two. This example depends on using `MPI_ANY_SOURCE` in both of the routines. While in this case the routines could be written to provide an explicit source instead, in other cases (particular master/worker examples), `MPI_ANY_SOURCE` cannot be avoided.

You might think that it is possible to fix this problem by never using `MPI_ANY_SOURCE`. The code in Figure 6.3 can have two different execution sequences, as shown in Figure 6.4. This example uses neither `MPI_ANY_SOURCE` nor `MPI_ANY_TAG`, but the messages are still delivered to the wrong places.

Both of these examples indicate the worst kind of error: a program that runs, but

```
void SendRight( int *buf, int rank, int size )
{
    MPI_Status status;
    if (rank + 1 < size)
        MPI_Send( buf, 1, MPI_INT, rank+1, 0, MPI_COMM_WORLD );
    if (rank > 0)
        MPI_Recv( buf, 1, MPI_INT, MPI_ANY_SOURCE, 0,
                  MPI_COMM_WORLD, &status );
}
void SendEnd( int *buf, int rank, int size )
{
    MPI_Status status;
    if (rank == 0)
        MPI_Send( buf, 1, MPI_INT, size-1, 0, MPI_COMM_WORLD );
    if (rank == size - 1)
        MPI_Recv( buf, 1, MPI_INT, MPI_ANY_SOURCE, 0,
                  MPI_COMM_WORLD, &status );
}
```

Figure 6.1
The two routines whose possible message patterns are shown in Figure 6.2

with wrong data. Similar examples can be shown where a program halts because a message was received by the wrong process.

Note that in this code, the routines of the first library are called on both sides of the routine in the second library. If both libraries use the same communicator, there is *nothing* that the second library can do to guarantee that it doesn't intercept the message sent in `StartSend`.

MPI communicators solve the problems illustrated in Figures 6.1 and 6.3 by providing distinct communication contexts; if the different routines (e.g., `SendRight` and `SendEnd` in Figure 6.1) use separate communicators, MPI guarantees that messages will be received by the intended routine.

Communicators also provide an elegant way to express other abstractions related to groups of processes. Incorporated into MPI are various kinds of abstraction: process groups describe participants in collective operations and rank-naming in point-to-point communication, contexts separate unrelated message traffic, topologies let users describe process relationships as they prefer, and communicators encapsulate all this information in a useful object that also abstracts all these details for the typical user.

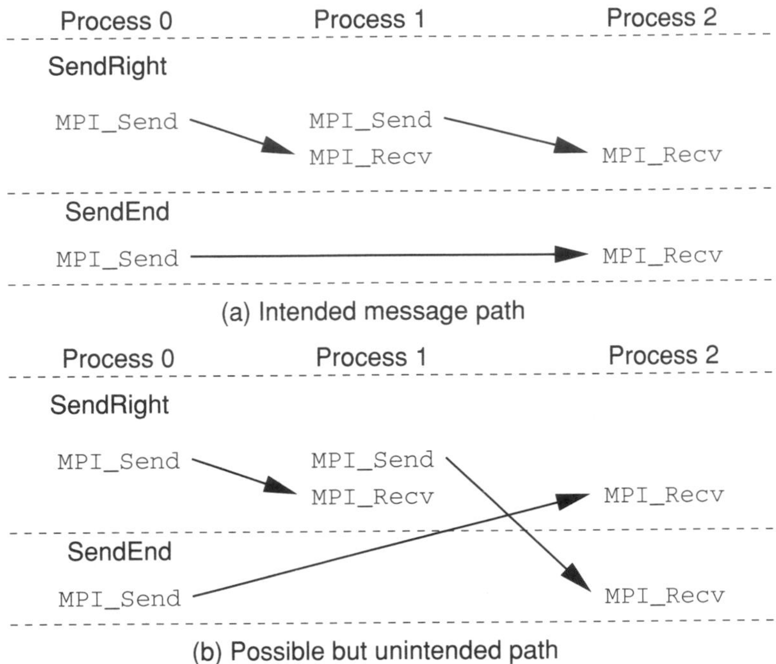

Figure 6.2
Possible message matching patterns for the code in Figure 6.1

6.1.3 Review of MPI Features That Support Libraries

The requirements for effective libraries can be summarized as follows:

- A safe communication space guarantees that a library can send and receive point-to-point messages without interference from other point-to-point messages generated in the system.
- Collective operations take a process group (from a communicator) as the set of participants; processes that do not participate continue unimpeded.
- Abstract names for processes are based on virtual topologies, or at least rank-in-group names, thereby avoiding hardware dependencies, and ideally making application code more intuitive.

MPI offers several features that implement these important requirements:

- **Process groups** define a rank-naming for processes in point-to-point communication relative to the group. In addition, these groups define the scope of collective

```
/* Code for library 1: Nonblocking send from 0 to 1 */
void StartSend( int *buf, int rank, int size, MPI_Request *req )
{
    if (rank == 0)
        MPI_Isend( buf, 1, MPI_INT, 1, 0, MPI_COMM_WORLD, req );
}

void EndSend( int *buf, int rank, MPI_Request *req )
{
    MPI_Status status;
    if (rank == 0)
        MPI_Wait( req, &status );
    else if (rank == 1)
        MPI_Recv( buf, 1, MPI_INT, 0, 0, MPI_COMM_WORLD, &status );
}

/* Code for library 2: send from 0 to 1 */
void DoSomething( int *buf, int rank, int size )
{
    MPI_Status status;
    if (rank == 0)
        MPI_Send( buf, 1, MPI_INT, 1, 0, MPI_COMM_WORLD );
    else if (rank == 1)
        MPI_Recv( buf, 1, MPI_INT, 0, 0, MPI_COMM_WORLD, &status );
}
```

Figure 6.3
Code whose message pattern is shown in Figure 6.4

operations. (Note that the internal representations of process names are not revealed at the application level; that would spoil portability.) This scope makes it possible to make strong statements about the noninterference of sequential collective operations in the same communication context.

- **Contexts** provide the ability to have separate safe "universes" (called contexts) of message passing in MPI. A context is conceptually implemented by a secondary or "hyper" tag that differentiates messages from one another. Unlike user-manipulated tags, these contexts provide totally separate communication space, each with a full complement of user-managed tags. Contexts are allocated by the system for safety; if users were to define contexts, two libraries might inadvertently define the same one. Users do not work directly with contexts; rather, they work with process

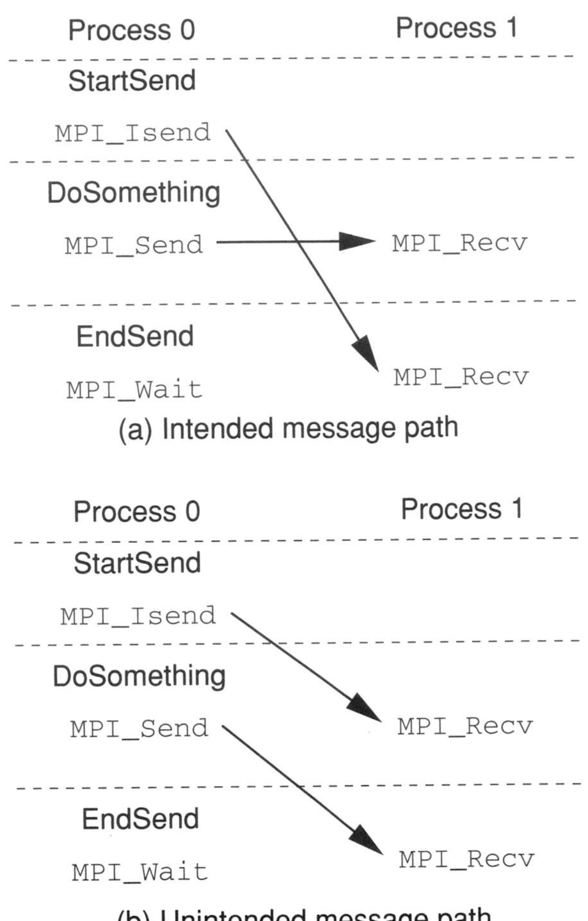

Figure 6.4
Possible message-matching patterns for the code in Figure 6.3

groups and communicators.

• **Communicators** encapsulate contexts, groups, and virtual topologies in an object that provides the appropriate scope for all communication operations in MPI. Communicators bind process groups and context information together to form a safe communication space within the group. The communicator also provides an object that can be used to maintain local (to the communicator) copies of data that the library needs to keep from one invocation to another. The MPI term for this is "attribute caching."

The use of separate communication contexts by distinct libraries (or distinct library invocations) insulates communication internal to the library execution from external communication (group safety). This approach allows one to invoke the library even if communications are pending. Moreover, it avoids the need to synchronize each entry into and exit from library code. Most such synchronizations are unnecessary, reduce performance, and can be avoided because of the context model.

6.2 A First MPI Library

In this section we describe a simple two-function library. It provides a feature that is not included in the MPI definition: a nonblocking broadcast. Recall that for all processes except the specified root, `MPI_Bcast` is a form of receive. Thus, it makes sense to post this "receive" and possibly others, then do whatever can be done, waiting for completion only when necessary. (This analogy with receive is not completely accurate, because intermediate processes in the broadcast tree must send as well as receive. However, the nonblocking broadcast may still be useful, particularly on multithreaded systems.) Use of this library is illustrated by the following sequence:

```
#include "ibcast.h"
Ibcast_handle *request;
...
Ibcast( buf, count, datatype, root, comm, &request );
...
Ibcast_wait( &request );
```

We first sketch the algorithm that is used by `Ibcast`. The call to `Ibcast` will start (using nonblocking communication routines) the sends from the root process. All other processes will start nonblocking receives. At the `Ibcast_wait`, we will wait for the sends and the receives to complete. We will use a tree of processes to perform the broadcast; hence, the processes that are not the root process will need to send the data (unless they are leaves of the distribution tree) to other processes during the `Ibcast_wait`.

This immediately raises a question: How can we do this safely? The algorithm described has exactly the same form as the second example on the need for communication contexts (Figure 6.3). To ensure that there is no interference with messages from other parts of the program, we will need to have a separate communicator. In addition, we would like to allow several `Ibcast` operations to be active at the same time. We could use separate communicators for each one, but in this example we'll show how to use unique message tag values, along with a private communicator, to ensure that different `Ibcast` calls, even on the same communicator, do not interfere with each other.

The approach that we will take is this: For each input communicator (the `MPI_Comm` argument to `Ibcast`, we will create a new, private communicator with `MPI_Comm_dup` and keep track of the message tags, starting at zero, that are being used to perform `Ibcast` calls on this private communicator. To do this, we need to keep track of the both the private communicator and the first unused tag value. The C structure that holds this information is shown in Figure 6.5 as `Ibcast_syshandle`. But where can we save this value so that, when `Ibast` is called with a communicator, we can find the appropriate private communicator and available tag value? We could keep a table of correspondences between communicators that we have seen before and the private `Ibcast_syshandle`s that we have created. But it would be better if we could somehow attach the `Ibcast_syshandle` value to the input communicator. Fortunately, MPI allows us to do just this. The MPI term for this is *caching of attributes*, and it is typically used to keep a pointer to a data structure used by the library to maintain information between calls. In Fortran, it is an integer. Attributes are identified by *key values*, which are system allocated so that multiple libraries can attach attributes to the same communicator without knowledge of one another.

In this case the cached information includes a communicator to be used for `ibcast`'s internal communication and an ordering tag to be used to separate multiple `ibcast`s using the same communicator. Thus the header file for the nonblocking broadcast library is as shown in Figure 6.5.

The complete nonblocking broadcast library is shown in Figures 6.6, 6.7, 6.8, 6.9, and 6.11. It demonstrates how to use communicators and caching. The way that attributes are attached to communicators allows for their selective propagation when the call `MPI_Comm_dup` is used, as we define further in this example. The already-discussed call `MPI_Comm_create` never copies attributes to the newly created

```
#include "mpi.h"
/* handle for ibcast operations on a communicator */
typedef struct
{
    MPI_Comm comm;
    int ordering_tag;
} Ibcast_syshandle;

/* handle for a particular ibcast operation */
typedef struct
{
    MPI_Request          *req_array;
    MPI_Status           *stat_array;
    int                   num_sends;
    int                   num_recvs;
} Ibcast_handle;
```

Figure 6.5
The header file for `Ibcast()`

communicator. The nonblocking broadcast library requires the use of caching to store persistent information; it requires the use of a cached communicator to protect the user from communication actions of the library; and it illustrates the need to use the tag (within that cached communication context) as a further mechanism for safety in a nondeterministically ordered library of this form. The code for the main routine of `Ibcast` is shown in Figures 6.6 and 6.7.

What's going on in this library? First, `Ibcast` checks to see whether it has ever been called before by this process, by seeing whether it has a valid value for the global integer `ibcast_keyval`. If not, `Ibcast` has to get an attribute *key value*, so that it can cache its information on this and all future communicators that may call `Ibcast` in this process; it does so with `MPI_Keyval_create`. Otherwise, `ibcast_keyval` is already the key value for use by this library.

Next, the code checks to see whether an `Ibcast` has ever been done on the current communicator, by looking up the attribute for the key value `ibcast_keyval`. If not, the system handle associated with this key value is created and attached to the communicator. The most notable call here is `MPI_Comm_dup`, which makes a complete duplicate of the input communicator, but with new contexts of communication. Any "other" attributes cached by the system will be selectively copied, according to the attribute-copying set up by the user when those attributes were attached. (See Table 6.1 for the bindings for attribute copying and deletion functions.) The next task for Ibcast is to determine all the specific data that needs to go in the user handle for this particular call, so that the work of transmitting data can begin, and so that the user can also legally call Ibcast_wait.

Ibcast builds a broadcast tree of sends and receives for the given root; for each such call, it assigns a new "ordering tag," to prevent any interference from in-progress Ibcast calls. We call this type of interference "back-masking," in that a subsequent call to the Ibcast could potentially interpose its data in advance of the data of an earlier Ibcast call, yielding an erroneous result. The duplicated context (which protects Ibcast from the user and other libraries), together with the incrementing tag strategy (which protects one call to Ibcast from others), eliminates this possibility. Thus, Ibcast is isolated from all other collective and point-to-point communication on its communicator because it uses a duplicated communicator. Furthermore, each call to Ibcast with a specific communicator is isolated from earlier ones because distinct tags are used for the sends and receives.[1]

Three general classes of process behavior arise with this library: the root, the leaves, and all other nodes of the broadcast tree. The root process only sends, the leaves only receive, and all other processes both send and receive. Specifics of the tree position of each process thus determine the number of persistent send and receive requests that Ibcast creates and stores in the "user handle." (The MPI calls MPI_Send_init and MPI_Recv_init generate the persistent operations, but do not start anything. They are used here not to allow the reuse of the MPI_-Requests, as in Section 5.2.2, but to provide an easy way to store the parameters for the MPI_Isend needed for processes that are neither the root nor the leaves of the broadcast tree.) Ibcast then calls Ibcast_work to do the main body of the broadcast transmission,

The root, which has no receives, immediately starts all its sends in Ibcast_-work, using the MPI call MPI_Startall. All the other nodes of the broadcast tree start their receives using MPI_Startall. After these calls are started, Ibcast_work terminates, returning control to Ibcast. Finally, Ibcast has but one additional bit of bookkeeping: to increment the ordering tag used by the next call to Ibcast, which can legally come before the call to Ibcast_wait. It returns with the handle containing the persistent information, which will be passed when the user calls Ibcast_wait, when the broadcast must be finalized.

[1]While the tag-incrementing strategy used here is probably overkill for Ibcast, which has only sends and receives without wild cards, and can consequently rely on *pairwise message ordering* (see the glossary) for correctness, the code illustrates an important general strategy for library design. For example, this can be used in libraries where MPI_ANY_SOURCE is used in receives, and hence tags must be used to order messages.

```
int MPI_Comm_dup(MPI_Comm comm, MPI_Comm *newcomm)

int MPI_Keyval_create(MPI_Copy_function *copy_fn,
                MPI_Delete_function *delete_fn, int *keyval, void* extra_state)

int MPI_Attr_put(MPI_Comm comm, int keyval, void* attribute_val)

int MPI_Attr_get(MPI_Comm comm, int keyval, void* attribute_val, int *flag)

int MPI_Keyval_free(int *keyval)

int MPI_Attr_delete(MPI_Comm comm, int keyval)

typedef int MPI_Copy_function(MPI_Comm *oldcomm, int *keyval,
                void *extra_state, void *attribute_value_in,
                void *attribute_value_out,int *flag)

typedef int MPI_Delete_function(MPI_Comm *comm, int *keyval,
                void *attribute_value, void *extra_state)
```

Table 6.1
C bindings for new MPI calls needed by `Ibcast` and related calls. The `attribute_value` in `MPI_Attr_get` is cast as a `void *` to simplify casts; the actual argument must be a pointer to a pointer of the correct type. The same applies to `attribute_value_out` in `MPI_Copy_function`.

`Ibcast_wait` picks up where `Ibcast_work` left off. For the root, it waits on the sends; for the leaves, it waits on the receives. For the other nodes of the broadcast tree, it waits on its receive, then starts its sends and waits on their completion. The calls `MPI_Startall` and `MPI_Waitall` figure in this process.

Communicators are frequently created by copying existing communicators (with `MPI_Comm_dup`) and are eventually freed, at which point one might wish to clean up storage associated with an attribute. In order to handle attached attributes during these operations, MPI specifies that when a key value is created, the user may supply functions to copy and delete the attribute value when the communicator is copied or freed.

In some cases, a library may want to ensure that the cached attribute information is propagated to new communicators created with `MPI_Comm_dup`. The version of `Ibcast` in Figure 6.6 does not do this, but a simple change is all that is required to add this feature. By changing one line of `Ibcast`, we can add the copy and delete callbacks:

```
#include "ibcast.h"
static int ibcast_keyval = MPI_KEYVAL_INVALID; /* keyval for
                                          attribute caching */
int Ibcast(void *buf, int count, MPI_Datatype datatype, int root,
           MPI_Comm comm, Ibcast_handle **handle_out)
{
    Ibcast_syshandle *syshandle;
    Ibcast_handle    *handle;
    int                  flag, mask, relrank;
    int                  retn, size, rank;
    int                  req_no = 0;
    /* get info about the communicator */
    MPI_Comm_size ( comm, &size );
    MPI_Comm_rank ( comm, &rank );
    /* If size is 1, this is trivially finished */
    if (size == 1) {
        (*handle_out) = (Ibcast_handle *) 0;
        return (MPI_SUCCESS);
    }
    /* first see if this library has ever been called. Generate new
       key value if not. */
    if (ibcast_keyval == MPI_KEYVAL_INVALID) {
        MPI_Keyval_create( MPI_NULL_COPY_FN, MPI_NULL_DELETE_FN,
                           &ibcast_keyval, NULL);
    }
    /* this communicator might already have used this collective
       operation, and so it would consequently have information
       of use to us cached on it. */
    MPI_Attr_get(comm, ibcast_keyval, (void **)&syshandle, &flag);
    if (flag == 0) { /* there was no attribute previously cached */
        syshandle =
            (Ibcast_syshandle *)malloc(sizeof(Ibcast_syshandle));
        /* fill in the attribute information */
        syshandle->ordering_tag = 0; /* start with tag zero */
        MPI_Comm_dup(comm, &(syshandle->comm)); /* duplicate comm */
        /* attach information to the communicator */
        MPI_Attr_put(comm, ibcast_keyval, (void *)syshandle);
    }
```

Figure 6.6
The first part of the main library routine of `Ibcast()`

```
    /* create a handle for this particular ibcast operation */
    handle = (Ibcast_handle *)malloc(sizeof(Ibcast_handle));
    handle->num_sends = 0;
    handle->num_recvs = 0;
    /* count how many send/recv handles we need */
    mask    = 0x1;
    relrank = (rank - root + size) % size;
    while ((mask & relrank) == 0 && mask < size) {
        if ((relrank | mask) < size)
            handle->num_sends++;
        mask <<= 1;
    }
    if (mask < size) handle->num_recvs++;
    /* allocate request and status arrays for sends and receives */
    handle->req_array  = (MPI_Request *)
        malloc(sizeof(MPI_Request) * (handle->num_sends +
                                      handle->num_recvs));
    handle->stat_array = (MPI_Status *)
        malloc(sizeof(MPI_Status) * (handle->num_sends +
                                     handle->num_recvs));
    /* create "permanent" send/recv requests */
    mask    = 0x1;
    relrank = (rank - root + size) % size;
    while ((mask & relrank) == 0 && mask < size) {
        if ((relrank|mask) < size)
            MPI_Send_init(buf, count, datatype,
                          ((relrank|mask)+root)%size,
                          syshandle->ordering_tag, syshandle->comm,
                          &(handle->req_array[req_no++]));
        mask <<= 1;
    }
    if (mask < size)
        MPI_Recv_init(buf, count, datatype,
                      ((relrank & (~ mask)) + root) % size,
                      syshandle->ordering_tag, syshandle->comm,
                      &(handle->req_array[req_no++]));
    retn = Ibcast_work(handle);
    /* prepare to update the cached information */
    ++(syshandle->ordering_tag); /* make bigger for next ibcast
                                    operation to avoid back-masking */
    (*handle_out) = handle;     /* return the handle */
    return(retn);
}
```

Figure 6.7
The second part of the main library routine of `Ibcast()`

Intracomm MPI::Intracomm::Dup() const

int MPI::Create_keyval(const Copy_function* copy_fn,
    const Delete_function* delete_fn, void* extra_state)

void MPI::Comm::Set_attr(int keyval, const void* attribute_val) const

bool MPI::Comm::Get_attr(int keyval, void* attribute_val) const

void MPI::Free_keyval(int& keyval)

void MPI::Comm::Delete_attr(int keyval) const

Table 6.2
C++ bindings for new MPI calls needed by `Ibcast` and related calls. Typedefs for the `Copy_function` and `Delete_function` are similar to the C case in Table 6.1

```
/* first see if this library has ever been called. */
if (ibcast_keyval == MPI_KEYVAL_INVALID) {
    /* our first mission is to create the process-local keyval
       for this library, while specifying callbacks */
    MPI_Keyval_create(Ibcast_copy, Ibcast_delete,
                      &ibcast_keyval, NULL);
...
```

We also define the functions there that do the copy (`Ibcast_copy`, see Figure 6.10) and delete (`Ibcast_delete`, see Figure 6.11) to complete the modifications. These changes will give the library the property that calls to `MPI_Comm_dup` and `MPI_Comm_free` on a communicator that has used `Ibcast` will behave as responsibly as possible about cleaning up memory. These functions should return the value zero unless some error has occurred. If they return a nonzero value, then the MPI routine that caused them to be called will also indicate an error. Note that the error value returned by the MPI routine (if the MPI error handler has been set to return a value on errors) will *not* be the nonzero value returned by the copy or delete function.

On systems that support threads, the ideas and code described above could be used to create a nonblocking reduce and a nonblocking barrier, as well as other collective calls not directly supported by the MPI Standard. The use of threads with MPI is discussed in more detail in *Using MPI-2* [66].

```
MPI_COMM_DUP(comm, newcomm, ierror)
        integer comm, newcomm, ierror

MPI_KEYVAL_CREATE(copy_fn, delete_fn, keyval, extra_state, ierror)
        integer copy_fn, delete_fn
        external copy_fn, delete_fn
        integer keyval, extra_state, ierror

MPI_ATTR_PUT(comm, keyval, attribute_val, ierror)
        integer comm, keyval, attribute_val, ierror

MPI_ATTR_GET(comm, keyval, attribute_val, flag, ierror)
        integer comm, keyval, attribute_val, ierror
        logical flag

MPI_KEYVAL_FREE(keyval, ierror)
        integer keyval, ierror

MPI_ATTR_DELETE(comm, keyval, ierror)
        integer comm, keyval, ierror

integer function COPY_FN(oldcomm, keyval, extra_state,attribute_value_in,
        attribute_value_out, flag)
        integer oldcomm, keyval,extra_state, attribute_value_in,
            attribute_value_out, flag

integer function DELETE_FN(comm, keyval, attribute_value,extra_state)
        integer comm, keyval, attribute_value, extra_state
        logical flag
```

Table 6.3
Fortran bindings for new MPI calls needed by `Ibcast` and related calls. `COPY_FN` and `DELETE_FN` are not MPI functions; instead, these show the calling sequences for the arguments with the same name to `MPI_KEYVAL_CREATE`.

```
#include "ibcast.h"
int Ibcast_work(Ibcast_handle *handle)
{
    /* if I don't have any recv's, start all my sends -- the root */
    if (handle->num_recvs == 0)
        MPI_Startall( handle->num_sends, handle->req_array );
    /* start all my recv's */
    else
        MPI_Startall( handle->num_recvs,
                      &handle->req_array[handle->num_sends] );
    return (MPI_SUCCESS);
}
```

Figure 6.8
The `Ibcast_work()` function, which does part of the broadcast for `Ibcast()`

6.2.1 MPI-2 Attribute-Caching Routines

One problem with the attribute-caching function is that the C and Fortran bindings cache a different kind of value. In C, the value cached is a pointer (`void *`); in Fortran, it is an `integer`. As discussed in Section 5.5, a Fortran `integer` may be smaller than a pointer. This makes it difficult to use attributes in cases where routines written in both C and Fortran must access the attribute. To fix this problem, the MPI Forum introduced new routines whose C bindings are the same as for the MPI-1 versions, but whose Fortran bindings use `integer (kind=MPI_ADDRESS_KIND)` instead of `integer` for the attribute value argument. These new routines are shown in Tables 6.4 and 6.5. The C++ bindings use these new forms.

6.2.2 A C++ Alternative to `MPI_Comm_dup`

In the C++ binding for MPI, there are five different types for the different kinds of communicators: `MPI::Comm`, `MPI::Intercomm`,`MPI::Intracomm`, `MPI::Graphcomm`, and `MPI::Cartcomm`. The class `MPI::Comm` is the abstract base class from which `MPI::Intercomm` and `MPI::Intracomm` are derived. The communicators `MPI::Cartcomm` and `MPI:Graphcomm` that contain topologies are derived from `MPI::Intracomm`. This contrasts with the C and Fortran bindings, where there is a single type (`MPI_Comm` in C) for all communicators. This finer division allows a C++ compiler to provide more compile-time checking for the correct kind of communicator (e.g., in collective routines where only intracommunicators are allowed in MPI-1). But it does have a disadvantage when an application wishes to work with an MPI communicator of any kind. To see the problem, consider `MPI_Comm_dup`. The

```
#include "ibcast.h"
int Ibcast_wait(Ibcast_handle **handle_out)
{
    Ibcast_handle *handle = (*handle_out);
    int retn, i;
    /* A NULL handle means there's nothing to do */
    if (handle == (Ibcast_handle *)0)
        return (MPI_SUCCESS);
    /* If I wasn't the root, finish my recvs and
       start & wait on sends */
    if (handle->num_recvs != 0) {
        MPI_Waitall(handle->num_recvs,
                    &handle->req_array[handle->num_sends],
                    &handle->stat_array[handle->num_sends]);
        MPI_Startall ( handle->num_sends, handle->req_array );
    }
    /* Wait for my receive and then start all my sends */
    retn = MPI_Waitall(handle->num_sends, handle->req_array,
                       handle->stat_array);
    /* free permanent requests */
    for (i=0; i < (handle->num_sends + handle->num_recvs); i++)
        MPI_Request_free (&(handle->req_array[i]));
    /* Free request and status arrays and ibcast handle */
    free (handle->req_array);
    free (handle->stat_array);
    free (handle);
    /* Return a NULL handle */
    (*handle_out) = (Ibcast_handle *)0;
    return(retn);
}
```

Figure 6.9
The `Ibcast_wait()` function, which effects the "wait" for `Ibcast()`

```
/* copier for ibcast cached information */
int Ibcast_copy(MPI_Comm  *oldcomm, int *keyval,
     void *extra, void *attr_in, void **attr_out, int *flag)
{
    Ibcast_syshandle *syshandle = (Ibcast_syshandle *)attr_in;
    Ibcast_syshandle *new_syshandle;
    /* do we have a valid keyval */
    if ( ( (*keyval)    == MPI_KEYVAL_INVALID )        ||
         ( (*keyval)    != ibcast_keyval )             ||
         ( (syshandle   == (Ibcast_syshandle *)0) ) ) {
        /* A non-zero return is an error and will cause MPI_Comm_dup
           to signal an error.  The return value here is *not* the
           MPI error code that MPI_Comm_dup will return */
      return 1;
    }
    /* create a new syshandle for the new communicator */
    new_syshandle =
        (Ibcast_syshandle *)malloc(sizeof(Ibcast_syshandle));
    /* fill in the attribute information */
    new_syshandle->ordering_tag = 0; /* start with tag zero */
    /* dup the "hidden" communicator */
    MPI_Comm_dup(syshandle->comm, &(new_syshandle->comm));
    /* return the new syshandle and set flag to true */
    (*attr_out) = (void *)new_syshandle;
    (*flag)     = 1;
    return MPI_SUCCESS;
}
```

Figure 6.10
The `Ibcast_copy()` function, which does copy-callback services for `Ibcast()`

```
/* destructor for ibcast cached information */
int Ibcast_delete(MPI_Comm *comm, int *keyval, void *attr_val,
                  void *extra)
{
    Ibcast_syshandle *syshandle = (Ibcast_syshandle *)attr_val;
    /* do we have a valid keyval */
    if ( ( (*keyval)    == MPI_KEYVAL_INVALID )         ||
         ( (*keyval)    != ibcast_keyval )              ||
         ( (syshandle   == (Ibcast_syshandle *)0) ) ) {
        /* Give a non-zero return code to indicate an error */
        return 1;
    }
    /* free the "hidden" communicator and memory for syshandle */
    MPI_Comm_free ( &(syshandle->comm) );
    free (syshandle);
    return MPI_SUCCESS;
}
```

Figure 6.11
The `Ibcast_delete()` function, which does delete-callback services for `Ibcast()`

int **MPI_Comm_create_keyval**(MPI_Comm_copy_attr_function *comm_copy_attr_fn, MPI_Comm_delete_attr_function *comm_delete_attr_fn, int *comm_keyval, void *extra_state)
int **MPI_Comm_free_keyval**(int *comm_keyval)
int **MPI_Comm_set_attr**(MPI_Comm comm, int comm_keyval, void *attribute_val)
int **MPI_Comm_get_attr**(MPI_Comm comm, int comm_keyval, void *attribute_val, int *flag)
int **MPI_Comm_delete_attr**(MPI_Comm comm, int comm_keyval)

Table 6.4
C bindings for attribute caching in MPI-2

MPI_COMM_CREATE_KEYVAL(comm_copy_attr_fn, comm_delete_attr_fn, comm_keyval, extra_state, ierror) external comm_copy_attr_fn, comm_delete_attr_fn integer comm_keyval, ierror integer(kind=MPI_ADDRESS_KIND) extra_state
MPI_COMM_FREE_KEYVAL(comm_keyval, ierror) integer comm_keyval, ierror
MPI_COMM_SET_ATTR(comm, comm_keyval, attribute_val, ierror) integer comm, comm_keyval, ierror integer(kind=MPI_ADDRESS_KIND) attribute_val
MPI_COMM_GET_ATTR(comm, comm_keyval, attribute_val, flag, ierror) integer comm, comm_keyval, ierror integer(kind=MPI_ADDRESS_KIND) attribute_val logical flag
MPI_COMM_DELETE_ATTR(comm, comm_keyval, ierror) integer comm, comm_keyval, ierror

Table 6.5
Fortran bindings for attribute caching routines in MPI-2

Dup method duplicates an `MPI::Intercomm`, `MPI::Intracomm`, `MPI::Graphcomm`, or `MPI::Cartcomm`, returning a communicator with the same type. If we want to manipulate the communicator as if it is a simple `MPI::Comm`, we can't, because `MPI::Comm` is an abstract base class and no variables can be declared as `MPI::Comm`. That is, you cannot have code like this

```
void mysample( MPI::Comm comm )
{
    MPI::Comm localcomm;
    localcomm = comm.Dup();
    ...
    localcomm.Free();
}
```

However, we can use a reference to an abstract base class, so it is possible to have

```
void mysample( MPI::Comm &comm )
{
```

Comm& MPI::Comm::Clone() const = 0
Intracomm& MPI::Intracomm::Clone() const
Intercomm& MPI::Intercomm::Clone() const
Cartcomm& MPI::Cartcomm::Clone() const
Graphcomm& MPI::Graphcomm::Clone() const

Table 6.6
C++ bindings for cloning a communicator

```
        MPI::Comm *localcomm;
        localcomm = &comm.Clone();
        ...
        localcomm->Free();
        delete localcomm;
    }
```

Note that instead of using `Dup` we have used `Clone` on the reference to `MPI::Comm comm`. The `Clone` method returns a new MPI communicator of the same type and with a new context (just like `Dup`), but by reference instead of by value. The bindings for `Clone` are shown in Table 6.6 (there are no C or Fortran versions of `Clone` because `MPI_Comm_dup` is sufficient for C and Fortran).

Note that when freeing a reference to a communicator created with `Clone`, you must both call the `Free` method so that MPI can free the communicator and you must tell C++ to recover the space allocated by `Clone` with `delete`.

6.3 Linear Algebra on Grids

Many applications can be written in terms of the standard vector operations performed on a grid or mesh. One such example is the Poisson problem presented in Chapter 4. As we saw in that chapter, a major issue is the choice of data decomposition, that is, how the elements of the vectors are distributed across the processes. This section describes the design and implementation of MPI libraries that address some of the issues in providing efficient and flexible routines for vector operations on grids that will operate correctly with many different distributions of the elements. These libraries are initially "object based" and alternatively "object oriented." The object-based libraries use C data structures and therefore provide abstractions like vectors and data distributions. The object-oriented libraries go one step further by exploiting inheritance and are consequently better able to optimize their run-time performance by making a number of decisions outside of inner loops. Typically, they do this with persistent objects that describe the details of a desired parallel computation. The hierarchy of objects is shown in Figure 6.14. We will discuss the objects in this figure, starting at the bottom.

6.3.1 Mappings and Logical Grids

Two basic abstractions help with data mapping. The first is a logical grid topology, which describes the names of processes and their relationships. This data structure is helpful for describing communication structures and data layout. Data layout itself is described by mapping functions, which describe transformations of indices of the data onto the logical grid topologies in each dimension. In this chapter, we will restrict our attention to two-dimensional logical grid topologies.

Logical 2-D Grid Topologies. As we saw in Chapter 4, MPI provides a set of routines that can be used to create virtual topologies. The routines provided by MPI for creating Cartesian virtual topologies are not always applicable, however. In some cases, it may be necessary to decompose or split a communicator into parts based on a more general criterion. MPI provides the function `MPI_Comm_split` for this purpose (see Section 3.9). Recall that this function takes as input a communicator, a color, and a key. All processes with the same `color` are placed into the same new communicator, which is returned in the fourth argument. The processes are ranked in the new communicator in the order given by `key`; if two processes have the same key value, they retain the same relative ordering as in the old communicator.

As an example of the use of `MPI_Comm_split`, in Figure 6.13 we show an alternative way to generate a 2-D Cartesian topology. The data structure for the logical grid that this routine creates is shown in Figure 6.12.

Multiple calls to `MPI_Comm_split` can be used to generate overlapping subgroup communicators, as we have done to get row communicators and column communicators in Figure 6.13, where the topology constructor is presented.

Revisiting Grids Using MPI Topology Functions. An alternative to `MPI_Comm_split` when using a Cartesian topology (created, for example, with `MPI_Cart_create`) is to use `MPI_Cart_sub`. This takes a communicator that has a Cartesian topology and returns a new communicator consisting of those processes that are in a hyperplane of the Cartesian topology of the input communicator.

```
typedef struct
{
    int P, Q;  /* global shape of grid */
    int p, q;  /* local position on grid */

    MPI_Comm grid_comm; /* parent communicator */
    MPI_Comm row_comm;  /* row    communicator */
    MPI_Comm col_comm;  /* column communicator */
} LA_Grid_2d;
```

Figure 6.12
The 2-D logical grid structure

int **MPI_Cart_sub**(MPI_Comm oldcomm, int *remain_dims, MPI_Comm *newcomm)

Table 6.7
C binding for MPI topology routine used in `la_grid_2d_new_II`

Cartcomm MPI::Cartcomm::Sub(const bool remain_dims[]) const

Table 6.8
C++ binding for `MPI_Cart_sub`

This hyperplane is described by the second argument; for each dimension in the original Cartesian topology, a true value indicates that that dimension remains in the Cartesian topology associated with the output communicator. One way to understand this is to think of a 2-D Cartesian topology, with rows numbered as the first dimension and columns the second. Then if `remain_dim = { 1, 0 }`, the output communicator represents the row containing the process; if `remain_dim = { 0, 1 }`, the output communicator represents the column containing the process. The use of `MPI_Cart_sub` to construct the row and column communicators for the virtual topology hierarchy is shown in Figure 6.15.

Note that the MPI Cartesian topology functions will map the processes to the Cartesian topology in a particular way: specifically, the ranks of the processes in the communicator created by `MPI_Cart_create` follow a row-major ordering; that is, if each process in a 3-D Cartesian topology has Cartesian coordinates (i, j, k), the next process in rank in the Cartesian communicator has Cartesian coordinates $(i, j, k+1)$, unless k is already at the maximum values (number of processes in that dimension), in which case j (or i if j is at the maximum value) is incremented by

```
LA_Grid_2d *la_grid_2d_new(MPI_Comm comm, int P, int Q)
{
    LA_Grid_2d *grid;
    MPI_Comm  row, col;
    int       my_rank, p, q;

    /* Determine row and column position */
    MPI_Comm_rank(comm, &my_rank);
    p = my_rank / Q;
    q = my_rank % Q;   /* pick a row-major mapping */

    /* Split comm into row and col comms */
    MPI_Comm_split(comm, p, q, &row); /* color by row,
                                         rank by column */
    MPI_Comm_split(comm, q, p, &col); /* color by column,
                                         rank by row */
    /* Make new grid */
    grid = (LA_Grid_2d *)malloc(sizeof(LA_Grid_2d));
    /* Fill in new grid structure */
    grid->grid_comm = comm;
    grid->row_comm  = row;
    grid->col_comm  = col;
    grid->P         = P;
    grid->Q         = Q;
    grid->p         = p;
    grid->q         = q;
    /* Return the newly built grid */
    return (grid);
}
```

Figure 6.13
The 2-D logical grid structure constructor

MPI_CART_SUB(oldcomm, remain_dims, newcomm, ierror) integer oldcomm, newcomm, ierror logical remain_dims(*)

Table 6.9
Fortran binding for MPI topology routine used in `la_grid_2d_new` (revisited)

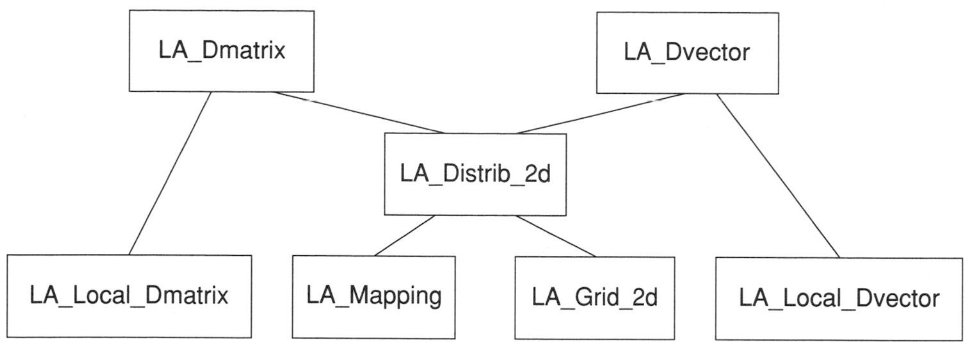

Figure 6.14
The hierarchy of data structures in the linear algebra examples

one. If another decomposition is preferred, for example, a column major (i.e., the first value in the coordinate tuple (i, j, k) changes first), then `MPI_Comm_split` can be used instead.

Mapping Functions and Distributions. Because we wish to provide flexible library routines, we let the user specify how data is laid out in the system. Specifically, we provide data mapping functions, particularly for common layouts (linear load balanced, scattered, and so on). Following the rules for these mappings, users can potentially add different mapping strategies for coefficients, but distributions we illustrate here will cover a lot of ground and will illustrate our design goal of "data distribution independence."

Single mappings aren't enough because they describe one-dimensional conversions between a global index space and local process naming for coefficients; they indicate which globally numbered coefficient goes where in a set of processes. For two-dimensional data structures (such as matrices), we need two such mappings to describe how information maps onto a process topology. To meet this need, we devise a data structure, called a distribution, that we make particular to two dimensions but that could generalize for higher-dimensional grids, too.

Figure 6.17 illustrates the data structure that encompasses both the logical grid information and a pair of mappings, which proves sufficient to describe basic linear algebra.

6.3.2 Vectors and Matrices

Given the logical grids, mappings, and the two-dimension distributions based on them, we can now turn to distributed data structures for linear algebra.

```
#define N_DIMS 2
#define FALSE 0
#define TRUE  1
LA_Grid_2d *la_grid_2d_new_II(MPI_Comm comm, int P, int Q)
{
    LA_Grid_2d *grid;
    MPI_Comm  comm_2d, row, col;
    int       my_rank, p, q;
    int dims[N_DIMS],          /* hold dimensions */
        local[N_DIMS],         /* local position */
        period[N_DIMS],        /* aperiodic flags */
        remain_dims[N_DIMS];   /* flags for sub-dimension
                                   computations */
    /* Generate a new communicator with virtual topology added */
    dims[0] = P; period[0] = FALSE;
    dims[1] = Q; period[1] = FALSE;
    MPI_Cart_create(comm, N_DIMS, dims, period, TRUE, &comm_2d);
    /* map back to topology coordinates: */
    MPI_Comm_rank(comm, &my_rank);
    MPI_Cart_coords(comm_2d, my_rank, N_DIMS, local);
    p = local[0]; q = local[1];  /* this is "my" grid location */
    /* Use cartesian sub-topology mechanism to get row/col comms */
    remain_dims[0] = FALSE; remain_dims[1] = TRUE;
    MPI_Cart_sub(comm_2d, remain_dims, &row);
    remain_dims[0] = TRUE; remain_dims[1] = FALSE;
    MPI_Cart_sub(comm_2d, remain_dims, &col);
    grid = (LA_Grid_2d *)malloc(sizeof(LA_Grid_2d));  /* new grid */

    /* rest of the code is the same as before */
}
```

Figure 6.15
2-D topology hierarchy with Cartesian topology functions

```
#define LA_MAPPING_BLINEAR  1
#define LA_MAPPING_BSCATTER 2

typedef struct
{
    int   map_type; /* Used for quick comparison of mappings */

    void (*mu)(int I, int P, int N, void *extra, int *p, int *i);
                    /* Mapping of I->(p,i) */
    void (*mu_inv)(int p, int i, int P, int N, void *extra, int *I);
                    /* Inverse (p,i)->I:   */
    void (*local_len)(int p, int P, int N, void *extra, int *n);
                    /* # of coefficients mapped to each process: */

    void *extra;    /* for mapping-specific parameters */
} LA_Mapping;

/* some pre-defined mappings ... */
extern LA_Mapping *LA_Mapping_Blk_Linear, *LA_Mapping_Blk_Scatter,
                  *LA_Mapping_Linear, *LA_Mapping_Scatter;
```

Figure 6.16
Definition of mapping function data structure

```
typedef struct
{
    LA_Grid_2d *grid; /* grid on which the distribution is based */
    LA_Mapping *row;  /* row mapping */
    LA_Mapping *col;  /* col mapping */
} LA_Distrib_2d;
```

Figure 6.17
Definition of mapping function data structure

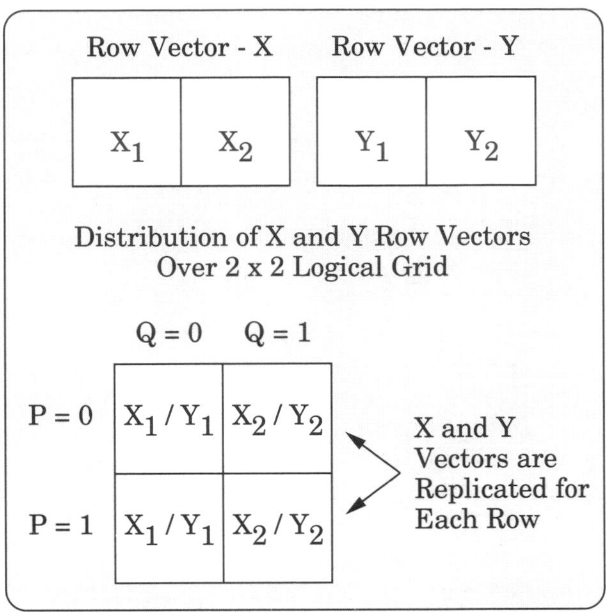

Figure 6.18
Layout of two row vectors over a 2 x 2 logical process grid. Column vectors are laid out in an analogous fashion, orthogonal to the row vectors.

Vectors. In a 2-D logical grid topology, vectors may be either row- or column-oriented vectors. We assume that each row (respectively, column) vector is replicated over each row (respectively, column) of a logical grid. Figure 6.18 shows schematically how two row vectors might be distributed in a grid. In this example, each vector is broken into two subvectors and is distributed along the columns of the grid. Through replication, each process row has a complete copy of both vectors; see also [43, 114].

Vector structure and construction. Distributed vectors are defined by the data structure illustrated in Figure 6.19. As an instance of a distributed object, a vector contains information including both its global and its local length, a pointer to local real data storage, and a type field that indicates the choice of row or column distribution. In addition, the vector data structure references an underlying logical grid topology data structure and a data distribution. This latter information completes the specification of how vector coefficients are mapped and replicated over the topology.

```
typedef struct la_local_dvector
{
    int m;                    /* local vector length */
    double *data;             /* vector data */
} LA_Local_Dvector;

typedef struct la_dvector
{
    LA_Local_Dvector v;       /* Local vector */
    int M;                    /* full length of vector */
    int type;                 /* row or column type */
    LA_Distrib_2d  *dis;      /* how to map data on grid */
} LA_Dvector;
```

Figure 6.19
Definition of the distributed vector on the logical grid

Matrices. Matrices on two-dimensional process grids are defined analogously to vectors, as depicted in Figure 6.20. A matrix is divided into submatrices, each with a local shape given by $m \times n$. The values of m and n generally differ in each process, just as the lengths of subvectors differ, in general, in each process. A matrix has a storage strategy, depending on whether it is row or column major. (The default constructor we use will make column-major local matrices; this detail remains an issue for fine optimizations of local memory access.) As with vectors, distributed matrices refer to an underlying logical process grid and distribution, through which thcy acquire the detailed information on topology shape and coefficient mapping.

6.3.3 Components of a Parallel Library

High-quality libraries must provide more than one version of a function that can perform efficiently over different conditions (we call such a set of methods a *poly-algorithm*). For example, we provide multiple versions of the vector sum and inner-product functions, both with the same sequential complexity. The "strided" version of these functions has a reduced computational load at the expense of more communication. Conversely, the "nonstrided" version is computationally more intensive but requires fewer messages because the algorithm exploits data redundancy; in the case of the vector sum (with compatibly stored data), no messages are needed at all. The most efficient function is determined by comparing issues such as message latency, bandwidth, and floating-point performance, all with reference to the size of the vector and the logical grid dimensions P, Q. (The `upshot` program and some empirical modeling will help decide which function is best for a given case on a real

```
typedef struct la_local_dmatrix
{
    int     storage_type; /* Storage strategy (row/column-major) */
    int     m, n;         /* Local dimensions */
    double  **data;       /* The local matrix, as set of pointers */
} LA_Local_Dmatrix;

typedef struct la_dmatrix
{
    LA_Local_Dmatrix a;   /* Local matrix */
    int     M, N;         /* Global dimensions of LA_Dmatrix. */
    LA_Distrib_2d *dis;   /* how to map data onto grid */
} LA_Dmatrix;
```

Figure 6.20
The distributed matrix structure

system.)

Vector sum. The vector sum is typically a noncommunicating operation provided the vectors being summed are stored compatibly, that is, corresponding coefficients appear in the same processes at aligned offsets. This is the simplest of the parallel vector operations possible on the distributed vectors. The operation to be performed is $\mathbf{z} = \alpha\mathbf{x} + \beta\mathbf{y}$, where α and β are real scalar constants. Good implementations handle special cases like $\alpha = 0$ and $\beta = 1.0$ for better performance. Even better implementations use sequential BLAS (for Basic Linear Algebra Subprograms [31, 30, 91]) when local vectors are long enough to make the cost of a subroutine call less important than the performance gain of an often-optimized sequential kernel.

Thus, a number of different versions of the vector sum must be available and must be selected appropriately for different situations. This is where the object-oriented and object-based approaches to the library design differ. For the object-oriented case, the user is forced to "commit" to certain operations in order to pre-evaluate all the data transformations, choices about use of BLAS, and so on. This approach makes these relatively expensive choices a one-time operation, and may even encourage further one-time overheads for better performance. The object-based versions, which are object extensions to the familiar BLAS, have to test for errors, data layout, and so on each time, making the overhead of general data layouts somewhat higher than the object-oriented versions. These concepts are illustrated in detail with the code and related documentation available in 'http://www.mcs.anl.gov/mpi/usingmpi' (Appendix D).

Inner product. The inner product offers a similar set of challenges to those presented by vector sum; in addition to offering the choices of replicated and non-replicated work versions, the use or nonuse of underlying BLAS remains. Here, we illustrate a version of the code that utilizes the object-oriented approach. For this approach, a "dot product" object is created once, describing the dot-product relationship between two vectors. Whenever a dot product is needed, `(*xy->op)()` is performed. The absence of arguments here appears to be a deficiency but is actually a sign that we have tightly optimized our code![2] We show the version that employs sequential BLAS, to remind the reader that we can access efficient local operations (in the limit of large enough data). See Figures 6.21 and 6.22.

Skew inner product. The skew inner product combines the idea of vector re-distribution and dot product into a single calculation, when the vectors are not distributed compatibly at the beginning of the operation. Specifically, it handles the case where one vector is a "row" vector, in any layout, and the other vector is a "column" vector. Until now, we have been assuming that the vectors are colinear (either row or column) and of the same distribution.

Both object-based and object-oriented versions of this call appear in the software distribution. The nice feature of this routine is that the object-oriented version is needed to achieve the right computational complexity, because it is essential to organize the operations in each process once and for all.

Matrix-Vector Product. To illustrate the use of the vectors together with dense matrices, we have also included the equivalent object-based and object-oriented libraries for the dense matrix-vector product. Here the number of choices for data optimization grows; hence, if the vectors and matrices are distributed incompatibly, a large number of `if` statements have to be handled. For the object-oriented strategy, this is done once and for all. For the object-based approach, lots of conditional branching gets done with each call.

---

[2]An alternative approach in C++ is to use operator overloading, so that the vectors and matrices are expressible as formulas and regain mathematical beauty. Unfortunately, in many C++ systems, overloading introduces overheads because of temporaries. In the C strategy used here, all temporaries are explicitly shown.

```
double ddot_stride(LA_Dvector *x, LA_Dvector *y, int *error)
{
    int    i, start, stride, m;
    double local_sum = 0.0, sum, *x_data, *y_data;

    if (x->type != y->type) { /* Check for compatible types */
        *error = LA_TYPE_ERROR;  /* FAILURE */
        return(0.0);
    }

    /* Determine the stride based on type */
    if (x->type == LA_GRID_ROW) {
        start = x->dis->grid->p; stride = x->dis->grid->P;
    }
    else {
        start = x->dis->grid->q; stride = x->dis->grid->Q;
    }

    /* Sum up my part (non-optimized) */
    m      = x->v.m;
    x_data = &(x->v.data[0]); y_data = &(y->v.data[0]);
    for (i =  start; i < m; i += stride)
        local_sum += x_data[i] * y_data[i];

    /* Get the sum of all parts */
    MPI_Allreduce(&local_sum, &sum, 1, MPI_DOUBLE, MPI_SUM,
                  x->dis->grid->grid_comm);

    /* Return result */
    *error = MPI_SUCCESS;
    return(sum);
}
```

Figure 6.21
Object-based, strided inner (dot) product on distributed vectors, without BLAS

```
void LAX_ddot_strided_blas(LA_Dvector_ddot_stride_binop *xy,
                           double *result)
{
    int    start, stride;
    double local_sum = 0.0;
    LA_Dvector *x, *y;

    /* Dereference the binary vector operands: */
    x = xy -> binop.x;  y = xy -> binop.y;

    /* Determine the stride based on type */
    start  = xy -> local_start;
    stride = xy -> local_stride;

    /* Sum up my part */
    blas_ddot(&(x->v.m), &(x->v.data[start]), &stride,
              &(y->v.data[start]), &stride);

    /* Get the sum of all parts */
    MPI_Allreduce(&local_sum, result, 1, MPI_DOUBLE, MPI_SUM,
                  xy->binop.comm);
    /* Return result */
    xy -> binop.error = 0;
}
```

Figure 6.22
Object-oriented, strided inner (dot) product on distributed vectors, with BLAS

6.4 The LINPACK Benchmark in MPI

The LINPACK benchmark is a well-known numerical code that is often used to benchmark computers for floating-point performance. LINPACK itself is an example of a successful numerical library, and it is interesting to briefly discuss some aspects of a parallel version of this program. We note that there is an active effort to produce a parallel version of LINPACK's successor, LAPACK; this package is known as ScaLAPACK (for Scalable LAPACK) [11]. We will discuss only a few of the issues involved in developing this code.

The benchmark program solves the linear system $Ax = b$ for x, given a matrix A and right-hand-side vector b. The matrix A is *dense* (i.e, all of its elements are nonzero). The code solves this problem by computing a factorization of A into PLU; here, L is a lower-triangular matrix, U is an upper triangular matrix, and P

```
double precision dtemp(2), ddummy(2)

dtemp(1) = dabs( work( j, j ) )
dtemp(2) = myrow

call MPI_ALLREDUCE( dtemp, ddummy, 2, MPI_DOUBLE_PRECISION, &
                    MPI_MAXLOC, colcomm, ierr )

ipivnode = ddummy(2)
if ( ddummy(1) .eq. 0.0d00 ) ipivnode = icurrow
```

Figure 6.23
Code fragment for finding a pivot row

is a permutation matrix. The permutation matrix represents the exchange of rows used in the *partial pivoting* algorithm that this code uses to improve numerical stability. In order to determine the permutation, as each row of the matrix is used to generate the factorization, the row of the matrix that contains the largest element is needed. We assume that the rows (and columns) of the matrix may be distributed across the processes. To find this element, we can use the code in Figure 6.23. This makes use of predefined reduction operation `MPI_MAXLOC` as the `MPI_Op` argument to `MPI_ALLREDUCE`; this routine returns just what we need (the maximum in the first element and the location of the maximum in the second element).

An interesting feature about this library is that once code is developed using a general communicator (instead of hard-wiring in `MPI_COMM_WORLD`), it immediately becomes useful on any subset of processes. Thus, if a parallel application is using task parallelism (dividing a job into tasks that may interact) and each of these tasks is itself parallel, then a parallel linear system solver library written in MPI can be used by any or all of the tasks. Without communicators (more precisely, the group component of the communicator), the library could not be used in this case (see [7]).

6.5 Strategies for Library Building

The nonblocking broadcast example is an example of an asynchronous library. The rest of this chapter concentrates on *loosely synchronous* parallel libraries. By loosely synchronous libraries we mean libraries that are essentially single program, multiple data. They compute on analogous parts of a dataset, however complex or irregular, and occasionally communicate. Perhaps this communication is collective; perhaps it is just selective point-to-point transfers. In any event, the number of messages produced and consumed is well characterized in advance for such libraries; and most often, both the size and sources for all messages are anticipated at the time the program is written. That processes may "get ahead" of other processes between synchronizing communications is the reason for the term loosely synchronous [43]. Also included in this model is the idea that certain processes may send messages and continue even though their counterpart has failed to complete a receive; for this purpose, we use MPI send routines that are nonblocking.

Particular strategies are now available to the library writer because of features in MPI:

- Duplicate communicators for safe communication space when entering calls to parallel libraries (`MPI_Comm_dup`, `MPI_Comm_create`).
- Define distributed structures based on communicators.
- Use MPI-defined virtual topology information to make algorithms easier to understand (e.g., `MPI_Cart_create`).
- Augment virtual topology technology as needed (e.g., topology hierarchies, as in Section 6.3.1).
- Use attributes on communicators (called attribute caching) when adding additional collective operations to a communicator (Section 6.2).
- If the library should handle any errors reported by an MPI routine (for example, to provide a more application-specific error message), attach a different error handler to the library's private communicator (see Section 7.7).

A number of mechanisms used in libraries before MPI to achieve correctness are no longer necessary and can be safely discarded:

- It is no longer necessary to publish tag usage by the library to avoid tag conflicts with user code. If the library uses its own communicator, both it and the user have access to a full range of tags.
- It is no longer necessary to make a parallel library mimic the behavior of a sequential library by synchronizing at the entry and exit of each parallel call in order to achieve quiescence. Communicators local to the library ensure that no library message will be intercepted by user code or vice versa.
- There is no need to restrict the library programming model to nonoverlapping process group assumptions, since communicators with overlapping groups pose no particular problem for MPI libraries.

• Many existing libraries work only over "all" processors (processes) of a user's allocation. With MPI it is easy to write a library so that it can use whatever group of processes is specified when it is called.

6.6 Examples of Libraries

One of the hopes of the MPI Forum was that the features in MPI intended for writing libraries would, in fact, enable the creation of portable libraries, allowing parallel programmers to use ever more powerful constructs in building their programs.

The following list provides a sampling of the libraries that are currently available.

PETSc is a library for the parallel solution of linear and nonlinear systems of equations arising from the discretization of partial differential equations [5].

ScaLAPACK includes routines for the parallel solution of dense and banded systems of linear equations and for eigensystem analysis [11].

PLAPACK is another library for dense matrix operations [124].

Parallel Print Function provides a convenient set of `printf`-like functions for C and Fortran programs. It is one of the projects in the Parallel Tools Consortium [94].

FFTW is a portable FFT library. The multidimensional FFTs use MPI [34].

These libraries vary in how much they exploit the features that MPI has provided for library developers. Some libraries, such as PETSc, make extensive use of the capabilities of MPI, exploiting persistent communication, communicator attributes, private communicators, and other features. Other libraries use a much smaller set of routines.

In some cases, you may find libraries that are simple ports of libraries written for previous message-passing systems. These can be very useful but, for the reasons given at the beginning of this chapter, may require care in their use. The most common limitation is for a library to use `MPI_COMM_WORLD` for all communication. A library that uses MPI to properly avoid the possible interference of messages in the library with ones outside of the library will either use `MPI_Comm_dup` or one of the other communicator construction routines (such as `MPI_Cart_create`), an explicit communicator argument, or `MPI_Barrier` to separate library messages from non-library messages. You can often use the Unix command `nm` to discover what routines are used in a library. For example,

```
nm /usr/local/lib/libpetsc.a | grep MPI_
```

lists all of the MPI routines used in the library `libpetsc.a`. Depending on the exact format of the output of the `nm` command, the command

```
nm /usr/local/lib/libpetsc.a | grep -i MPI_ | \
            awk '{print $8}' | sort | uniq
```

will print a sorted list containing the MPI routines in use (along with other symbols containing `MPI_`). If this list contains only a subset of the MPI point-to-point functions (e.g., `MPI_Send` and `MPI_Recv`), along with the communicator information functions `MPI_Comm_size` and `MPI_Comm_rank`, then you know that the library does not use the MPI features for providing communication safety and hence must be used with care.

This command shows that PETSc, for example, uses some 46 MPI functions, including those for attributes, persistent communication, and multiple completions, as well as `MPI_Comm_dup`.

7 Other Features of MPI

This chapter describes the more advanced routines from the MPI Standard that have not arisen in the discussion so far. We use the opportunity to introduce several interesting example programs.

7.1 Simulating Shared-Memory Operations

Throughout this book we have been concentrating on the message-passing computational model. Some applications are more naturally written for a *shared-memory* model, in which all of the parallel machine's memory is directly available to each process. In this section we discuss what is necessary in order to provide the basic functionality of the shared-memory model in a distributed-memory environment, and what MPI routines might be used in doing so.

7.1.1 Shared vs. Distributed Memory

The essential feature of the message-passing model is that at least two processes are involved in every communication; send and receive operations must be paired. The essential feature of the shared-memory model is that any process can access all the memory in the machine. On a distributed-memory architecture, where each memory address is local to a specific processor, this means that each process must be able to access the local memory of other processes, without any particular action on the part of the process whose local memory is being read or written to.

In a sense, then, every processor (CPU plus memory) must be host to two different functions: a compute process that does the main work, and a data server process that provides the other processes in the computation access to that processor's memory (see Figure 7.1). These two processes need not be separate MPI processes. In many cases the machine's operating system or message-passing software will not permit it, and in other cases the overhead of switching between the two processes is prohibitive.

Several approaches exist, depending on what level of extension to the message-passing model is offered by the underlying system. One approach is to use a separate thread to handle the data management requests. In MPI-2, a more direct approach, called one-sided or remote memory access, is available; this is discussed in *Using MPI-2* [66]. Here we assume that we have to do everything within the message-passing environment defined by MPI-1 and with single-threaded processes.

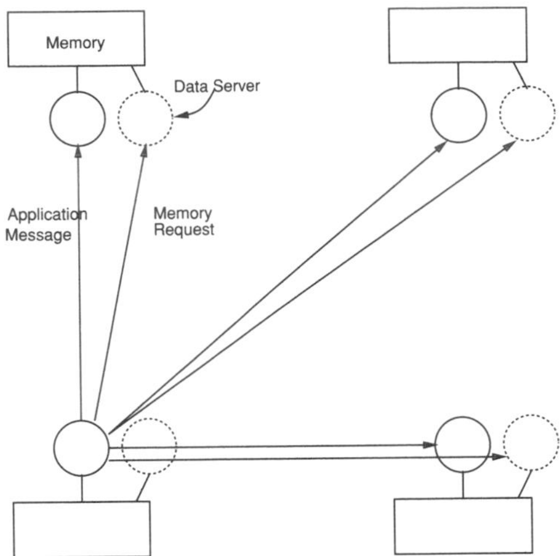

Figure 7.1
Sharing distributed memory

7.1.2 A Counter Example

We begin with the simplest possible case: simulating a single shared-memory location. Having a single "shared" variable that can be updated atomically by any process is surprisingly useful. In a true shared-memory environment, the counter is read and updated by normal memory operations, but the updating must be protected by a lock of some kind. In the message-passing environment, no lock is needed because only one process is actually updating the memory location. Hence, one easy way to implement the shared counter with MPI is to give one MPI process the job of holding the counter and servicing requests to retrieve and update its value. To make things particularly straightforward, let us suppose we wish to implement something like the `NXTVAL` counter in the message-passing library TCGMSG [74].) The function `NXTVAL` returns the value of a built-in counter that is initialized to 0 at startup. Each retrieval of its value increments the value by one. With many processes calling `NXTVAL`, it is guaranteed that no two will ever retrieve the same value and that all values of the counter will handed out consecutively, with no value being skipped.

We dedicate one process[1] to being the "server" for this variable. It can be set

[1]In some MPI implementations, multiple MPI processes per processor are allowed. The MPI standard neither requires nor prohibits it. This example makes the most sense in such an environment; otherwise, one processor is idle most of the time waiting for counter requests.

```
int MPI_Rsend(void* buf, int count, MPI_Datatype datatype, int dest, int tag,
              MPI_Comm comm)

int MPI_Iprobe(int source, int tag, MPI_Comm comm, int *flag,
               MPI_Status *status)
```

Table 7.1
C bindings for MPI routines in counter example

up much the same way in which we established the server for random numbers in Chapter 3. Let us encapsulate the counter by defining of set of three routines to manage it for the MPE library: `MPE_Counter_create`, `MPE_Counter_free`, and `MPE_Counter_nxtval`. `MPE_Counter_create` will be a collective operation (must be called by all processes in a given communicator); it will split off one process of the communicator's group to hold the counter and return two new communicators. One communicator, `counter_comm`, will be used in calls to to `MPE_Counter_nxtval`; the other, `smaller_comm`, will be used by the remaining processes for the main computation. `MPE_Counter_free` cleans up these communicators and ends the server process function, terminating its original call to `MPI_Counter_create`. This strategy relies on the fact that MPI, unlike many other systems, supports collective and point-to-point operations on communicators based on arbitrary subgroups of processes. Thus, the communicator `smaller_comm` is just as capable as the communicator passed to `MPI_Counter_create`, except that it has one less process available.

This client-server computation is easy enough that we can include all the necessary code here. `MPE_Counter_create` is shown in Figure 7.2, including the handling of an unexpected tag (signifying an error in our program) that uses `MPI_Abort` to cause the program to exit (see Section 7.7.4). `MPE_Counter_nxtval` is shown in Figure 7.3. `MPE_Counter_free` is shown in Figure 7.4; it is also a collective operation. The process with rank 0 in the counter's communicator sends a message to the counter process to make it call `MPE_Counter_free` as well.

We use `MPI_Comm_split` to create the smaller communicator `smaller_comm`. We do this by using the special value `MPI_UNDEFINED` as the value of `color` for the process that is the counter process and is not in the `smaller_comm` communicator. For this process, `MPI_Comm_split` returns a value of `MPI_COMM_NULL`. All other processes are placed in the new communicator; because we used `myid` as the `key` argument, they are ordered in `smaller_comm` the same as in `old_comm`.

```
void MPE_Counter_create( MPI_Comm old_comm, MPI_Comm *smaller_comm,
                         MPI_Comm *counter_comm )
{
    int counter = 0;
    int message, done = 0, myid, numprocs, server, color;
    MPI_Status status;

    MPI_Comm_size(old_comm, &numprocs);
    MPI_Comm_rank(old_comm, &myid);
    server = numprocs-1;     /*   last proc is server */
    MPI_Comm_dup( old_comm, counter_comm ); /* make one new comm */
    if (myid == server) color = MPI_UNDEFINED;
    else color = 0;
    MPI_Comm_split( old_comm, color, myid, smaller_comm );

    if (myid == server) {       /* I am the server */
        while (!done) {
            MPI_Recv(&message, 1, MPI_INT, MPI_ANY_SOURCE,
                     MPI_ANY_TAG, *counter_comm, &status );
            if (status.MPI_TAG == REQUEST) {
                MPI_Send(&counter, 1, MPI_INT, status.MPI_SOURCE,
                         VALUE, *counter_comm );
                counter++;
            }
            else if (status.MPI_TAG == GOAWAY) {
                done = 1;
            }
            else {
                fprintf(stderr, "bad tag %d sent to MPE counter\n",
                        status.MPI_TAG );
                MPI_Abort( *counter_comm, 1 );
            }
        }
        MPE_Counter_free( smaller_comm, counter_comm );
    }
}
```

Figure 7.2
MPE_Counter_create

```
int MPE_Counter_nxtval( MPI_Comm counter_comm, int *value )
{
    int server,numprocs;
    MPI_Status status;
    MPI_Comm_size(counter_comm, &numprocs);
    server = numprocs-1;
    MPI_Send(NULL, 0, MPI_INT, server, REQUEST, counter_comm);
    MPI_Recv(value, 1, MPI_INT, server, VALUE, counter_comm,
             &status);
    return 0;
}
```

Figure 7.3
MPE_Counter_nxtval

```
int MPE_Counter_free( MPI_Comm *smaller_comm,
                      MPI_Comm *counter_comm )
{
    int myid, numprocs;
    MPI_Comm_rank( *counter_comm, &myid );
    MPI_Comm_size( *counter_comm, &numprocs );
    /* Make sure that all requests have been serviced */
    if (myid == 0)
        MPI_Send(NULL, 0, MPI_INT, numprocs-1, GOAWAY,
                 *counter_comm);
    MPI_Comm_free( counter_comm );
    if (*smaller_comm != MPI_COMM_NULL) {
        MPI_Comm_free( smaller_comm );
    }
    return 0;
}
```

Figure 7.4
MPE_Counter_free

MPI_RSEND(buf, count, datatype, dest, tag, comm, ierror)
<type> buf(*)
integer count, datatype, dest, tag, comm, ierror

MPI_IPROBE(source, tag, comm, flag, status, ierror)
logical flag
integer source, tag, comm, status(MPI_STATUS_SIZE), ierror

Table 7.2
Fortran bindings for MPI routines in counter example

7.1.3 The Shared Counter Using Polling instead of an Extra Process

The disadvantage of the implementation we have just described is, of course, that one process is "wasted" minding the counter when it could perhaps be used in computation. To get around this disadvantage, this process must do useful work and manage the counter simultaneously. One way to do so within the restrictions of the message-passing mode, where all communication requires explicit receives, is to periodically probe the system to see whether a request for "counter service" has arrived. This is called *polling*. If a message *has* arrived, the message is received and responded to; otherwise the computation is resumed. The check can be carried out with a call to `MPI_Iprobe`, which determines whether messages have arrived that match a source, tag, and communicator given as arguments. The difference between using `MPI_Test` and using `MPI_Iprobe` is that `MPI_Test` is associated with a specific nonblocking send or receive operation that created a request. In particular, in the case of the receive, this means that the buffer has already been supplied by the user program. `MPI_Iprobe` (and its blocking version, `MPI_Probe`), on the other hand, are not associated with a particular request. Rather, they check for receipt of messages arriving with certain characteristics. To periodically check for counter requests and service them, then, the application program periodically calls

```
MPE_Counter_service( comm )
```

where `comm` is the communicator built for use by the counter. Let us suppose that this time we let process 0 be responsible for the counter and define `COUNTER` as the tag to be used in counter-related communication. The code for `MPE_Counter_-service` is shown in Figure 7.5. Assorted generalizations are of course possible (multiple counters, separate communicators), but we show here just the simplest case.

The programmer is responsible for seeing that this routine gets called often enough by the server process to service requests. One way to do this might be to use the profiling interface described in Section 7.6 to intercept MPI calls and probe for messages. The requests themselves are made with

```
MPI_Send( NULL, 0, MPI_INT, 0, COUNTER, comm );
MPI_Recv( &val, 1, MPI_INT, 0, COUNTER, comm, &status );
```

Note the explicit known server and tag. The `count` field in the send is `0` because no data is associated with the request; the tag is enough. Note that we also could have used `MPI_Sendrecv` here.

```
void MPE_Counter_service( MPI_Comm comm )
{
    static int counter = 0;
    int requester, flag;
    MPI_Status status;
    /* Process all pending messages */
    do {
       MPI_Iprobe(MPI_ANY_SOURCE, COUNTER, comm, &flag, &status );
       if (flag) {
          requester = status.MPI_SOURCE;
          MPI_Recv(MPI_BOTTOM, 0, MPI_INT, requester, COUNTER,
                   comm, &status );
          counter++;
          MPI_Send(&counter, 1, MPI_INT, requester,
                   COUNTER, comm );
       }
    } while (flag);
}
```

Figure 7.5
MPE_Counter_service

7.1.4 Fairness in Message Passing

In the preceding example, one process that makes a large number of requests very quickly can prevent other processes from receiving counter values. For example, consider what happens in Figure 7.5 if MPI_Iprobe always returns the process with the lowest rank in the communicator that matches the source, tag, and communicator values. If the process with rank zero, for example, makes many requests for the counter in a short period of time, the code in Figure 7.5 will give preference to that process over other processes with larger rank. MPI does not guarantee that MPI_Recv or MPI_Iprobe will be *fair* in selecting a message when a wildcard such as MPI_ANY_SOURCE or MPI_ANY_TAG is used.

What behavior would we like in this case? Basically, we don't want any one process to monopolize the counter; we want MPE_Counter_service to respond to all processes that are requesting a value once before responding to a process that "has come back for seconds." To do this, we need to eliminate the use of MPI_-ANY_SOURCE. But if we do this, we must turn the call to MPI_Iprobe into

```
for (rank=0; rank<size; rank++) {
    MPI_Iprobe( rank, COUNTER, comm, &flag, &status );
```

```
        if (flag) { ... }
    }
```

This will work, but there is a better way in MPI. Instead of using MPI_Iprobe followed by MPI_Recv, we can use MPI_Irecv, followed by MPI_Test. Since every receive in MPI must have a specified source (or MPI_PROC_NULL), we need one MPI_-Irecv for each process in the communicator. Then we want MPE_Counter_service to test each of these receive requests and determine which are ready; those processes are sent the updated counter value.

We could use code similar to the loop with MPI_Iprobe, but MPI provides a single function that does just what we want: MPI_Testsome. This routine tests each of the requests and indicates which of them have completed. It returns the number of completed requests in outcount, the indices of the completed requests in array_of_indices, and the corresponding status values in the first outcount elements of array_of_statuses. This "fair" version of MPE_Counter_service is shown in Figure 7.6.

Because this example uses MPI_Irecv, the array of requests that MPE_Counter_-service is testing must be created first. The routine MPE_Counter_service_setup is used for that purpose.

The approach arguably has some awkward pieces. The global variable reqs is one. As a result of using this global variable, this version of MPE_Counter_service can be used with only one communicator at a time. In addition, the MPE_Counter_-service routine must use malloc and free to provide temporary arrays for MPI_-Testsome. This is a place where attributes attached to the communicator, using the approach from Section 6.2, are a natural and powerful way to improve the usability of a library routine.

The approach used by MPI to provide fairness in message passing is very similar to the approach used in Unix to provide fairness in handling read and write operations with file descriptors. See Section 9.1 for details.

7.1.5 Exploiting Request-Response Message Patterns

In the preceding two sections, "shared memory" has consisted of a single value held by a single process. At this point, however, it is not difficult to see how to generalize the concept to treat all, or nearly all, the machine's memory as shared. If multiple processes per processor are allowed, then we can use the approach of Section 7.1.2, where the memory of each node is managed by a separate process. If they are not, or we cannot tolerate the overhead of constantly switching processes on a single processor, then we can use the approach of Section 7.1.3, at the expense of having

```
/* We will see later how to remove the global variable reqs */
static MPI_Request *reqs;
void MPE_Counter_service( MPI_Comm comm )
{
    static int counter = 0;
    int requester, outcount, size, i;
    MPI_Status *statuses;
    int        *indices;

    MPI_Comm_size( comm, &size );
    /* Allocate space for arrays */
    statuses = (MPI_Status *)malloc( size * sizeof(MPI_Status) );
    indices  = (int *)malloc( size * sizeof(int) );
    /* Process all pending messages FAIRLY */
    do {
        MPI_Testsome( size, reqs, &outcount, indices, statuses );
        if (outcount) {
            for (i=0; i<outcount; i++) {
                requester = statuses[i].MPI_SOURCE;
            counter++;
            MPI_Send(&counter, 1, MPI_INT, requester,
                     COUNTER, comm );
            /* Repost the nonblocking receive */
            MPI_Irecv( MPI_BOTTOM, 0, MPI_INT, requester,
                       COUNTER, comm, &reqs[indices[i]] );
            }
        }
    } while (outcount);
    free( statuses ); free( indices );
}

void MPE_Counter_service_setup( MPI_Comm comm )
{
    int i, size;
    MPI_Comm_size( comm, &size );
    for (i=0; i<size; i++) {
        MPI_Irecv( MPI_BOTTOM, 0, MPI_INT, i, COUNTER, comm,
                   &reqs[i] );
    }
}
```

Figure 7.6
A fair version of `MPE_Counter_service`

to call the service routine often enough to provide timely service to requests. It is precisely the desire to avoid both of these drawbacks (multiple processes per node or frequent calls to a "polling" routine) that has motivated the approaches that go beyond the message-passing model. We touch on these in Chapter 10.

There is one way in which we might be able to improve the performance of the mechanism we have used here. We note that whenever a process requests data from another one, it knows that the request will be answered. Similarly, the "server" process knows that every request is expecting a reply. This means that the request for data, which earlier had the form

```
MPI_Send
MPI_Recv
```

can be recoded as

```
MPI_Irecv
MPI_Send
MPI_Wait
```

On some architectures, particularly more loosely coupled systems that use networks to communicate data between processes, the protocol that takes place between sending and receiving processes can be greatly simplified if the sending process can assume that the matching receive has already been posted. The reason the protocol can be simpler is that if the sending side knows that a buffer has been supplied (this is the main function of `MPI_Irecv`), any negotiations between the processes over buffer space can be bypassed. In fact, some network approaches, such as VIA [125], require that receive buffers exist, and require additional coding and message traffic to ensure that these buffers are available. MPI provides a special form of the send for this situation. If the sender is assured that the receive has already been posted, then it may use `MPI_Rsend`. (The "R" is for "receiver ready," the MPI Standard calls this kind of send a "ready send".) The MPI implementation may treat this as a normal send (the semantics are the same as those of `MPI_Send`) but is allowed to optimize the protocol if it can. If the corresponding receive is *not* posted, then this is treated as a programmer error, and MPI's behavior is undefined in this case. Because it is important when using `MPI_Rsend` to consider both the sending and receiving side, we show a sketch of the code for the two processes below.

Requester	Server
`MPI_Irecv`	
`MPI_Send`	`MPI_Recv`
	`MPI_Rsend`
`MPI_Wait`	

A further refinement is to use `MPI_Rsend` in both the requester and the server.

Note that `MPI_Rsend` should be used only when it is known that the receive is already issued. For the most part, message-passing programming purposely allows few opportunities for writing code whose correct execution depends on the exact timing and order of events, but `MPI_Rsend` makes it possible to write code that is formally incorrect (because the program does not guarantee that `MPI_Rsend` is never called unless the matching `MPI_Recv` has already been issued) but that runs correctly most of the time. This means that `MPI_Rsend` should be used only when it can be shown to improve performance, and only with great care. In addition, few implementations currently exploit the opportunities offered to an MPI implementation, though at least one does, and performance tests have shown some benefits to using it on that implementation of MPI.

7.2 Application: Full-Configuration Interaction

Ab initio chemistry attempts to compute chemical results from the first principles of the quantum theory of charged particles and their interactions. Solution of the Schrödinger equation leads to linear algebra problems that are amenable to solution on parallel computers. Several of the techniques discussed above are used in an actual production chemistry code, currently running on the Intel Delta and being ported to MPI.

Full-configuration interaction (FCI) provides the *exact* solution of the electronic Schrödinger equation within the initial algebraic approximation of finite 1-particle basis set. The only errors present in an FCI result derive from either the underlying finite one-particle basis set or approximations in the nonrelativistic, Born-Oppenheimer Hamiltonian. The ability to compute FCI wave functions thus confers the ability to adjudicate among all approximate methods (e.g., SCF, many-body methods, and truncated CI*) and, by comparison with experiment, permits assessment of deficiencies in the one-particle basis set and the Hamiltonian approximations.

In the one application, a large full-CI calculation was successfully completed, included 94,930,032 configurations, or 418,639,400 determinants. Methane ($r =$ 1.085600Å) in a cc-p VDZ basis set was run in a C_{2v} subgroup of T_4, again with a frozen canonical SCF core orbital. This is just one point in a series of calculations. Details are given in [75].

The particular code described there uses "shared memory" in two different ways. First, because there is no locality to the computation, all processes act as data servers, responding to requests for data using a mechanism similar to the one just outlined. When originally implemented on the Intel Delta, a 512 node system that preceded the Intel Paragon, the program used Intel `hrecv` (corresponding to a `MPI_Recv` in a separate thread) along with "force-type" messages (corresponding to `MPI_Rsend`) to return the requested data.

Second, the workload is distributed through access to a shared counter, of the type we have used as an example in this section. In TCGMSG [74], which this code was originally written in, it uses `NXTVAL`, implemented on the Intel Delta with `hrecv`.

7.3 Advanced Collective Operations

In the book so far, we have introduced new collective operations of MPI as a consequence of trying to create a parallel algorithm, code, or library. At this stage, a few routines remain that we haven't needed in our palette of examples. Since these routines are important, and may be just what is needed to get the job done, we present them here all at once.

7.3.1 Data Movement

MPI provides many operations for collective data movement. We have already seen `MPI_Bcast` and the gather routines. In addition to these, MPI provides the opposite of gather, called scatter (`MPI_Scatter` and `MPI_Scatterv`), and a kind of "all scatter" called alltoall (`MPI_Alltoall` and `MPI_Alltoallv`). MPI-2 introduced an additional variation of `MPI_Alltoallv` called `MPI_Alltoallw`. These are illustrated in Figure 7.7.

7.3.2 Collective Computation

We have already seen several collective computation routines; `MPI_Reduce` performs a reduction of data from each process onto the specified root process. We have seen the use of `MPI_SUM` as the operation given to `MPI_Reduce` to sum up entries from all of the processes in a communicator. MPI provides a number of additional operations, shown in Table 7.3, that can be used with any of the collective computation routines. Most of these are self-explanatory. The last two, `MPI_MAXLOC` and `MPI_MINLOC`, are similar to `MPI_MAX` and `MPI_MIN` except that they also return the rank of the process where the maximum or minimum was found (if several processes have the maximum or minimum, the rank of the first one is returned). The datatype that is used for `MPI_MAXLOC` and `MPI_MINLOC` contains both the value and the

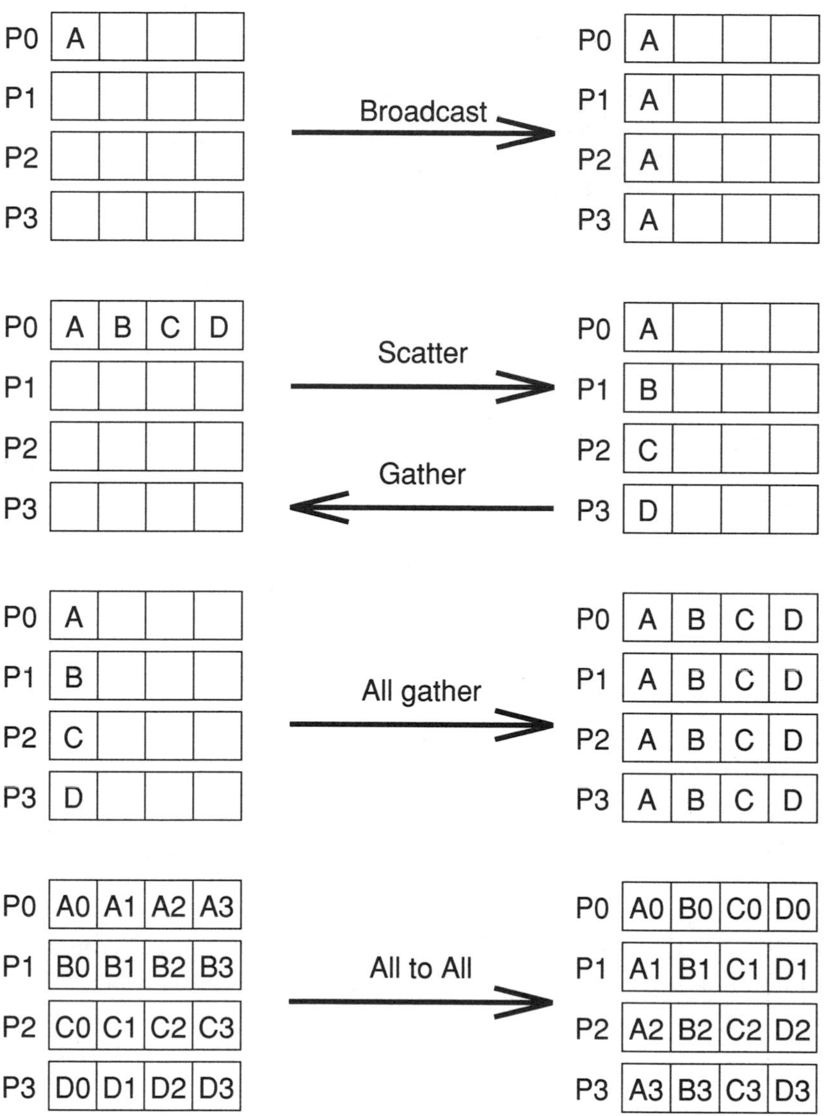

Figure 7.7
Schematic representation of collective data movement in MPI

MPI Name	Operation
MPI_MAX	Maximum
MPI_MIN	Minimum
MPI_PROD	Product
MPI_SUM	Sum
MPI_LAND	Logical and
MPI_LOR	Logical or
MPI_LXOR	Logical exclusive or (xor)
MPI_BAND	Bitwise and
MPI_BOR	Bitwise or
MPI_BXOR	Bitwise xor
MPI_MAXLOC	Maximum value and location
MPI_MINLOC	Minimum value and location

Table 7.3
Predefined operations for MPI collective computation

rank; see the MPI Standard or the implementation's `man` pages on `MPI_MAXLOC` and `MPI_MINLOC` for more details.

One additional predefined operation was introduced in MPI-2 called `MPI_REPLACE`. This is intended for use with the MPI-2 remote memory access operations and is covered in *Using MPI-2* [66].

User-Defined Operations. MPI also allows you to define your own operations that can be passed to the collective computation routines. For example, you may want to perform a more complex arithmetic operation (e.g., arguments are matrices to be multiplied together). A new operation is defined by using the routine `MPI_Op_create`; the output (third argument) of this routine is a new operation (in C, of type `MPI_Op`) that can be passed to routines such as `MPI_Allreduce`. There are two input values; the first is a function, and the second indicates whether the operation is commutative. The form of the function is the same for C and Fortran; the bindings are shown in Tables 7.4 and 7.5. A user-defined operation is deleted by calling `MPI_Op_free`.

The second argument to `MPI_Op_create` allows you to indicate that the operation is not commutative; that is, `a op b` does not give the same results as `b op a`. Matrix multiplication is a well-known example of a noncommutative operation. The presence of the commutative flag allows an MPI implementation more freedom in determining the order in which it computes the result.

```
int MPI_Op_create(MPI_User_function *function, int commute, MPI_Op *op)

int MPI_Op_free(MPI_Op *op)

typedef int MPI_User_function(void *invec, void *inoutvec, int *len,
                MPI_Datatype *datatype)
```

Table 7.4
C bindings for defining collective computation

```
MPI_OP_CREATE(function, commute, op, ierror)
                external function
                logical commute
                integer op, ierror

MPI_OP_FREE(op, ierror)
                integer op, ierror

User_function(invec, inoutvec, len, datatype)
                <type> invec(*),inoutvec(*)
                integer len, datatype
```

Table 7.5
Fortran bindings for defining collective computation. The `User_function` is not part of MPI; rather, it shows the calling sequence for the `function` argument to `MPI_OP_CREATE`.

Other Collective Computation Operations. MPI provides two more collective computation operations that users may find valuable. One is `MPI_Scan`. This is much like an `MPI_Allreduce` in that the values are formed by combining values contributed by each process and that each process receives a result. The difference is that the result returned by the process with rank r is the result of operating on the input elements on processes with rank $0, 1, \ldots, r$. If the operation is `MPI_SUM`, `MPI_Scan` computes all of the partial sums. MPI-2 adds a variation of `MPI_Scan` called `MPI_Exscan`. This is an exclusive scan: whereas in `MPI_Scan` the value returned on each process includes the contribution from that process, in `MPI_Exscan` the value of the calling process is not included in the result returned on that process. That is, the result of `MPI_Exscan` on the process with rank r is the result of applying the specified operation on the values contributed by processes $0, 1, \ldots, r-1$.

As an example of where `MPI_Scan` and `MPI_Exscan` can be used, consider the problem of balancing the work (computational effort) across processors. For example, in the one-dimensional decomposition that we used in Chapter 4, we can order all processes by rank, and consider the work "to the left" relative to the total work. That is, if the work is evenly distributed, each process will find that the sum of work to the left, not counting the current process, will be `rank * total_work / nprocs`. The following code provides a simple sketch:

```
t1 = MPI::Wtime();
... work ...
my_time = MPI::Wtime() - t1;
COMM_WORLD.Scan( &my_time, &time_to_me, 1, MPI::DOUBLE,
                 MPI::SUM );
total_work = time_to_me;   // Only for the last process
COMM_WORLD.Bcast( &total_work, 1, MPI::DOUBLE, nprocs - 1 );
fair_share = (rank + 1) * total_work / nprocs;
if ( fair_share > time_to_me + EPS) {
   ... shift work to rank-1
}
else if ( fair_share < time_to_me - EPS) {
   ... shift work to rank+1
}
```

With `MPI_Exscan`, the `fair_share` term would use `rank` instead of `rank + 1`.

The other collective computation routine is `MPI_Reduce_scatter`. The effect of this routine is to combine an `MPI_Reduce` and a `MPI_Scatterv`. This routine can be used to perform multiple `MPI_Reduce` operations concurrently and, in a sophisticated MPI implementation, can run faster than using `MPI_Reduce` and `MPI_Scatterv`. To see how this can be used, consider the problem of forming a matrix-vector product where the matrix and the vector are distributed across the processes. The vectors are distributed as follows: each process has some contiguous section of the vector, and these sections are in rank order. That is, process zero has the first chunk of values, process one the next chunk, and so on. More precisely, if the full vector is of size `n` and there are `nprocs` processes, then process zero has elements (starting from 1) `1:n/nprocs`, the second has elements `n/nprocs+1:2n/nprocs`, and so on (we are assuming that `nprocs` divides `n` here for simplicity).

The matrix is distributed across the processes by *columns*: the process with rank zero has columns `1:n/nprocs` and all of the rows, process one has columns `n/nprocs+1:2n/nprocs`, and so on. The distribution of the matrix and the vectors across the processes is shown in Figure 7.8.

We want to form the matrix-vector product $y = Ax$. Let A_i denote the part of the matrix A that is on process i, and let x_i denote the part of the vector

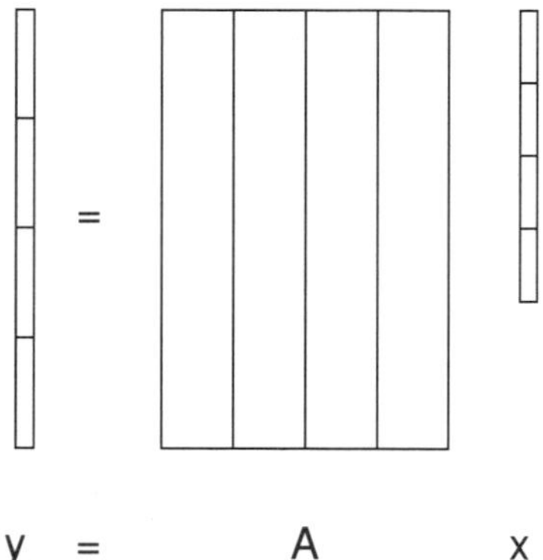

Figure 7.8
Distribution of a matrix and vector across a communicator

```
int MPI_Reduce_scatter(void *sendbuf, void *recvbuf, int *recvcounts,
                MPI_Datatype datatype, MPI_Op op, MPI_Comm comm)
```

Table 7.6
C binding for `MPI_Reduce_scatter`

x that is on process i. Because we have distributed A across the processes by column, we can form the product $w^i = A_i x_i$ on each process independently, that is, without any communication with any other process. The result vector w^i is a vector of size `n`, not `n/nprocs`; we use a superscript i to remind us that w^i is *not* the part of w on the ith process but is instead the result from the local matrix-vector product on the ith process. To get the result y, we must combine all of the contributions w^i. Specifically, on process zero, we must sum up the first `n/nprocs` elements from all of the w^i's, on the second process, we must sum up the second `n/nprocs` elements of the w^i's, and so forth. This is what `MPI_Reduce_scatter` does. It takes a `sendbuf` and an array of counts `recvcounts` and forms a result in `recvbuf` by combining the first `recvcounts(1)` (in Fortran notation) elements from `sendbuf` on all processes to the `recvbuf` on process zero; on process one, the `recvcounts(2)` elements in `sendbuf`, starting at the `recvcounts(1)+1`th element are combined from all processes, and so on. This is just what we need to form y_i from the corresponding parts of the w^ks. The code for the matrix-vector product is shown in Figure 7.9. Bindings for `MPI_Reduce_scatter` are shown in Tables 7.6, 7.7, and 7.8.

```
subroutine matvec( n, m, lmatrix, lx, ly, counts, comm )
use mpi
integer n, m, comm, counts(*)
real lmatrix(n,m), lx(m), ly(m)
integer i, j
real sum
real, allocatable :: tmp(:)

allocate (tmp(n))

! Perform the local matrix-vector multiply
! Should use the level-2 BLAS routine SGEMV
do i=1,n
   sum = 0
   do j=1,m
      sum = sum + lmatrix(i,j)*lx(j)
   enddo
   tmp(i) = sum
enddo

! Perform the local matrix-vector product
call MPI_REDUCE_SCATTER( tmp, ly, counts, &
                         MPI_REAL, MPI_SUM, comm, ierr)
deallocate (tmp)

! We're done!
end
```

Figure 7.9
Dense matrix-vector multiplication using `MPI_Reduce_scatter`

MPI_REDUCE_SCATTER(sendbuf, recvbuf, recvcounts,datatype, op, comm, ierror) <type> sendbuf(*), recvbuf(*) integer recvcounts(*), datatype, op, comm, ierror

Table 7.7
Fortran binding for `MPI_Reduce_scatter`

void MPI::Intracomm::Reduce_scatter(const void* sendbuf, void* recvbuf, int recvcounts[], const Datatype& datatype, const Op& op) const

Table 7.8
C++ binding for MPI_Reduce_scatter

7.3.3 Common Errors and Misunderstandings

Four errors are more common than others in using the collective routines. The first two apply to all collective routines. MPI requires that collective routines on the same communicator be called by all processes in that communicator, in the same order. The most common error that violates this rule is using a collective operation within one branch of an if-test on rank, and either forgetting or mis-ordering the collective routine in the other branch of the if.

The second common error is to assume that because a routine is collective, all processes making a collective call will complete that call at (roughly) the same time. Even `MPI_Barrier` guarantees only that no process will exit the barrier before all have entered; MPI says nothing about how far apart in time different processes may be when they exit the barrier. In collective routines such as `MPI_Bcast`, the root process may exit the call, having performed its task, before some or any of the other processes enter the collective routine. In the MPI standard, the collective routines are allowed to be synchronizing, but, with the exception of `MPI_Barrier`, are not required to be synchronizing. Of course some routines, such as `MPI_Allreduce`, because of their very definition, cannot complete on any process until all processes have contributed their data.

The third common error applies to all the routines where it might make sense to use the input buffer as the output buffer. A good example is `MPI_Allreduce`, where code like the following is often desired:

```
call MPI_ALLREDUCE( a, a, 1, MPI_REAL, MPI_SUM, comm, ierror )
```

Unfortunately, this violates the Fortran standard, and hence MPI cannot allow it. For consistency, MPI also prohibits this in C and C++ code. MPI-2 has introduced an extension, described in Appendix E, that addresses this problem.

The last common error is specific to `MPI_Bcast`. All processes, both the root (sender) and the other processes (those receiving the data), must call `MPI_Bcast`. Some message-passing systems had a "multicast" or "multisend" routine that sent messages to many processes; these processes used a regular receive call to receive the message. The MPI Forum considered such a "multisend" but felt that it would interfere with the performance of regular receives (that would now need to check for broadcasts) and the scalability of the broadcast itself.

7.4 Intercommunicators

Despite the convenience of communicators discussed thus far, a more general form of communicators, specifically targeted for group-to-group communication, proves a useful addition to MPI. Such "extended communicators" are called *intercommunicators* in the Standard, and the regular communicators discussed thus far are more formally called *intracommunicators.* MPI defines a minimal number of operations for these intercommunicators; these operations are, however, a powerful starting point for group-to-group communication.

Figure 7.10 illustrates the relationship of processes and groups in an intercommunicator. Each intercommunicator contains two groups. A process that is a member of an intercommunicator is, by definition, in one of these two groups. We call the group that the process is in the *local group*; the other group is called *remote group.* Accessor functions (mainly used by libraries built on top of MPI) permit queries about whether a communicator is an intercommunicator, via `MPI_Comm_test_inter`, and access to information about the remote group, via `MPI_Comm_remote_size` and `MPI_Comm_remote_group`. The local group, of which the owner of the intercommunicator is always a member, is accessible with the usual commands `MPI_Comm_size` and `MPI_Comm_group`, as before.

The remote group is the destination of messages sent with `MPI_Send` and its relatives. When sending a message, one names processes in the remote group by rank in the remote group. Messages are received with `MPI_Recv` and its relatives. The value of the `source` in the arguments to the receive call and in the `MPI_SOURCE` field of `MPI_Status` refers to a rank in the sending group (and hence remote group to the receiving process). This is illustrated in Figure 7.10.

The two groups in an intercommunicator do not overlap; that is, no process in the remote group may also be part of the local group. In MPI-1, only point-to-point communication is defined on intercommunicators, in addition to special operations used to construct and destroy them. These operations are summarized for C in Table 7.9, for Fortran in Table 7.10, and for C++ in Table 7.11. The most commonly used function is `MPI_Intercomm_create`; regular `MPI_Send` and `MPI_Recv` calls are valid with an intercommunicator as their argument, as well as the usual intracommunicator already introduced.

MPI-1 did not define general collective operations for intercommunicators. How-

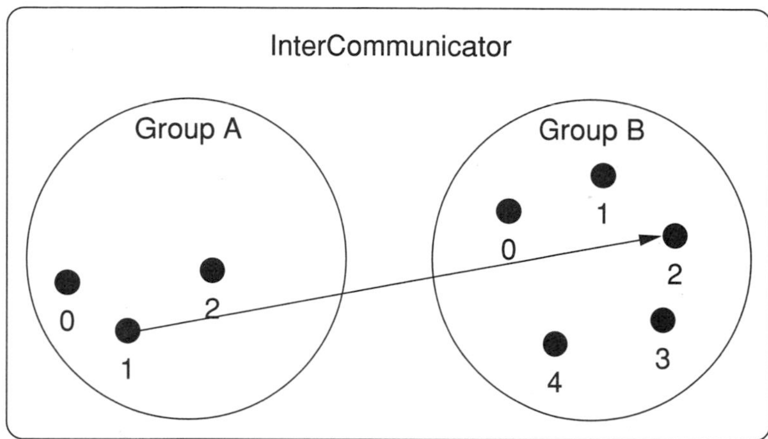

Figure 7.10
Schematic of an MPI intercommunicator. A send from process 1 of one group to process 2 of the other group is shown. From the point of view of the sending process in group A, the local group is group A and the remote group is group B. From the point of view of the receiving process (process 2 in group B), the local group is group B and the remote group is group A. All point-to-point communication in an intercommunicator takes place between the two groups that make up the intercommunicator.

ever, it is possible to turn an intercommunicator into an intracommunicator, with `MPI_Intercomm_merge`. This command provides a means to get an intracommunicator suitable for use with collective operations (as well as point-to-point operations). The operation is also summarized in the three tables just mentioned. MPI-2 did define general collective operations for intercommunicators. These exploit the two-group nature of intercommunicators are different from the MPI-1 intracommunicator collective operations. For example, `MPI_Bcast` on an intercommunicator sends data from one process in one group to *all* processes in the other group.

NXTVAL Revisited. Earlier in this chapter, we defined a client-server computation to provide the NXTVAL counter service. It turns out that using intercommunicators is another way to implement this service, and actually simplifies the coding of some features. Therefore, we've reimplemented the earlier service, as displayed in Figures 7.11, 7.12, and 7.13. While the service provided is equivalent, the bookkeeping of an intercommunicator is simpler, because the remote group of the clients is a server, at known rank 0. As before, the clients get their own "`smaller_comm`" in which to work; unlike the earlier examples, `counter_comm` is an intercommunicator. The only interaction that makes sense is for the server to communicate with

```
int MPI_Comm_test_inter(MPI_Comm comm, int *flag)

int MPI_Comm_remote_size(MPI_Comm comm, int *size)

int MPI_Comm_remote_group(MPI_Comm comm, MPI_Group *group)

int MPI_Intercomm_create(MPI_Comm local_comm, int local_leader,
              MPI_Comm peer_comm, int remote_leader, int tag,
              MPI_Comm *newintercomm)

int MPI_Intercomm_merge(MPI_Comm intercomm, int high,
              MPI_Comm *newintracomm)
```

Table 7.9
C bindings for intercommunicator routines

```
MPI_COMM_TEST_INTER(comm, flag, ierror)
              integer comm, ierror
              logical flag

MPI_COMM_REMOTE_SIZE(comm, size, ierror)
              integer comm, size, ierror

MPI_COMM_REMOTE_GROUP(comm, group, ierror)
              integer comm, group, ierror

MPI_INTERCOMM_CREATE(local_comm, local_leader, peer_comm,
              remote_leader, tag, newintercomm, ierror)
              integer local_comm, local_leader, peer_comm, remote_leader, tag,
                  newintercomm, ierror

MPI_INTERCOMM_MERGE(intercomm, high, intracomm, ierror)
              integer intercomm, intracomm, ierror
              logical high
```

Table 7.10
Fortran bindings for intercommunicator routines

```
#define ICTAG 0
int MPE_Counter_create_ic(MPI_Comm oldcomm, MPI_Comm *smaller_comm,
                          MPI_Comm *counter_comm)
{
    int counter = 0, message, done = 0, myid, numprocs, server;
    int color, remote_leader_rank;
    MPI_Status status;
    MPI_Comm oldcommdup, splitcomm;

    MPI_Comm_dup(oldcomm, &oldcommdup);
    MPI_Comm_size(oldcommdup, &numprocs);
    MPI_Comm_rank(oldcommdup, &myid);
    server = numprocs-1;       /* last proc is server */

    color = (myid == server);  /* split into server and rest */
    MPI_Comm_split(oldcomm, color, myid, &splitcomm);

    /* build intercommunicator using bridge w/ oldcommdup */
    if(!color) { /* I am not the server */
        /* 1) the non-server leader process is chosen to have rank
              "0" in the peer comm. oldcommdup != rank of server
           guaranteed that this leader "0" has rank "0" in both
           oldcommdup and in this splitcomm too, by virtue of
           MPI_Comm_split
           2) server has rank "server" in oldcommdup */

        remote_leader_rank = server; /* server rank, oldcommdup */
        *smaller_comm = splitcomm; /* return new, smaller world */
    }
    else
        remote_leader_rank = 0; /* non-server leader, oldcommdup */

    MPI_Intercomm_create(splitcomm, 0, oldcommdup,
                         remote_leader_rank, ICTAG, counter_comm);
    MPI_Comm_free(&oldcommdup); /* not needed after
                                   Intercomm_create */

    /* rest of code unchanged from before... */
}
```

Figure 7.11
MPE_Counter_create using intercommunicators

```
#define SERVER_RANK 0
int MPE_Counter_nxtval_ic( MPI_Comm counter_comm, int *value )
{
    MPI_Status status;
    /* always request/receive services from
       intercomm (remote) rank=0 */
    MPI_Send(NULL, 0, MPI_INT, SERVER_RANK, REQUEST, counter_comm );
    MPI_Recv(value, 1, MPI_INT, SERVER_RANK, VALUE, counter_comm,
             &status );
    return(0);
}
```

Figure 7.12
MPE_Counter_nxtval using intercommunicators

```
#define SERVER_RANK 0
int MPE_Counter_free_ic( MPI_Comm *smaller_comm,
                         MPI_Comm *counter_comm )
{
    int myid;
    MPI_Comm_rank( *smaller_comm, &myid );
    MPI_Barrier( *smaller_comm );
    if (myid == 0)
        MPI_Send(NULL, 0, MPI_INT, SERVER_RANK, GOAWAY,
                 *counter_comm);

    MPI_Comm_free( counter_comm );
    MPI_Comm_free( smaller_comm );

    return(0);
}
```

Figure 7.13
MPE_Counter_free using intercommunicators

bool MPI::Comm::Is_inter() const
int MPI::Intercomm::Get_remote_size() const
Group MPI::Intercomm::Get_remote_group() const
Intercomm MPI::Intracomm::Create_intercomm(int local_leader, const Comm& peer_comm, int remote_leader, int tag) const
Intracomm MPI::Intercomm::Merge(bool high) const

Table 7.11
C++ bindings for intercommunicator routines

the clients (and the clients with the server) when referring to `counter_comm`. This provides a nice separation from any communication that might have been intended in `old_comm` (which might have well been `MPI_COMM_WORLD`).

This simple example, while introducing the use of intercommunicators, does not demonstrate the convenience that they bring when both groups have, in general, more than one process. In that case, intercommunicators provide a clean way to implement "parallel-client, parallel-server" computations [115].

To give more of a flavor for intercommunicators, we outline two interesting services that could be supported by them: first, peer-oriented intercommunicators to allow separately devised "modules" to be interfaced at a higher level (an abstraction of an atmospheric/ocean model communication); second, a bulletin-board system analogous to the Linda tuple space [21].

Atmospheric and Ocean Intercommunication. A Grand Challenge application that is often discussed is modeling the ocean and atmosphere in a single, comprehensive code. Several groups are developing such codes, or evolving them from their sequential counterparts—often the atmospheric and oceanic codes are developed separately, with the intent to couple them at a higher level later on and to transfer boundary information at the ocean-atmosphere boundary via messages.

Intercommunicators are natural for this situation. The separate codes can both work with intracommunicators, allowing them to be developed and tested separately. The intercommunicator for the ocean will have as its local group the ocean's processes, just as they appear in the intracommunicator used for ocean-only messages. Similarly, the intercommunicator for the atmosphere will have as its local group the atmosphere's processes. The remote group for the ocean will be the atmospheric processes that interface on the ocean, and vice versa. Other strategies are possible too, depending on the details of the communication across the boundary.

For example, assume that the two parts of the application have been written to use a specified communicator comm instead of MPI_COMM_WORLD. We'll name the two parts do_ocean(comm) and do_atmos(comm). There is also a routine, ocean_and_-atmos(intercomm), that communicates data between the ocean and atmosphere models. The main program that sets these up is shown in Figure 7.14.

Note that the result of MPI_Comm_split is a communicator that is either for the ocean routine (if color = OCEAN) or for the atmosphere routine (if color = ATMOS). MPI_Comm_split always returns either a single new communicator (if color is non-negative) or MPI_COMM_NULL.

In *Using MPI-2* [66], we will see how to use the MPI-2 dynamic process features to bring together two separate MPI programs, rather than using this approach of splitting MPI_COMM_WORLD.

Building a Bulletin Board (or Linda Tuple-Space). A group of parallel data servers is another possibility with intercommunicators. The Linda tuple-space model provides a bulletin board of data that can be accessed by name, in the style of a virtual shared memory. In order to get reasonable scalability with this strategy, multiple processes must be involved in the process of serving these requests. Obvious operations are to place a named object into the space, to retrieve its value, or to retrieve its value and remove it. A process that is a client of the bulletin board service would have as its local group itself, or itself and others who are receiving the same class, or priority of service. The remote group for such clients is the set of servers (or subset of servers) that is allowed to post and retrieve information.

A key facet of these requests is that the clients need not know *where* the data is and need not specify where it should be stored. Rather, a request will be made, possibly to a master server, which will then scatter the request. One of the servers will provide the service. The communication isolation of an intercommunicator helps with the possibility that the client receive a response from any of the servers, not just the server that took the client's original request.

7.5 Heterogeneous Computing

Heterogeneous computing refers to using a collection of computers of different types as a parallel computer. In many settings, a powerful parallel computer can be constructed by connecting workstations together. If workstations from several vendors

```
program main
use mpi
integer ocean_or_atmos_comm, intercomm, ocean_comm, atmos_comm
integer nprocs, rank, ierr, color
integer OCEAN, ATMOS
parameter (OCEAN=0,ATMOS=1)

call MPI_INIT( ierr )
call MPI_COMM_SIZE( MPI_COMM_WORLD, nprocs, ierr )
call MPI_COMM_RANK( MPI_COMM_WORLD, rank, ierr )
if (rank .lt. size/2) then
    color = OCEAN
else
    color = ATMOS
endif
call MPI_COMM_SPLIT( MPI_COMM_WORLD, color, rank, &
                     ocean_or_atmos_comm, ierr )
call MPI_INTERCOMM_CREATE( ocean_or_atmos_comm, 0, &
                     MPI_COMM_WORLD, 0, 0, intercomm, ierr )
if (color .eq. OCEAN) then
    ocean_comm = ocean_or_atmos_comm
    call do_ocean( ocean_comm )
else
    atmos_comm = ocean_or_atmos_comm
    call do_atmos( atmos_comm )
endif
call ocean_and_atmos( intercomm )
...
end
```

Figure 7.14
Program to combine two applications using separate communicators

are combined, however, the workstations may not share a common format for data. For example, the order of bytes within an integer may differ. Systems may even use different numbers of bytes to represent integers and floating-point values.

MPI has been designed to operate correctly in this environment. MPI ensures that if data is sent and received with MPI datatypes with the same type signature, then the correct data will be received (if the data is representable on both the sender and the receiver). No special steps need be taken to port an MPI program to a heterogeneous parallel computer. Note also that this flexibility can be provided by an MPI implementation at no cost on a homogeneous system; this helps to encourage the creation of programs that are truly portable between dedicated MPPs and workstation clusters.

From the very beginning, certain implementations of MPI supported heterogeneous computing, including MPICH [63] and LAM [17]. More recently, versions that include support for more advanced security, resource, and scheduling issues have been developed; see [40] for some of the issues and [37] for a description of one such implementation. Another wide-area implementation is [92].

One of the benefits of MPI as a standard is that computer and software vendors can produce optimized versions for specific platforms. But these implementations of MPI could not interoperate with MPI implementations from other vendors. Thus, users who wanted to exploit heterogeneous parallel computing could not use most optimized versions of MPI. To address this issue, a group was formed to define an interoperable MPI standard [24] (IMPI). This effort is nearing its completion as this book is being written, and should allow MPI implementations from several sources to interoperate. Already, several MPI implementors have promised to provide IMPI-compliant versions.

7.6 The MPI Profiling Interface

The MPI Forum recognized that profiling and other forms of performance measurement were vital to the success of MPI. At the same time, it seemed far too early to standardize on any particular performance measurement approach. Common to all approaches, however, is the requirement that something particular happens at the time of every MPI call, for example, to take a time measurement, or write a log record, or perform some more elaborate action.

The MPI Forum decided, therefore, to include in MPI a specification for allowing anyone, even without the source code for the MPI implementation, to intercept calls to the MPI library and perform *arbitrary* actions.

```
int MPI_Bcast( void *buf, int count, MPI_Datatype datatype,
               int root, MPI_Comm comm )
{
    int result;

    MPE_Log_event( S_BCAST_EVENT, Bcast_ncalls, (char *)0 );
    result = PMPI_Bcast( buf, count, datatype, root, comm );
    MPE_Log_event( E_BCAST_EVENT, Bcast_ncalls, (char *)0 );
    return result;
}
```

Figure 7.15
Profiling version of MPI_Bcast

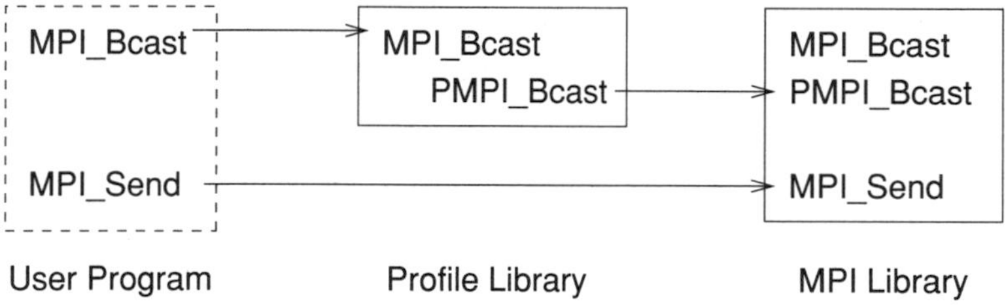

Figure 7.16
Resolution of routines when using profiling library

The trick is to perform this interception of calls at link time rather than compile time. The MPI specification requires that every MPI routine be callable by an alternative name. In particular, every routine of the form `MPI_xxx` must also be callable by the name `PMPI_xxx`. Moreover, users must be able to provide their own versions of `MPI_xxx`.

This scheme allows users to write a limited number of "wrappers" for the MPI routines and perform whatever actions they wish in the wrappers. To call the "real" MPI routine, they address it with its `PMPI_` prefix. For example, suppose that we wished to create logfiles automatically instead of explicitly as we did in Chapter 3. Then we might write our own version of, say, `MPI_Bcast`, as shown in Figure 7.15.

We then need only ensure that our version of `MPI_Bcast` is the one used by the linker to resolve references to it from the application code. Our routine calls `PMPI_Bcast` to do the normal work. The sequence of libraries presented to the linker is as shown in Figure 7.16.

The MPE logging routines require an initialization of their data structures. This can be provided by having a "profile" version of `MPI_Init`, as shown in Figure 7.17.

```
int MPI_Init( int *argc, char ***argv )
{
    int procid, returnVal;
    returnVal = PMPI_Init( argc, argv );
    MPE_Initlog();
    MPI_Comm_rank( MPI_COMM_WORLD, &procid );
    if (procid == 0) {
        MPE_Describe_state( S_SEND_EVENT, E_SEND_EVENT,
                            "Send", "blue:gray3" );
        MPE_Describe_state( S_RECV_EVENT, E_RECV_EVENT,
                            "Recv", "green:light_gray" );
        ...
    }
    return returnVal;
}
```

Figure 7.17
Profiling version of MPI_Init

Similarly, a profiling version of MPI_Finalize can be used to do any termination processing, such as writing out log files or printing statistics accumulated during the individual calls to profiled versions of the MPI routines.

Various profiling libraries are likely to want to enable user control of some of their functions at run time. A simple example is the MPE_Stoplog and MPE_Startlog that we defined in Chapter 3. The problem for the profiling interface is that the types of control are likely to vary widely from one profiling library to another. The solution is to define a single MPI profiling control routine, MPI_Pcontrol, with a variable length argument list. The first argument is assumed to be a level number, used to control the amount or type of profiling that is to occur. The amusing feature about this routine is that it is not defined to do anything. But a profiling library writer can redefine it, just as he redefines other MPI routines. The bindings for MPI_Pcontrol are shown in Tables 7.12, 7.13, and 7.14.

For example, to provide the MPE_Stoplog and MPE_Startlog functions to the automatic MPE logging profiling library, one could do something like the following:

int **MPI_Pcontrol**(const int level, . . .)

Table 7.12
C binding for MPI profiling control

MPI_PCONTROL(level) integer level

Table 7.13
Fortran binding for MPI profiling control. Note that this is one of the few MPI routines whose Fortran binding does *not* include an error return code.

void MPI::Pcontrol(const int level, . . .)

Table 7.14
C++ binding for MPI profiling control

```
int MPI_Pcontrol(const int flag, ...)
{
   if (flag)
       MPE_Startlog();
   else
       MPE_Stoplog();
   return 0;
}
```

The beauty of this arrangement is that the supplier of the profiling library need not provide profiling versions of any routines other than those in which he is interested.

With the MPICH implementation of MPI come three profiling libraries that use the MPI profiling interface, and that will work with any MPI implementation, not just MPICH.

- The first is extremely simple. It simply writes to `stdout` when each MPI routine is entered and exited. This can be helpful in identifying in which MPI routine a program is hanging.
- The second creates MPE logfiles, which can be examined with a variety of tools, such as Jumpshot. This profiling library was used to create the logfile data used to examine communication alternatives in Chapter 4.
- The third profiling library implements a simple form of real-time program animation, using the MPE graphics library to show process states and message traffic

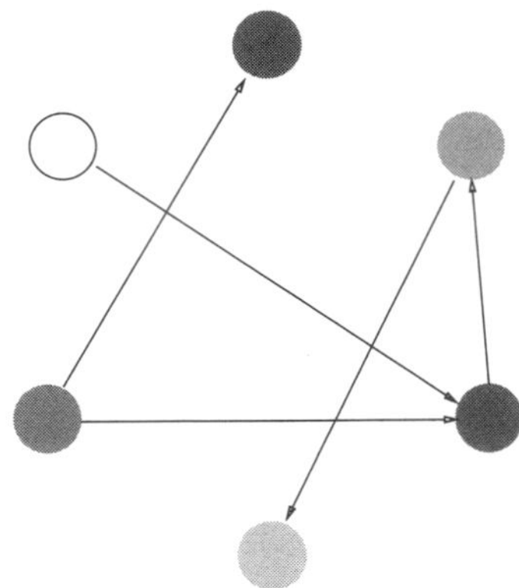

Figure 7.18
Program animation created with MPI profiling interface

as it happens. A single frame looks roughly like Figure 7.18.

Once the style of profiling has been chosen, of course, most of what goes into the profiled version of each routine is the same. It is not difficult to develop a meta-profiling mechanism that automates the wrapping of all, or a specific subset, of the MPI routines at once, provided that the action taken for each routine is the same. In fact, such a tool is provided with the MPICH implementation (see "Automatic generation of profiling libraries" in [58]).

The profiling interface can also be used to answer questions about an application without changing the source code of the application. We will illustrate this with two examples.

7.6.1 Finding Buffering Problems

The routine `MPI_Send` is often implemented with some internal buffering, allowing some programs that are formally unsafe (because they depend on buffering) to run in practice. Depending on such buffering is poor practice, however. Is there any easy way to check to see if a program depends on buffering in `MPI_Send`?

This is a very hard problem to answer in general, but the following approaches will often reveal codes that depend on buffering. Our first solution is very simple. We will write our own version of `MPI_Send` that provides no buffering:

```
subroutine MPI_SEND( buf, count, datatype, dest, &
                     tag, comm, ierr )
include 'mpif.h'
```

int **MPI_Issend**(void* buf, int count, MPI_Datatype datatype, int dest,int tag, MPI_Comm comm, MPI_Request *request)

Table 7.15
C binding for the nonblocking synchronous send

MPI_ISSEND(buf, count, datatype, dest, tag, comm, request, ierror) <type> buf(*) integer count, datatype, dest, tag, comm, request, ierror

Table 7.16
Fortran binding for the nonblocking synchronous send

```
integer buf(*), count, datatype, dest, tag, comm, ierr
call PMPI_SSEND( buf, count, datatype, dest, tag, comm, ierr )
end
```

With this version of `MPI_Send`, many programs that depend on `MPI_Send` providing buffering will deadlock; specifically, the program will enter this routine but never complete because the matching receive, required to start before `MPI_Ssend` and `PMPI_Ssend` can complete, is never started. If a parallel debugger is available, it can be used to find out where the program has stopped.

Note that you cannot just use `use mpi` in the profiling replacement for `include 'mpif.h'` because the Fortran compiler will not allow you to redefine `MPI_SEND` in this way.

The approach of using `MPI_Ssend` is a little awkward because it depends on having the program deadlock and then using a parallel debugger. Can we write a version of `MPI_Send` that will detect that there is a problem? We can, if we require that any `MPI_Send` complete within a specific length of time. For example, in many scientific applications, no send operation should take more than a few seconds. Let us assume that any `MPI_Ssend` that takes more than ten seconds indicates a problem. Hence, what we need is a send operation that is nonblocking (so that we can start it and then time how long it takes, waiting no more than ten seconds) and that cannot complete until the matching receive begins. In other words, we want to use the nonblocking synchronous send `MPI_Issend`. The bindings for this routine are the same as for the other nonblocking sends, are shown in Tables 7.15, 7.16, and 7.17.

The code is shown in Figure 7.19. This code busy-waits for the `PMPI_Issend` to complete by calling `PMPI_Test` repeatedly. More refined versions might poll `PMPI_-`

Request MPI::Comm::Issend(const void* buf, int count, const Datatype& datatype, int dest, int tag) const

Table 7.17
C++ binding for the nonblocking synchronous send

`Test` for a short period of time, then sleep (using the Unix `sleep` call) for a second or two, then test again, and so on, until ten seconds elapse. Another version could use `MPI_Pcontrol` to allow the user to control the length of time delay rather than fixing the time limit at ten seconds.

7.6.2 Finding Load Imbalances

Consider an application that uses `MPI_Allreduce` and where profiling results, using, for example, the MPE profiling library, indicate that `MPI_Allreduce` is very slow, hurting parallel performance. In many cases, the problem is not in the implementation of `MPI_Allreduce`; rather, the problem is in a load imbalance in the application. Because `MPI_Allreduce` is synchronizing (since no process can complete this operation before all processes have contributed their values), any load imbalance shows up in the execution time of `MPI_Allreduce`. We can estimate the size of the load imbalance by measuring the time that an `MPI_Barrier` takes right before the `MPI_Allreduce`. Figure 7.20 shows one simple implementation; it also shows how to use `MPI_Finalize` to report final statistics.

7.6.3 The Mechanics of Using the Profiling Interface

The MPI standard does not specify how to compile or link programs with MPI (other than specifying that the header files `mpi.h`, `mpif.h`, and, for Fortran 90, an `mpi` module, must exist). Similarly, the names of the MPI library and the name of any separate library containing the profiling versions of the MPI routines are not specified.

In some system, both the `MPI` and `PMPI` routines will be in a single library. This is the simplest case. In other cases, the `PMPI` routines will be in a separate library. For example, let us assume that the `MPI` routines are in `libmpi` and the `PMPI` versions are in `libpmpi`. Then a link line for a program in `myprog.o` with a profiling library `libprof` might look like

```
cc -o myprog myprog.o -lprof -lmpi -lpmpi
```

Note that the profiling library *follows* the regular (`-lmpi`) library. In some cases, it may be necessary to repeat the library names. Using Fortran or C++ may

```
      subroutine MPI_SEND( buf, count, datatype, dest, &
                           tag, comm, ierr )
      include 'mpif.h'
      integer buf(*), count, datatype, dest, tag, comm, ierr
      integer request, status(MPI_STATUS_SIZE)
      logical flag
      double precision tstart

      tstart = MPI_WTIME()
      call PMPI_ISSEND( buf, count, datatype, dest, tag, comm, &
                        request, ierr )
      ! wait until either ten seconds have passed or
      ! the issend completes.
   10 continue
      call PMPI_TEST( request, flag, status, ierr )
      if (.not. flag .and. MPI_WTIME() - tstart .lt. 10.0) goto 10
      ! Signal error if we timed out.
      if (.not. flag) then
          print *, 'MPI_SEND call has hung!'
          call PMPI_ABORT( comm, ierr )
      endif
      end
```

Figure 7.19
Version of MPI_Send that uses MPI_Issend to detect unsafe programs

also require special libraries. You should check the documentation for your MPI implementation; do not assume that `cc ... -lmpi -lpmpi` is all that you need to do.

7.7 Error Handling

Error handling and error recovery are important and difficult issues. Errors can be the result of user mistakes (e.g., invalid arguments), hardware errors (e.g., power supply failure), resource exhaustion (e.g., no more memory), or bugs in the base software. MPI provides some facilities for handling error reporting, particularly by libraries.

```
static double t_barrier = 0, t_allreduce = 0;
int MPI_Allreduce(void* sendbuf, void* recvbuf, int count,
              MPI_Datatype datatype, MPI_Op op, MPI_Comm comm)
{
    double t1, t2, t3;
    t1 = MPI_Wtime();
    MPI_Barrier( comm );
    t2 = MPI_Wtime();
    PMPI_Allreduce(sendbuf, recvbuf, count, datatype, op, comm);
    t3 = MPI_Wtime();
    t_barrier += (t2 - t1);
    t_allreduce += (t3 - t2);
    if (t3 - t2 < t2 - t1) {
        int myrank;
        MPI_Comm_rank( comm, &myrank );
        printf("Barrier slower than Allreduce on %d\n", myrank);
    }
    return MPI_SUCCESS;
}
int MPI_Finalize()
{
    printf("Barrier time in Allreduce %f; Allreduce time %f\n",
            t_barrier, t_allreduce);
    return PMPI_Finalize();
}
```

Figure 7.20
C version of MPI_Allreduce that uses MPI_Barrier to estimate the amount of load imbalance

7.7.1 Error Handlers

MPI associates an error handler with each communicator. When an error is detected, MPI calls the error handler associated with the communicator being used; if there is no communicator, MPI_COMM_WORLD is used. When MPI_Init is called, the initial (default) error handler is one that causes the program to abort (i.e., all processes exit). Most MPI implementations will print an error message as well.

Instead of aborting on an error, MPI can return an error code. In Fortran, this is the ierror argument in most of the MPI routines. In C, this is the return value of the MPI function. In C++, following C++ practice, an exception is thrown rather than returning an error code. The only exceptions are MPI_Wtime and MPI_Wtick. MPI provides two predefined error handlers: MPI_ERRORS_ARE_-FATAL (the default) and MPI_ERRORS_RETURN. MPI_ERRORS_RETURN causes the MPI routines to return an error value instead of aborting. In C++, the default error handler is MPI::ERRORS_THROW_EXCEPTIONS; this causes an MPI::Exception to be thrown. If there is no code to catch the exception, this has the same effect as MPI_ERRORS_ARE_FATAL. The routine MPI_Errhandler_set is used to change the error handler.

The error codes returned, with the exception of MPI_SUCCESS, are defined by each MPI implementation. This approach allows an MPI implementation to encode additional data into the error code. MPI also specifies a small set of error *classes*: integers that divide the errors codes into a small number of categories. For example, for an error class such as MPI_ERR_TAG, the error code could encode information on what was wrong with the tag value (e.g., too big? too small?) and the MPI routine that detected the error. The MPI-1 error classes are shown in Table 7.18. MPI-2 adds error classes for the new functions in MPI-2; these are covered in *Using MPI-2* [66].

The difference between MPI_ERR_UNKNOWN and MPI_ERR_OTHER is that MPI_-Error_string can return useful information about MPI_ERR_OTHER. The error class MPI_ERR_UNKNOWN can be used by an MPI implementation for unexpected situations, such as an error return from code that the MPI implementation itself uses.

The two error classes MPI_ERR_IN_STATUS and MPI_ERR_PENDING are special cases. MPI-1 has four routines that complete multiple requests and return an array of statuses; these are MPI_Waitsome, MPI_Waitall, MPI_Testsome, and MPI_-Testall. For these four functions, errors could occur for any subset of the requests. In this case, there is no single error code to return from the routine. In this case, the error value returned is MPI_ERR_IN_STATUS. This indicates that the actual error codes are in the array of statuses, in the MPI_ERROR element (status.MPI_ERROR in C; status(MPI_ERROR) in Fortran). To understand MPI_ERR_PENDING, consider the case of MPI_Waitall. For each request that was passed to MPI_Waitall, there are three possibilities. First, the request completed successfully. In this case, the MPI_ERROR field of the corresponding status element is set to MPI_SUCCESS. Second, the request failed because of an error; in that case, the MPI_ERROR field of the corresponding status element is set to the MPI error code that indicates the reason the request failed. The third case is that the request has neither completed nor failed. In this case, the MPI_ERROR field is set to MPI_ERR_PENDING to indicate that the request is still pending without error.

To convert an error code into a error class, use MPI_Error_class. As an example, consider the code in Figure 7.21.

MPI_SUCCESS	No error
MPI_ERR_BUFFER	Invalid buffer pointer
MPI_ERR_COUNT	Invalid count argument
MPI_ERR_TYPE	Invalid datatype argument
MPI_ERR_TAG	Invalid tag argument
MPI_ERR_COMM	Invalid communicator
MPI_ERR_RANK	Invalid rank
MPI_ERR_REQUEST	Invalid request (handle)
MPI_ERR_ROOT	Invalid root
MPI_ERR_GROUP	Invalid group
MPI_ERR_OP	Invalid operation
MPI_ERR_TOPOLOGY	Invalid topology
MPI_ERR_DIMS	Invalid dimension argument
MPI_ERR_ARG	Invalid argument of some other kind
MPI_ERR_UNKNOWN	Unknown error
MPI_ERR_TRUNCATE	Message truncated on receive
MPI_ERR_OTHER	Known error not in this list
MPI_ERR_INTERN	Internal MPI error
MPI_ERR_IN_STATUS	Look in the status array for the error
MPI_ERR_PENDING	Operation not complete (see text)
MPI_ERR_LASTCODE	Last standard error code (not class)

Table 7.18
Error classes defined by MPI-1

```
/* Install a new error handler */
MPI_Errhandler_set( MPI_COMM_WORLD, MPI_ERRORS_RETURN );
/* Send a message to an invalid destination */
dest = -1;
errcode = MPI_Send( ..., dest, ... );
if (errcode != MPI_SUCCESS) {
    MPI_Error_class( errcode, &errclass );
    if (errclass == MPI_ERR_RANK) {
        puts( "Invalid rank (%d) in call to MPI_Send", dest );
    }
}
```

Figure 7.21
Code to check the error class of an error code returned by an MPI routine. Note that the MPI Standard does not specify which error class a particular error returns; other possibilities for this error include MPI_ERR_ARG.

All MPI implementations provide a way to translate an MPI error code or class) into a string. The routine MPI_Error_string takes an error code or class and a user-provided string buffer and returns a description of the error in the string, along with the length of the text in the string. The string buffer must be MPI_-MAX_ERROR_STRING in size.

For example, instead of using MPI_Error_class in the example above, we could use

```
...
if (errcode != MPI_SUCCESS) {
    MPI_Error_class( errcode, &errclass );
    if (errclass == MPI_ERR_RANK) {
        char buffer[MPI_MAX_ERROR_STRING];
        int  resultlen;
        MPI_Error_string( errcode, buffer, &resultlen );
        puts( buffer );
    }
}
```

The value of MPI_MAX_ERROR_STRING in C is one greater than the value of MPI_-MAX_ERROR_STRING in Fortran to allow for the string terminator in C. That is, the same maximum number of characters are allowed in both C and Fotran; however, C requires a declaration of char buf[11] to hold ten characters while Fortran requires character*10 buf. Fortran users should also note that character*10 buf and character buf(10) are very different declarations. Error strings in Fortran must be declared as

```
character*(MPI_MAX_ERROR_STRING) buf
```

7.7.2 An Example of Error Handling

Figure 7.22 shows code that reports on any errors that occur during the execution of one of the four MPI routines that can complete multiple requests. This code assumes that the error handler has been set to be MPI_ERRORS_RETURN.

The C++ version of this code, using an exception handler, is shown in Figure 7.23.

The nice part of the C++ exception mechanism is that the code is not cluttered with error-handling code. In addition, the catch part of the exception handling could be in any routine that is above the routine throwing the exception in the call stack. Figure 7.23 also shows the Get_error_string method of an

```
MPI_Request     req_array[100];
MPI_Status      status_array[100];
char            msg[MPI_MAX_ERROR_STRING];
...
err = MPI_Waitall( n, req_array, status_array );
if (err == MPI_ERR_IN_STATUS) {
    for (i=0; i<n; i++) {
        switch (status_array[i].MPI_ERROR) {
        case MPI_SUCCESS:     /* request has completed */
        break;
        case MPI_ERR_PENDING: /* request hasn't completed */
        break;
        default:              /* error on this request */
        MPI_Error_string( status_array[i].MPI_ERROR, msg,
                          &msglen );
        printf( "Error in request %d: %s\n", i, msg );
        }
    }
}
```

Figure 7.22
Handling error returns from MPI_Waitany

MPI::Exception, which may be used instead of the MPI::Get_error_string routine.

This code does illustrate a drawback of the C++ bindings. Note the use of MPI_-MAX_ERROR_STRING instead of MPI::MAX_ERROR_STRING, and MPI_ERR_IN_STATUS instead of MPI::ERR_IN_STATUS. The C++ versions of these values are not compile-time constants suitable for use in declearations or switch statements. In this case, we can use the C values instead.

7.7.3 User-Defined Error Handlers

MPI also allows the user to define additional error handlers.

A user-defined error handler has the form

```
void user_function( MPI_Comm *comm, int *error_code, ... )
```

The first argument is the communicator of the operation; the second is the error code. Pointers are used so that Fortran programmers may write MPI error handlers without resorting to C. Additional arguments are available to C programmers

```
MPI::Request    req_array[100];
MPI::Status     status_array[100];
...
try {
    MPI::REQUEST_NULL.Waitall( n, req_array, status_array );
}
catch (MPI::Exception e) {
    char msg[MPI_MAX_ERROR_STRING];
    int  resultlen;
    int  err = e.Get_error_code();

    if (err == MPI::ERR_IN_STATUS) {
        for (i=0; i<n; i++) {
            switch (status_array[i].Get_error()) {
              case MPI_SUCCESS:     /* request has completed */
                break;
              case MPI_ERR_PENDING: /* request not completed */
                break;
              default:              /* error on this request */
                MPI::Get_error_string( status_array[i].Get_error(),
                                       msg, resultlen );
                cout <<"Error in request "<< i <<": "<< msg <<"\n";
            }
        }
    }
    else {
        cout << "Error " << e.Get_error_string() << "\n";
    }
}
```

Figure 7.23
Handling error returns from MPI_Waitany

through a "stdargs" interface; their meaning is defined by each MPI implementation.

Often, it is desirable to temporarily replace one error handler with another one. For example, in Fortran we can use

```
integer old_handler, new_handler
call MPI_Errhandler_get( comm, old_handler, ierr )
call MPI_Errhandler_set( comm, new_handler, ierr )
<.... code .... >
call MPI_Errhandler_set( comm, old_handler, ierr )
call MPI_Errhandler_free( old_handler, ierr )
```

For Fortran users to be able to do this, the error handler must be an object that can be assigned to a variable. Since Fortran has no variable type that can be assigned the pointer to a function, an MPI error handler is an opaque object that is created and freed much like an `MPI_Request`. The routine `MPI_Errhandler_create` creates an MPI error handler that Fortran and C users can assign to a variable.

Once an error handler is created, it can be attached to a communicator with `MPI_Errhandler_set`. This is done so that a library that uses its own communicator can have its own error handler. The error handler for a communicator can be retrieved with `MPI_Errhandler_get` and freed with `MPI_Errhandler_free`.

The last line of this example calls `MPI_Errhandler_free` to free the error handler returned by `MPI_Errhandler_get`. In general, most MPI routines that return an MPI object, such as the group associated with a communicator (`MPI_Comm_group` and `MPI_Comm_remote_group`), return (semantically[2]) a *copy* of the object; this copy must be freed by the user when it is no longer needed. The MPI standard, as written, is unclear about whether the error handler returned by `MPI_Errhandler_get` should be freed; this matter is currently under discussion by the MPI Forum. Many implementations currently require that the error handler acquired by `MPI_Errhandler_get` be freed with `MPI_Errhandler_free`, and this is likely to be the outcome of the MPI Forum discussions. You can check by consulting the errata pages at the MPI Forum Web site, `http://www.mpi-forum.org`.

Error handlers are inherited from the parent communicator. That is, when a new communicator is created with a function such as `MPI_Comm_dup`, the error handler in the new communicator is set to be the same one as the input communicator. Thus, to change the "global" error handler, one might change the error handler

[2]By this we mean that the object behaves as if it is a copy. An implementation can implement this operation in many ways; many implementations use a reference count mechanism to avoid making an actual copy.

associated with MPI_COMM_WORLD before any other communicators are created (for example, right after the MPI_Init call).

Users should be careful with error handlers. The MPI standard does not require that a program that encounters an error be continuable; that is, once an error has occurred, it may not be possible for the program to continue to use MPI. This is a common position for standards: a standard does not specify the behavior of erroneous programs.

In the most general case, where nothing is known about the ability of the MPI implementation to continue from errors, the user should terminate the program (see the next section). User-defined error handlers can be used to ensure that program termination proceeds in an orderly way and that important information is preserved. For example, a user-defined error handler might flush all file output buffers and write out some information on the cause of the error.

However, most MPI implementations will allow a program to continue and operate correctly after an error is encountered. In fact, many of the error classes represent cases where error recovery is particularly easy. These classes include all of the "invalid xxx" errors: MPI_ERR_BUFFER, MPI_ERR_COUNT, MPI_ERR_TYPE, ..., MPI_ERR_ARG. Most MPI implementations will also continue after MPI_ERR_TRUNCATE, which is usually generated when the specified buffer size in a receive operation is too small to hold the message received (the usual behavior is to discard either the entire message or the part that does not fit in the buffer). The error classes MPI_ERR_UNKNOWN and MPI_ERR_INTERN are usually *not* continuable since they indicate a problem within the MPI implementation itself. The other error class, MPI_ERR_OTHER, may or may not be continuable, depending on the particular MPI implementation.

7.7.4 Terminating MPI Programs

To force an MPI program to exit, MPI provides the function MPI_Abort. This function has two arguments: the communicator of tasks to abort, and the error code that should, where possible, be returned to the calling environment (for example, by exit(code) or stop code). This function should only be used for unusal termination, for example, in the case of an error.

An implementation is always free to abort all processes; that is, it can act as if the communicator argument was MPI_COMM_WORLD. The presence of the communicator argument is intended for compatibility with future extensions of MPI that may include dynamic process management.

```
int MPI_Abort(MPI_Comm comm, int errorcode)

int MPI_Errhandler_create(MPI_Handler_function *function,
                          MPI_Errhandler *errhandler)

int MPI_Errhandler_set(MPI_Comm comm, MPI_Errhandler errhandler)

int MPI_Errhandler_get(MPI_Comm comm, MPI_Errhandler *errhandler)

int MPI_Errhandler_free(MPI_Errhandler *errhandler)

int MPI_Error_string(int errorcode, char *string, int *resultlen)

int MPI_Error_class(int errorcode, int *errorclass)

typedef void MPI_Handler_function(MPI_Comm *, int *, ...)
```

Table 7.19
C bindings for error handling and the `typedef` for the user-provided error handling function

```
MPI_ABORT(comm, errorcode, ierror)
          integer comm, errorcode, ierror

MPI_ERRHANDLER_CREATE(function, handler, ierror)
          external function
          integer errhandler, ierror

MPI_ERRHANDLER_SET(comm, errhandler, ierror)
          integer comm, errhandler, ierror

MPI_ERRHANDLER_GET(comm, errhandler, ierror)
          integer comm, errhandler, ierror

MPI_ERRHANDLER_FREE(errhandler, ierror)
          integer errhandler, ierror

MPI_ERROR_STRING(errorcode, string, resultlen, ierror)
          integer errorcode, resultlen, ierror
          character*(*) string

MPI_ERROR_CLASS(errorcode, errorclass, ierror)
          integer errorcode, errorclass, ierror
```

Table 7.20
Fortran bindings for error handling

```
void MPI::Comm::Abort(int errorcode)

void MPI::Errhandler::Init(const Handler_function* function)

void MPI::Comm::Set_errhandler(const Errhandler& errhandler)

Errhandler MPI::Comm::Get_errhandler() const

void MPI::Errhandler::Free()

void MPI::Get_error_string(int errorcode, char* name, int& resultlen)

int MPI::Get_error_class(int errorcode)
```

Table 7.21
C++ bindings for error handling

```
int MPI_Comm_create_errhandler(MPI_Comm_errhandler_fn *function,
                MPI_Errhandler *errhandler)

int MPI_Comm_set_errhandler(MPI_Comm comm, MPI_Errhandler errhandler)

int MPI_Comm_get_errhandler(MPI_Comm comm, MPI_Errhandler *errhandler)
```

Table 7.22
C bindings for MPI-2 versions of routines to manage error handlers on communicators

7.7.5 MPI-2 Functions for Error Handling

In MPI-2, two new objects were introduced that are similar to communicators in the sense that they provide a container for operations among a group of processes. These two new objects are `MPI_Win` for remote memory access and `MPI_File` for parallel I/O. Each of these can has its own error handler and its own set of routines for managing its error handlers. These routines contain the name `Win` or `File`; for example, `MPI_Win_set_errhandler`. For consistency, MPI-2 provides routines for managing error handlers on communicators that are named similarly; these are shown in Tables 7.22, 7.23, and 7.24. These routines should be used instead of the MPI-1 versions in programs that use MPI-2. The MPI-1 functions remain in MPI-2 for backward compatibility.

MPI_COMM_CREATE_ERRHANDLER(function, errhandler, ierror) external function integer errhandler, ierror
MPI_COMM_SET_ERRHANDLER(comm, errhandler, ierror) integer comm, errhandler, ierror
MPI_COMM_GET_ERRHANDLER(comm, errhandler, ierror) integer comm, errhandler, ierror

Table 7.23
Fortran bindings for MPI-2 versions of routines to manage error handlers on communicators

Errhandler MPI::Comm::Create_errhandler(MPI::Comm::Errhandler_fn* function)
void MPI::Comm::Set_errhandler(const MPI::Errhandler& errhandler)
Errhandler MPI::Comm::Get_errhandler() const

Table 7.24
C++ bindings for MPI-2 versions of routines to manage error handlers on communicators

7.8 The MPI Environment

In writing portable programs, it is often necessary to determine some implementation limits. For example, even a sequential program may need to know how many open files it can have. In many cases, this information is available only from the documentation of the system; this documentation may be incorrect or out of date. MPI provides access to some of the implementation limits through predefined attribute keys defined for the communicator `MPI_COMM_WORLD` (see Section 6.2 for information about attribute keys).

Currently, there are only four predefined attribute keys:

`MPI_TAG_UB` Largest message tag value (smallest is zero).

`MPI_HOST` Rank in `MPI_COMM_WORLD` of host process, if any.

`MPI_IO` Which process can do I/O (see below).

`MPI_WTIME_IS_GLOBAL` If true, the values returned by `MPI_Wtime` are synchronized across all processes in `MPI_COMM_WORLD` (that is, `MPI_Wtime` returns the value of a gloabl clock).

In some parallel processing systems, there is a distinguished process called the *host*. The value of MPI_HOST is the rank of this process in MPI_COMM_WORLD. If there is no host process, the value MPI_PROC_NULL is used.

MPI makes some requirements for how system operations are provided *if* they are provided. For example, any system operation, whether it be (in C) a malloc or a printf or (in Fortran) an open or write, must operate independently of other processes. This means that all I/O is independent *if it can be performed at all*. To determine whether I/O is available, one uses the attribute key MPI_IO. The value associated with this key can be MPI_ANY_SOURCE, indicating that any and all processes can perform I/O; MPI_PROC_NULL, indicating that no process can perform I/O; or a rank of a process that can perform I/O.

The definition of "perform I/O" is that any of the language-specified I/O operations are allowed. For example, for C users, this means that printf and scanf are supported. For Fortran, this means that read (including read *, ...) and print are supported. If a system cannot provide the full functionality of the language-specified I/O, it is required to return MPI_PROC_NULL as the value of the key MPI_IO. (This does not mean that the system cannot provide any I/O, just that it must return MPI_PROC_NULL if it cannot provide all of the language-specified I/O. On some systems, providing access to standard input is not possible; these systems must return MPI_PROC_NULL.)

When MPI was first specified, some parallel computers did not have good facilities for providing I/O to all MPI processes, or could provide only a subset of the language-specified I/O. Some MPI implementations also chose not to provide I/O from every process. While there are still cases where I/O is not available from each process, these are now much less common. Many MPI applications assume that I/O is available from every process and operate on a wide variety of platforms.

Note that because the key values are defined by MPI, future versions of MPI can define additional key values. In fact, MPI_WTIME_IS_GLOBAL is an example; this key value was added in MPI 1.1. In addition, each MPI implementation may define key values that refer to a particular implementation. As a hypothetical example, an implementation might provide MPIV_REQUESTS (MPIV for MPI vendor) that would give the number of MPI_Requests that can be active at any time. To data, few such vendor-specific key values have been implemented, although some research projects are investigating the use of key values to provide run-time control of parameters within a particular MPI implementation to an application.

int **MPI_Get_processor_name**(char *name, int *resultlen)

int **MPI_Initialized**(int *flag)

Table 7.25
C bindings for inquiry functions

7.8.1 Processor Name

It is often helpful to be able to identify the processor on which a process is running. Having the program provide the names of the processors on which the program has run is much more reliable than having the user remember to do so. In MPI, the routine `MPI_Get_processor_name` performs this task. It also returns the length of the string. The buffer provided to this routine should be at least `MPI_MAX_PROCESSOR_NAME` characters long. Note that some systems, such as symmetric multiprocessors (SMPs), may migrate a process from one processor to another during the course of a run. On these systems, an MPI implementation may choose to indicate the processor that was running the process at the time of the call. Other implementations may simply return the name of the multiprocessor without indicating which processor within the SMP running the process at the time of the call.[3]

7.8.2 Is MPI Initialized?

We pointed out in Chapter 3 that `MPI_Init` had to be called before any other MPI routine and that it could be called at most once by each process. These requirements can cause problems for modules that wish to use MPI and are prepared to call `MPI_Init` if necessary. To solve this problem, MPI has one routine that can always be called, even if `MPI_Init` has not been called. The routine, `MPI_Initialized`, returns a flag whose value is true if `MPI_Init` has been called and false otherwise. The value is true even in `MPI_Finalize` has been called. MPI-2 introduces `MPI_Finalized` to discover whether `MPI_Finalize` has been called.

[3]This interpretation of the Standard meets the letter but not the spirit of the Standard, which was intended to allow users to gather enough information about the execution environment to reproduce a computational experiment. On SMPs that are not perfectly symmetrical in hardware (for example, have non-uniform memory access (NUMA)), returning the name of the SMP without indicating the specific processor used is not sufficient.

MPI_GET_PROCESSOR_NAME(name, resultlen, ierror)
character*(MPI_MAX_PROCESSOR_NAME) name
integer resultlen, ierror
MPI_INITIALIZED(flag, ierror)
logical flag
integer ierror

Table 7.26
Fortran bindings for inquiry functions

void MPI::Get_processor_name(char* name, int& resultlen)
bool MPI::Is_initialized()

Table 7.27
C++ bindings for inquiry functions

7.9 Determining the Version of MPI

MPI is a standard, which means that it is documented and changes very slowly. It has changed, however. There are three versions of MPI-1: MPI-1.0, MPI-1.1, and MPI-1.2. MPI-1.0 was the original version of MPI. MPI-1.1 was primarily a "bug fix" version, fixing obvious errors in the document. It also removed the function `MPI_Type_count`, because the standard was vague about its meaning and implementations had chosen different interpretations (and no applications were using it). MPI-1.1 also introduced the `MPI_ERR_IN_STATUS` and `MPI_ERR_PENDING` error classes for multiple completions. MPI-1.2 contained a few additional clarifications and one new function: `MPI_Get_version`. This function returns the version of MPI as two integers: the version and the subversion. For MPI-1.2, the version is one and the subversion is two. The bindings of this function are shown in Tables 7.28, 7.29, and 7.30.

In addition to this new function, constants are also defined containing the version and subversion numbers. For MPI-1.2, these are

```
#define MPI_VERSION    1
#define MPI_SUBVERSION 2
```

in C and C++ and

```
INTEGER MPI_VERSION, MPI_SUBVERSION
```

int **MPI_Get_version**(int *version, int *subversion)

Table 7.28
C routine to return the version of MPI

MPI_GET_VERSION(version, subversion, ierror) integer version, subversion, ierror

Table 7.29
Fortran routine to return the version of MPI

void MPI::Get_version(int& version, int& subversion);

Table 7.30
C++ routine to return the version of MPI

```
PARAMETER (MPI_VERSION    = 1)
PARAMETER (MPI_SUBVERSION = 2)
```

in Fortran.

Why are there both constants and functions? In creating an MPI application, a programmer needs both compile-time information, provided by the 'mpi.h' and 'mpif.h' files or the MPI module (in Fortran), and link-time information, provided by the library containing the MPI implementation. In a perfect world, these would always be consistent. By providing both constants and a function, careful programmers can test that the version of MPI that they compiled for (and included header files for) matches the one that they linked with.

C and C++ users can also use the constant forms, because they are preprocessor constants, to arrange for conditional compilation. For example, the code

```
#if MPI_VERSION < 2
  /* Do I/O by sending data to root process with MPI_Gatherv */
  ...
#else
  /* We can use MPI-2 parallel I/O */
  ...
#endif
```

allows an application to select more powerful and efficient MPI-2 features when MPI-2 is available, and to function using MPI-1 when MPI-2 isn't available.

Note that MPI version 2.0 is primarily a set of entirely new functions, but also impacts MPI-1 programs, because MPI 1.0 deprecates certain MPI-1 functions and encourages new functions in their place, which will not be available in an implementation with version 1.x. Version 2.0 of MPI also introduces the C++ bindings for the MPI-1 functions and such variations on the MPI-1 functions as the use of `NULL` for the arguments to `MPI_Init`.

7.10 Other Functions in MPI

We have tried to introudce as many of the MPI functions as possible by having them appear in examples. This means that some MPI functions have not appeared at all. The routines that we have not discussed fall into seven categories:

- Routines to create new groups from an existing group or groups: `MPI_Group_incl`, `MPI_Group_range_incl`, `MPI_Group_range_excl`, `MPI_Group_union`, `MPI_Group_intersection`, and `MPI_Group_difference`. These are rarely needed; normally, `MPI_Comm_split` should be used to create new communicators. Groups are used in MPI-2 scalable remote memory synchronization.
- Routines to get information about a group: `MPI_Group_compare`, `MPI_Group_size`, `MPI_Group_rank`, and `MPI_Group_translate_ranks`. The one routine here that sees some use is `MPI_Group_translate_ranks`. This can be used to determine the rank in `MPI_COMM_WORLD` that corresponds to a particular rank in another communicator.
- Routine to determine the type of virtual topology: `MPI_Topo_test`.
- Routines to manipulate Cartesian virtual topologies: `MPI_Cartdim_get`, `MPI_Cart_rank`, and `MPI_Cart_map`.
- Routines to manipulate graph virtual topologies: `MPI_Graph_create`, `MPI_Graphdims_get`, `MPI_Graph_neighbors_count`, `MPI_Graph_neighbors`, and `MPI_Graph_map`.
- Routines to cancel a point-to-point operation: `MPI_Cancel` and `MPI_Test_cancelled`.
- Miscellaneous point-to-point routines: `MPI_Bsend_init`, `MPI_Ibsend`, `MPI_Rsend_init`, `MPI_Irsend`, `MPI_Ssend_init`, `MPI_Sendrecv_replace`, `MPI_Get_elements`, and `MPI_Waitsome`.

Although these routines did not find a natural place in our book, they may be just what you need. For example, the routines for manipulating virtual topologies may provide exactly the operations needed for a PDE application on a complicated mesh. We encourage you to consider these routines when developing an application.

7.11 Application: Computational Fluid Dynamics

The following application illustrates the usefulness of user-defined virtual topologies and collective communication over these virtual topologies, all within a computational fluid dynamics code. It illustrates the use of operations on communicators to define topologies not provided directly by MPI. The computation of flow regimes over complex configurations involves the numerical solution of a system of coupled nonlinear partial differential equations known as the Navier-Stokes equations. Researchers in the CFD lab at the Mississippi State University NSF Engineering Research Center for Computational Field Simulation have developed an implicit, finite-volume code (known as UNCLE) for solving the unsteady three-dimensional incompressible Euler and Navier-Stokes equations using an artificial compressibility approach [123, 122, 128]. The flow solver can be used in a variety of applications ranging from maneuvering underwater vehicles to centrifugal compressors.

This code uses dynamic multiblock grids with relative motion in order to account for complex moving geometries. Key elements of the solution method include high-resolution, flux-based, upwind finite-volume approximations in time-varying transformed coordinates and a multiple-pass solution algorithm based on discretized Newton relaxation [128]. The equations in the fully coupled unsteady form are solved by using third-order spatial differencing for both steady and unsteady flows and second-order time differencing for unsteady flows. Relaxation at each time step is carried out by using a simple symmetric Gauss-Seidel sweeps. Turbulent flows are simulated by using the Baldwin-Lomax turbulence model.

Large memory requirements and large run times severely restrict the size and complexity of the problems that can be handled using the sequential version of the code. Therefore, the need was identified for a scalable portable parallel version that could take advantage of existing and emerging parallel platforms. The message-passing interface required for the parallel implementation had to support collective operations within user-defined groups as well as provide safe communication contexts for overlapping sets of collective operations (we will see an example of overlapping communicators later in this section).

7.11.1 Parallel Formulation

The parallel formulation employs spatial decomposition of the overall grid into subblocks that are assigned to separate processes [109]. To exploit coarse-grained parallelism and message passing, the implicit subiteration algorithm was modified at block interfaces to provide a block-decoupled algorithm. This decoupled algorithm utilizes Gauss-Seidel relaxation sweeps within each process but is effectively explicit at block boundaries, allowing parallel solution for all blocks. The solution at points shared by neighboring processes is updated between each subiteration by means of a message exchange.

The implementation of the Baldwin-Lomax turbulence model [6] introduces additional complexity into the parallel implementation of the flow code. This mainly affects the set-up phase of the solution process. The model requires the normal derivative of the tangential velocity at all impermeable surfaces in order to calculate the turbulent viscosity. This derivative is calculated in any block that includes an impermeable surface. The values of the derivatives then are propagated along the blocks that lie on any of the computational domain axes that begin with or terminate in an impermeable boundary. The blocks that satisfy the above condition are grouped together to share the derivative information. The turbulence model further requires the calculation of the maxima and minima of quantities that are distributed among the blocks of the above group.

The time-dependent equations in Cartesian coordinates are transformed into general curvilinear coordinates while introducing the artificial compressibility terms into the equations. The coordinate transformation essentially maps the arbitrary shape of the region of interest to a computational domain that is a rectangular parallelepiped. The solution procedure consists of two different phases. The first involves setting up a linear system using appropriate flux formulation and linearization techniques. The second phase is the solution of the linear system. The size of the system is equal to four times the number of grid points in the domain and could be of order 10^4–10^6 unknowns for realistic problems. However, the coefficient matrix of the linear system is extremely sparse and is generally solved by using iterative methods. From the parallel processing point of view, the set-up phase is easily parallelizable, having local data dependencies and being confined to at most 13-point stencils for three-dimensional problems.

Mapping of the physical domain into a single rectangular parallelepiped is often not possible for complex geometries. This problem is resolved by resorting to what are known as multiblock grids, where the physical domain is partitioned appropriately before being mapped into a number of rectangular three-dimensional domains that share common faces. This is shown in Figure 7.24. The linear system in each block is solved by using symmetric Gauss-Seidel iterations with boundary information being exchanged at the end of each forward and backward iteration [122].

Key areas of the parallel implementation include (a) initialization of the flow field, (b) duplication of stored data for points near block interfaces, (c) exchange of data during subiterations, for points having duplicated storage, and (d) treatment

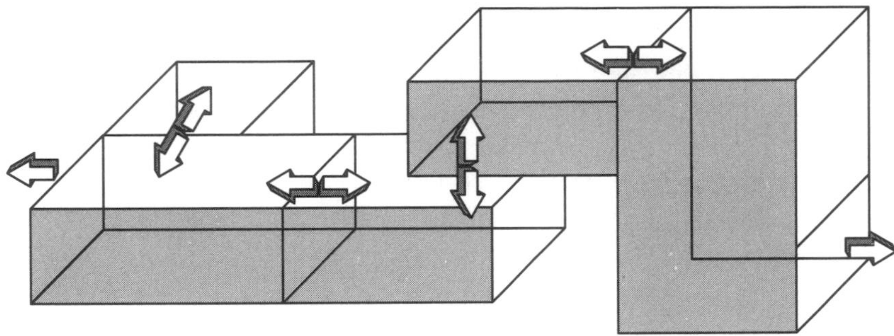

Figure 7.24
Multiblock grid of physical domain for CFD problem

of line searches along coordinates emanating from solid boundaries, which arise from the particular algebraic turbulence model used. These issues are discussed below.

7.11.2 Parallel Implementation

In the parallel implementation of this code [109], the domain is partitioned into a number of nearly equally sized subdomains, each of which is assigned to a different process. The local data dependencies at the boundary of each block are taken into account by a two-cell-deep layer of buffer cells whose values are updated from the appropriate block, as shown in Figure 7.25.

These values are used for setting up and solving the linear system. Each node independently performs Gauss-Seidel iterations and exchanges information through point-to-point messages. Thus each block goes through the sequence of operations shown in Figure 7.26.

The data duplication and updating at the block boundaries are implemented using the `MPI_Sendrecv` routine. Since this is a locally blocking routine, tight synchronization is achieved among the blocks. A message is exchanged after each forward and backward sweep of the symmetric Gauss-Seidel iteration, as shown in Figure 7.27.

The connectivity of the processes gives rise to a Cartesian virtual topology having empty nodes in it. Each process is tagged by using an ordered triplet `P,Q,R` that represents its coordinate on the virtual Cartesian grid. These coordinates are then

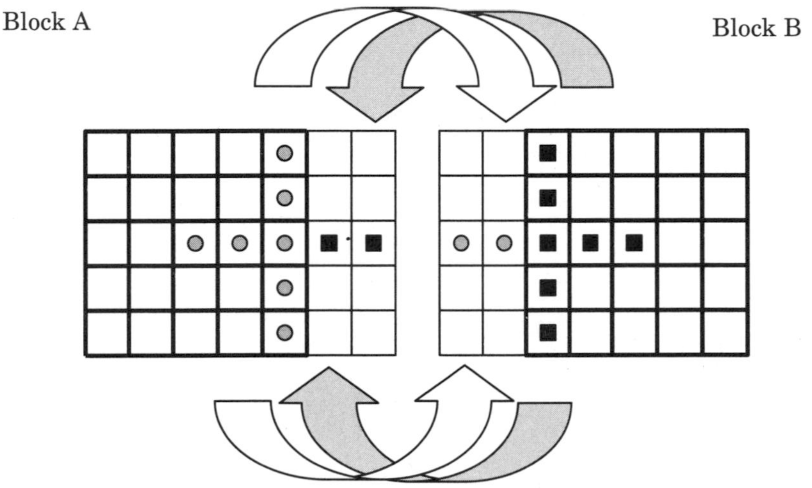

Figure 7.25
Information interchange between grid blocks in CFD application

used to define communicators for processes that are oriented along any of the three axes of the grid. This technique involves repeated use of the MPI_COMM_SPLIT, by using the values of the coordinate triplet at the color value. For example, in creating the communicator in the second coordinate, we could use

```
call MPI_COMM_SPLIT( MPI_COMM_WORLD, p+r*p_max, q, &
                     q_comm, ierror )
```

The communicators that are defined in this way form the basis for all the collective operations needed for implementing the turbulence model.

The details of the parallel turbulence model implementation are shown in Figure 7.27. The blocks with the shaded borders have impermeable boundaries and therefore calculate the velocity derivatives. The values of the derivative are then broadcast to the blocks through which the arrows pass. This is done using the MPI_BCAST routine within an appropriately defined communicator. Thus each arrow represents a separate process group and its associated communicator. A global

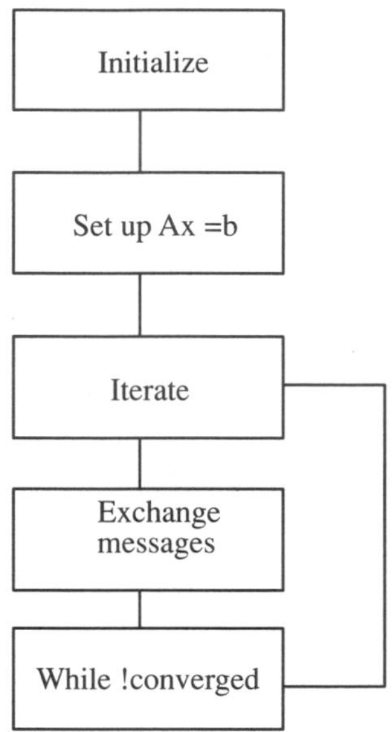

Figure 7.26
Simple flowchart of algorithm for CFD application

MPI_ALLREDUCE operation using the local minimum and maximum leaves the global minimum and maximum with each process that participates. The pattern here shows overlapping communicators, as promised above. For each process, there are two communicators: one for the row that the process is in and one for the column. The code for the broadcasts in this step looks very rougly like

```
call MPI_BCAST( deriv, count, MPI_DOUBLE_PRECISION, row_root, &
                row_comm, ierror )
call MPI_BCAST( deriv, count, MPI_DOUBLE_PRECISION, col_root, &
                col_comm, ierror )
```

This application illustrates how MPI can simplify the coding of a complex application. The key simplifications that result come from the use of virtual topologies and collective communication with the virtual topologies. Although the researchers chose to use their own virtual topologies in this case, the availability of communicators and the ease of building subset communicators with MPI_COMM_SPLIT made

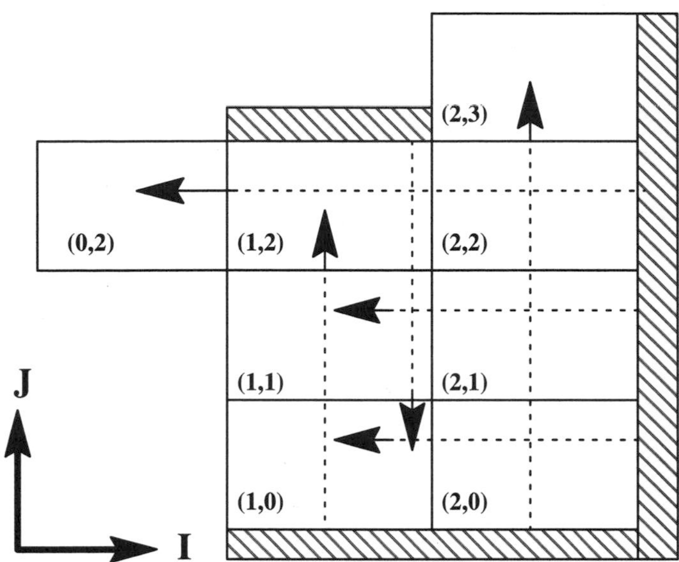

Figure 7.27
Communication pattern for CFD application with turbulence model

programming easy. This application would be extremely difficult on a system that was strictly a point-to-point message-passing interface without contexts of message passing.

8 Understanding how MPI Implementations Work

Understanding how MPI may be implemented can provide greater insight into the particular design choices made by the MPI Forum. Looking at the implementation reveals the motivation for some of the MPI design decisions. This motivation might be missed if one considered the library design only from the viewpoint of programmer convenience and failed to take into account the interface between the MPI library and the underlying message-passing hardware. In this chapter, we will briefly discuss one possible implementation approach for an MPI implementation that sends messages between computers connected by a network.

The approach taken for the implementation here separates the complicated part of an MPI implementation (managing communicators, derived datatypes, topologies, etc.) from the part that makes contact with the communication device. The upper layers can remain open and independent of a particular communication device, while the communication part can be optimized for a particular device and environment.

A more detailed and specific description of the design of several MPI implementations can be found in the literature. The MPICH implementation is described in more detail in [56, 63]. Several projects have developed variations on the MPICH implementation [14, 35, 44, 78, 79, 90]. Details of other MPI implementations are also available. For example, [4] surveys MPI implementations for Windows NT.

It is important to remember that it is impossible to say "how MPI is implemented." It is only possible to discuss how a particular implementation of MPI works.

8.1 Introduction

In order to understand how an MPI implementation might work, we will start by considering how an `MPI_Send` might be implemented and follow the message to the matching `MPI_Recv`. Along the way, we will discover that we will need to add features to our design.

8.1.1 Sending Data

When MPI sends data, it must include with the buffer that the user is sending information on the message tag, communicator, length, and source and destination of the message. We will call this additional information the *envelope*. Sending a message consists of sending the envelope, followed by the data. This method of sending the data immediately is call an *eager* protocol.

8.1.2 Receiving Data

When a message arrives, there are two possible cases. Either a matching receive (e.g., `MPI_Recv`, `MPI_Irecv`, `MPI_Sendrecv`, etc.) has already been made or it hasn't. In the case where a matching receive already exists, the receive provides a location for the data that is arriving behind the envelope. To keep track of what receives are available (particularly for the nonblocking varieties), the MPI implementation can maintain a queue[1] of receives that have been posted. We can think of this as a queue of messages that are expected, and call it the expected queue. When an incoming message matches a receive in this queue, the receive is marked as completed and is removed from the queue.

In the case where there is no matching receive, the situation is more complicated. The receiving process must remember that a message has arrived, and it must store the data somewhere. Let us look at these two requirements. The first requirement, to remember that a message has arrived but has not matched a receive, is relatively easy to handle. We keep a queue (in the same sense as the expected messages are in a queue) of messages that were unexpected. When a program tries to receive a message with `MPI_Recv`, it first checks this unexpected queue to see if the message has already arrived. If it has, the receive can remove the message and data from that queue and complete. What about the data? The receiving process must store the data somewhere. Here we have a problem. What if the message is too big to fit in the available memory space? This can happen, for example, if in a master-worker algorithm such as the one described in Section 3.6, many workers send large messages (say, 100 MBytes each) to the master at nearly the same time. The MPI standard requires the implementation to handle this case and not to fail. This is the reason that we discussed buffering in Chapter 4; no matter how much memory space is provided for unexpected messages, at some point, the receiver can run out.

8.1.3 Rendezvous Protocol

To solve the problem of delivering too much data to the destination, we need to control how much data arrives at the destination and when that data is delivered. One simple solution is to send only the envelope to the destination process. When the receiver wants the data (and has a place to put the data), it sends back to the sender a message that says, in effect, "send the data for this message now." The sender can then send the data, knowing that the receiver has a place to put the

[1]Strictly speaking, it isn't exactly a queue, since we don't always take the top element off of it. But it is ordered in the sense that if two messages have the same source, communicator, and message tag, the first to arrive is the first to be removed from the queue.

MPI Call	Message Size	Protocol
MPI_Ssend	any	Rendezvous always
MPI_Rsend	any	Eager always
MPI_Send	$\leq$ 16KB	Eager
MPI_Send	$>$ 16KB	Rendezvous

Table 8.1
One possible mapping of MPI send modes onto the eager and rendezvous protocols. Other mappings are possible. See text.

data. This approach is called a *rendezvous* protocol, because the sender and the receiver must meet and agree when to send the data.

A careful reader will note that the rendezvous approach addresses the issue of the space taken up by the data but not the space needed by the receiving process to store the envelopes. Any MPI implementation is limited to the number of unmatched (unexpected) messages that can be handled. This number is usually reasonably large (e.g., thousands), but can sometimes be exceeded by applications that send large numbers of messages to other processes without receiving any messages. See [16] for a discussion of how the LAM implementation of MPI controls envelope resources.

8.1.4 Matching Protocols to MPI's Send Modes

The reason for the various MPI send modes now becomes clear. Each represents a different style of communication and each can be implemented naturally using a combination of the eager and rendezvous protocols. One possible mapping of MPI send modes onto the protocols is shown in Table 8.1.

It is important to remember that MPI does not specify a particular implementation approach. For example, an MPI implementation could choose to implement `MPI_Send`, `MPI_Rsend`, and `MPI_Ssend` with the rendezvous protocol and never use the eager protocol. It could also choose to implement `MPI_Ssend` with a modified eager protocol, where the message is send eagerly but the `MPI_Ssend` does not complete until the sending process receives an acknowledgment from the receiving process, thus enforcing the requirement that `MPI_Ssend` not complete until the matching receive has started (this would make `MPI_Ssend` slightly faster than an implementation that used only the rendezvous protocol, and was in fact used by early versions of MPICH).

Protocol	Time
Eager (expected)	$s + r(n + e)$
Eager (unexpected)	$s + r(n + e) + cn$
Rendezvous	$3s + r(n + 3e)$

Table 8.2
Comparison of the costs of eager and rendezvous protocols

8.1.5 Performance Implications

The major advantage of the rendezvous protocol is that it can handle arbitrarily large messages in any number. Why not use this method for all messages? The reason is that the eager method can be faster, particularly for short messages. To understand this, we can go back to the time complexity analysis in Chapter 4, but now apply the terms to the messages that the MPI implementation itself sends. Let the cost of sending a message of n bytes be $s + rn$. Let the envelope be e bytes in size. Also, since in the eager case we may need to copy the message from a temporary buffer to the buffer provided by the receive, let the cost of this copy be c seconds/byte. The relative costs of the eager and rendezvous protocols are shown in Table 8.2.

If messages are expected, eager is always faster than rendezvous. Even for unexpected messages, eager is faster for messages smaller than $2(s + re)/c$ bytes. For small messages, the cost of sending the message is dominated by the latency term s; in this limit, the rendezvous method is three times slower than the eager method. This is why implementations often have a mix of methods. Typically, s/c is 10^3 to 10^4, so for many applications that send relatively short messages (of around a thousand elements or less), the eager protocol is always faster.

Given this analysis, we might choose to always use the fastest method (under the assumption that either all or some fraction of the eager messages will be unexpected). However, if we do this, we must provide roughly $2s/c$ space for each message that we might eagerly receive. If we simply consider receiving one message from every other process (say we have p processes), and one in every communicator (u for unique communication spaces), we need $2spu/c$ bytes for each process (or $2sp^2u/c$ over all). On a system with many processes this is a significant amount of space. Many implementations currently address this by limiting the amount of space available, giving each possible source process the same amount of space for eagerly delivered messages. Other approaches are possible; for example, the space for eager messages could be dynamically assigned as needed.

8.1.6 Alternative MPI Implementation Strategies

Here we have briefly sketched one implementation approach. There are others. For example, it is possible for a receive to send a message to the source of the message (when `MPI_ANY_SOURCE` is not used) indicating that a message is expected [105]. This can reduce the latency introduced by the rendezvous protocol by eliminating one message exchange. Other approaches can be used when the hardware supports remote memory access or some form of shared memory.

8.1.7 Tuning MPI Implementations

Most MPI implementations provides some parameters to allow MPI users to tune the performance for their applications. From the preceding discussion, we know that both the amount of space available for eager delivery of messages and the message size at which an `MPI_Send` or `MPI_Isend` switches from eager to rendezvous protocol are natural parameters, and many MPI implementations allow the user some control over these. For example, the IBM implementation has an environment variable `MP_EAGER_LIMIT` that sets the message size above which the rendezvous protocol is used. Note, however, that you can't just set this to 4000000000; there is usually a range of valid values.

These parameters are implementation-dependent, and can change with time. For example, the SGI implementation of MPI used to provide `MPI_THRESHOLD` for the eager to rendezvous threshold, but at this writing provides a set of environment variables that closely match SGI's implementation of MPI (and that involves a generalization of the rendezvous approach). Each vendor's documentation for MPI should be checked to see what environment variables are available.

In some cases, there are options that you may want to use during program development. For example, by default, the SGI implementation of MPI does no error checking. During program development, it is important to set the environment variable `MPI_CHECK_ARGS`.

8.2 How Difficult Is MPI to Implement?

MPI has many functions. How difficult is it to implement all of these functions? How difficult is it to develop a high performance MPI implementation? MPI was carefully designed so that the features of MPI are orthogonal, allowing an implementation to both build a full MPI implementation on top of a smaller number of routines, and to incrementally improve the implementation by replacing parts of the MPI implementation with more sophisticated techniques as the implementation matures.

This is a common approach. For example, in graphics and printing, most graphical displays provide for drawing a single pixel at an arbitrary location. Any other graphical function can be built using this single, elegant primitive. However, high-performance graphical displays offer a wide variety of additional functions, ranging from block copy and line drawing to 3-D surface shading. MPI implementations tend to follow this same approach: at the very bottom of the MPI implementation are routines to communicate data between processes. An MPI implementation, early in its life, may implement all of MPI in terms of these operations. As time goes on, it can add more advanced features. For example, special routines to provide faster collective operations might exploit special features of the parallel computer's hardware. The topology routines (i.e., `MPI_Cart_create` and `MPI_Graph_create`) can become aware of the parallel computer's interconnect topology.

One example of a feature in MPI that implementations are improving incrementally is the handling of MPI's derived datatypes. Early implementations of MPI often did the equivalent of using `MPI_Pack` followed by a send of contiguous data. As implementations have matured, they have addressed the issue of providing better performance on MPI derived datatypes; see [65], for example.

8.3 Device Capabilities and the MPI Library Definition

Earlier we commented that considering the device interface illuminates some of the design decisions in MPI. Any message-passing library imposes a certain view of the characteristics of the devices it is intended for. MPI was carefully designed to impose as few restrictions as possible, thus allowing implementations that take full advantage of modern, powerful communications hardware.

For a simple example, consider the case of `MPI_Probe`, the blocking "probe" function. Recall that MPI also has a nonblocking version, `MPI_Iprobe`. Not all message-passing libraries support probe at all, and those that do tend to supply only the nonblocking version, since the blocking one can be implemented at the user level by calling the nonblocking one in a loop. However, this "busy waiting" is not really acceptable in a multithreaded or even multiprogramming environment. If the library supplies the blocking probe as well, then the implementation can use whatever resources it may have, such as an intelligent communication controller, to free the CPU while waiting for a message.

Similarly, from the programmer's point of view there is no *need* for the (blocking) function MPI_Recv, since its functionality can be obtained with MPI_Irecv followed by MPI_Wait. On the other hand, the library can make more efficient use of the device if it does not have to return to the user halfway through the operation. Another case in point is the use of a datatype parameter on all MPI communication calls, rather than using MPI_Pack and MPI_Unpack together with sending untyped data. Explicit packing and unpacking, while sometimes necessary, forces a memory copy operation that usually is not.

Other parts of the MPI library, such as MPI_Waitany, clearly could be implemented at the user level, and thus are not necessary in order for the programmer to implement an algorithm. Eliminating them would make MPI a smaller and simpler library. On the other hand, it would also eliminate opportunities for optimization by the communications layer. One reason that MPI is a relatively large library is that the MPI Forum deliberately sacrificed the notion of a "minimalist" library in favor of enabling high performance.

8.4 Reliability of Data Transfer

The MPI standard specifies that the message-passing operations are *reliable*. This means that the application programmer who uses MPI need not worry about whether the data sent has been delivered correctly. However, it does mean that the MPI implementation must take steps to ensure that messages are delivered reliably.

No mechanism for delivering data is 100% reliable. Even direct, memory-to-memory interconnects have a small probability of failure. This is what parity and ECC (error correcting code) memories and data paths are for. Parity allows errors to be detected, ECC allows some (usually single-bit) errors to be corrected and others (usually double-bit) detected. In the case of more loosely-connected systems, the probability of a uncorrectable failure is higher.

For example, take the commonly-used network protocol TCP. TCP provides *reliable* data connections between two points. But what does "reliable" mean in this context? It turns out that, since 100% reliability is impossible, any TCP implementation must be prepared to decide that a connection has failed. At that point, TCP terminates the connection and reliably notifies the users of the connection that the connection has been closed. This is the meaning of "reliable" in TCP: data is delivered or it is possible to discover that something went wrong.

This level of reliability is adequate in some circumstances but not in others. Many of the MPI Forum participants intended for MPI to provide what is often called "guaranteed delivery": MPI is expected to ensure that the message is delivered, correcting for any errors that may occur in the lower-level data-movement layers. In the TCP case, this might mean keeping track of how much data has been successfully delivered, and if a connection fails, having MPI automatically re-establish the connection and continue sending the data. However, being able to ensure that data has been delivered adds extra overhead and can reduce the performance of MPI (or any other message-passing or data-delivery system).

Another example is a system connected by a high-speed network such as HiPPI. HiPPI (now called HiPPI-800 to distinguish it from a second-generation version called HiPPI-6400) provides 100 MB/sec (800 Mb/sec) bandwidth. HiPPI has an error rate of no more than 10^{-12} errors/second. This appears to be a very small rate until you realize how fast HiPPI is: At 8×10^8 bits/second, an error can be expected every 1250 seconds, or roughly 20 minutes. Of course, the actual error rates will be somewhat less than the specified value, and so errors will occur, on average, less often than once every 20 minutes. However, a long-running MPI application will depend on the MPI implementation to provide error detection and recovery so that the application can run successfully, and a correct MPI implementation will provide this capability.

9 Comparing MPI with Other Systems for Interprocess Communication

In the first edition of this book, we provided a chapter on how to convert programs using different message-passing systems to MPI. This is no longer necessary; most programs using previous message-passing systems have already been re-written in MPI or discarded. The first edition also showed how MPI built on the successes of previous message-passing systems, such as Chameleon [71], Zipcode [116], and commercial systems such as Intel NX and IBM's EUI (later called MPL). That chapter was also useful in drawing attention to differences and similarities between MPI and other systems. Understanding the differences between systems, in particular, can help in understanding why certain design choices were made and can also aid in deciding which approach is appropriate for a given task. The chapter from the first edition is available at `http://www.mcs.anl.gov/mpi/usingmpi`.

In this chapter, we will discuss two other systems for interprocess communication in detail. The first is sockets; this is a common, low-level mechanism for communicating between different computers. The second is PVM [47], a popular and widely-used message-passing model emphasizing communication between computer systems, and one for which porting to MPI is still taking place.

9.1 Sockets

The socket application programmer interface (API) is the basic programming interface for using TCP (among other methods) to send data between processes that are connected by many networks, including the Internet. The details of this interface are not covered here; see, for example, [121] for detailed coverage of the use of sockets. In this discussion we focus on using TCP with sockets. We will cover only a subset of the socket interface that illuminates the differences from MPI and similarities with it.

Sockets are used primarily to establish a point-to-point communication path between two processes. Once a connection is established between two processes (using `socket`, `bind`, `listen`, `accept`, and `connect`), the two processes have file descriptors (fds) with which they can read from and write to the socket. At the very simplest level, a `read` on a socket is similar to an `MPI_Recv` and a `write` on a socket is similar to an `MPI_Send`. However, it is the differences between MPI and sockets that are interesting.

Let us look first at how data can be sent with sockets. In the case of sockets, a `write` call can return with a positive value, indicating that that number of bytes were written, or a negative value, indicating a problem (and no bytes written). The

```
void Sender( int fd, char *buf, int count )
{
    int n;
    while (count > 0) {
        n = write( fd, buf, count );
        if (n < 0) { ... special handling ... }
        count -= n;
        buf += n;
    }
}

void Receiver( int fd, char *buf, int count )
{
    int n;
    while (count > 0) {
        n = read( fd, buf, count );
        if (n < 0) { ... special handling ... }
        count -= n;
        buf += n;
    }
}
```

Figure 9.1
Partial code to send data between two processes

behavior of `read` is similar: the returned value indicates the number of bytes read, with an negative value indicating a problem (and no bytes read).

For sockets, as for MPI, the handling of message buffers is key to understanding what happens. The first thing to note is that an attempt to write `count` bytes to the socket may be only partially successful. What happens depends on whether the socket has been set to be nonblocking (with the flag `O_NONBLOCK` or `O_NDELAY` set using the `fcntl` call on the sockets file descriptor). If the socket has *not* been set as nonblocking, then the `write` will succeed, that is, it will return with value `count` as long as `count` is no larger than the size of the socket buffer (this also assumes that the socket buffer is empty, for example, when no data has yet been sent on the socket). If `count` is greater than the socket size, then the `write` call will block until enough data has been read from the other end of the socket. In this mode, a `write` is very much like an `MPI_Send`: small enough data buffers are sent even if there is no receive waiting for them, while sending (writing) larger data buffers can block the process, waiting for a receive to occur at the other end of the communication.

For the same reasons that we discussed in Chapter 4, it can be difficult in some cases to guarantee that a program using `write` and `read` won't deadlock because two processes are both trying to write data to a socket that is already full of data.

To avoid this problem, a socket can be marked as nonblocking. In this case, the behavior of `read` and `write` are different from the blocking case. For `write`, if there is no room for the data, the `write` call returns the value `-1` and sets `errno` to `EAGAIN`[1]. This keeps the process from blocking, but requires the programmer to take other steps to deliver the data. For example, when a `write` fails, the programmer might try to `read` from the socket, in the event that the socket is being written to from both ends (the "unsafe" case of each process executing a write to the other, intending to follow that with a read). In this mode, `write` and `read` are somewhat like `MPI_Isend` and `MPI_Irecv`, but with a different way of handling `MPI_Wait`. Note that this nonblocking mode for sockets is provided to allow applications to function correctly in the presence of limited buffering, just as for the MPI nonblocking modes.

Some operating systems provide asynchronous read and write operations called `aio_read` and `aio_write` respectively. These are an alternative interface for non-blocking read and write operations, and are closer to the MPI nonblocking operations in spirit. Note, however, that there is no requirement in MPI (or in the definitions of `aio_read` or `aio_write` for that matter) that these operations take place concurrently with computation.

Continuing the analogy with the MPI nonblocking operations, the socket API provides its own counterpart to `MPI_Waitsome` and `MPI_Testsome`. These are the `select` and `poll` calls, whose arguments are file descriptor masks. `Select` and `poll` can return immediately, in analogy with `MPI_Testsome` (when called with a timeout value of zero), or block until at least one of the fds is ready to be read from or written to. The difference is that `select` and `poll` only indicate that a file descriptor may be used; in MPI, a successful test or wait completes the related communication. A sketch of what an implementation of `MPI_Testsome` might look like in an implementation that communicates over sockets is shown in Figure 9.2.

9.1.1 Process Startup and Shutdown

When describing a message-passing library or application, most of the time is spent discussing the mechanisms for sending data between processes. This overlooks the difficulty in simply getting the processes started, particularly in a scalable way. To illustrate the issues, we will briefly describe some of the possibilities.

[1] In a multithreaded environment, you must access the per-thread value of `errno`.

```
int Testsome( int *flag )
{
    fd_set readmask, writemask;
    int nfds;
    struct timeval timeout;

    ... setup read and write masks
    ... set timeout to zero (don't block)
    timeout.tv_sec  = 0;
    timeout.tv_usec = 0;
    nfds = select( maxfd+1, &readmask, &writemask,
                   (fd_set*)0, &timeout );
    if (nfds == 0) { *flag = 0; return 0; }
    if (nfds < 0) { return nfds; }  /* Error! */
    for (fds to read on) {
        if (FD_ISSET(fd,&readmask)) {
            Receive(fd,....);
            }
    }
    for (fds to write on) {
        if (FD_ISSET(fd,&writemask)) {
            Sender(fd,....);
        }
    }
    return 0;
}
```

Figure 9.2
A sketch of a `Testsome` implementation using `select` with sockets

Starting a parallel job consists of two steps: starting the processes and putting those processes in contact with one another. Different approaches may be taken for each of these steps.

One of the simplest approaches is for the first process, for example, the single process that is started by `mpiexec`, to start all of the other processes by using a remote shell program such as `rsh` or `ssh`. This initial process is called the *master* process. In this approach, a command-line argument can be used to give the new processes the port number of a socket on the first process that can be connected to in order to get information on all of the processes in the MPI job.

This approach has the advantage of making use of existing facilities for starting processes and for routing standard in, out, and error. The disadvantages are many. For example, it is not scalable (all processes are connected to the master process) and it relies on remote shell (considered a security risk) or a secure variant. In environments where a process manager is used for load-balancing, this approach cannot be used because only the process manager is allowed to start tasks.

Another approach is to run daemons on the processors that will allow processes to be started for MPI jobs. An MPI job is started by contacting one more more of these demons and requesting that the MPI process be started. This can be organized in a scalable way, but adds the extra burden of providing reliable, fault tolerant, and secure process management services to the MPI implementor. In addition, some mechanism must be provided to allow the MPI processes to discover each other, such as a separate data server.

If starting processes seems hard, ensuring that processes are all stopped under all conditions is even harder. Consider the case where one MPI process in an MPI job is killed, either by a signal (such as `SIGINT` or `SIGFPE`) or by `MPI_Abort`. When this happens, all processes in the MPI job should exit. Making this happen can be difficult. For example, it would be incorrect to rely on catching a signal, since some Unix signals are uncatchable (e.g., `SIGKILL` and `SIGSTOP`). Similarly, relying on a "watchdog" process is also unreliable, since the watchdog itself may fail or be killed (for example, some operating systems will kill processes when the OS starts to run short of critical resources like swap space; this might happen as a result of a runaway parallel program, thus causing the OS to kill the one process (the watchdog) that could save the day).

9.1.2 Handling Faults

The MPI standard says little about what happens when something goes wrong. In large part, this is because standards rarely specify the behavior of erroneous programs or the consequences of events beyond the standard (such as a power failure). This is a good match to highly-scalable systems where communications between processes is guaranteed by the underlying operating environment and where scalable and high-performance implementation of the MPI collective routines is important. However, in a more loosely-coupled network environment, such as a collection of workstations, there is a much greater likelihood of losing contact with another process, and applications written using sockets (or PVM) often include code to handle this event.

One reason that this is easier to handle in the socket case than it is in the MPI case is that there are only two parties to the socket: if one fails, then it is reasonably clear what needs to be done. This is much harder in the case of MPI, since the failure of one process among a thousand during an MPI collective operation such as an `MPI_Allreduce` makes it very difficult to recover (it is possible to ensure that the `MPI_Allreduce` operation succeeds for all members of the communicator before allowing the MPI program to continue, but only at a significant performance cost).

An MPI implementation could provide the same level of support for communication failures in the case of communicators of size two; this is a "quality of implementation" issue. That is, there is no reason why an MPI implementation cannot provide the same level of support for failures in communication as sockets long as only two-party communicators are used. A generalization of this, to intercommunicators, where the two "parties" are the groups of processes, can also be made.

9.2 PVM 3

PVM is an important library of message-passing models developed at Oak Ridge National Laboratory, University of Tennessee, and Emory University by Vaidy Sunderam, Al Geist, Jack Dongarra, Robert Manchek, and others (see [51]). PVM stands for "Parallel Virtual Machine," heralding its support for process management, heterogeneous clusters, and message passing. PVM version 2 and earlier versions ran on heterogeneous networks of workstations and on front ends of parallel machines. PVM 3.x (the most recent as of this writing is 3.4, with the user's manual documenting 3.3) is the currently supported version of the PVM library described in [47]. Unlike PVM version 2, PVM 3 has support for specific parallel machines as well as for heterogeneous networks of workstations. Furthermore, the Version 3 release constituted a complete redesign of the system. Yet, version 3's message-passing aspects remain quite simple, and translation to MPI is consequently straightforward.

The Version 3 release uses a systematic naming convention for functions and constants. In C, `pvm_` is prepended to all the names of routines to avoid the many potential conflicts in short, common names. In Fortran, this is modified to `pvmf`.

For ease in summarizing the similarities and differences between MPI and PVM version 3, the topics are separated into six separate subsections:

Basics Initialization and cleanup, identifying one's self and one's peers, and basic (blocking) send and receive

Miscellaneous Functions Nonblocking send and receive operations, wait, test, probe, status information, and error handling

Collective operations Synchronizing processes, collective data movement and computations, process subgroups

MPI Counterparts of Other Features Special features in the library that have MPI counterparts

Features not in MPI Special features in the library that do not have MPI counterparts

Process Startup Features outside MPI, but worth considering and comparing

9.2.1 The Basics

Table 9.1 shows the correspondences between basic PVM 3 functions and their MPI counterparts. The table shows Fortran bindings for both PVM 3 and MPI; the full C translations are similar. We show only certain of the arguments to each routine; the correspondences for the others can be readily inferred. Group arguments for PVM 3 correspond to the dynamic group concept added in this Version 3 release. In MPI, the communicator would hold a corresponding static group. Use of dynamic addition or subtraction of processes after an initial group formulation is not within the MPI model and requires a more complex porting strategy than what which is shown in Table 9.1. Intercommunicators provide one alternative means for handling complex group management in MPI. (The rank of a task and the number of tasks can also be determined without using the PVM group operations at the time the PVM processes are started. We will not discuss this approach here.)
PVM 3 has replaced the notion of "components" and "instances" used in PVM version 2 with TIDs (task IDs) and dynamic process groups. This change makes porting to MPI somewhat simpler than with the earlier versions of PVM, unless dynamic groups are used extensively. Furthermore, PVM 3 has replaced the restriction of single buffers with multiple buffers, each identified by its "bufid." PVM 3 buffers are created, deleted and selected; these operations are unneeded in MPI. In Table 9.1, the "`buf_type`" argument in `MPI_SEND()` and `MPI_RECV()` refers either to a simple type like `MPI_BYTE` or `MPI_INTEGER` or to a more complex data type, covered below.

The PVM design makes no claims about buffering, though the most widely distributed implementation provides significant (though not infinite) buffering. PVM users who depend on the buffering in the implementation can use the buffered sends (`MPI_Bsend`) of MPI.

```
pvmfmytid(mytid)             MPI_INIT(...)
pvmfexit(info)               MPI_FINALIZE(ierr)
pvmfgetinst(grp,mytid,me)    MPI_COMM_RANK(comm,me,ierr)
pvmfgsize(grp,np)            MPI_COMM_SIZE(comm,np,ierr)
pvmfpack(...);pvmfsend(tid,tag,info)
                             MPI_BSEND(.., buf_type,...)
                             or
                             MPI_SEND(.., buf_type,...)
pvmfrecv(tid,tag,bufid);pvmfunpack(...)
                             MPI_RECV(.., buf_type,...)
pvmfpsend(tid,tag,buf,len,datatype,info)
                           MPI_SEND(buf,len,datatype...)
pvmfprecv(tid,tag,buf,len,datatype,...)
                           MPI_RECV(buf,len,datatype...)
```

Table 9.1
Translating PVM 3 to MPI: basic functions

```
pvmfnrecv(src,tag,bufid)   MPI_IPROBE(...);
                           if(flag) MPI_RECV(...);
pvmfprobe(src,tag,bufid)   MPI_IPROBE(src,tag,
                             MPI_COMM_WORLD,flag,status)
pvmfperror(str,info)       MPI_ABORT(comm, val)
```

Table 9.2
Translating PVM 3 to MPI: miscellaneous functions

9.2.2 Miscellaneous Functions

PVM 3 has both "probe" and nonblocking receive. Note that PVM's non-blocking receive is not like MPI's `MPI_Irecv`; rather is combines the effects of `MPI_Iprobe` and `MPI_Recv`.

9.2.3 Collective Operations

PVM 3 has no counterpart to the a wide variety of global data-movement routines in MPI. To get access to most of PVM 3's collective operations, one needs to use dynamic groups. Note that the broadcast operation `pvmfmcast` in PVM is really a multisend; whereas in MPI messages sent with `MPI_BCAST` are received with `MPI_-BCAST`. The sender is specified by the `root` parameter; the other processes receive. The semantics of a PVM 3 barrier are quite different from those of an MPI barrier, in that MPI barriers are over a specific group and synchronize, whereas PVM 3

pvmfmcast(ntask,tids,tag,info)	MPI_BCAST(buf,count,datatype, root,comm,ierr)
pvmfbcast(grp,tag,info)	MPI_BCAST(buf,count,datatype, root,comm,ierr)
pvmfbarrier(grp,count,info)	MPI_BARRIER(comm,ierr)

Table 9.3
Translating PVM 3 to MPI: collective operations

barriers wait for any n processes to call the function, with possible race conditions. MPI has no non-blocking collective communications; these must be implemented via thread extensions.

The problem with dynamic groups, unlike MPI's static groups, is that there are race conditions associated with "joining" and "leaving" these groups (since a dynamic group is a distributed data structure, it may be out of date in some processes unless it is synchronized properly). Assuming one is careful to form a group and then barrier synchronize, Table 9.3 gives an accurate picture of how to map from PVM 3's groups to MPI communicators. Note that the tag argument of PVM 3's broadcast has no corresponding entry in MPI.

9.2.4 MPI Counterparts of Other Features

Communication among heterogeneous machines in PVM 3 is provided by packing and unpacking functions that apply to the current-send and specified-receive buffers on each process. The first pack command is normally preceded by `pvmfinitsend()` (when `pvmfmkbuf()/pvmffreebuf` are used, `pvmfinitsend()` may not be necessary). Multiple pending sends are possible.

In MPI every *send* has a datatype argument; this matches PVM's use of different routines for different types of data.

PVM 3 has support for most of the the basic datatypes supported by the host language, whether Fortran or C. In converting string transmissions from PVM to MPI, the correspondence between `pvm_pkstr()` (in C) and `pvmfpack` with `STRING` as the `what` argument (in Fortran) and the use of `MPI_CHARACTER` is not exact, in that the send must elect to send or not send the null termination when it sizes the character array. (The detailed issues of Fortran character strings vs. character arrays and substrings are thorny, as described in the MPI Standard [97, Chapters 2 and 3].)

The approach of PVM and MPI to handling data of different basic datatypes is somewhat different. The MPI `MPI_Pack` and `MPI_Unpack` routines, discussed in Section 5.2.5 were added to MPI to provide a closer correspondence with the approach used in PVM of incrementally packing data into a buffer. Following MPI's approach of making more explicit the buffers used, the buffer in MPI must be provided directly by the user rather than being managed by the system, as PVM does.

We need to call attention to one subtle difference between MPI and PVM. MPI is designed to require no buffering of data within the system; this allows MPI to be implemented on the widest range of platforms, and with great efficiency, since buffering often results in performance-draining copies. On the other hand, providing buffering can make programming much easier, and PVM provides extensive (though not unbounded) buffering for the programmer. Thus, the closest correspondence with the PVM send routines (such as `pvmfsend` is really with `MPI_Bsend`, not with `MPI_Send`. However, few if any MPI implementations contain an efficient `MPI_Bsend`, since MPI programmers are encouraged to manage their memory more carefully. Thus, porting a PVM program to MPI can be done relatively easily by using combinations of `MPI_Pack`, `MPI_Unpack`, and `MPI_Bsend`, but a high-quality port will require examining the uses of `MPI_Bsend` and replacing them with `MPI_Send`, `MPI_Isend`, or other MPI send routines.

9.2.5 Features Not in MPI

Key features in PVM 3 that are not in MPI are as follows:

- Interactive process management as described in the following section is not in MPI-1. MPI-2 defined dynamic process management extensions for MPI, but these are slightly different from the PVM routines.
- Routines for adding and deleting hosts from the virtual machine dynamically (in addition to dynamic process management). This is not part of MPI-2, as the MPI Forum, after considering the options, felt that this should be part of the operating environment outside of MPI.
- Timeouts on communications routines. This aids in writing applications that are tolerant of faults.

A more detailed discussion of the differences between MPI and PVM may be found in [70, 60].

9.2.6 Process Startup

Parallel programs written using PVM 3 are started by running the first instance of the program (or the master program executable, if the slaves and master have different executables) from the Unix shell, after the master PVM daemon has also been started as a regular Unix process. The first process then starts the other processes via a `pvmfspawn()` call, which can specify location either by architecture or by machine name. The virtual machine is specified to PVM 3 through a "hostfile" with a specific format (see [10]), and a default location in the user's directory structure. Note that the `pvmfmytid()` that appears in the master program does *not* start the PVM master daemon. The daemon must be started beforehand (perhaps as a separate program, running interactively in a separate window); it in turn subsequently starts slave daemons. The PVM console may be run interactively and interacts with the daemons; this feature is particularly useful when passwords are needed to achieve startup on remote nodes or when the user wishes to observe the behavior of processes (see [10]). There is also a group server for dynamic group management, which gets started automatically if needed. In contrast, MPI-1 did not specify any analogous portable mechanism for process startup or dynamic management, and the MPI-2 dynamic process mechanism is designed to support scalable formation of new, yet static, intercommunicators. The reason that MPI-1 did not specify process startup or management were twofold:

- On parallel machines, vendor-specific mechanisms were currently too diverse to coerce into a single style.
- On workstation networks, the problems of process startup and management were intertwined with the difficulties of workstation management and parallel job queuing, which were being addressed by a variety of both proprietary and public-domain systems. (DQS is one example of such a system.) These systems are being designed to interface to a number of different parallel programming systems being run on the networks, including MPI.

In MPI-2, the MPI Forum provides a method to start new processes and to connect to existing ones but did not directly address many of the resource management issues. Some of the reasons are covered in [70].

9.2.7 MPI and PVM related tools

Several projects have looked at providing interoperability of MPI and PVM programs; that is, single programs that could use both MPI and PVM libraries within the same executable. One such project, by Fei Cheng of Mississippi State University, provided a large subset of both PVM and MPI with a single underlying implementation [22]. The PVMPI [32] project and its follow-on MPI_Connect [33] use PVM to interconnect different MPI implementations; they also allow the application to make use of PVM's process control and resource management tools. PHIS [95] allows MPI and PVM applications to communicate.

9.3 Where to Learn More

In this chapter, we have discussed two message passing systems and compared and contrasted their features with those in MPI. Additional information about porting and about detailed features of the other systems is available. The Internet newsgroups *comp.parallel*, *comp.parallel.pvm*, and *comp.parallel.mpi* provide access to up-to-the-minute discussions on message-passing systems, including details of real experience with porting. See also the discussion in Appendix D for other ways to access information on MPI as well as many of the systems described in this chapter on the Internet.

10 Beyond Message Passing

As we've discussed all along, MPI is a standard library (and notation) specification for supporting the message-passing model of parallel computation. The MPI Forum interpreted its mission broadly (not without considerable discussion), and "message passing" in MPI includes not only many varieties of point-to-point communication, but also contexts, groups, collective operations, and process topologies, and profiling and environmental inquiry functions. Making MPI a large specification widened the scope of its applicability.

On the other hand, programmers are already experimenting with facilities that extend beyond the message-passing model. Vendors are starting to provide such features as part of their operating environments, whereas these features were previously included only in research systems; the most notable example is threads, discussed further below. As described in the Preface, the MPI Forum has extended the MPI Standard to include some of these features. Although we leave to [66] our own discussion of the MPI-2 Standard [55, 101], it is appropriate to discuss here the directions to be explored beyond the strict message-passing model.

In this chapter, we focus on several broad topics:

- **Generalizing the fixed nature of `MPI_COMM_World`.** The MPI (-1) process model described in this book assumes that the number of processes participating in the parallel computation is fixed before the program begins. A more dynamic approach is to allow a computation to create new processes during the run or to establish MPI communication with processes already running in a separate `MPI_COMM_WORLD`.
- **Generalizing the notion of process.** The MPI process model implicitly characterizes MPI processes as existing statically and having disjoint address spaces. The *thread* model postulates "lightweight" processes that come into and go out of existence quickly and that share memory with one another. This latter model has important implications for message passing and for parallel performance.
- **Generalizing the notion of message passing.** The idea here is to explore ways that a process can cause events to occur on another process or processor without sending a message that the other process must explicitly receive, such as a remote signal or remote memory copy.
- **Generalizing the notion of computation.** As parallel machines have become larger, many applications based on scalable algorithms for their core computations have seen their bottlenecks shift from computation and interprocess communication to input and output of data. New parallel computers have parallel hardware in the

file system, but what a "parallel file" *means* or what parallel I/O should be in general is still an open research question.

We will consider these areas in turn.

10.1 Dynamic Process Management

The MPI specification describes the effects of calls made to MPI subroutines after each process calls `MPI_Init` and before it calls `MPI_Finalize`. In particular, the MPI specification is silent on the topic of how processes come into existence. In current systems, a wide variety of mechanisms are in use: specialized program startup programs and scripts, custom daemons running on other processors, remote shells, and other mechanisms. The reason MPI does not address this problem is that it is complicated and there is no consensus about common methods, particularly among vendors.

To start a process, one must specify at least an executable file and a processor on which to run it. Although the examples in this book typically show the same program (executable file) being executed by all processes, in what is called the SPMD (single program, multiple data) model, this is not required by MPI, and a different program text may be run by each process.

Bringing new processes into existence is only the first part of what needs to be done. It is also necessary to establish communication between new and previously existing processes. In MPI terms, this means that a communicator must be provided that includes at least one of the "old" processes and one of the "new" processes. A related problem arises when one wants to establish communication between two already-running MPI programs.

Note that MPI addresses this problem currently by

- omitting the definition of how processes are created,
- disallowing new processes to be born or die after the call to `MPI_Init`,
- providing the communicator `MPI_Comm_world`, and
- not allowing communication between processes in separate `MPI_COMM_WORLD`s.

These restrictions are all lifted in the MPI-2 Standard. Intercommunicators, which are a minor part of MPI-1, play a larger role in MPI-2. MPI-2 introduces the `MPI_Spawn` function, which is collective over one communicator and returns a new *inter*communicator (see Section 7.4 for the definition of an intercommunicator) containing the new processes as the remote group. The new processes have their own MPI_COMM_WORLD and can access the new intercommunicator with a call to MPI_Comm_get_parent. Communication between the parents and the children can take place in this intercommunicator, and it can even be turned into a normal (intra) communicator by calling MPI_Intercomm_merge.

Intercommunicators also play a role in connecting two separate communicators that are not subsets of a containing communicator. The paired collective calls MPI_Accept and MPI_Connect create an intercommunicator, thus allowing two separately started MPI programs to communicate.

10.2 Threads

Throughout this book we have referred constantly to *processes* as the entities that communicate with one another. A process may be defined loosely as an address space together with a current state consisting of a program counter, register values, and a subroutine call stack. The fact that a process has only one program counter means that it is doing only one thing at a time; we call such a process *single threaded.* Multiple processes may be executed on a single processor through timesharing, so in some sense the processor is doing more than one thing at a time, but the process isn't.

An important generalization of the process introduces multiple program counters (and call stacks) within a single address space. Each program counter and call stack defines a *thread*. The MPI Forum was aware of threads and was careful to design MPI to be *thread safe.* That is, there is nothing about the MPI interface (with one exception, for which see Section 5.2.3) that interferes with using MPI in a multithreaded program. However, at the time MPI-1 was defined, there was no clear thread interface; for example, many vendors had their own different thread interface, and there were many research systems. The POSIX (pthreads) interface was still being developed. Thus MPI-1 simply designed for a future that contained threads, without having a specific implementation or practice in mind.

Since then, the picture with respect to threads has cleared up somewhat. Threads are now much more prevalent; many systems support POSIX pthreads. In addition, some MPI implementors built thread-safe *implementations* of MPI and gained experience with using multithreaded processes in an MPI setting. The result was some additional functions defined in MPI-2 to provide better support for multithreaded programs. Because these additions and clarifications were made as part of the MPI-2 process, they are discussed in our companion book, *Using MPI-2.*

10.3 Action at a Distance

The most characteristic feature of the message-passing model is that one process cannot access the memory of another process without its explicit consent: send has no effect without a corresponding receive. This isolation of processes increases modularity and arguably makes message-passing programs easier to debug than those in which processes can access one another's memory directly. On the other hand, sometimes a process would like to cause some event on another processor, typically to access its memory, without involving the other process.

In a true shared-memory machine, the process of accessing remote memory is transparent; a process does not even know which accesses are "local" and which are "remote." One of the first extensions to message-passing distributed-memory machines was the *interrupt-driven receive.* This extension was pioneered by Intel. The idea is that an interrupt handler is associated with a message tag; when a matching message arrives, the user-defined interrupt handler is called. After the interrupt is serviced, control is returned to wherever it was when the interrupt occurred. Thus the methods of Section 7.1.3 could be used without the need for polling. The code to receive and respond to a request for the counter value, or for memory access in general, can reside in an interrupt handler. One can also think of the interrupt-handler code as taking place in a separate thread.

A more elaborate mechanism is provided by *active messages.* Active messages, as described in [126], formed the low-level communication mechanism on the TMC CM-5. An active message is one whose arrival triggers the execution of a specific subroutine in the target process. Active messages are sometimes used to initiate *remote memory copying,* in which data is moved from one process's address space to another's by the action of only one process. On the CM-5, this was made possible by the requirement that each process be executing the exact same code, so that addresses refer to the same objects on all processors. Because active messages cause the execution of code on the destination processor, they can be costly if this forces a context-switch, particularly for parallel machines built with commodity RISC processors. Another complication facing the programmer is the need to coordinate the active messages. In data-parallel applications, however, active messages can be an attractive approach.

The MPI-2 Forum defined an `MPI_Put` and `MPI_Get` in such a way that they can be implemented without shared memory hardware support, even on heterogeneous networks. See [101, 55, 66] for details.

10.4 Parallel I/O

Parallel I/O means providing access by a collection of processes to external devices. The most common device is an external disk containing a file system; other devices include tape systems, graphical displays, and real-time signal sources.

Many of these external devices are themselves parallel, often for the same reason that a parallel processor is used. For example, the speed at which data can be moved on and off of a spinning disk necessitates the use of arrays of disks in order to get data transfer rates of more than about 10 MB/sec.

This situation leads to a problem with files. Many programmers (and the Unix operating system) view files as a single stream of bytes, making it difficult to exploit parallelism in this mode. Therefore, much current research has considered various kinds of file layout organized by parallel objects [27, 108, 28, 46]. Existing I/O systems for parallel computers have tended to concentrate on providing access to the file system at a fairly low level; users often need to know details of disk-blocking and read-write caching strategies to get acceptable performance.

Fortunately, MPI datatypes provide a powerful way to describe data layouts; MPI's communicators provide an effective means of organizing the processes that are responsible for I/O. MPI's thread safety will help in providing nonblocking (often called asynchronous) I/O operations. Choosing the appropriate extensions to MPI (including new datatypes and datatype constructors) as well as handling the nonuniformity in access to the external devices has been a challenging research area. The approach taken in MPI-2 was to explore the analogy between message-passing and I/O (writing to a file is in many ways like sending a message). Parallel I/O is a major component of the MPI-2 Standard, which exploits MPI datatypes and communicators and provides MPI-like nonblocking and collective operations, together with other convenient features, such as a portable file format.

10.5 MPI-2

The MPI Forum deliberately limited the scope of its decisions to the message-passing model, partly in order to complete the MPI specification quickly and partly because there was so much experience with the message-passing model. The first edition of the book concluded with a section entitled "Will There Be an MPI-2?" There was. The MPI Forum reconvened during 1995-1997 and debated standards for dynamic process management, parallel I/O, and remote memory operations, all of which became parts of MPI-2, as well as a complete thread interface, active messages, and interrupt-driven receives, all of which didn't (although user-defined requests have some related properties). For details on MPI as extended by the MPI-2 Forum, see the Standard itself [101], the book version of the Standard [55], or the companion to this book, *Using MPI-2* [66].

10.6 Will There Be an MPI-3?

MPI-2 introduced a lot of new, sophisticated technology into MPI, and it will take some time before enough experience has been gained by applications with MPI-2 implementations to see what gaps need to be filled in another round. Topics that one can see on the horizon are new language bindings (e.g., Java), extensions to MPI for real-time computing and wide area networks, interoperability among MPI implementations, and the interaction of MPI with newly emerging programming models involving shared memory.

10.7 Final Words

In this book we have illustrated the use of MPI in a wide variety of parallel programs from elementary examples to libraries and complex applications. Along the way we have touched on some of the subtler aspects of the message-passing approach and how MPI deals with these issues. We have introduced parts of a parallel computing environment that enhances programming with MPI. Guidance has been offered both for implementing MPI and for porting existing programs to MPI.

MPI offers the potential of a spurt in the growth of parallel software, long identified as the principal obstacle to the widespread use of parallel computing technology. The combination of efficiency, portability, and functionality offered by MPI on both parallel supercomputers and workstation networks will form the basis of parallel computing for years to come.

Glossary of Selected Terms

The following is a glossary of the most commonly used terms in this book. It is far from complete, but is intended to provide a number of useful definitions in one place.

Active Messages An active message is normally a short message that causes remote execution on the receiving process of a specified section of code, while delivering to that code the active-message "payload." Analogous to remote procedure calls used in most Unix systems, the active-message paradigm is a means both for implementing higher-level protocols like MPI and for direct programming in certain situations. Active messages are an extension to the message-passing model envisaged by MPI.

Application Topology Application topologies are the natural process interconnection implied by the algorithm, in parallel. MPI supports the mapping of application topologies onto virtual topologies, and virtual topologies onto physical hardware topologies.

Attributes Attributes in MPI are integers (in Fortran) or pointers (in C) that can be attached, by key value, to a communicator.

Asynchronous Communication Asynchronous communication is often used interchangably with nonblocking communication. This is generally communication in which the sender and receiver place no constraints on each other in terms of completion, and which may also overlap as much as possible with computation. The term asynchronous communication is not used in MPI.

Bandwidth The bandwidth of a message transmission is the reciprocal of the time needed to transfer a byte (the incremental per-byte cost).

Blocking Communication Blocking communication refers to communication in which the call does not complete until the buffer is available for reuse (in the case of the send) or use (in the case of a receive). See *Blocking Send* and *Blocking Receive.*

Blocking Receive A receive that blocks until the data buffer contains the selected message. See *Nonblocking Receive.*

Blocking Send A send that blocks until the data buffer is available for reuse. This may or may not require recipient to begin the process of receiving the message. The details of the blocking depend on the implementation, and the amount of buffering that the system may choose to do or be able to do.

Buffered Communication Communication in which the send operation (which may be blocking or nonblocking) may make use of a user-provided buffer, in order to ensure that the send does not block while waiting for space to store the user's message. This is primarily of use with blocking sends, where it removes the possibility that the matching receive may need to start before the blocking, buffered send call can return. Buffering may involve additional copying of data and can impact performance.

Buffering Buffering refers to the amount or act of copying (or the amount of memory) that the system uses as part of its transmission protocols. Generally, buffering helps avoid deadlocks, making programming easier for specific cases but less portable and predictable.

Caching of Attributes The process of attaching attributes in MPI to a communicator. See *Attributes.*

Cartesian Topology Cartesian topology is the type of virtual topology that supports regular mapping of processes into an N-dimensional name space. Examples include two- and three-dimensional logical process topologies used for linear algebra and PDE computations.

Collective Communication Collective communication involves operations such as "broadcast" (`MPI_Bcast`) and "all reduce" (`MPI_Allreduce`) that involve the entire group of a communicator, rather than just two members, as in point-to-point communication.

Communication Modes MPI provides buffered, ready, standard, and synchronous communication modes for point-to-point communication.

Communication Processor A communication processor is generally the hardware component that provides the local access of a processor to the parallel computer network. Such processors are also called "router chips" and "mesh-routing chips" or MRCs on some systems. As time passes, the communication processor and its "glue chips" are becoming capable of more than simple transfers to and from CPUs, and may be capable of "gather/scatter"-type operations and other high-speed memory accesses without direct CPU intervention.

Communicator A communicator is a group of processes plus the notion of safe communication context. There are two types of communicators in MPI: intracommunicators (the default), and intercommunicators. Communicators guarantee that communication is isolated from other communication in the system and also that collective communication is isolated from point-to-point communication.

Context In MPI, the context is not a user-visible quantity, but it is the internal mechanism by which a communicator endows a group with safe communication space, separating such communication from all others in the system and also separating point-to-point and collective communication of a communicator's group.

Contiguous Data The simplest message buffers consist of data that is not dispersed in memory, but rather is contiguous. MPI deals with this case, and also with more general noncontiguous data, through datatypes.

Datatypes The MPI objects that support general gather and scatter of complicated data specifications are called datatypes. The simple ones are built in, and user-defined data types are called derived datatypes.

Deadlock The state of execution where the computation cannot proceed because an impasse is reached where two or more processes depend directly or indirectly on each other for a result before continuing. A good example is two processes trying to receive from each other, then send to each other, in a blocking communication mode.

Event The unit of logging for program instrumentation. Events are considered to have no duration.

Graph Topology Graph topology is the type of virtual topology that allows general relationships between processes, where processes are represented by nodes of a graph.

Group A group (or process group) is an ordered collection of processes. Each process has a rank in the group. The rank runs from 0 to one less than the number of processes.

Group Safety Group safety is the type of insulation from message-passing provided by contexts of communication in MPI. Each communicator has a group, and that group communicates in a specific context, independent of all other communication for that group (with different communicators) and all other groups.

Heterogeneous Computing An environment that has distinct data formats, and/or distinct computational capabilities is considered heterogeneous.

InterCommunicator Intercommunicators support both a "local" and "remote" group view of the world, and can be used in client-server-oriented point-to-point computation.

Interconnection Network The hardware that connects processors to form a parallel computer.

IntraCommunicator Intracommunicators (conventionally, communicators), are less general than intercommunicators, in that they have only a "local" view of processes, but support both point-to-point and collective communication.

Key Value The MPI-defined integer that is used to name a particular attribute to be cached is called the key value. The names are process local, so that all communicators on a process can easily share similar attributes.

Latency Latency in the sense of a message-passing system refers to the cost to set up a message transmission. It is the "startup cost" before any bytes of data can be sent. High latency means that messages are costly up front, and may be cheap in the limit of large messages only if the per-byte rate is small (respectively, the bandwidth is high).

MPE MPE is the MultiProcessing Environment add-on software provided with this book to enhance message-passing programming with MPI, including graphics and profiling capabilities.

Message Passing Interface Forum (MPIF) The MPI Forum convened to create a "de facto" standard for message passing, independent of standards bodies. The group consisted of representatives from vendors, universities, and natial laboratories. Researchers from both the United States and Europe were represented.

Multicomputer A term sometimes used to describe a parallel computer where processors with their own private memories are networked.

Node "Node" is used in two senses in this book. In one sense, it is synonymous with processor; in the other it refers to the nodes of a graph, which is a standard computer science data structure.

NonBlocking Communication In a nonblocking communication, the call does not wait for the communication to be completed. See NonBlocking Receive and NonBlocking Send.

Nonblocking Receive A receive operation that may return before the data buffer contains an incoming message. This is often used to provide the location and layout of the data buffer to the lower-level message passing hardware to provide better performance.

Nonblocking Send The send may return before the data buffer is available for re-use. The intent is that the send returns almost immediately. A nonblocking send must not require a matching receive to start before returning.

Object-Based Library Libraries (as defined in Chapter 6) are object-based when they take advantage of hierarchical data structures, uniform calling sequences, and information hiding but do not use inheritance to build complex codes from simpler codes. The resulting programs are similar to functional decompositions. Though the use of data objects is a great help to organization and understanding, there is not the full potential for optimizations nor for code reuse.

Object-Oriented Library Object-oriented libraries (as mentioned in Chapter 6) go beyond object-based libraries in their use of inheritance. Inheritance is used to build up complex relationships from simpler relationships. Simpler class structures are used to build more complex ones, leading to code reuse and, more important, to sources of optimization for the kinds of libraries considered in this book.

Pairwise Ordering The "pairwise ordering" property of message-passing systems is essential to the message-passing programming paradigm of MPI and its ancestor systems. This property guarantees that two messages sent between a pair of processes arrives in the order they were sent. With the introduction of "contexts," this requirement is weakened to require that two messages sent between a pair of processes using the same communicator arrive in the same order they were sent. MPI does weaken this further by changing the order of messages of different tags between the same processor pair.

Parallel Library A library is an "encapsulation" of an algorithm in a way that is meant to be convenient for multiple uses in a single application and/or reuse in multiple applications. Library writers for parallel computers can build robust libraries because MPI specifically provides features to help libraries to isolate their communication from that of users, and other libraries.

Libraries are a mainstay of scientific programming in a number of technical computing environments, but their additional complexity in the parallel computing world has limited their wide use thus far. MPI will help promote a significant body of library codes, since it provides a convenient, and portable basis for robust libraries.

Persistent Requests Persistent requests are used when multiple communications are to be started, tested, or completed, in order to reduce costs and provide the user with access to higher performance.

Physical Topology Physical topology is the topology of the parallel computer interconnection network, such as a mesh or hypercube.

Point-to-Point Communication Point-to-point communication is between two members of a communicator; (generically, a send-receive type call).

Portability Portability is the concept of f moving a program from one environment to another. The degree of portability indicates the amount of work needed to get the program to run again. High-quality portability (also called performance portability, or transportability) implies that reasonable performance is retained as a product of that porting process. MPI is designed to help ensure that high performance is possible across a number of different parallel platforms.

Process A process is the smallest addressable unit of computation in the MPI model. A process resides on a processor (or node). MPI does not discuss how processes are born, die, or are otherwise managed.

Processor A processor is (loosely) the CPU, memory, and I/O capabilities of a subset of a parallel machine (or a workstation in a workstation cluster). A processor supports the execution of one or more processes in the MPI model, but MPI makes only limited connection between processes and processors in environmental inquiry routines and in two topology-related mapping routines.

Quiesence The quiesence property requires that programmers guarantee that no outside communication will impinge on a group of processes during a specific period of execution, in order for a given operation to execute correctly. Quiescence demands that no pending point-to-point communication is in place and that no other processes will send any messages between two points of synchronization for a group of processes. This strategy is not required for most of MPI; the notable exception is during the creation of intercommunicators, where a quiescence guarantee is required of two "leader" processes in the "peer communicator."

Race Condition A race condition is the situation in which two or more processes or threads strive for a resource and obtain it in an unpredictable fashion. Race conditions often mean that a program sometimes works and sometimes breaks.

Ready Communication Mode Also known as *Ready send.* In a ready communication mode, the system is allowed to assume that the receiver has already posted the receive prior to the sender posting the send. If the receive has not been issued when the send occurs, the send is erroneous and the behavior is undefined (error detection is encourage but not required by MPI). The ready send may also be either blocking or nonblocking, as defined above.

Reduce An operation that reduces many data items by combining them together to form a result.

Request Object A request object is returned by MPI in response to an operation that will have a subsequent "wait" before it is completed. A good example is `MPI_Irecv`. The request object is used with `MPI_Wait` and similar calls to find out whether the original operation is complete.

Safe Programs In this book, and in the MPI standard, reference is made to "safe" and "unsafe" programs, independent of the concept of thread safety. A safe program is a program that does not rely on any buffering for its correct execution.

Standard Mode The standard communication mode of MPI corresponds most closely to current common practice.

Status Object The status object is the MPI means for returning information about an operation, notably a receive. For thread safety, this object is returned at the time the receive completes; for efficiency, the format of the receive object is an array for Fortran and a structure for C.

Subgroup MPI works on communicators that have groups. Other communicators based on subgroups of the "world group" are also possible. Subgroups are just as flexible as groups from which they are defined, and no distinction is necessary, except that it is convenient to call certain groups "subgroups" and certain communicators "subcommunicators" when describing algorithms.

Synchronization A synchronization is an operation that forces a group of processes all to pass through a critical section of code before any can continue. Many MPI collective operations are potentially synchronizations, but not all are required to be implemented with this property (except `MPI_Barrier`, which is specifically designed to be a synchronization). See also *Synchronous Communication Mode.*

Synchronous Communication Mode The sender in the synchronous communication mode may not return until the matching receive has been issued on the destination process. Synchronous sends may be either blocking or nonblocking, depending on whether the data buffer provided to the send is available for reuse when the send call returns.

Thread A thread is the atomic notion of execution within an MPI process. Each MPI process has a main thread and may have additional threads, provided a thread-safe programming environment and threads package are available. The MPI interface is thread safe, but does not tie MPI specifically to any thread paradigm or standard. Implementations of MPI may or may not be thread safe. The precise level of thread safety offered in an MPI implementation can be found in an MPI program with functions introduced in MPI-2.

Thread Safety Thread safety is the quality of software semantics that guarantees that independently executing threads will not interfere with each other by accessing data intended for a different thread. Implementing thread safety requires eliminating most global state and explicitly managing use of any global state that can not be eliminated. MPI is designed to be thread safe.

Topology See *Virtual Topology.*

Type Map A type map is the sequence of pairs of basic MPI datatypes and displacements that make up, in part, a derived datatype.

Type Signature The type signature is the MPI concept that extracts just the sequence of datatypes from a type map.

User-Defined Topology If MPI's virtual topologies are insufficient, then users can easily build their own topologies. Such topologies are often application-oriented.

Virtual Shared Memory Virtual shared memory is a software and/or hardware model in which the system provides the user with the impression that there is a single address space for the purpose of programming the system.

Virtual Topology Virtual topologies are a naming of processes in a communicator other than the rank naming. Graphs, Cartesian grids, and user-defined arrangements are all possible. Virtual topologies link applications more closely to communicators because the names of processes reflect the communication pattern needed for it. See also *Application Topology.*

A Summary of MPI-1 Routines and Their Arguments

The Appendix contains the bindings for the MPI-1 routines in C, Fortran, and C++. For the routines that are deprecated, we have indicated the MPI-2 replacement with text like "Deprecated. Use MPI_Get_address instead". We have added to this list the MPI-2 functions that replace deprecated MPI-1 functions.

A.1 C Routines

This section describes the C routines from [99].

```
int MPI_Abort(MPI_Comm comm, int errorcode)
```
Terminates MPI execution environment

```
int MPI_Address(void* location, MPI_Aint *address)
```
Gets the address of a location in memory

Deprecated. Use MPI_Get_address instead

```
int MPI_Allgather(void* sendbuf, int sendcount,
          MPI_Datatype sendtype, void* recvbuf, int recvcount,
          MPI_Datatype recvtype, MPI_Comm comm)
```
Gathers data from all tasks and distribute it to all

```
int MPI_Allgatherv(void* sendbuf, int sendcount,
          MPI_Datatype sendtype, void* recvbuf, int *recvcounts,
          int *displs, MPI_Datatype recvtype, MPI_Comm comm)
```
Gathers data from all tasks and deliver it to all

```
int MPI_Allreduce(void* sendbuf, void* recvbuf, int count,
          MPI_Datatype datatype, MPI_Op op, MPI_Comm comm)
```
Combines values from all processes and distribute the result back to all processes

```
int MPI_Alltoall(void* sendbuf, int sendcount,
          MPI_Datatype sendtype, void* recvbuf, int recvcount,
          MPI_Datatype recvtype, MPI_Comm comm)
```
Sends data from all to all processes

```
int MPI_Alltoallv(void* sendbuf, int *sendcounts, int *sdispls,
          MPI_Datatype sendtype, void* recvbuf, int *recvcounts,
          int *rdispls, MPI_Datatype recvtype, MPI_Comm comm)
```
Sends data from all to all processes, with a displacement

```
int MPI_Attr_delete(MPI_Comm comm, int keyval)
```
Deletes attribute value associated with a key

Deprecated. Use MPI_Comm_delete_attr instead

```
int MPI_Attr_get(MPI_Comm comm, int keyval, void *attribute_val,
         int *flag)
```
Retrieves attribute value by key

Deprecated. Use MPI_Comm_get_attr instead

```
int MPI_Attr_put(MPI_Comm comm, int keyval, void* attribute_val)
```
Stores attribute value associated with a key

Deprecated. Use MPI_Comm_set_attr instead

```
int MPI_Barrier(MPI_Comm comm)
```
Blocks until all process have reached this routine

```
int MPI_Bcast(void* buffer, int count, MPI_Datatype datatype,
         int root, MPI_Comm comm)
```
Broadcasts a message from the process with rank "root" to all other processes of the group

```
int MPI_Bsend(void* buf, int count, MPI_Datatype datatype, int dest,
         int tag, MPI_Comm comm)
```
Basic send with user-specified buffering

```
int MPI_Bsend_init(void* buf, int count, MPI_Datatype datatype,
         int dest, int tag, MPI_Comm comm, MPI_Request *request)
```
Builds a handle for a buffered send

```
int MPI_Buffer_attach(void* buffer, int size)
```
Attaches a user-defined buffer for sending

```
int MPI_Buffer_detach(void* buffer, int* size)
```
Removes an existing buffer (for use in MPI_Bsend, etc.)

```
int MPI_Cancel(MPI_Request *request)
```
Cancels a communication request

```
int MPI_Cart_coords(MPI_Comm comm, int rank, int maxdims,
         int *coords)
```
Determines process coords in Cartesian topology given rank in group

```
int MPI_Cart_create(MPI_Comm comm_old, int ndims, int *dims,
         int *periods, int reorder, MPI_Comm *comm_cart)
```
Makes a new communicator to which topology information has been attached

```
int MPI_Cart_get(MPI_Comm comm, int maxdims, int *dims,
         int *periods, int *coords)
```
Retrieve Cartesian topology information associated with a communicator

```
int MPI_Cart_map(MPI_Comm comm, int ndims, int *dims, int *periods,
         int *newrank)
```
Maps process to Cartesian topology information

```
int MPI_Cart_rank(MPI_Comm comm, int *coords, int *rank)
```
Determines process rank in communicator given Cartesian location

```
int MPI_Cart_shift(MPI_Comm comm, int direction, int disp,
         int *rank_source, int *rank_dest)
```
Returns the shifted source and destination ranks given a shift direction and amount

```
int MPI_Cart_sub(MPI_Comm comm, int *remain_dims, MPI_Comm *newcomm)
```
Partitions a communicator into subgroups that form lower-dimensional cartesian subgrids

```
int MPI_Cartdim_get(MPI_Comm comm, int *ndims)
```
Retrieves Cartesian topology information associated with a communicator

```
int MPI_Comm_compare(MPI_Comm comm1, MPI_Comm comm2, int *result)
```
Compares two communicators

```
int MPI_Comm_create(MPI_Comm comm, MPI_Group group,
         MPI_Comm *newcomm)
```
Creates a new communicator

```
int MPI_Comm_create_errhandler(MPI_Comm_errhandler_fn *function,
         MPI_Errhandler *errhandler)
```
MPI-2: Creates an MPI-style error handler

```
int MPI_Comm_create_keyval(MPI_Comm_copy_attr_function *copy_fn,
         MPI_Comm_delete_attr_function *delete_fn, int *keyval,
         void* extra_state)
```
MPI-2: Generates a new attribute key

```
int MPI_Comm_delete_attr(MPI_Comm comm, int keyval)
```
MPI-2: Deletes attribute value associated with a key

```
int MPI_Comm_dup(MPI_Comm comm, MPI_Comm *newcomm)
```
Duplicates an existing communicator with all its cached information

```
int MPI_Comm_free(MPI_Comm *comm)
```
Marks the communicator object for deallocation

```
int MPI_Comm_free_keyval(int *keyval)
```
MPI-2: Frees attribute key for communicator cache attribute

```
int MPI_Comm_get_attr(MPI_Comm comm, int keyval,
         void *attribute_val, int *flag)
```
MPI-2: Retrieves attribute value by key

```
int MPI_Comm_get_errhandler(MPI_Comm comm,
          MPI_Errhandler *errhandler)
```
MPI-2: Gets the error handler for a communicator

```
int MPI_Comm_group(MPI_Comm comm, MPI_Group *group)
```
Accesses the group associated with given communicator

```
int MPI_Comm_rank(MPI_Comm comm, int *rank)
```
Determines the rank of the calling process in the communicator

```
int MPI_Comm_remote_group(MPI_Comm comm, MPI_Group *group)
```
Returns the remote group in an intercommunicator

```
int MPI_Comm_remote_size(MPI_Comm comm, int *size)
```
Returns the number of processes in the remote group

```
int MPI_Comm_set_attr(MPI_Comm comm, int keyval,
          void* attribute_val)
```
Stores attribute value associated with a key

```
int MPI_Comm_set_errhandler(MPI_Comm comm,
          MPI_Errhandler errhandler)
```
MPI-2: Sets the error handler for a communicator

```
int MPI_Comm_size(MPI_Comm comm, int *size)
```
Determines the size of the group associated with a communictor

```
int MPI_Comm_split(MPI_Comm comm, int color, int key,
          MPI_Comm *newcomm)
```
Creates new communicators based on colors and keys

```
int MPI_Comm_test_inter(MPI_Comm comm, int *flag)
```
Tests to see whether a communicator is an intercommunicator

```
int MPI_Dims_create(int nnodes, int ndims, int *dims)
```
Creates a division of processes in a Cartesian grid

```
int MPI_Errhandler_create(MPI_Handler_function *function,
          MPI_Errhandler *errhandler)
```
Creates an MPI-style error handler

Deprecated. Use MPI_Comm_create_errhandler instead

```
int MPI_Errhandler_free(MPI_Errhandler *errhandler)
```
Frees an MPI-style error handler

```
int MPI_Errhandler_get(MPI_Comm comm, MPI_Errhandler *errhandler)
```
Gets the error handler for a communicator

Deprecated. Use MPI_Comm_get_errhandler instead

`int MPI_Errhandler_set(MPI_Comm comm, MPI_Errhandler errhandler)` *Sets the error handler for a communicator* *Deprecated. Use MPI_Comm_set_errhandler instead*
`int MPI_Error_class(int errorcode, int *errorclass)` *Converts an error code into an error class*
`int MPI_Error_string(int errorcode, char *string, int *resultlen)` *Returns a string for a given error code*
`int MPI_Finalize(void)` *Terminates MPI execution environment*
`int MPI_Gather(void* sendbuf, int sendcount, MPI_Datatype sendtype, void* recvbuf, int recvcount, MPI_Datatype recvtype, int root, MPI_Comm comm)` *Gathers together values from a group of tasks*
`int MPI_Gatherv(void* sendbuf, int sendcount, MPI_Datatype sendtype, void* recvbuf, int *recvcounts, int *displs, MPI_Datatype recvtype, int root, MPI_Comm comm)` *Gathers into specified locations from all tasks in a group*
`int MPI_Get_address(void* location, MPI_Aint *address)` *MPI-2: Gets the address of a location in memory*
`int MPI_Get_count(MPI_Status *status, MPI_Datatype datatype, int *count)` *Gets the number of "top-level" elements*
`int MPI_Get_elements(MPI_Status *status, MPI_Datatype datatype, int *elements)` *Returns the number of basic elements in a Datatype*
`int MPI_Get_processor_name(char *name, int *resultlen)` *Gets the name of the processor*
`int MPI_Get_version(int *version, int *subversion)` *Return the version of MPI*
`int MPI_Graph_create(MPI_Comm comm_old, int nnodes, int *index, int *edges, int reorder, MPI_Comm *comm_graph)` *Makes a new communicator to which topology information has been attached*
`int MPI_Graph_get(MPI_Comm comm, int maxindex, int maxedges, int *index, int *edges)` *Retrieves graph topology information associated with a communicator*

```
int MPI_Graph_map(MPI_Comm comm, int nnodes, int *index, int *edges,
         int *newrank)
```
Maps process to graph topology information

```
int MPI_Graph_neighbors_count(MPI_Comm comm, int rank,
         int *nneighbors)
```
Returns the number of neighbors of a node associated with a graph topology

```
int MPI_Graph_neighbors(MPI_Comm comm, int rank, int *maxneighbors,
         int *neighbors)
```
Returns the neighbors of a node associated with a graph topology

```
int MPI_Graphdims_Get(MPI_Comm comm, int *nnodes, int *nedges)
```
Retrieves graph topology information associated with a communicator

```
int MPI_Group_compare(MPI_Group group1, MPI_Group group2,
         int *result)
```
Compare two groups

```
int MPI_Group_difference(MPI_Group group1, MPI_Group group2,
         MPI_Group *newgroup)
```
Makes a group from the difference of two groups

```
int MPI_Group_excl(MPI_Group group, int n, int *ranks,
         MPI_Group *newgroup)
```
Produces a group by reordering an existing group and taking only unlisted members

```
int MPI_Group_free(MPI_Group *group)
```
Frees a group

```
int MPI_Group_incl(MPI_Group group, int n, int *ranks,
         MPI_Group *newgroup)
```
Produces a group by reordering an existing group and taking only listed members

```
int MPI_Group_intersection(MPI_Group group1, MPI_Group group2,
         MPI_Group *newgroup)
```
Produces a group as the intersection of two existing groups

```
int MPI_Group_range_excl(MPI_Group group, int n, int ranges[][3],
         MPI_Group *newgroup)
```
Produces a group by excluding ranges of processes from an existing group

```
int MPI_Group_range_incl(MPI_Group group, int n, int ranges[][3],
         MPI_Group *newgroup)
```
Creates a new group from ranges of ranks in an existing group

```
int MPI_Group_rank(MPI_Group group, int *rank)
```
Returns the rank of this process in the given group

```
int MPI_Group_size(MPI_Group group, int *size)
```
Returns the size of a group

```
int MPI_Group_translate_ranks (MPI_Group group1, int n, int *ranks1,
         MPI_Group group2, int *ranks2)
```
Translates the ranks of processes in one group to those in another group

```
int MPI_Group_union(MPI_Group group1, MPI_Group group2,
         MPI_Group *newgroup)
```
Produces a group by combining two groups

```
int MPI_Ibsend(void* buf, int count, MPI_Datatype datatype,
         int dest, int tag, MPI_Comm comm, MPI_Request *request)
```
Starts a nonblocking buffered send

```
int MPI_Init(int *argc, char ***argv)
```
Initializes the MPI execution environment

```
int MPI_Initialized(int *flag)
```
Indicates whether MPI_Init has been called

```
int MPI_Intercomm_create(MPI_Comm local_comm, int local_leader,
         MPI_Comm peer_comm, int remote_leader, int tag,
         MPI_Comm *newintercomm)
```
Creates an intercommunicator from two intracommunicators

```
int MPI_Intercomm_merge(MPI_Comm intercomm, int high,
         MPI_Comm *newintracomm)
```
Creates an intracommunicator from an intercommunicator

```
int MPI_Iprobe(int source, int tag, MPI_Comm comm, int *flag,
         MPI_Status *status)
```
Nonblocking test for a message

```
int MPI_Irecv(void* buf, int count, MPI_Datatype datatype,
         int source, int tag, MPI_Comm comm, MPI_Request *request)
```
Begins a nonblocking receive

```
int MPI_Irsend(void* buf, int count, MPI_Datatype datatype,
         int dest, int tag, MPI_Comm comm, MPI_Request *request)
```
Starts a nonblocking ready send

```
int MPI_Isend(void* buf, int count, MPI_Datatype datatype, int dest,
         int tag, MPI_Comm comm, MPI_Request *request)
```
Starts a nonblocking send

```
int MPI_Issend(void* buf, int count, MPI_Datatype datatype,
        int dest, int tag, MPI_Comm comm, MPI_Request *request)
```
Starts a nonblocking synchronous send

```
int MPI_Keyval_create(MPI_Copy_function *copy_fn,
        MPI_Delete_function *delete_fn, int *keyval,
        void* extra_state)
```
Generates a new attribute key

Deprecated. Use MPI_Comm_create_keyval instead

```
int MPI_Keyval_free(int *keyval)
```
Frees attribute key for communicator cache attribute

Deprecated. Use MPI_Comm_free_keyval instead

```
int MPI_Op_create(MPI_Uop function, int commute, MPI_Op *op)
```
Creates a user-defined combination function handle

```
int MPI_Op_free(MPI_Op *op)
```
Frees a user-defined combination function handle

```
int MPI_Pack(void *inbuf, int incount, MPI_Datatype datatype,
        void *outbuf, int outcount, int *position, MPI_Comm comm)
```
Packs data into a contiguous buffer

```
int MPI_Pack_size(int incount, MPI_Datatype datatype, MPI_Comm comm,
        int *size)
```
Return the size needed to pack a datatype

```
int MPI_Pcontrol(const int level, ...)
```
Controls profiling

```
int MPI_Probe(int source, int tag, MPI_Comm comm,
        MPI_Status *status)
```
Blocking test for a message

```
int MPI_Recv(void* buf, int count, MPI_Datatype datatype,
        int source, int tag, MPI_Comm comm, MPI_Status *status)
```
Basic receive

```
int MPI_Recv_init(void* buf, int count, MPI_Datatype datatype,
        int source, int tag, MPI_Comm comm, MPI_Request *request)
```
Creates a handle for a receive

```
int MPI_Reduce(void* sendbuf, void* recvbuf, int count,
        MPI_Datatype datatype, MPI_Op op, int root, MPI_Comm comm)
```
Reduces values on all processes to a single value

```
int MPI_Reduce_scatter(void* sendbuf, void* recvbuf,
         int *recvcounts, MPI_Datatype datatype, MPI_Op op,
         MPI_Comm comm)
```
Combines values and scatters the results

```
int MPI_Request_free(MPI_Request *request)
```
Frees a communication request object

```
int MPI_Rsend(void* buf, int count, MPI_Datatype datatype, int dest,
         int tag, MPI_Comm comm)
```
Basic ready send

```
int MPI_Rsend_init(void* buf, int count, MPI_Datatype datatype,
         int dest, int tag, MPI_Comm comm, MPI_Request *request)
```
Builds a handle for a ready send

```
int MPI_Scan(void* sendbuf, void* recvbuf, int count,
         MPI_Datatype datatype, MPI_Op op, MPI_Comm comm)
```
Computes the scan (partial reductions) of data on a collection of processes

```
int MPI_Scatter(void* sendbuf, int sendcount, MPI_Datatype sendtype,
         void* recvbuf, int recvcount, MPI_Datatype recvtype,
         int root, MPI_Comm comm)
```
Sends data from one task to all other tasks in a group

```
int MPI_Scatterv(void* sendbuf, int *sendcounts, int *displs,
         MPI_Datatype sendtype, void* recvbuf, int recvcount,
         MPI_Datatype recvtype, int root, MPI_Comm comm)
```
Scatters a buffer in parts to all tasks in a group

```
int MPI_Send(void* buf, int count, MPI_Datatype datatype, int dest,
         int tag, MPI_Comm comm)
```
Basic send

```
int MPI_Send_init(void* buf, int count, MPI_Datatype datatype,
         int dest, int tag, MPI_Comm comm, MPI_Request *request)
```
Builds a handle for a standard send

```
int MPI_Sendrecv(void *sendbuf, int sendcount,
         MPI_Datatype sendtype, int dest, int sendtag,
         void *recvbuf, int recvcount, MPI_Datatype recvtype,
         int source, int recvtag, MPI_Comm comm, MPI_Status *status)
```
Sends and receives a message

```
int MPI_Sendrecv_replace(void* buf, int count,
         MPI_Datatype datatype, int dest, int sendtag, int source,
         int recvtag, MPI_Comm comm, MPI_Status *status)
```
Sends and receives using a single buffer

```
int MPI_Ssend(void* buf, int count, MPI_Datatype datatype, int dest,
         int tag, MPI_Comm comm)
```
Basic synchronous send

```
int MPI_Ssend_init(void* buf, int count, MPI_Datatype datatype,
         int dest, int tag, MPI_Comm comm, MPI_Request *request)
```
Builds a handle for a synchronous send

```
int MPI_Start(MPI_Request *request)
```
Initiates a communication with a persistent request handle

```
int MPI_Startall(int count, MPI_Request *array_of_requests)
```
Starts a collection of requests

```
int MPI_Test(MPI_Request *request, int *flag, MPI_Status *status)
```
Tests for the completion of a send or receive

```
int MPI_Testall(int count, MPI_Request *array_of_requests,
         int *flag, MPI_Status *array_of_statuses)
```
Tests for the completion of all previously initiated communications

```
int MPI_Testany(int count, MPI_Request *array_of_requests,
         int *index, int *flag, MPI_Status *status)
```
Tests for completion of any previously initiated communication

```
int MPI_Testsome(int incount, MPI_Request *array_of_requests,
         int *outcount, int *array_of_indices,
         MPI_Status *array_of_statuses)
```
Tests for some given communications to complete

```
int MPI_Test_cancelled(MPI_Status *status, int *flag)
```
Tests to see whether a request was cancelled

```
int MPI_Topo_test(MPI_Comm comm, int *top_type)
```
Determines the type of topology (if any) associated with a communicator

```
int MPI_Type_commit(MPI_Datatype *datatype)
```
Commits the datatype

```
int MPI_Type_contiguous(int count, MPI_Datatype oldtype,
         MPI_Datatype *newtype)
```
Creates a contiguous Datatype

```
int MPI_Type_create_hindexed(int count, int *array_of_blocklengths,
          MPI_Aint *array_of_displacements, MPI_Datatype oldtype,
          MPI_Datatype *newtype)
```
MPI-2: Creates an indexed Datatype with offsets in bytes

```
int MPI_Type_create_hvector(int count, int blocklength,
          MPI_Aint stride, MPI_Datatype oldtype,
          MPI_Datatype *newtype)
```
MPI-2: Creates a vector (strided) Datatype with offset in bytes

```
int MPI_Type_create_struct(int count, int *array_of_blocklengths,
          MPI_Aint *array_of_displacements,
          MPI_Datatype *array_of_types, MPI_Datatype *newtype)
```
MPI-2: Creates a struct Datatype

```
int MPI_Type_extent(MPI_Datatype datatype, MPI_Aint *extent)
```
Returns the extent of Datatype

Deprecated. Use MPI_Type_get_extent instead

```
int MPI_Type_free(MPI_Datatype *datatype)
```
Marks the Datatype object for deallocation

```
int MPI_Type_get_extent(MPI_Datatype datatype, MPI_Aint *lb,
          MPI_Aint *extent)
```
MPI-2: Return the lower bound and extent of a datatype

```
int MPI_Type_hindexed(int count, int *array_of_blocklengths,
          MPI_Aint *array_of_displacements, MPI_Datatype oldtype,
          MPI_Datatype *newtype)
```
Creates an indexed Datatype with offsets in bytes

Deprecated. Use MPI_Type_create_hindexed instead

```
int MPI_Type_hvector(int count, int blocklength, MPI_Aint stride,
          MPI_Datatype oldtype, MPI_Datatype *newtype)
```
Creates a vector (strided) Datatype with offset in bytes

Deprecated. Use MPI_Type_create_hvector instead

```
int MPI_Type_indexed(int count, int *array_of_blocklengths,
          int *array_of_displacements, MPI_Datatype oldtype,
          MPI_Datatype *newtype)
```
Creates an indexed Datatype

```
int MPI_Type_lb(MPI_Datatype datatype, MPI_Aint *displacement)
```
Returns the lower-bound of a datatype

Deprecated. Use MPI_Type_get_extent instead

```
int MPI_Type_size(MPI_Datatype datatype, int *size)
```
Return the number of bytes occupied by entries in the datatype

```
int MPI_Type_struct(int count, int *array_of_blocklengths,
         MPI_Aint *array_of_displacements,
         MPI_Datatype *array_of_types, MPI_Datatype *newtype)
```
Creates a struct Datatype

Deprecated. Use MPI_Type_create_struct instead

```
int MPI_Type_ub(MPI_Datatype datatype, MPI_Aint *displacement)
```
Returns the upper bound of a Datatype

Deprecated. Use MPI_Type_get_extent instead

```
int MPI_Type_vector(int count, int blocklength, int stride,
         MPI_Datatype oldtype, MPI_Datatype *newtype)
```
Creates a vector (strided) Datatype

```
int MPI_Unpack(void *inbuf, int insize, int *position, void *outbuf,
         int outcount, MPI_Datatype datatype, MPI_Comm comm)
```
Unpacks data from a contiguous buffer

```
int MPI_Wait(MPI_Request *request, MPI_Status *status)
```
Waits for an MPI send or receive to complete

```
int MPI_Waitall(int count, MPI_Request *array_of_requests,
         MPI_Status *array_of_statuses)
```
Waits for all given communications to complete

```
int MPI_Waitany(int count, MPI_Request *array_of_requests,
         int *index, MPI_Status *status)
```
Waits for any specified send or receive to complete

```
int MPI_Waitsome(int incount, MPI_Request *array_of_requests,
         int *outcount, int *array_of_indices,
         MPI_Status *array_of_statuses)
```
Waits for some given communications to complete

```
double MPI_Wtick(void)
```
Returns the resolution of MPI_Wtime

```
double MPI_Wtime(void)
```
Returns an elapsed time on the calling processor

A.2 Fortran Routines

This section describes the Fortran routines from [99].

```
MPI_Abort(comm, errorcode, ierror)
integer comm, errorcode, ierror
```
Terminates MPI execution environment

```
MPI_Address(location, address, ierror)
<type> location
integer address, ierror
```
Gets the address of a location in memory

Deprecated. Use MPI_Get_address instead

```
MPI_Allgather(sendbuf, sendcount, sendtype, recvbuf, recvcount,
          recvtype, comm, ierror)
<type> sendbuf(*), recvbuf(*)
integer sendcount, sendtype, recvcount, recvtype, comm, ierror
```
Gathers data from all tasks and distribute it to all

```
MPI_Allgatherv(sendbuf, sendcount, sendtype, recvbuf, recvcounts,
          displs, recvtype, comm, ierror)
<type> sendbuf(*), recvbuf(*)
integer sendcount, sendtype, recvcounts(*), displs(*), recvtype,
comm, ierror
```
Gathers data from all tasks and deliver it to all

```
MPI_Allreduce(sendbuf, recvbuf, count, datatype, op, comm, ierror)
<type> sendbuf(*), recvbuf(*)
integer count, datatype, op, comm, ierror
```
Combines values from all processes and distribute the result back to all processes

```
MPI_Alltoall(sendbuf, sendcount, sendtype, recvbuf, recvcount,
          recvtype, comm, ierror)
<type> sendbuf(*), recvbuf(*)
integer sendcount, sendtype, recvcount, recvtype, comm, ierror
```
Sends data from all to all processes

```
MPI_Alltoallv(sendbuf, sendcounts, sdispls, sendtype, recvbuf,
         recvcounts, rdispls, recvtype, comm, ierror)
<type> sendbuf(*), recvbuf(*)
integer sendcounts(*), sdispls(*), sendtype, recvcounts(*),
rdispls(*), recvtype, comm, ierror
```

Sends data from all to all processes, with a displacement

```
MPI_Attr_delete(comm, keyval, ierror)
integer comm, keyval, ierror
```

Deletes attribute value associated with a key

Deprecated. Use MPI_Comm_delete_attr instead

```
MPI_Attr_get(comm, keyval, attribute_val, flag, ierror)
integer comm, keyval, attribute_val, ierror
logical flag
```

Retrieves attribute value by key

Deprecated. Use MPI_Comm_get_attr instead

```
MPI_Attr_put(comm, keyval, attribute_val, ierror)
integer comm, keyval, attribute_val, ierror
```

Stores attribute value associated with a key

Deprecated. Use MPI_Comm_set_attr instead

```
MPI_Barrier(comm, ierror)
integer comm, ierror
```

Blocks until all process have reached this routine.

```
MPI_Bcast(buffer, count, datatype, root, comm, ierror)
<type> buffer(*)
integer count, datatype, root, comm, ierror
```

Broadcasts a message from the process with rank "root" to all other processes of the group

```
MPI_Bsend(buf, count, datatype, dest, tag, comm, ierror)
<type> buf(*)
integer count, datatype, dest, tag, comm, ierror
```

Basic send with user-specified buffering

```
MPI_Bsend_init(buf, count, datatype, dest, tag, comm, request,
         ierror)
<type> buf(*)
integer count, datatype, dest, tag, comm, request, ierror
```

Builds a handle for a buffered send

```
MPI_Buffer_attach(buffer, size, ierror)
<type> buffer(*)
integer size, ierror
```
Attaches a user-defined buffer for sending

```
MPI_Buffer_detach(buffer, size, ierror)
<type> buffer(*)
integer size, ierror
```
Removes an existing buffer (for use in MPI_Bsend, etc.)

```
MPI_Cancel(request, ierror)
integer request, ierror
```
Cancels a communication request

```
MPI_Cart_coords(comm, rank, maxdims, coords, ierror)
integer comm, rank, maxdims, coords(*), ierror
```
Determines process coords in Cartesian topology, given rank in group

```
MPI_Cart_create(comm_old, ndims, dims, periods, reorder, comm_cart,
          ierror)
integer comm_old, ndims, dims(*), comm_cart, ierror
logical periods(*), reorder
```
Makes a new communicator to which topology information has been attached

```
MPI_Cart_get(comm, maxdims, dims, periods, coords, ierror)
integer comm, maxdims, dims(*), coords(*), ierror
logical periods(*)
```
Retrieves Cartesian topology information associated with a communicator

```
MPI_Cart_map(comm, ndims, dims, periods, newrank, ierror)
integer comm, ndims, dims(*), newrank, ierror
logical periods(*)
```
Maps process to Cartesian topology information

```
MPI_Cart_rank(comm, coords, rank, ierror)
integer comm, coords(*), rank, ierror
```
Determines process rank in communicator, given Cartesian location

```
MPI_Cart_shift(comm, direction, disp, rank_source, rank_dest,
          ierror)
integer comm, direction, disp, rank_source, rank_dest, ierror
```
Returns the shifted source and destination ranks given a shift direction and amount

```
MPI_Cart_sub(comm, remain_dims, newcomm, ierror)
integer comm, newcomm, ierror
logical remain_dims(*)
```
Partitions a communicator into subgroups that form lower-dimensional Cartesian subgrids

```
MPI_Cartdim_get(comm, ndims, ierror)
integer comm, ndims, ierror
```
Retrieves Cartesian topology information associated with a communicator

```
MPI_Comm_compare(comm1, comm2, result, ierror)
integer comm, group, newcomm, ierror
```
Compares two communicators

```
MPI_Comm_create(comm, group, newcomm, ierror)
integer comm, group, newcomm, ierror
```
Creates a new communicator

```
MPI_Comm_create_errhandler(function, errhandler, ierror)
external function
integer errhandler, ierror
```
MPI-2: Creates an MPI-style error handler

```
MPI_Comm_create_keyval(copy_fn, delete_fn, keyval, extra_state,
          ierror)
external copy_fn, delete_fn
integer keyval, ierror
integer (kind=MPI_ADDRESS_KIND) extra_state
```
MPI-2: Generates a new attribute key

```
MPI_Comm_delete_attr(comm, keyval, ierror)
integer comm, keyval, ierror
```
MPI-2: Deletes attribute value associated with a key

```
MPI_Comm_dup(comm, newcomm, ierror)
integer comm, newcomm, ierror
```
Duplicates an existing communicator with all its cached information

```
MPI_Comm_free(comm, ierror)
integer comm, ierror
```
Marks the communicator object for deallocation

```
MPI_Comm_free_keyval(keyval, ierror)
integer keyval, ierror
```
MPI-2: Frees and attribute key for communicator cache attribute

MPI_Comm_get_attr(comm, keyval, attribute_val, flag, ierror) integer comm, keyval, ierror integer (kind=MPI_ADDRESS_KIND) attribute_val logical flag *MPI-2: Retrieves attribute value by key*
MPI_Comm_get_errhandler(comm, errhandler, ierror) integer comm, errhandler, ierror *MPI-2: Gets the error handler for a communicator*
MPI_Comm_group(comm, group, ierror) integer comm, group, ierror *Accesses the group associated with given communicator*
MPI_Comm_rank(comm, rank, ierror) integer comm, rank, ierror *Determines the rank of the calling process in the communicator*
MPI_Comm_remote_group(comm, group, ierror) integer comm, group, error *Returns the remote group in an intercommunicator*
MPI_Comm_remote_size(comm, size, ierror) integer comm, size, ierror *Returns the number of processes in the remote group*
MPI_Comm_set_attr(comm, keyval, attribute_val, ierror) integer comm, keyval, ierror integer (kind=MPI_ADDRESS_KIND) attribute_val *MPI-2: Stores attribute value associated with a key*
MPI_Comm_set_errhandler(comm, errhandler, ierror) integer comm, errhandler, ierror *MPI-2: Sets the error handler for a communicator*
MPI_Comm_size(comm, size, ierror) integer comm, size, ierror *Determines the size of the group associated with a communictor*
MPI_Comm_split(comm, color, key, newcomm, ierror) integer comm, color, key, newcomm, ierror *Creates new communicators based on colors and keys*

```
MPI_Comm_test_inter(comm, flag, ierror)
integer comm, ierror
logical flag
```
Tests to see whether a communicator is an intercommunicator

```
MPI_Dims_create(nnodes, ndims, dims, ierror)
integer nnodes, ndims, dims(*), ierror
```
Creates a division of processes in a Cartesian grid

```
MPI_Errhandler_create(function, errhandler, ierror)
external function
integer errhandler, ierror
```
Creates an MPI-style error handler

Deprecated. Use MPI_Comm_create_errhandler instead

```
MPI_Errhandler_free(errhandler, ierror)
integer errhandler, ierror
```
Frees an MPI-style error handler

```
MPI_Errhandler_get(comm, errhandler, ierror)
integer comm, errhandler, ierror
```
Gets the error handler for a communicator

Deprecated. Use MPI_Comm_get_errhandler instead

```
MPI_Errhandler_set(comm, errhandler, ierror)
integer comm, errhandler, ierror
```
Sets the error handler for a communicator

Deprecated. Use MPI_Comm_set_errhandler instead

```
MPI_Error_class(errorcode, errorclass, ierror)
integer errorcode, errorclass, ierror
```
Converts an error code into an error class

```
MPI_Error_string(errorcode, string, resultlen, ierror)
integer errorcode, resultlen, ierror
character*(MPI_MAX_ERROR_STRING) string
```
Returns a string for a given error code

```
MPI_Finalize(ierror)
integer ierror
```
Terminates MPI execution environment

```
MPI_Gather(sendbuf, sendcount, sendtype, recvbuf, recvcount,
         recvtype, root, comm, ierror)
<type> sendbuf(*), recvbuf(*)
integer sendcount, sendtype, recvcount, recvtype, root, comm, ierror
```
Gathers together values from a group of tasks

```
MPI_Gatherv(sendbuf, sendcount, sendtype, recvbuf, recvcounts,
         displs, recvtype, root, comm, ierror)
<type>sendbuf(*), recvbuf(*)
integer sendcount, sendtype, recvcounts(*), displs(*), recvtype,
root, comm, ierror
```
Gathers into specified locations from all tasks in a group

```
MPI_Get_address(location, address, ierror)
<type> location(*)
integer (kind=MPI_ADDRESS_KIND) address
integer ierror
```
MPI-2: Gets the address of a location in memory

```
MPI_Get_count(status, datatype, count, ierror)
integer status(*), datatype, count, ierror
```
Gets the number of "top level" elements

```
MPI_Get_elements(status, datatype, elements, ierror)
integer status(*), datatype, elements, ierror
```
Returns the number of basic elements in a datatype

```
MPI_Get_processor_name(name, resultlen, ierror)
character*(MPI_MAX_PROCESSOR_NAME) name
integer resultlen, ierror
```
Gets the name of the processor

```
MPI_Get_version(version, subversion, ierror)
integer version, subversion, ierror
```
Return the version of MPI

```
MPI_Graph_create(comm_old, nnodes, index, edges, reorder,
         comm_graph, ierror)
integer comm_old, nnodes, index(*), edges(*), comm_graph, ierror
logical reorder
```
Makes a new communicator to which topology information has been attached

`MPI_Graph_get(comm, maxindex, maxedges, index, edges, ierror)`
`integer comm, maxindex, maxedges, index(*), edges(*), ierror`
Retrieves graph topology information associated with a communicator

`MPI_Graph_map(comm, nnodes, index, edges, newrank, ierror)`
`integer comm, nnodes, index(*), edges(*), newrank, ierror`
Maps process to graph topology information

`MPI_Graph_neighbors_count(comm, rank, nneighbors, ierror)`
`integer comm, rank, nneighbors, ierror`
Returns the number of neighbors of a node associated with a graph topology

`MPI_Graph_neighbors(comm, rank, maxneighbors, neighbors, ierror)`
`integer comm, rank, maxneighbors, neighbors(*), ierror`
Returns the neighbors of a node associated with a graph topology

`MPI_Graphdims_Get(comm, nnodes, nedges, ierror)`
`integer comm, nnodes, nedges, ierror`
Retrieves graph topology information associated with a communicator

`MPI_Group_compare(group1, group2, result, ierror)`
`integer group1, group2, result, ierror`
Compare two groups

`MPI_Group_difference(group1, group2, newgroup, ierror)`
`integer group1, group2, newgroup, ierror`
Makes a group from the difference of two groups

`MPI_Group_excl(group, n, ranks, newgroup, ierror)`
`integer group, n, ranks(*), newgroup, ierror`
Produces a group by reordering an existing group and taking only unlisted members

`MPI_Group_free(group, ierror)`
`integer group, ierror`
Frees a group

`MPI_Group_incl(group, n, ranks, newgroup, ierror)`
`integer group, n, ranks(*), newgroup, ierror`
Produces a group by reordering an existing group and taking only listed members

`MPI_Group_intersection(group1, group2, newgroup, ierror)`
`integer group1, group2, newgroup, ierror`
Produces a group as the intersection of two existing groups.

`MPI_Group_range_excl(group, n, ranges, newgroup, ierror)`
`integer group, n, ranges(3,*), newgroup, ierror`
Produces a group by excluding ranges of processes from an existing group

```
MPI_Group_range_incl(group, n, ranges, newgroup, ierror)
integer group, n, ranges(3,*), newgroup, ierror
```
Creates a new group from ranges of ranks in an existing group

```
MPI_Group_rank(group, rank, ierror)
integer group, rank, ierror
```
Returns the rank of this process in the given group

```
MPI_Group_size(group, size, ierror)
integer group, size, ierror
```
Returns the size of a group

```
MPI_Group_translate_ranks(group1, n, ranks1, group2, ranks2, ierror)
integer group1, n, ranks1(*), group2, ranks2(*), ierror
```
Translates the ranks of processes in one group to those in another group

```
MPI_Group_union(group1, group2, newgroup, ierror)
integer group1, group2, newgroup, ierror
```
Produces a group by combining two groups

```
MPI_Ibsend(buf, count, datatype, dest, tag, comm, request, ierror)
<type> buf(*)
integer count, datatype, dest, tag, comm, request, ierror
```
Starts a nonblocking buffered send

```
MPI_Init(ierror)
integer ierror
```
Initializes the MPI execution environment

```
MPI_Initialized(flag, ierror)
logical flag
integer ierror
```
Indicates whether MPI_Init has been called

```
MPI_Intercomm_create(local_comm, local_leader, peer_comm,
          remote_leader, tag, newintercomm, ierror)
integer local_comm, local_leader, peer_comm, remote_leader, tag,
newintercomm, ierror
```
Creates an intercommunicator from two intracommunicators

```
MPI_Intercomm_merge(intercomm, high, intracomm, ierror)
integer intercomm, intracomm, ierror
logical high
```
Creates an intracommunicator from an intercommunicator

```
MPI_Iprobe(source, tag, comm, flag, status, ierror)
integer source, tag, comm, status(*), ierror
logical flag
```
Nonblocking test for a message

```
MPI_Irecv(buf, count, datatype, source, tag, comm, request, ierror)
<type> buf(*)
integer count, datatype, source, tag, comm, request, ierror
```
Begins a nonblocking receive

```
MPI_Irsend(buf, count, datatype, dest, tag, comm, request, ierror)
<type> buf(*)
integer count, datatype, dest, tag, comm, request, ierror
```
Starts a nonblocking ready send

```
MPI_Isend(buf, count, datatype, dest, tag, comm, request, ierror)
<type> buf(*)
integer count, datatype, dest, tag, comm, request, ierror
```
Starts a nonblocking send

```
MPI_Issend(buf, count, datatype, dest, tag, comm, request, ierror)
<type> buf(*)
integer count, datatype, dest, tag, comm, request, ierror
```
Starts a nonblocking synchronous send

```
MPI_Keyval_create(copy_fn, delete_fn, keyval, extra_state, ierror)
external copy_fn, delete_fn
integer keyval, extra_state, ierror
```
Generates a new attribute key

Deprecated. Use MPI_Comm_create_keyval instead

```
MPI_Keyval_free(keyval, ierror)
integer keyval, ierror
```
Frees attribute key for communicator cache attribute

Deprecated. Use MPI_Comm_free_keyval instead

```
MPI_Op_create(function, commute, op, ierror)
external function
logical commute
integer op, ierror
```
Creates a user-defined combination function handle

```
MPI_Op_free(op, ierror)
integer op, ierror
```
Frees a user-defined combination function handle

```
MPI_Pack(inbuf, incount, datatype, outbuf, outcount, position, comm,
         ierror)
<type>inbuf(*), outbuf(*)
integer incount, datatype, outcount, position, comm, ierror
```
Packs data into a contiguous buffer

```
MPI_Pack_size(incount, datatype, size, ierror)
integer incount, datatype, size, ierror
```
Return the size needed to pack a datatype

```
MPI_Pcontrol(level)
integer level
```
Controls profiling (no ierror *argument; see A.14 in [97])*

```
MPI_Probe(source, tag, comm, status, ierror)
integer source, tag, comm, status(*), ierror
```
Blocking test for a message

```
MPI_Recv(buf, count, datatype, source, tag, comm, status, ierror)
<type> buf(*)
integer count, datatype, source, tag, comm, status(*), ierror
```
Basic receive

```
MPI_Recv_init(buf, count, datatype, source, tag, comm, request,
         ierror)
<type> buf(*)
integer count, datatype, source, tag, comm, request, ierror
```
Creates a handle for a receive

```
MPI_Reduce(sendbuf, recvbuf, count, datatype, op, root, comm,
         ierror)
<type> sendbuf(*), recvbuf(*)
integer count, datatype, op, root, comm, ierror
```
Reduces values on all processes to a single value

```
MPI_Reduce_scatter(sendbuf, recvbuf, recvcounts, datatype, op, comm,
         ierror)
<type> sendbuf(*), recvbuf(*)
integer recvcounts(*), datatype, op, comm, ierror
```
Combines values and scatters the results

```
MPI_Request_free(request, ierror)
integer request, ierror
```
Frees a communication request object

```
MPI_Rsend(buf, count, datatype, dest, tag, comm, ierror)
<type> buf(*)
integer count, datatype, dest, tag, comm, ierror
```
Basic ready send

```
MPI_Rsend_init(buf, count, datatype, dest, tag, comm, request,
         ierror)
<type> buf(*)
integer count, datatype, dest, tag, comm, request, ierror
```
Builds a handle for a ready send

```
MPI_Scan(sendbuf, recvbuf, count, datatype, op, comm, ierror)
<type> sendbuf(*), recvbuf(*)
integer count, datatype, op, comm, ierror
```
Computes the scan (partial reductions) of data on a collection of processes

```
MPI_Scatter(sendbuf, sendcount, sendtype, recvbuf, recvcount,
         recvtype, root, comm, ierror)
<type> sendbuf(*), recvbuf(*)
integer sendcount, sendtype, recvcount, recvtype, root, comm, ierror
```
Sends data from one task to all other tasks in a group

```
MPI_Scatterv(sendbuf, sendcounts, displs, sendtype, recvbuf,
         recvcount, recvtype, root, comm, ierror)
<type> sendbuf(*), recvbuf(*)
integer sendcounts(*), displs(*), sendtype, recvcount, recvtype,
root, comm, ierror
```
Scatters a buffer in parts to all tasks in a group

```
MPI_Send(buf, count, datatype, dest, tag, comm, ierror)
<type> buf(*)
integer count, datatype, dest, tag, comm, ierror
```
Basic send

```
MPI_Send_init(buf, count, datatype, dest, tag, comm, request,
         ierror)
<type> buf(*)
integer count, datatype, dest, tag, comm, request, ierror
```
Builds a handle for a standard send

```
MPI_Sendrecv(sendbuf, sendcount, sendtype, dest, sendtag, recvbuf,
        recvcount, recvtype, source, recvtag, comm, status, ierror)
<type>sendbuf(*), recvbuf(*)
integer sendcount, sendtype, dest, sendtag, recvcount, recvtype,
source, recvtag, comm, status(*), ierror
```
Sends and receives

```
MPI_Sendrecv_replace(buf, count, datatype, dest, sendtag, source,
        recvtag, comm, status, ierror)
<type> buf(*)
integer count, datatype, dest, sendtag, source, recvtag, comm,
status(*), ierror
```
Sends and receives using a single buffer

```
MPI_Ssend(buf, count, datatype, dest, tag, comm, ierror)
<type> buf(*)
integer count, datatype, dest, tag, comm, ierror
```
Basic synchronous send

```
MPI_Ssend_init(buf, count, datatype, dest, tag, comm, request,
        ierror)
<type> buf(*)
integer count, datatype, dest, tag, comm, request, ierror
```
Builds a handle for a synchronous send

```
MPI_Start(request, ierror)
integer request, ierror
```
Initiates a communication with a persistent request handle

```
MPI_Startall(count, array_of_requests, ierror)
integer count, array_of_requests(*), ierror
```
Starts a collection of requests

```
MPI_Test(request, flag, status, ierror)
integer request, status(*), ierror
logical flag
```
Tests for the completion of a send or receive

```
MPI_Testall(count, array_of_requests, flag, array_of_statuses,
        ierror)
integer count, array_of_requests(*),
array_of_statuses(MPI_STATUS_SIZE,*), ierror
logical flag
```
Tests for the completion of all previously initiated communications

```
MPI_Testany(count, array_of_requests, index, flag, status, ierror)
integer count, array_of_requests(*), index, status(*), ierror
logical flag
```
Tests for completion of any previously initiated communication

```
MPI_Testsome(incount, array_of_requests, outcount, array_of_indices,
         array_of_statuses, ierror)
integer incount, array_of_requests(*), outcount,
array_of_indices(*), array_of_statuses(MPI_STATUS_SIZE,*), ierror
```
Tests for some given communications to complete

```
MPI_Test_cancelled(status, flag, ierror)
integer status(*), ierror
logical flag
```
Tests to see whether a request was canceled

```
MPI_Topo_test(comm, top_type, ierror)
integer comm, top_type, ierror
```
Determines the type of topology (if any) associated with a communicator

```
MPI_Type_commit(datatype, ierror)
integer datatype, ierror
```
Commits the datatype

```
MPI_Type_contiguous(count, oldtype, newtype, ierror)
integer count, oldtype, newtype, ierror
```
Creates a contiguous datatype

```
MPI_Type_create_hindexed(count, array_of_blocklengths,
         array_of_displacements, oldtype, newtype, ierror)
integer count, array_of_blocklengths(*), oldtype, newtype, ierror
integer (kind=MPI_ADDRESS_KIND) array_of_displacements(*)
```
MPI-2: Creates an indexed datatype with offsets in bytes

```
MPI_Type_create_hvector(count, blocklength, stride, oldtype,
         newtype, ierror)
integer count, blocklength, oldtype, newtype, ierror
integer (kind=MPI_ADDRESS_KIND) stride
```
MPI-2: Creates a vector (strided) datatype with offset in bytes

```
MPI_Type_create_struct(count, array_of_blocklengths,
          array_of_displacements, array_of_types, newtype, ierror)
integer count, array_of_blocklengths(*), array_of_types(*), newtype,
ierror
integer (kind=MPI_ADDRESS_KIND) array_of_displacements(*)
```
MPI-2: Creates a structure datatype

```
MPI_Type_extent(datatype, extent, ierror)
integer datatype, extent, ierror
```
Returns the size of datatype

Deprecated. Use MPI_Type_get_extent instead

```
MPI_Type_free(datatype, ierror)
integer datatype, ierror
```
Marks the datatype object for deallocation

```
MPI_Type_get_extent(datatype, lb, extent, ierror)
integer datatype, ierror
integer (kind=MPI_ADDRESS_KIND) lb, extent
```
MPI-2: Return the lower bound and extent of a datatype

```
MPI_Type_hindexed(count, array_of_blocklengths,
          array_of_displacements, oldtype, newtype, ierror)
integer count, array_of_blocklengths(*), array_of_displacements(*),
oldtype, newtype, ierror
```
Creates an indexed datatype with offsets in bytes

Deprecated. Use MPI_Type_create_hindexed instead

```
MPI_Type_hvector(count, blocklength, stride, oldtype, newtype,
          ierror)
integer count, blocklength, stride, oldtype, newtype, ierror
```
Creates a vector (strided) datatype with offset in bytes

Deprecated. Use MPI_Type_create_hvector instead

```
MPI_Type_indexed(count, array_of_blocklengths,
          array_of_displacements, oldtype, newtype, ierror)
integer count, array_of_blocklengths(*), array_of_displacements(*),
oldtype, newtype, ierror
```
Creates an indexed datatype

```
MPI_Type_lb(datatype, displacement, ierror)
integer datatype, displacement, ierror
```
Returns the lower-bound of a datatype

Deprecated. Use MPI_Type_get_extent instead

```
MPI_Type_size(datatype, size, ierror)
integer datatype, size, ierror
```
Return the number of bytes occupied by entries in the datatype

```
MPI_Type_struct(count, array_of_blocklengths,
          array_of_displacements, array_of_types, newtype, ierror)
integer count, array_of_blocklengths(*), array_of_displacements(*),
array_of_types(*), newtype, ierror
```
Creates a structure datatype

Deprecated. Use MPI_Type_create_struct instead

```
MPI_Type_ub(datatype, displacement, ierror)
integer datatype, displacement, ierror
```
Returns the upper bound of a datatype

Deprecated. Use MPI_Type_get_extent instead

```
MPI_Type_vector(count, blocklength, stride, oldtype, newtype,
          ierror)
integer count, blocklength, stride, oldtype, newtype, ierror
```
Creates a vector (strided) datatype

```
MPI_Unpack(inbuf, insize, position, outbuf, outcount, datatype,
          comm, ierror)
<type> inbuf(*), outbuf(*)
integer insize, position, outcount, datatype, comm, ierror
```
Unpacks data from a contiguous buffer

```
MPI_Wait(request, status, ierror)
integer request, status(*), ierror
```
Waits for an MPI send or receive to complete

```
MPI_Waitall(count, array_of_requests, array_of_statuses, ierror)
integer count, array_of_requests(*),
array_of_statuses(MPI_STATUS_SIZE,*), ierror
```
Waits for all given communications to complete

```
MPI_Waitany(count, array_of_requests, index, status, ierror)
integer count, array_of_requests(*), index, status(*), ierror
```
Waits for any specified send or receive to complete

```
MPI_Waitsome(incount, array_of_requests, outcount, array_of_indices,
         array_of_statuses, ierror)
integer incount, array_of_requests(*), outcount,
array_of_indices(*), array_of_statuses(MPI_STATUS_SIZE,*), ierror
```
Waits for some given communications to complete

```
double precision MPI_Wtick()
```
Returns the resolution of MPI_Wtime

```
double precision MPI_Wtime()
```
Returns an elapsed time on the calling processor

A.3 C++ Routines

This section describes the C++ routines from [100]. To save space, the `MPI::` namespace identifier is not shown.

```
void Comm::Abort(int errorcode)
```
Terminates MPI execution environment

```
void Intracomm::Allgather(const void* sendbuf, int sendcount,
         const Datatype& sendtype, void* recvbuf, int recvcount,
         const Datatype& recvtype) const
```
Gathers data from all tasks and distribute it to all

```
void Intracomm::Allgatherv(const void* sendbuf, int sendcount,
         const Datatype& sendtype, void* recvbuf,
         const int recvcounts[], const int displs[],
         const Datatype& recvtype) const
```
Gathers data from all tasks and deliver it to all

```
void Intracomm::Allreduce(const void* sendbuf, void* recvbuf,
         int count, const Datatype& datatype, const Op& op) const
```
Combines values from all processes and distribute the result back to all processes

```
void Intracomm::Alltoall(const void* sendbuf, int sendcount,
         const Datatype& sendtype, void* recvbuf, int recvcount,
         const Datatype& recvtype) const
```
Sends data from all to all processes

```
void Intracomm::Alltoallv(const void* sendbuf,
         const int sendcounts[], const int sdispls[],
         const Datatype& sendtype, void* recvbuf,
         const int recvcounts[], const int rdispls[],
         const Datatype& recvtype) const
```
Sends data from all to all processes, with a displacement

```
void Attach_buffer(void* buffer, int size)
```
Attaches a user-defined buffer for sending

```
void Intracomm::Barrier() const
```
Blocks until all process have reached this routine

```
void Intracomm::Bcast(void* buffer, int count,
         const Datatype& datatype, int root) const
```
Broadcasts a message from the process with rank "root" to all other processes of the group

```
void Comm::Bsend(const void* buf, int count,
         const Datatype& datatype, int dest, int tag) const
```
Basic send with user-specified buffering

```
Prequest Comm::Bsend_init(const void* buf, int count,
         const Datatype& datatype, int dest, int tag) const
```
Builds a handle for a buffered send

```
void Request::Cancel() const
```
Cancels a communication request

```
Comm& Comm::Clone() const
```
Like Dup, but return by reference

```
void Datatype::Commit()
```
Commits the datatype

```
int Comm::Compare(const Comm& comm1, const Comm& comm2)
```
Compares two communicators

```
int Group::Compare(const Group& group1, const Group& group2)
```
Compare two groups

```
void Compute_dims(int nnodes, int ndims, int dims[])
```
Creates a division of processes in a Cartesian grid

```
Intracomm Intracomm::Create(const Group& group) const
```
Creates a new communicator

```
Cartcomm Intracomm::Create_cart(int ndims, const int dims[],
         const bool periods[], bool reorder) const
```
Makes a new communicator to which topology information has been attached

```
Datatype Datatype::Create_contiguous(int count) const
```
Creates a contiguous datatype

```
Graphcomm Intracomm::Create_graph(int nnodes, const int index[],
         const int edges[], bool reorder) const
```
Makes a new communicator to which topology information has been attached

```
Datatype Datatype::Create_hindexed(int count,
         const int array_of_blocklengths[],
         const Aint array_of_displacements[]) const
```
Creates an indexed datatype with offsets in bytes

```
Datatype Datatype::Create_hvector(int count, int blocklength,
         Aint stride) const
```
Creates a vector (strided) datatype with offset in bytes

```
Datatype Datatype::Create_indexed(int count,
         const int array_of_blocklengths[],
         const int array_of_displacements[]) const
```
Creates an indexed datatype

```
Intercomm Intracomm::Create_intercomm(int local_leader,
         const Comm& peer_comm, int remote_leader, int tag) const
```
Creates an intercommunicator from two intracommunicators

```
int Create_keyval(const Copy_function* copy_fn,
         const Delete_function* delete_fn, void* extra_state)
```
Generates a new attribute key

```
Datatype Datatype::Create_struct(int count,
         const int array_of_blocklengths[],
         const Aint array_of_displacements[],
         const Datatype array_of_types[])
```
Creates a struct datatype

```
Datatype Datatype::Create_vector(int count, int blocklength,
         int stride) const
```
Creates a vector (strided) datatype

```
void Comm::Delete_attr(int keyval) const
```
Deletes attribute value associated with a key

```
int Detach_buffer(void*& buffer)
```
Removes an existing buffer (for use in MPI_Bsend, etc.)

```
Group Group::Difference(const Group& group1, const Group& group2)
```
Makes a group from the difference of two groups

```
Intercomm Intercomm::Dup() const
```
Duplicates an existing communicator with all its cached information

```
Intracomm Intracomm::Dup() const
```
Duplicates an existing communicator with all its cached information

```
Group Group::Excl(int n, const int ranks[]) const
```
Produces a group by reordering an existing group and taking only unlisted members

```
void Finalize()
```
Terminates MPI execution environment

```
void Comm::Free()
```
Marks the communicator object for deallocation

```
void Datatype::Free()
```
Marks the datatype object for deallocation

```
void Errhandler::Free()
```
Frees an MPI-style error handler

```
void Group::Free()
```
Frees a group

```
void Op::Free()
```
Frees a user-defined combination function handle

```
void Request::Free()
```
Frees a communication request object

```
void Free_keyval(int& keyval)
```
Frees attribute key for communicator cache attribute

```
void Intracomm::Gather(const void* sendbuf, int sendcount,
          const Datatype& sendtype, void* recvbuf, int recvcount,
          const Datatype& recvtype, int root) const
```
Gathers together values from a group of tasks

```
void Intracomm::Gatherv(const void* sendbuf, int sendcount,
          const Datatype& sendtype, void* recvbuf,
          const int recvcounts[], const int displs[],
          const Datatype& recvtype, int root) const
```
Gathers into specified locations from all tasks in a group

`Aint Get_address(const void* location)` *Gets the address of a location in memory*
`bool Comm::Get_attr(int keyval, void* attribute_val) const` *Retrieves attribute value by key*
`int Cartcomm::Get_cart_rank(const int coords[]) const` *Determines process rank in communicator given Cartesian location*
`void Cartcomm::Get_coords(int rank, int maxdims, int coords[]) const` *Determines process coords in Cartesian topology given rank in group*
`int Status::Get_count(const Datatype& datatype) const` *Gets the number of "top-level" elements*
`int Cartcomm::Get_dim() const` *Retrieves Cartesian topology information associated with a communicator*
`void Graphcomm::Get_dims(int nnodes[], int nedges[]) const` *Retrieves graph topology information associated with a communicator*
`int Status::Get_elements(const Datatype& datatype) const` *Returns the number of basic elements in a datatype*
`Errhandler Comm::Get_errhandler() const` *Gets the error handler for a communicator* *Deprecated. Use MPI_Comm_get_errhandler instead*
`int Status::Get_error() const` *Get error field from status*
`int Exception::Get_error_class() const` *Return error class of an MPI exception*
`int Get_error_class(int errorcode)` *Converts an error code into an error class*
`int Exception::Get_error_code() const` *Return error code of an MPI exception*
`const char* Exception::Get_error_string() const` *Get error string for an MPI exception*
`void Get_error_string(int errorcode, char* name, int& resultlen)` *Returns a string for a given error code*
`Aint Datatype::Get_extent() const` *Returns the extent of datatype*
`Group Comm::Get_group() const` *Accesses the group associated with given communicator*

```
Aint Datatype::Get_lb() const
```
Returns the lower-bound of a datatype

```
void Graphcomm::Get_neighbors(int rank, int maxneighbors,
          int neighbors[]) const
```
Returns the neighbors of a node associated with a graph topology

```
int Graphcomm::Get_neighbors_count(int rank) const
```
Returns the number of neighbors of a node associated with a graph topology

```
void Get_processor_name(char* name, int& resultlen)
```
Gets the name of the processor

```
int Comm::Get_rank() const
```
Determines the rank of the calling process in the communicator

```
int Group::Get_rank() const
```
Returns the rank of this process in the given group

```
Group Intercomm::Get_remote_group() const
```
Returns the remote group in an intercommunicator

```
int Intercomm::Get_remote_size() const
```
Returns the number of processes in the remote group

```
int Comm::Get_size() const
```
Determines the size of the group associated with a communictor

```
int Datatype::Get_size() const
```
Return the number of bytes occupied by entries in the datatype

```
int Group::Get_size() const
```
Returns the size of a group

```
int Status::Get_source() const
```
Return the source field from status

```
int Status::Get_tag() const
```
Return the tag field from status

```
void Cartcomm::Get_topo(int maxdims, int dims[], bool periods[],
          int coords[]) const
```
Retrieve Cartesian topology information associated with a communicator

```
void Graphcomm::Get_topo(int maxindex, int maxedges, int index[],
          int edges[]) const
```
Retrieves graph topology information associated with a communicator

```
int Comm::Get_topology() const
```
Determines the type of topology (if any) associated with a communicator

```
Aint Datatype::Get_ub() const
```
Returns the upper bound of a datatype

```
void Get_version(int& version, int& subversion)
```
Return the version of MPI

```
Request Comm::Ibsend(const void* buf, int count,
          const Datatype& datatype, int dest, int tag) const
```
Starts a nonblocking buffered send

```
Group Group::Incl(int n, const int ranks[]) const
```
Produces a group by reordering an existing group and taking only listed members

```
void Errhandler::Init(const Handler_function* function)
```
Creates an MPI-style error handler

```
void Init()
```
Initializes the MPI execution environment

```
void Init(int& argc, char**& argv)
```
Initializes the MPI execution environment

```
void Op::Init(User_function* function, bool commute)
```
Creates a user-defined combination function handle

```
Group Group::Intersect(const Group& group1, const Group& group2)
```
Produces a group as the intersection of two existing groups

```
bool Comm::Iprobe(int source, int tag) const
```
Nonblocking test for a message

```
bool Comm::Iprobe(int source, int tag, Status& status) const
```
Nonblocking test for a message

```
Request Comm::Irecv(void* buf, int count, const Datatype& datatype,
          int source, int tag) const
```
Begins a nonblocking receive

```
Request Comm::Irsend(const void* buf, int count,
          const Datatype& datatype, int dest, int tag) const
```
Starts a nonblocking ready send

```
bool Status::Is_cancelled() const
```
Tests to see whether a request was cancelled

```
bool Is_initialized()
```
Indicates whether MPI_Init has been called

```
bool Comm::Is_inter() const
```
Tests to see whether a communicator is an intercommunicator

```
Request Comm::Isend(const void* buf, int count,
         const Datatype& datatype, int dest, int tag) const
```
Starts a nonblocking send

```
Request Comm::Issend(const void* buf, int count,
         const Datatype& datatype, int dest, int tag) const
```
Starts a nonblocking synchronous send

```
int Cartcomm::Map(int ndims, const int dims[], const bool periods[])
         const
```
Maps process to Cartesian topology information

```
int Graphcomm::Map(int nnodes, const int index[], const int edges[])
         const
```
Maps process to graph topology information

```
Intracomm Intercomm::Merge(bool high) const
```
Creates an intracommunicator from an intercommunicator

```
void Datatype::Pack(const void* inbuf, int incount, void *outbuf,
         int outsize, int& position, const Comm &comm) const
```
Packs data into a contiguous buffer

```
int Datatype::Pack_size(int incount, const Comm& comm) const
```
Return the size needed to pack a datatype

```
void Pcontrol(const int level, ...)
```
Controls profiling

```
void Comm::Probe(int source, int tag) const
```
Blocking test for a message

```
void Comm::Probe(int source, int tag, Status& status) const
```
Blocking test for a message

```
Group Group::Range_excl(int n, const int ranges[][3]) const
```
Produces a group by excluding ranges of processes from an existing group

```
Group Group::Range_incl(int n, const int ranges[][3]) const
```
Creates a new group from ranges of ranks in an existing group

```
void Comm::Recv(void* buf, int count, const Datatype& datatype,
         int source, int tag) const
```
Basic receive

```
void Comm::Recv(void* buf, int count, const Datatype& datatype,
         int source, int tag, Status& status) const
```
Basic receive

```
Prequest Comm::Recv_init(void* buf, int count,
         const Datatype& datatype, int source, int tag) const
```
Creates a handle for a receive

```
void Intracomm::Reduce(const void* sendbuf, void* recvbuf,
         int count, const Datatype& datatype, const Op& op,
         int root) const
```
Reduces values on all processes to a single value

```
void Intracomm::Reduce_scatter(const void* sendbuf, void* recvbuf,
         int recvcounts[], const Datatype& datatype, const Op& op)
         const
```
Combines values and scatters the results

```
void Comm::Rsend(const void* buf, int count, const
         Datatype& datatype, int dest, int tag) const
```
Basic ready send

```
Prequest Comm::Rsend_init(const void* buf, int count,
         const Datatype& datatype, int dest, int tag) const
```
Builds a handle for a ready send

```
void Intracomm::Scan(const void* sendbuf, void* recvbuf, int count,
         const Datatype& datatype, const Op& op) const
```
Computes the scan (partial reductions) of data on a collection of processes

```
void Intracomm::Scatter(const void* sendbuf, int sendcount,
         const Datatype& sendtype, void* recvbuf, int recvcount,
         const Datatype& recvtype, int root) const
```
Sends data from one task to all other tasks in a group

```
void Intracomm::Scatterv(const void* sendbuf,
         const int sendcounts[], const int displs[],
         const Datatype& sendtype, void* recvbuf, int recvcount,
         const Datatype& recvtype, int root) const
```
Scatters a buffer in parts to all tasks in a group

```
void Comm::Send(const void* buf, int count,
         const Datatype& datatype, int dest, int tag) const
```
Basic send

```
Prequest Comm::Send_init(const void* buf, int count,
         const Datatype& datatype, int dest, int tag) const
```
Builds a handle for a standard send

```
void Comm::Sendrecv(const void *sendbuf, int sendcount,
        const Datatype& sendtype, int dest, int sendtag,
        void *recvbuf, int recvcount, const Datatype& recvtype,
        int source, int recvtag) const
```
Sends and receives a message

```
void Comm::Sendrecv(const void *sendbuf, int sendcount,
        const Datatype& sendtype, int dest, int sendtag,
        void *recvbuf, int recvcount, const Datatype& recvtype,
        int source, int recvtag, Status& status) const
```
Sends and receives a message

```
void Comm::Sendrecv_replace(void* buf, int count,
        const Datatype& datatype, int dest, int sendtag,
        int source, int recvtag) const
```
Sends and receives using a single buffer

```
void Comm::Sendrecv_replace(void* buf, int count,
        const Datatype& datatype, int dest, int sendtag,
        int source, int recvtag, Status& status) const
```
Sends and receives using a single buffer

```
void Comm::Set_attr(int keyval, const void* attribute_val) const
```
Stores attribute value associated with a key

Deprecated. Use MPI_Comm_set_attr instead

```
void Comm::Set_errhandler(const Errhandler& errhandler)
```
Sets the error handler for a communicator

Deprecated. Use MPI_Comm_set_errhandler instead

```
void Status::Set_error(int error)
```
Sets the error field in status

```
void Status::Set_source(int source)
```
Set the source field in status

```
void Status::Set_tag(int tag)
```
sets the tag field in status

```
void Cartcomm::Shift(int direction, int disp, int& rank_source,
        int& rank_dest) const
```
Returns the shifted source and destination ranks given a shift direction and amount

```
Intracomm Intracomm::Split(int color, int key) const
```
Creates new communicators based on colors and keys

```
void Comm::Ssend(const void* buf, int count,
        const Datatype& datatype, int dest, int tag) const
```
Basic synchronous send

```
Prequest Comm::Ssend_init(const void* buf, int count,
        const Datatype& datatype, int dest, int tag) const
```
Builds a handle for a synchronous send

```
void Prequest::Start()
```
Initiates a communication with a persistent request handle

```
void Prequest::Startall(int count, Prequest array_of_requests[])
```
Starts a collection of requests

```
Cartcomm Cartcomm::Sub(const bool remain_dims[]) const
```
Partitions a communicator into subgroups that form lower-dimensional cartesian subgrids

```
bool Request::Test()
```
Tests for the completion of a send or receive

```
bool Request::Test(Status& status)
```
Tests for the completion of a send or receive

```
bool Request::Testall(int count, Request array_of_requests[])
```
Tests for the completion of all previously initiated communications

```
bool Request::Testall(int count, Request array_of_requests[],
        Status array_of_statuses[])
```
Tests for the completion of all previously initiated communications

```
bool Request::Testany(int count, Request array_of_requests[],
        int& index)
```
Tests for completion of any previously initiated communication

```
bool Request::Testany(int count, Request array_of_requests[],
        int& index, Status& status)
```
Tests for completion of any previously initiated communication

```
int Request::Testsome(int incount, Request array_of_requests[],
        int array_of_indices[])
```
Tests for some given communications to complete

```
int Request::Testsome(int incount, Request array_of_requests[],
        int array_of_indices[], Status array_of_statuses[])
```
Tests for some given communications to complete

```
void Group::Translate_ranks (const Group& group1, int n,
        const int ranks1[], const Group& group2, int ranks2[])
```
Translates the ranks of processes in one group to those in another group

```
Group Group::Union(const Group& group1, const Group& group2)
```
Produces a group by combining two groups

```
void Datatype::Unpack(const void* inbuf, int insize, void *outbuf,
        int outcount, int& position, const Comm& comm) const
```
Unpacks data from a contiguous buffer

```
void Request::Wait()
```
Waits for an MPI send or receive to complete

```
void Request::Wait(Status& status)
```
Waits for an MPI send or receive to complete

```
void Request::Waitall(int count, Request array_of_requests[])
```
Waits for all given communications to complete

```
void Request::Waitall(int count, Request array_of_requests[],
        Status array_of_statuses[])
```
Waits for all given communications to complete

```
int Request::Waitany(int count, Request array_of_requests[])
```
Waits for any specified send or receive to complete

```
int Request::Waitany(int count, Request array_of_requests[],
        Status& status)
```
Waits for any specified send or receive to complete

```
int Request::Waitsome(int incount, Request array_of_requests[],
        int array_of_indices[])
```
Waits for some given communications to complete

```
int Request::Waitsome(int incount, Request array_of_requests[],
        int array_of_indices[], Status array_of_statuses[])
```
Waits for some given communications to complete

```
double Wtick()
```
Returns the resolution of Wtime

```
double Wtime()
```
Returns an elapsed time on the calling processor

B The MPICH Implementation of MPI

In Chapter 8 we described some of the methods that an MPI implementation can use to implement MPI on top of a simpler communication layer. Here we describe the concrete implementation of MPI that has resulted from building on top of a number of different communications layers, together with other aspects of a convenient parallel programming environment.

The MPICH implementation is a complete implementation of MPI-1 and is freely available from `http://www.mcs.anl.gov/mpi/mpich` and `ftp://ftp.mcs.anl.gov/pub/mpi`. The name is derived from MPI and Chameleon; Chameleon both because MPICH can run (adapt its color) on a wide range of environments and because the initial implementation of MPICH used the Chameleon [71] message-passing portability system. MPICH is pronounced "Em Pee Eye See Aych," not "Emm Pitch."

B.1 Features of the Model Implementation

Although the MPI Standard specifies what user programs will look like, actual implementations of the MPI library will differ in various ways. In this section we describe some of the characteristic features of the MPICH implementation, developed originally by Argonne National Laboratory and Mississippi State University and now being further developed by Argonne National Laboratory.

B.1.1 User Features

The model implementation is a complete implementation of the MPI-1.2 Standard and is freely available over the web from `http://www.mcs.anl.gov/mpi/mpich`. The authors of MPICH were members of the MPI Forum and tracked the development of the standard as it evolved [62]. Many MPI-2 features are also included, and the authors intend for MPICH to provide a complete MPI-2 implementation as well.

MPICH is distributed with all source code. Both the C and Fortran bindings are part of MPICH; in addition, the C++ bindings developed by the University of Notre Dame [102] are also distributed with MPICH. Fortran 90 module support is also available. Full documentation is included in Unix man page form (nroff using the man macros) for use with `man` or other man-page viewers, HTML for viewing with web browsers, and in Postscript for printing. A User's Manual [58] contains more detailed information in using MPICH and the tools that come with it.

MPICH is portable to a wide variety of parallel computers and workstation networks. It supports heterogeneous computation while exacting no overhead when in a homogeneous environment. The implementation includes all the tools described in this book, including the MPE library, the `upshot-jumpshot` family of performance visualization tools, and the tools for creating profiling libraries.

Configuration is carried out with the aid of the GNU `autoconf` program, which allows great flexibility in installation. Precise installation instructions are supplied with the distribution in an installation manual [57].

In addition to the code that implements MPI itself, the MPICH distribution contains a number of MPI programs. There is an extensive test suite that allows the installer to check that the implementation is operating correctly. A set of performance test programs [61] allows the user to measure the performance of any MPI implementation and the computers that it is running on. Simple example programs, such as programs for computing π, and more complex ones, such as for computing the Mandelbrot set (and interactively displaying selected portions of it graphically), are included.

B.1.2 Portability

The portability of the MPICH implementation is based on the concept of an abstract device interface (ADI) that provides a set of basic services, including interprocess communication, process start and stop, and some miscellaneous functions (e.g., support for `MPI_Wtime`). This ADI has evolved over time (see Section B.3), but has always been a thin layer between the MPI routines such as `MPI_Send` and the communication mechanism provided by the parallel computer. Porting MPICH to a new parallel computer requires implementing only the small number of routines defined by the ADI. In addition, the ADI itself is designed in a layered fashion: a basic yet functional port of MPICH to a new platform requires implementing only a few routines. The port can be improved (in terms of performance) by implementing additional routines that the ADI provides functional versions for otherwise. This design of MPICH has enabled many groups to use MPICH as the basis of their own MPI implementations, and remains an important part of the MPICH design.

B.1.3 Efficiency

The portable, freely available MPICH implementation must, of course, yield a slight performance edge to a proprietary one, since it cannot access proprietary low-level system primitives. However, we have been able to achieve quite respectable performance from the very beginning, as shown in Figure B.1, which compares the performance of an early IBM implementation of MPI with MPICH, where MPICH is implemented on top of IBM's earlier message-passing system MPL (previously known as EUI). This graph was generated shortly after the MPI standard was released in 1993.

In fact, the MPICH implementation can be faster than the vendor implementations in some cases. For example, when handling certain kinds of MPI derived datatypes, the MPICH implementation is faster, as is shown in Figure B.2. This experience is the basis of our encouragement of the use of MPI datatypes at the end of Chapter 5. The approach used in MPICH for improving the performance of MPI datatypes is discussed in more detail in [65], and is an example of how MPICH provides a platform for conducting research into efficient implementations of MPI.

B.1.4 Auxiliary Tools

The distribution comes with a number of useful tools, many of which have been introduced in this book. The MPE library, including event logging and a simple parallel graphics interface, is included; see Appendix C. The `upshot` logfile examination tool described below is also included, along with its successor, `jumpshot`. As demonstrations of what can be done with the MPI profiling interface, three different profiling libraries are included, for simple counting and time accumulation, for performance visualization with `jumpshot`, and for real-time graphical display of message traffic. Finally, a program called the "wrapper generator" helps the user create simple profiling libraries by taking a simple description of the code to be executed before and after the PMPI version of the call and writing the rest of the MPI "wrapper".

Because MPICH has been adopted by so many, a number of groups have developed tools that work with MPICH. One example is the message-queue display and process management available in the TotalView debugger [26] (TotalView can now display message queues in some vendor MPI implementations as well.)

B.1.5 MPICH as a Research Vehicle

The MPICH implementation was designed to be easily transported to other parallel computing environments. Both research projects and computer vendors have used MPICH as the basis for developing MPI implementations. For example, a number of research groups have used MPICH to provide a way to port applications to their own, lower level communications layers. Two examples are Fast Messages [23, 90] and Globus [39, 37, 42]. Other projects have used MPICH to explore issues in the implementation of MPI; in the area of wide-area collective communications, see [86].

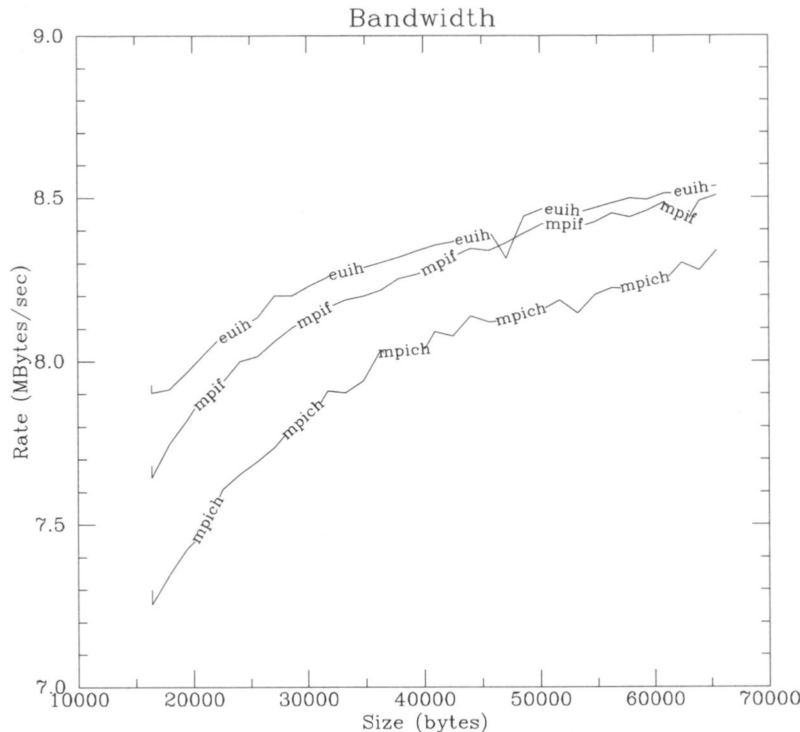

Figure B.1
Bandwidth comparisons on the IBM SP1

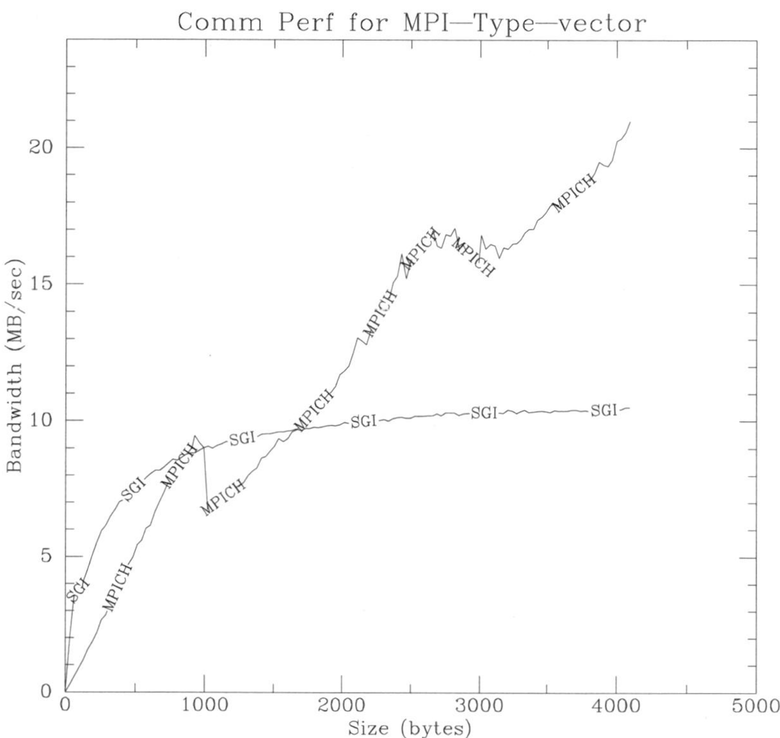

Figure B.2
Bandwidth comparisons on the SGI Origin 2000 for `MPI_Type_vector`. MPICH starts slower (the SGI implementation has lower latency) but MPICH optimizes for `MPI_Type_vector`.

Two of the authors of this book (Gropp and Lusk) have based their MPI research on MPICH. This research has included implementing MPI on vector supercomputers [53], MPICH as an example of developing and managing distributable software [59], and improving the performance of MPI implementations [65].

B.2 Installing and Running the Model Implementation

Installation of MPI consists of executing `configure` to create the makefiles appropriate for an installation, followed by running `make`. Details are given in the installation manual [57] that comes with the distribution, including a section on troubleshooting the installation. For problems that the user can't fix, there is a list of known bugs and patches at

```
http://www.mcs.anl.gov/mpi/mpich/buglist-tbl.html
```

If that doesn't help, bug reports may be sent to `mpi-bugs@mcs.anl.gov`.

MPI-1 did not specify a standard way of starting MPI programs, partly because of the diversity of mechanisms in use. The MPICH implementation hid these differences as much as possible through the use of a common startup program called `mpirun`. MPICH now provides the `mpiexec` command recommended by the MPI-2 standard, and continues to support the use of `mpirun` for those users who have built scripts that rely on the MPICH `mpirun`.

B.3 History of MPICH

MPI may be the first parallel programming model for scientific computing to survive long enough to justify a second edition of books about it (starting with [118]). MPICH has been around long enough that MPICH itself has a history.

MPICH has had three generations of implementation that reflect three generations of abstract device interface. The first generation of ADI was designed to be efficient on massively parallel computers where the interprocess communication mechanism provided was a proprietary message-passing system. This ADI was able to deliver good performance with low overhead, as is shown in Figure B.1, which compares MPICH with an early native MPI implementation (MPI-F) [44] and IBM's EUI message-passing system.

This early version of MPICH was portable to a very wide range of systems. These included many massively parallel computers, such as the Intel iPSC/860, Delta, and Paragon, and the nCUBE, using implementation of the ADI in terms of the Intel and nCUBE proprietary message-passing libraries. The other implementation of the ADI used Chameleon [71], itself a portable message passing system. Chameleon supported many different communication libraries; one of the most important is p4 [13]. P4 supports communication over heterogeneous, widely distributed computers (including systems on separate continents); p4 also supports *multi-method* communication, for example, using TCP between network-connected computers and specialized communication, such as shared-memory in an SMP or proprietary message-passing, within a parallel computer. Thus, MPICH supported heterogeneous, multi-method communication from the very beginning.

The second generation ADI, called ADI-2, was introduced to provide greater flexibility in the implementation and to efficiently support communication mechanisms that provide more functionality. For example, the implementation of the second generation ADI on top of Globus [37] exploits the option in ADI-2 for the "device" to provide its own implementation of the MPI derived datatype routines. This allows MPICH-G, the name used for this Globus-based implementation of the ADI, to use the heterogeneous data communication capabilities within Globus. ADI-2 also provided a mechanism that allowed an abstract device to replace, on a communicator-by-communicator basis, each and any of the MPI collective routines. That is, the ADI could replace just `MPI_Barrier` and just on `MPI_COMM_WORLD`, or it could replace any combination of routines; this has allowed devices to make use of special hardware or algorithms for implementing collective routines.

The third generation ADI, called ADI-3, has been developed to provide a better match to the emerging remote-memory access networks, multithreaded execution environments, and to support MPI-2 operations such as remote memory access and dynamic process management. ADI-3 is the first version of the MPICH ADI that is not designed to closely match the capabilities of other message-passing libraries, since MPI has displaced most other message-passing systems in scientific computing. ADI-3 is, like all previous ADIs, designed to encourage the porting of MPICH to new platforms and communication methods.

C The MPE Multiprocessing Environment

Here we describe the MPE library that has been used in the examples throughout this book. It consists of functions that are

- consistent in style with MPI,
- not in MPI,
- freely available, and
- will work with any MPI implementation.

These tools are extremely rudimentary and lack many desirable features. Nonetheless, we have found them useful even in their present state. They are continuing to evolve.

The files '`mpe.h`' and '`mpef.h`' should be included for C and Fortran programs respectively.

C.1 MPE Logging

The logging routines in MPE are used to create logfiles of events that occur during the execution of a parallel program. These files can then be studied after the program has ended. These routines were introduced and discussed in Chapter 3, Section 3.7.3. Currently there are two logfile formats. The first, called ALOG, is used by `upshot` and `nupshot`; the second, called CLOG, is used by `jumpshot`, the latest in the series (see Section C.4). The ALOG format is roughly that described in [80]. The C bindings for the logging routines are given in Table C.1 and the Fortran bindings in Table C.2.

These routines allow the user to log events that are meaningful for specific applications, rather than relying on automatic logging of MPI library calls. The basic routines are `MPE_Init_log`, `MPE_Log_event`, and `MPE_Finish_log`. `MPE_Init_log` must be called (by all processes) to initialize MPE logging data structures. `MPE_Finish_log` collects the log data from all the processes, merges it, and aligns the timestamps with respect to the times at which `MPE_Init_log` and `MPE_Finish_log` were called. Then, the process with rank 0 in `MPI_COMM_WORLD` writes the log into the file whose name is given as an argument. A single event is logged with the `MPE_Log_event` routine, which specifies an event type (completely up to the user), and one integer and one character string for user data. In order to place in the logfile data that might be useful for a logfile analysis or visualization program (like `upshot`), the routines `MPE_Describe_event` and `MPE_Describe_state` allow one to add event and state descriptions and to define states by specifying a starting and

```
int MPE_Init_log(void)

int MPE_Start_log(void)

int MPE_Stop_log(void)

int MPE_Finish_log(char *logfilename)

int MPE_Describe_state(int start, int end, char *name, char *color)

int MPE_Describe_event(int event, char *name)

int MPE_Log_event(int event, int intdata char *chardata)
```

Table C.1
C bindings for MPE logging routines

```
MPE_INIT_LOG()

MPE_FINISH_LOG(logfilename)
        character*(*) logfilename

MPE_START_LOG()

MPE_STOP_LOG()

MPE_DESCRIBE_STATE(start, end, name, color)
        integer start, end
        character*(*) name, color

MPE_DESCRIBE_EVENT(event, name)
        integer event
        character*(*) name

MPE_LOG_EVENT(event, intdata, chardata)
        integer event, intdata
        character*(*) chardata
```

Table C.2
Fortran bindings for MPE logging

ending event for each state. One can also suggest a state color to be used by the logfile visualizations program. In the case of `upshot`, the color can be of the form `"red:vlines"` in order to specify simultaneously a color for a color display and a bitmap for black-and-white displays (such as books).

Finally, `MPE_Stop_log` and `MPE_Start_log` can be used to dynamically turn logging on and off. By default, it is on after `MPE_Init_log` is called.

These routines are used in one of the profiling libraries supplied with the distribution for automatic event logging for MPI library calls.

C.2 MPE Graphics

Many application programmers would like to enhance the output of their programs with some simple graphics, but find learning the X11 programming model too much of a burden. To make it easier, we have defined a small set of simple graphics primitives that can be used in MPI programs. An introduction to this library is given in Chapter 3, Section 3.8. The C bindings for these routines are given in Table C.3. (We note that some MPI implementations may not be compatible with X11; our implementation assumes that X11 routines can be called directly from programs that are also using MPI.)

C.3 MPE Helpers

In addition to the logging and graphics code, the MPE library contains a number of routines to aid programmers in producing parallel applications. The routine shown in Tables C.5 and C.6, `MPE_Decomp1d`, was used in Chapter 4 to compute decompositions of an array. Additional routines will be added to the MPE library as we use it.

C.4 The Upshot Program Visualization System

The `upshot` logfile analysis program [80] has been in use for several years. Recently it has been re-implemented in Tcl/Tk [106, 107]. Useful features of `upshot`, some of which are indicated in Figure C.1, are the following:

- The ability to scroll and zoom in an out both horizontally and vertically
- The ability to display multiple windows on the same or different files at once. (In Figure C.1 the middle window is a detailed view of a portion of the upper window.)

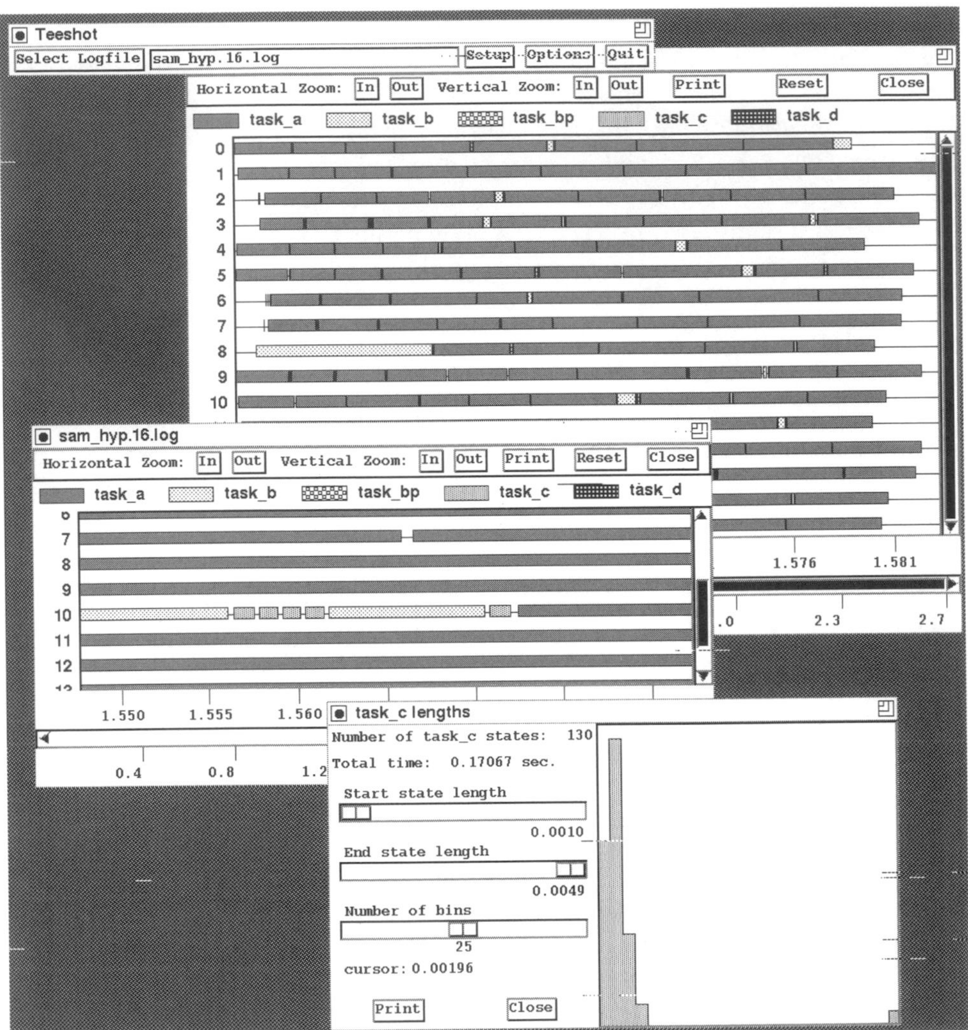

Figure C.1
A screendump of upshot

int **MPE_Open_graphics**(MPE_XGraph *handle, MPI_comm comm, char *display, int x, int y, int is_collective)
int **MPE_Draw_point**(MPE_XGraph handle, int x, int y, MPE_Color color)
int **MPE_Draw_line**(MPE_XGraph handle, int x1, int y1, int x2, int y2, MPE_Color color)
int **MPE_Draw_circle**(MPE_XGraph handle, int centerx, int centery, int radius, MPE_Color color)
int **MPE_Fill_rectangle**(MPE_XGraph handle, int x, int y, int w, int h, MPE_Color color)
int **MPE_Update**(MPE_XGraph handle)
int **MPE_Num_colors**(MPE_XGraph handle, int *nc)
int **MPE_Make_color_array**(MPE_XGraph handle, int ncolors, MPE_Color array[])
int **MPE_Close_graphics**(MPE_XGraph *handle)

Table C.3
C bindings for MPE graphics routines

• Histograms of state durations. One can also vary the range and number of bins in the histogram.

As this is being written, we are in the process of replacing the Tcl/Tk version of `upshot`, as well as its faster Tcl/Tk/C version `nupshot`, with a Java version called (what else?) `jumpshot` [132]. `Jumpshot` is now distributed with MPICH. A screen shot is shown in Figure C.2

MPE_OPEN_GRAPHICS(handle, comm, display, x, y,is_collective, ierror)
integer handle, comm, x, y, ierror
character*(*) display
logical is_collective

MPE_DRAW_POINT(handle, x, y, color, ierror)
integer handle, x, y,color, ierror

MPE_DRAW_LINE(handle, x1, y1, x2, y2, color, ierror)
integer handle, x1, y1, x2, y2, color, ierror

MPE_DRAW_CIRCLE(handle, centerx, centery, radius, color,ierror)
integer handle, centerx, centery, radius, color, ierror

MPE_FILL_RECTANGLE(handle, x, y, w, h, color, ierror)
integer handle, x, y, w, h, color, ierror

MPE_UPDATE(handle, ierror)
integer handle, ierror

MPE_NUM_COLORS(handle, nc, ierror)
integer handle, nc, ierror

MPE_MAKE_COLOR_ARRAY(handle, ncolors, array, ierror)
integer handle, ncolors, array(*), ierror

MPE_CLOSE_GRAPHICS(handle, ierror)
integer handle, ierror

Table C.4
Fortran bindings for MPE graphics routines

int **MPE_Decomp1d**(int n, int size, int rank, int *s, int *e)

Table C.5
C bindings for Miscellaneous MPE routines

MPE_DECOMP1D(n, size, rank, s, e)
integer n, size, rank, s, e

Table C.6
Fortran bindings for Miscellaneous MPE routines

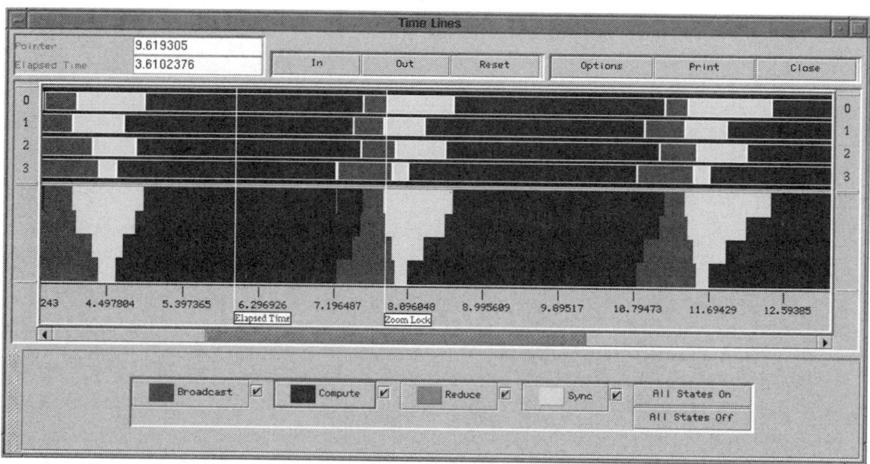

Figure C.2
A screendump of `jumpshot`

D MPI Resources on the World Wide Web

Here we describe how to get access to MPI-related material on the Internet.

MPI Home Pages. There are many MPI "home pages" on the World Wide Web. The most important is the MPI Forum's home page, `http://www.mpi-forum.org`. The page at `http://www.mcs.anl.gov/mpi` contains links to other home pages, as well as links to tools, tutorials, implementations, and documentation on MPI.

Examples of MPI programs. All of the examples used in this book are available on the web at `http://www.mcs.anl.gov/mpi/usingmpi` or by anonymous `ftp` from `ftp.mcs.anl.gov` in directory `pub/mpi/using/examples`. This directory is organized by book chapter. The file '`README`' lists the files by chapter. A Unix '`tar`' file (compressed) containing all of the examples is available in '`examples.tar.Z`'. Instructions for unpacking this file are in the '`README`' file.

MPI Implementations. The MPICH implementation, written by the authors of this book and others, is freely available and may be downloaded from the web at `http://www.mcs.anl.gov/mpi/mpich` or by anonymous ftp from `ftp.mcs.anl.gov`. The '`README`' file in directory '`pub/mpi`' describes how to fetch and install the most recent version of the model implementation. The MPICH implementation includes examples and test programs, as well as performance measurement programs. Most of the test and performance programs may be used with any MPI implementation.

A list of implementations is maintained at `http://www.mpi.nd.edu/MPI/` ; this includes both freely available and commercial implementations.

The MPI Standard. The MPI Standard is available on the web in both Postscript and HTML forms at `http://www.mpi-forum.org`. Errata for both MPI-1 and MPI-2 are also available here. In addition, archives of the MPI Forum, including e-mail discussions, meeting notes, and voting records, can be viewed here.

Discussion on MPI. A newsgroup, `comp.parallel.mpi`, is devoted to the discussion of all aspects of MPI. Discussion of MPI-related issues also sometimes occurs in the more general group, `comp.parallel`, devoted to parallel computers and computation.

A "frequently asked questions" (FAQ) page is available at

`http://www.erc.msstate.edu/mpi/mpi-faq.html`

A great deal of information on parallel programming projects and tools is available on the WWW. We encourage you to investigate other sites on the Web for other resources on MPI and parallel computing.

E Language Details

In this appendix we briefly discuss some details of C and Fortran that interact with MPI.

E.1 Arrays in C and Fortran

This section discusses the layout of Fortran arrays in memory and talks very briefly about how implicit "reshapes" of arrays are handled in Fortran 77. All arrays are stored in memory according to some rule, defined by the language, that says how to map the indices of an array reference such as `a(i,j,k,l)` into a computer's memory. Understanding and exploiting this rule is important in creating efficient representations of data.

E.1.1 Column and Row Major Ordering

Many discussions of the differences between Fortran and C arrays refer to "column" and "row" major ordering. These terms come from looking at a two-dimensional array as representing a matrix. To understand this, consider the $m \times n$ matrix

$$\begin{pmatrix} a_{11} & a_{12} & a_{13} & \cdots & a_{1n} \\ a_{21} & a_{22} & a_{23} & \cdots & a_{2n} \\ \vdots & \vdots & \vdots & \vdots & \vdots \\ a_{m1} & a_{m2} & a_{m3} & \cdots & a_{mn} \end{pmatrix}$$

If we use the Fortran declaration

```
real a(m,n)
```

and represent the matrix element a_{ij} with `a(i,j)`, then *column major ordering*, used in the Fortran language, means that the elements are stored by columns; that is, they are stored in the order `a(1,1)`, `a(2,1)`, ..., `a(m,1)`, `a(1,2)`, ..., `a(m,n)`. *Row major ordering*, used in the C language, means that the elements are stored by rows; that is, `a[0][0]`, `a[0][1]`, ..., `a[0][n-1]`, `a[1][0]`, ..., `a[m-1][n-1]`. We have used Fortran and C array notation here to emphasize how each is stored in memory.

E.1.2 Meshes vs. Matrices

While a matrix-based view of arrays is very common and often helpful, a different view of arrays is more natural for many applications. For instance, the 2-d Poisson example in Chapter 4. The solution to the problem had a natural representation as a function $u(x, y)$. We solved this on a discrete mesh of points (x_i, y_j) and used the Fortran element `u(i,j)` to represent $u(x_i, y_j)$. While this approach seems entirely natural, consider how this appears:

```
  u(1,m)      u(2,m)     ...    u(n,m)
 u(1,m-1)    u(2,m-1)    ...   u(n,m-1)
    :           :         :       :
  u(1,1)      u(2,1)     ...    u(n,1)
```

Viewed this way, the *rows* are stored together! What is going on?

The real story is that Fortran arrays are (always) stored so that, when we look at how the elements are placed in memory, we see that the first index varies most rapidly. In fact, the rule for mapping a Fortran array into memory is quite simple: If the array is declared as `A(N1,N2,...)`, then `A(I1,I2,...)` is the `(I1-1) + N1*((I2-1) + N2*(...))`th element (starting from zero).

The rule for C is the opposite; the *last* index varies most rapidly. When considering the special case of two dimensions, and looking at the arrays as representing matrices, we see how these lead to the row- and column-major interpretations.

E.1.3 Higher Dimensional Arrays

Once we know how arrays are laid out in the computer's memory, we can use that information to design ways to access sections of multidimensional arrays, planes with one coordinate constant, for example. If we wish to send a plane of data out of a 3-d array, we can form three different datatypes, one for each coordinate direction.

For concreteness, consider a Fortran array dimensioned as

```
double precision a(nx,ny,nz)
```

We will consider two different situations. In the first, we wish to send an entire face of this 3-D rectangular array. In the second, we wish to send only a rectangular part of the face. We will see that exploiting the knowledge of how data is laid out in memory will allow use to use a single `MPI_Type_vector` call for the first situation, while in the second situation (involving a part of a face), we will need to build a derived type from another derived type.

This is a good place to mention that most MPI implementations do not understand Fortran-90 array sections. That is, you should not pass a part of an array using, for example, `a(3:10,19:27,4)`. Instead, you should pass the first element that you wish to send; for example, `a(3,19,4)`. In some Fortran environments, even this may not work. In that case, the MPI-2 standard [100], which covers the issues of MPI and Fortran in detail, should be consulted.

A prototype version of an MPI implementation that worked with HPF programs, including handling array sections, is described in [41].

Sending an Entire Face. To send the elements `a(1:nx,1:ny,k)` for some value of k, we can do not even need a datatype, since this selects `nx*ny` contiguous memory locations, starting at `a(1,1,k)`. However, it can be convenient to have a datatype for each face; we can construct the datatype for this face with

```
call MPI_TYPE_CONTIGUOUS( nx * ny, MPI_DOUBLE_PRECISION, &
                          newz, ierror )
```

The next face to send is `a(1:nx,j,1:nz)`. This is a vector: there are `nx` elements in each block, there are `nz` blocks, and the blocks are separated by a stride of `nx*ny`. The datatype representing full faces in the $x - z$ plane is

```
call MPI_TYPE_VECTOR( nz, nx, nx * ny, MPI_DOUBLE_PRECISION, &
                          newy, ierror )
```

Finally, consider the $y - z$ face `a(i,1:ny,1:nz)`. There are `ny*nz` elements, each of size 1, separated by `nx`. To see this, remember that the formula for the locations of the elements of `a(i,j,k)` is `offset + (i-1) + nx * ((j-1) + ny * (z-1))`. The value of j runs from 1 to ny, and k runs from 1 to nz. Thus the elements are

$$
\begin{array}{lcl}
\mathit{offset} + (i-1) & + & 0 \\
\mathit{offset} + (i-1) & + & nx \\
 & \cdots & \\
\mathit{offset} + (i-1) & + & nx * (ny-1) \\
\mathit{offset} + (i-1) & + & nx * (0 + ny * 1) \\
 & \cdots & \\
\mathit{offset} + (i-1) & + & nx * ((ny-1) + ny * (nz-1))
\end{array}
$$

Note that the element at `a(i,ny,k)` is `nx` elements from the element at `a(i,1,k+1)`, as of course are all the elements `a(i,j,k)` are `nx` elements from `a(i,j+1,k)`. Thus, we can use the vector type

```
call MPI_TYPE_VECTOR( ny * nz, 1, nx * ny, &
                      MPI_DOUBLE_PRECISION, newx, ierror )
```

These examples show the power of the `blockcount` argument in the MPI vector datatype creation calls.

Sending a Partial Face. If instead of sending the entire face of the cube, we want to send or receive the elements `a(sx:ex,sy:ey,k)` for some value of `k`, we can define a vector datatype `newz`:

```
call MPI_TYPE_VECTOR( ey-sy+1, ex-sx+1, nx, &
                      MPI_DOUBLE_PRECISION, newz, ierror )
call MPI_TYPE_COMMIT( newz, ierror )
call MPI_SEND( a(sx,sy,k), 1, newz, dest, tag, comm, ierror )
```

To understand this, we need only look at the discussion of arrays above. For the elements `a(sx:ex,sy:ey,k)`, we see that the data consists of `ey-sy+1` groups ("columns") of `ex-sx+1` elements ("rows"); the rows are contiguous in memory. The stride from one group to another (i.e., from `a(sx,j,k)` to `a(sx,j+1,k)`) is just `nx` double precision values. Note that this is an example of a vector type with a block count that is different from one.

Similarly, to send or receive the elements `a(sx:ex,j,sz:ez)` we can use

```
call MPI_TYPE_VECTOR( ez-sz+1, ex-sx+1, nx*ny, &
                      MPI_DOUBLE_PRECISION, newy, ierror )
call MPI_TYPE_COMMIT( newy, ierror )
```

The explanation for this is the same as for `a(sx:ex,sy:ey,k)` except that the stride between elements is `nx*ny` double precision values.

The final case, to send or receive the elements `a(i,sy:ey,sz:ez)` requires a little more work because we can not use the blocklength argument in `MPI_Type_vector`. In this case, we take advantage of MPI's ability to form a datatype from an MPI datatype. First, we for a datatype for the elements `a(i,sy:ey,k)`:

```
call MPI_TYPE_VECTOR( ey-sy+1, 1, nx, &
                      MPI_DOUBLE_PRECISION, newx1, ierror )
```

(We do not need to commit `newx1` because we will not be using it in a communication operation.) Next, we form a vector of these types. Since the stride between these elements is probably not an integral multiple of `ey-sy+1`, we use `MPI_Type_-hvector`; this routine measures the stride in bytes.

```
call MPI_TYPE_EXTENT( MPI_DOUBLE_PRECISION, sizeof, ierror )
call MPI_TYPE_HVECTOR( ez-sz+1, 1, nx*ny*sizeof, &
                       newx1, newx, ierror )
call MPI_TYPE_COMMIT( newx, ierror )
```

An approach similar to that in Section 5.4 can be used to generate more general datatypes.

E.2 Aliasing

MPI routines such as `MPI_Allreduce` have both input and output buffers. It might seem natural to use code like this:

```
sum = ...
call MPI_ALLREDUCE( sum, sum, 1, MPI_INT, MPI_SUM, &
                    MPI_COMM_WORLD, ierr )
```

This code is incorrect; we mentioned in Section 3.1 that the input and output buffers had to be distinct (nonoverlapping). This is a requirement of Fortran of which some programmers are not aware. The ANSI Fortran 77 standard [36], in Section 15.9.3.6, states that if an actual argument is repeated, then the routine may not assign a value to it. Repeating an argument is called *aliasing*. This prohibits the form of use of the `MPI_Allreduce` call given above, because the second use of the repeated argument `sum` has a value assigned to it by the routine. For consistency, the C versions of the MPI routines share this restriction (even though the C language does not prohibit aliasing).

In MPI-2, this restriction was eased somewhat. Many of the collective routines allow the use of the value `MPI_IN_PLACE` as the value of the `sendbuf` or `recvbuf`. For example, `MPI_Allreduce` allows `MPI_IN_PLACE` as the `sendbuf` argument. In that case, the input data is taken from `recvbuf`. `MPI_IN_PLACE` is discussed in Section 4.5 of [118] on page 197.

References

[1] Jeanne C. Adams, Walter S. Brainerd, Jeanne T. Martin, Brian T. Smith, and Jerrold L. Wagener. *Fortran 95 Handbook.* MIT Press, 1997.

[2] Srinivas Aluru, G. M. Prabju, and John Gustafson. A random-number generator for parallel computers. *Parallel Computing*, 18:839–847, 1992.

[3] Andrew W. Appel. An efficient program for many-body simulation. *SIAM Journal of Sci. and Stat. Comp.*, 6, January 1985.

[4] Mark Baker. MPI on NT: The current status and performance of the available environments. In Vassuk Alexandrov and Jack Dongarra, editors, *Recent Advances in Parallel Virtual Machine and Message Passing Interface*, volume 1497 of *Lecture Notes in Computer Science*, pages 63–73. Springer, 1998. 5th European PVM/MPI Users' Group Meeting.

[5] Satish Balay, William Gropp, Lois Curfman McInnes, and Barry Smith. *PETSc 2.0 Users Manual.* Mathematics and Computer Science Division, Argonne National Laboratory, 1997. ANL-95/11.

[6] B. S. Baldwin and H. Lomax. Thin-layer approximation and algebraic model for separated turbulent flows. *AIAA*, January 1978. AIAA-78-257.

[7] Purushotham V. Bangalore. The Data-Distribution-Independent Approach to Scalable Parallel Libraries. Technical report, Mississippi State University — Dept. of Computer Science, October 1994. Master's Thesis. (Available from `ftp://cs.msstate.edu/pub/reports/bangalore_ms.ps.Z`).

[8] Joshua E. Barnes and Piet Hut. A hierarchical O(N log N) force calculation algorithm. *Nature*, 324(4), December 1986.

[9] A. Beguelin, J. Dongarra, G. A. Geist, R. Manchek, and V. Sunderam. A user's guide to PVM: Parallel virtual machine. Technical Report TM-11826, Oak Ridge National Laboratory, Oak Ridge, TN, 1991.

[10] A. Beguelin, G. A. Geist, W. Jiang, R. Manchek, K. Moore, and V. Sunderam. The PVM project. Technical report, Oak Ridge National Laboratory, February 1993.

[11] L. S. Blackford, J. Choi, A. Cleary, E. DÁzevedo, J. Demmel, I. Dhillon, J. Dongarra, S. Hammarling, G. Henry, A. Petitet, K. Stanley, D. Walker, and R. C. Whaley. *ScaLAPACK Users' Guide.* SIAM, Philadelphia, 1997.

[12] L. Bomans, D. Roose, and R. Hempel. The Argonne/GMD macros in FORTRAN for portable parallel programming and their implementation on the Intel iPSC/2. *Parallel Computing*, 15:119–132, 1990.

[13] James Boyle, Ralph Butler, Terrence Disz, Barnett Glickfeld, Ewing Lusk, Ross Overbeek, James Patterson, and Rick Stevens. *Portable Programs for Parallel Processors.* Holt, Rinehart, and Winston, 1987.

[14] David Brightwell. The Design and Implementation of a Datagram Protocol (UDP) Device for MPICH. Master's thesis, University of Maryland, December 1995. Dept. of Computer Science.

[15] T. A. Brody. Random-number generation for parallel processors. *Computer Physics Communications*, 56:147–153, 1989.

[16] Greg Burns and Raja Daoud. Robust MPI message delivery with guaranteed resources. MPI Developers Conference, June 1995. `http://www.itl.nist.gov/div895/sasg/LAM/delivery.paper.html`.

[17] Greg Burns, Raja Daoud, and James Vaigl. LAM: An open cluster environment for MPI. In John W. Ross, editor, *Proceedings of Supercomputing Symposium '94*, pages 379–386. University of Toronto, 1994.

[18] Ralph Butler, William Gropp, and Ewing Lusk. Developing applications for a heterogeneous computing environment. In Mary Eshaghian and Vaidy Sunderam, editors, *Workshop on Heterogeneous Processing*, pages 77–83. IEEE Computer Society Press, April 1993.

[19] Ralph Butler and Ewing Lusk. User's guide to the p4 parallel programming system. Technical Report ANL-92/17, Argonne National Laboratory, October 1992.

[20] Ralph Butler and Ewing Lusk. Monitors, messages, and clusters: The p4 parallel programming system. *Parallel Computing*, 20:547–564, April 1994.

[21] N. Carriero and D. Gelernter. How to write parallel programs. *ACM Computing Surveys*, 21(3):323–356, September 1989.

[22] Fei-Chen Cheng. Unifying the MPI and PVM 3 systems. Technical report, Mississippi State University — Dept. of Computer Science, May 1994. Master's Report. (Available from `ftp://ftp.cs.msstate.edu/pub/reports/feicheng.ps`).

[23] Andrew Chien, Scott Pakin, Mario Lauria, Matt Buchanan, Kay Hane, Louis Giannini, and Jane Prusakova. High performance virtual machines (HPVM): Clusters with supercomputing APIs and performance. In *Eighth SIAM Conference on Parallel Processing for Scientific Computing*, March 1997.

[24] IMPI Steering Committee. IMPI - interoperable message-passing interface, 1998. `http://impi.nist.gov/IMPI/`.

[25] Parasoft Corporation. Express version 1.0: A communication environment for parallel computers, 1988.

[26] James Cownie and William Gropp. A standard interface for debugger access to message queue information in MPI. Technical Report ANL/MCS-P754-0699, Mathematics and Computer Science Division, Argonne National Laboratory, June 1999.

[27] T. Crockett. File concepts for parallel I/O. In *Proceedings of Supercomputing'89*, pages 574–579, 1989.

[28] J. M. del Rosario and A. Choudhary. High performance I/O for parallel computers: Problems and prospects. *IEEE Computer*, March 1994.

[29] Eric D. Demaine. A threads-only MPI implementation for the development of parallel programs. In *Proceedings of the 11th International Symposium on High Performance Computing Systems*, pages 153–163, July 1997.

[30] J. J. Dongarra, J. DuCroz, I. Duff, and R. Hanson. A set of Level 3 basic linear algebra subprograms. ACM Trans. on Math. Soft., 5, December 1989.

[31] J. J. Dongarra, J. DuCroz, S. Hammarling, and R. Hanson. An extended set of Fortran basic linear algebra subprograms. ACM Trans. on Math. Soft., 5, 1988.

[32] G. Fagg, J. Dongarra, and A. Geist. PVMPI provides interoperability between MPI implementations. In *Proc. 8th SIAM Conf. on Parallel Processing*. SIAM, 1997.

[33] Graham E. Fagg, Kevin S. London, and Jack J. Dongarra. MPI_Connect managing heterogeneous MPI applications interoperation and process control. In Vassuk Alexandrov and Jack Dongarra, editors, *Recent advances in Parallel Virtual Machine and Message Passing Interface*, volume 1497 of *Lecture Notes in Computer Science*, pages 93–96. Springer, 1998. 5th European PVM/MPI Users' Group Meeting.

[34] FFTW. `http://www.fftw.org/`.

[35] Marco Fillo and Richard B. Gillett. Architecture and implementation of MEMORY CHANNEL2. *DIGITAL Technical Journal*, 9(1), 1997. `http://www.digital.com/info/DTJP03/DTJP03HM.HTM`.

[36] American National Standard Programming Language Fortran. ANSI X3.9-1978.

[37] I. Foster, J. Geisler, W. Gropp, N. Karonis, E. Lusk, G. Thiruvathukal, and S. Tuecke. A wide-area implementation of the Message Passing Interface. *Parallel Computing*, 24(11), 1998.

[38] I. Foster, W. Gropp, and R. Stevens. The parallel scalability of the spectral transform method. *Monthly Weather Review*, 120(5):835–850, 1992.

[39] I. Foster and C. Kesselman. Globus: A metacomputing infrastructure toolkit. *International Journal of Supercomputer Applications*, 11(2):115–128, 1997.

[40] I. Foster and C. Kesselman, editors. *The Grid: Blueprint for a Future Computing Infrastructure*. Morgan Kaufmann Publishers, 1999.

[41] I. Foster, D. R. Kohr, Jr., R. Krishnaiyer, and A. Choudhary. MPI as a coordination layer for communicating HPF tasks. In *Proceedings of the 1996 MPI Developers Conference*, pages 68–78. IEEE Computer Society Press, 1996.

[42] Ian Foster and Nicholas T. Karonis. A grid-enabled MPI: Message passing in heterogeneous distributed computing systems. In *Proceedings of SC98*. IEEE, November 1999. `http://www.supercomp.org/sc98`.

[43] Geoffrey C. Fox, Mark A. Johnson, Gregory A. Lyzenga, Steve W. Otto, John K. Salmon, and David W. Walker. *Solving Problems on Concurrent Processors*, volume 1. Prentice Hall, 1988.

[44] Hubertus Franke, Peter Hochschild, Pratap Pattnaik, Jean-Pierre Prost, and Marc Snir. MPI-F: an MPI prototype implementation on IBM SP1. In Jack J. Dongarra and Bernard Tourancheau, editors, *Environments and Tools for Parallel Scientific Computing*, pages 43–55. SIAM, 1994.

[45] N. Galbreath, W. Gropp, D. Gunter, G. Leaf, and D. Levine. Parallel solution of the three-dimensional, time-dependent Ginzburg-Landau equation. In *Proceedings of the SIAM Parallel Processing for Scientific Computing Conference*, pages 160–164. SIAM, 1993.

[46] N. Galbreath, W. Gropp, and D. Levine. Applications-driven parallel I/O. In *Proceedings of Supercomputing '93*, pages 462–471, Los Alamitos, California, November 1993. IEEE computer Society Press.

[47] Al Geist, Adam Beguelin, Jack Dongarra, Weicheng Jiang, Bob Manchek, and Vaidy Sunderam. *PVM: Parallel Virtual Machine—A User's Guide and Tutorial for Network Parallel Computing.* MIT Press, 1994.

[48] G. A. Geist, M. T. Heath, B. W. Peyton, and P. H. Worley. PICL: A portable instrumented communications library, C reference manual. Technical Report TM-11130, Oak Ridge National Laboratory, Oak Ridge, TN, July 1990. See also `http://www.epm.ornl.gov/picl`.

[49] G. A. Geist, M. T. Heath, B. W. Peyton, and P. H. Worley. A users' guide to PICL, a portable instrumented communication library. Technical Report ORNL/TM-11616, Oak Ridge National Laboratory, Oak Ridge, TN, October 1990.

[50] John R. Gilbert and Robert Schreiber. Optimal data placement for distributed memory architectures. In *Parallel Processing for Scientific Computing*, pages 462–471. SIAM, March 1991.

[51] Brian K. Grant and Anthony Skjellum. The PVM Systems: An in-depth analysis and documenting study: Concise edition. Technical Report UCRL-JC-112016, Lawrence Livermore National Laboratory, August 1992. (Revised).

[52] Leslie Greengard. *The Rapid Evaluation of Potential Fields in Particle Systems.* ACM Press, 1987.

[53] W. Gropp and E. Lusk. A high-performance MPI implementation on a shared-memory vector supercomputer. *Parallel Computing*, 22(11):1513–1526, January 1997.

[54] W. Gropp and E. Smith. Computational fluid dynamics on parallel processors. *Computers and Fluids*, 18:289–304, 1990.

[55] William Gropp, Steven Huss-Lederman, Andrew Lumsdaine, Ewing Lusk, Bill Nitzberg, William Saphir, and Marc Snir. *MPI—The Complete Reference: Volume 2, The MPI-2 Extensions.* MIT Press, Cambridge, MA, 1998.

[56] William Gropp and Ewing Lusk. An abstract device definition to support the implementation of a high-level message-passing interface. Technical Report MCS-P342-1193, Argonne National Laboratory, 1993.

[57] William Gropp and Ewing Lusk. Installation guide for `mpich`, a portable implementation of MPI. Technical Report ANL-96/5, Argonne National Laboratory, 1996.

[58] William Gropp and Ewing Lusk. User's guide for `mpich`, a portable implementation of MPI. Technical Report ANL-96/6, Argonne National Laboratory, 1996.

[59] William Gropp and Ewing Lusk. Sowing MPICH: A case study in the dissemination of a portable environment for parallel scientific computing. *IJSA*, 11(2):103–114, Summer 1997.

[60] William Gropp and Ewing Lusk. PVM and MPI are completely different. *Future Generation Computer Systems*, 1999.

[61] William Gropp and Ewing Lusk. Reproducible measurements of MPI performance characteristics. Technical Report ANL/MCS-P755-0699, Mathematics and Computer Science Division, Argonne National Laboratory, June 1999.

[62] William Gropp and Ewing Lusk. A test implementation of the MPI draft message-passing standard. Technical Report ANL-92/47, Mathematics and Computer Science Division, Argonne National Laboratory, December 92.

[63] William Gropp, Ewing Lusk, Nathan Doss, and Anthony Skjellum. A high-performace, portable implementation of the MPI Message Passing Interface standard. *Parallel Computing*, 22(6):789–828, 1996.

[64] William Gropp, Ewing Lusk, and Anthony Skjellum. *Using MPI: Portable Parallel Programming with the Message Passing Interface,* 2nd edition. MIT Press, Cambridge, MA, 1999.

[65] William Gropp, Ewing Lusk, and Debbie Swider. Improving the performance of MPI derived datatypes. In Anthony Skjellum, Purushotham V. Bangalore, and Yoginder S. Dandass, editors, *Proceedings of the Third MPI Developer's and User's Conference*, pages 25–30, Starkville, MS, 1999. MPI Software Technology Press.

[66] William Gropp, Ewing Lusk, and Rajeev Thakur. *Using MPI-2: Advanced Features of the Message-Passing Interface.* MIT Press, Cambridge, MA, 1999.

[67] William D. Gropp. Solving PDEs on loosely-coupled parallel processors. *Parallel Computing*, 5:165–173, 1987.

[68] William D. Gropp and I. C. F. Ipsen. Recursive mesh refinement on hypercubes. *BIT*, pages 186–211, 1989.

[69] William D. Gropp and Ewing Lusk. A test implementation of the MPI draft message-passing standard. Technical Report ANL-92/47, Argonne National Laboratory, Argonne, IL, December 1992.

[70] William D. Gropp and Ewing Lusk. Why are PVM and MPI so different? In Marian Bubak, Jack Dongarra, and Jerzy Waśniewski, editors, *Recent Advances in Parallel Virtual Machine and Message Passing Interface*, volume 1332 of *Lecture Notes in Computer Science*, pages 3–10. Springer Verlag, 1997. 4th European PVM/MPI Users' Group Meeting, Cracow, Poland, November 1997.

[71] William D. Gropp and Barry Smith. Chameleon parallel programming tools users manual. Technical Report ANL-93/23, Argonne National Laboratory, Argonne, IL, March 1993.

[72] William D. Gropp and Barry Smith. Users manual for KSP: Data-structure-neutral codes implementing Krylov space methods. Technical Report ANL-93/30, Argonne National Laboratory, Argonne, IL, August 1993.

[73] Erik Hagersten, Anders Landin, and Seif Haridi. DDM — a cache-only memory architecture. *IEEE Computer*, pages 44–54, September 1992.

[74] R. J. Harrison. Portable tools and applications for parallel computers. *Intern. J. Quantum Chem.*, 40(847), 1991.

[75] R. J. Harrison and E. A. Stahlberg. Massively parallel full configuration interaction. benchmark electronic structure calculations on the Intel Touchstone Delta, 1993.

[76] M. T. Heath. Recent developments and case studies in performance visualization using ParaGraph. In G. Haring and G. Kotsis, editors, *Performance Measurement and Visualization of Parallel Systems*, pages 175–200, Amsterdam, The Netherlands, 1993. Elsevier Science Publishers.

[77] M. T. Heath and J. A. Etheridge. Visualizing the performance of parallel programs. *IEEE Software*, 8(5):29–39, September 1991.

[78] L. Shane Hebert, Walter G. Seefeld, and Anthony Skjellum. MPICH on the Cray T3E. In Anthony Skjellum, Purushotham V. Bangalore, and Yoginder S. Dandass, editors, *Proceedings of the Third MPI Developer's and User's Conference*, pages 69–76, Starkville, MS, 1999. MPI Software Technology Press.

[79] Rolf Hempel, Hubert Ritzdorf, and Falk Zimmermann. Implementation of MPI on NEC's SX-4 multi-node architecture. In Marian Bubak, Jack Dongarra, and Jerzy Waśniewski, editors, *Recent advances in Parallel Virtual Machine and Message Passing Interface*, volume 1332 of *Lecture Notes in Computer Science*, pages 185–193. Springer, 1997. 4th European PVM/MPI Users' Group Meeting.

[80] Virginia Herrarte and Ewing Lusk. Studying parallel program behavior with `upshot`. Technical Report ANL–91/15, Argonne National Laboratory, 1991.

[81] C.-T. Ho and L. Johnsson. On the embedding of arbitrary meshes in Boolean cubes with expansion two dilation two. In *Proc. 1987 ICPP*, pages 188–191, 1987.

[82] R. W. Hockney and J. W. Eastwood. *Computer simulation using particles.* Adam Hilger, Bristol, UK, 1988.

[83] Hybrid technology multithreaded architecture. `http://htmt.cacr.caltech.edu/index.html`.

[84] Institute of Electrical and Electronics Engineers, New York. *Draft Standard for Information Technology–Portable Operating System Interface (POSIX) – Part 1: System Application Program Interface (API) – Amendment 2: Threads Extension [C Language], Draft 8*, October 1993.

[85] L. Johnsson. Communication efficient basic linear algebra computations on hypercube architectures. *J. Par. Dist. Comp.*, 4:133–172, 1987.

[86] T. Kielmann, R.F.H. Hofman, H.E. Bal, A. Plaat, and R.A.F. Bhoedjang. MagPIe: MPI's collective communication operations for clustered wide area systems. In *ACM SIGPLAN Symposium on Principles and Practice of Parallel Programming (PPoPP'99)*, pages 131–140. ACM, May 1999.

[87] Charles H. Koelbel, David B. Loveman, Robert S. Schreiber, Guy L. Steele Jr., and Mary E. Zosel. *The High Performance Fortran Handbook.* MIT Press, Cambridge, MA, 1993.

[88] Vipin Kumar, Ananth Grama, Anshui Gupta, and George Karypis. *Introduction to Parallel Computing: Design and Analysis of Algorithms.* Benjamin/Cummings, 1994.

[89] Leon Lapidus and George F. Pinder. *Numerical Solution of Partial Differential Equations in Science and Engineering.* Wiley-Interscience, New York, NY, 1982.

[90] Mario Lauria and Andrew Chien. MPI-FM: High performance MPI on workstation clusters. *Journal of Parallel and Distributed Computing*, 1997.

[91] C. Lawson, R. Hanson, D. Kincaid, and F. Krogh. Basic linear algebra subprograms for Fortran usage. ACM Trans. on Math. Soft., 14:308–325, 1989.

[92] Cookbook: Running an MPI code in Legion with the fewest changes. `http://legion.virginia.edu/documentation/tutorials/MPI_cookbook.html`.

[93] Benoit B. Mandelbrot. *The Fractal Geometry of Nature.* W. H. Freeman and Company, 1983.

[94] John May. Parallel Print Function. `http://www.llnl.gov/sccd/lc/ptcprint`.

[95] Pedro D. Medeiros and José C. Cunha. Interconnecting PVM and MPI applications. In Vassuk Alexandrov and Jack Dongarra, editors, *Recent advances in Parallel Virtual Machine and Message Passing Interface*, volume 1497 of *Lecture Notes in Computer Science*, pages 105–112. Springer, 1998. 5th European PVM/MPI Users' Group Meeting.

[96] Piyush Mehrotra, Joel Saltz, and Robert Voigt, editors. *Unstructured Scientific Computation on Scalable Multiprocessors.* MIT Press, Cambridge, MA, 1992.

[97] Message Passing Interface Forum. Document for a standard message-passing interface. Technical Report Technical Report No. CS-93-214 (revised), University of Tennessee, April 1994. Available on **netlib**.

[98] Message Passing Interface Forum. MPI: A message-passing interface standard. Computer Science Dept. Technical Report CS-94-230, University of Tennessee, Knoxville, TN, April 1994. (Also appeared in the International Journal of Supercomputer Applications, Volume 8, Number 3/4, 1994, and is available at `http://www.mpi-forum.org`).

[99] Message Passing Interface Forum. MPI: A Message-Passing Interface standard. *International Journal of Supercomputer Applications*, 8(3/4):165–414, 1994.

[100] Message Passing Interface Forum. MPI2: A message passing interface standard. *International Journal of High Performance Computing Applications*, 12(1–2):1–299, 1998.

[101] Message Passing Interface Forum. MPI-2: Extensions to the message-passing interface. World Wide Web, July 1997. `http://www.mpi-forum.org/docs/mpi2-report.html`.

[102] MPI-2 C++ bindings, 1999. `http://www.mpi.nd.edu/research/mpi2c++`.

[103] OpenMP Fortran Application Program Interface, Version 1.0. World Wide Web, `http://www.openmp.org`, October 1997.

[104] OpenMP C and C++ Application Program Interface, Version 1.0. World Wide Web, `http://www.openmp.org`, October 1998.

[105] Satoshi Sekiguchi Osamu Tatebe, Yuetsu Kodama and Yoshinori Yamaguchi. Highly efficient implementation of MPI point-to-point communication using remote memory operations. In *Proceedings of ICS98*, pages 267–273. ACM, 1998.

[106] John Osterhout. Tcl: An embeddable command language. In *Proceedings of the Winter 1990 USENIX Conference*, pages 133–146. USENIX Association, January 1990.

[107] John Osterhout. An X11 toolkit based on the Tcl language. In *Proceedings of the Winter 1991 USENIX Conference*, pages 105–115. USENIX Association, January 1991.

[108] John Ousterhout and Fred Douglis. Beating the I/O bottleneck: A case for log-structured file systems. *ACM Operating Systems Review*, 23(1):11–28, January 1989.

[109] Ramesh Pankajakshan and W. Roger Briley. Parallel solution of unsteady incompressible viscous flows. (in preparation).

[110] H.-O. Peitgen and D. Saupe. *The Beauty of Fractals.* Springer-Verlag, 1988.

[111] S. C. Pieper, R. B. Wiringa, and V. R. Pandharipande. Variational calculation of the ground state of ^{16}o. *Physical Review C*, 46:1741–1756, 1992.

[112] B. S. Pudliner, V. R. Pandharipande, J. Carlson, S. C. Pieper, and R. B. Wiringa. Quantum monte carlo calculations of nuclei with $a \leq 7$. *Phus. Rev. C*, 56:1720–1750, 1997.

[113] Gautam Shah, Jarek Nieplocha, Jamshed Mirza, Chulho Kim, Robert Harrison, Rama K. Govindaraju, Kevin Gildea, Paul DiNicola, and Carl Bender. Performance and experience with LAPI—a new high-performance communication library for the IBM RS/6000 SP. In *Proceedings of the International Parallel Processing Symposium*, 1998.

[114] Anthony Skjellum and Chuck H. Baldwin. *The Multicomputer Toolbox:* Scalable parallel libraries for large-scale concurrent applications. Technical Report UCRL-JC-109251, Lawrence Livermore National Laboratory, Livermore, CA, December 1991.

[115] Anthony Skjellum, Nathan E. Doss, and Kishore Viswanathan. Inter-communicator extensions to MPI in the MPIX (MPI eXtension) Library. Technical report, Mississippi State University — Dept. of Computer Science, April 1994. Draft version.

[116] Anthony Skjellum, Steven G. Smith, Nathan E. Doss, Alvin P. Leung, and Manfred Morari. The design and evolution of zipcode. *Parallel Computing*, 20, April 1994.

[117] Anthony Skjellum, Steven G. Smith, Charles H. Still, Alvin P. Leung, and Manfred Morari. The Zipcode message-passing system. In Geoffrey C. Fox, editor, *Parallel Computing Works!* Morgan Kaufman, 1994.

[118] Marc Snir, Steve W. Otto, Steven Huss-Lederman, David W. Walker, and Jack Dongarra. *MPI—The Complete Reference: Volume 1, The MPI Core,* 2nd edition. MIT Press, Cambridge, MA, 1998.

[119] Jeffrey M. Squyres, Brian C. McCandless, and Andrew Lumsdaine. Object oriented MPI: A class library for the message passing interface. In *Parallel Object-Oriented Methods and Applications (POOMA '96)*, Santa Fe, 1996.

[120] Thomas L. Sterling, John Salmon, Donald J. Becker, and Daniel F. Savarese. *How to Build a Beowulf.* MIT Press, 1999.

[121] W. Richard Stevens. *Unix Network Programming: Networking APIs: Sockets and XTI*, volume 1. Prentice Hall PTR, second edition, 1998.

[122] Lafe K. Taylor, Judy A. Busby, Min Yee Jiang, Abdollah Arabshahi, Kidambi Sreenivas, and David L. Whitfield. Time accurate incompressible Navier-Stokes simulation of the flapping foil experiment, August 2–5 1993. Presented at the Sixth International Conference on Numerical Ship Hydrodynamics, Iowa City, Iowa.

[123] Lafe K. Taylor and David L. Whitfield. Unsteady three-dimensional incompressible Euler and Navier-Stokes solver for stationary and dynamic grids, June 24–26 1991. AIAA 91-1650. Presented at the AIAA 22nd Fluid Dynamics, Plasma Dynamics and Lasers Conference, Honolulu, Hawaii.

[124] Robert A. van de Geijn. *Using PLAPACK: Parallel Linear Algebra Package.* MIT Press, Cambridge, MA, 1997.

[125] VI Architecture. `http://www.viarch.org`.

[126] Thorsten von Eicken, David E. Culler, Seth Copen Goldstein, and Klaus Erik Schauser. Active messages: A mechanism for integrated communication and computation. In *Proc. of the 19th Int'l. Symposium on Computer Architecture*, Gold Coast, Australia, May 1992. (Also available as Technical Report UCB/CSD 92/675, Computer Science Div., University of California at Berkeley).

[127] David Walker. Standards for message passing in a distributed memory environment. Technical Report ORNL/TM-12147, Oak Ridge National Laboratory, Oak Ridge, TN, August 1992.

[128] David L. Whitfield and Lafe K. Taylor. Discretized Newton-relaxation solution of high resolution flux-difference split schemes, June 24–26 1991. AIAA-91-1539. Presented at the AIAA 10th Computational Fluid Dynamics Conference, Honolulu, Hawaii.

[129] R. B. Wiringa. Variational calculations of few-body nuclei. *Physical Review C*, 43:1585–1598, 1991.

[130] P. H. Worley. A new PICL trace file format. Technical Report ORNL/TM-12125, Oak Ridge National Laboratory, Oak Ridge, TN, October 1992.

[131] Patrick H. Worley. MPICL, 1999. `http://www.epm.ornl.gov/picl`.

[132] Omer Zaki, Ewing Lusk, William Gropp, and Debbie Swider. Scalable performance visualization with jumpshot. *International Journal of High Performance Computing Applications*, 1999. (to appear).

Subject Index

Function and Term Index

P

R

S

T

U

W

X